MENTAL HEALTH AND ACHIEVEMENT

MENTAL HEALTH AND ACHIEVEMENT

Increasing Potential and Reducing School Dropout

edited by E. PAUL TORRANCE *and* ROBERT D. STROM

John Wiley & Sons, Inc. | *New York London Sydney*

"Maternal Teaching Styles and Educational Retardation" by Robert D. Hess is a revised version of a presentation to the 'Invitational Meeting on Secondary School Curriculum for Potential Dropouts' sponsored by Project School Dropouts of the National Education Association, Washington, D. C.

A revised version of Chapter 7 appeared in the Catholic Educational Review and appears through their courtesy.

Library of Congress Card Number: 65-26853
Printed in the United States of America

CONTRIBUTORS

Gordon W. Allport, Professor of Psychology, Harvard University

Roderick A. Armstrong, Director, Digby-Annapolis Mental Health Service, Digby, Nova Scotia

David P. Ausubel, Professor of Education, University of Illinois

Paul H. Bowman, Director, Department of Prevention, Kansas City Mental Health Foundation

Francis J. Braceland, Psychiatrist in Chief, Institute of Living, Hartford, Connecticut

Milton Brown, Director, Neighborhood Services, Community Progress, Inc., New Haven, Connecticut

James S. Coleman, Director of Social Relations, Johns Hopkins University

James Conner, President, Wheelock College, Boston, Massachusetts

Martin Deutsch, Director, Institute for Developmental Studies, New York Medical College

Dana L. Farnsworth, Director, University Health Service, Harvard University

Lois French, School Social Worker, Middletown, Connecticut

Jacob W. Getzels, Professor of Educational Psychology and Human Development, University of Chicago

Charlotte Hayman, Supervisor, Bureau of Child Guidance, New York City

Robert D. Hess, Director, Committee on Human Development, University of Chicago

Kenneth Hoyt, Professor of Education and Guidance, University of Iowa

Paul R. Hunt, Director of Rehabilitation for Youth, Detroit Public Schools

Philip W. Jackson, Associate Professor, University of Chicago

Roy J. Jones, Director, Washington Action for Youth, Washington, D. C.

Merle B. Karnes, Director of Special Education, Champaign, Illinois

Frank Riessman, Consultant, Mobilization for Youth, New York City

A. Raymond Rogers, Principal, Manchester High School, Manchester, Connecticut

Mary Ellen Saterlie, Supervisor of Junior High Schools, Baltimore County, Maryland

Charles Savitsky, Coordinator, School to Employment Program, New York City

Daniel Schreiber, Director, Project: School Dropouts, National Education Association, Washington, D. C.

Howard C. Seymour, Superintendent of Schools, Phoenix, Arizona

Robert D. Strom, Associate Professor of Education, The Ohio State University (formerly Assistant Director of Project: School Dropouts, National Education Association)

E. Paul Torrance, Professor of Educational Psychology, University of Minnesota

Gordon E. Wesner, Assistant Superintendent for Instruction, Kansas City, Missouri

Percy Williams, Supervisor, Senior High Schools, Maryland State Department of Education

George A. Xydis, Professor of Educational Psychology, Teachers College, Ioannina, Greece

"I believe in an America where every child is educated, not according to his means or his race, but according to his capacity — where there are no literacy tests for voting that mean anything because there are no illiterate citizens."

John F. Kennedy

PREFACE

Although not exclusive to modernity, the quest for mental health and achievement has never been so pursued as it is today. In this era of rapid change, ever-increasing numbers of professionals are devoting their time and talent to helping young people grow and develop. Promising efforts in this regard are not confined to a given field of academic endeavor but include the work of men and women engaged in such differing occupations as medicine, psychology, education, psychiatry, and social work.

Frequently there is a conjunction of focus among those who write and conduct research in these various disciplines. Even on matters of mutual concern, however, there is not the access and exchange of data that could most profit children. Surely teachers would seem to be one group of consumers for new findings in child behavior and learning since this knowledge could appreciably improve their role. Yet the benefit of some studies is rendered forfeit when results are not made available to persons who could most use them. To better help the young, therefore, some mental-health leaders are urging an increase of interdisciplinary confrontation on problems of common interest.

By invitation of the editors, a selected group of professional and lay leaders representing diverse backgrounds were requested to address themselves to an assigned topic concerning personal development. Since many of the writers are currently involved in new and exciting programs for improving home, school, and community influences on child development, they were asked to go beyond the usual citation of obstacles to mental health and suggest positive measures for intervention. The effective way in which each contributor fulfilled his responsibility has made the singular purpose of this interdisciplinary book possible—namely, to assist school personnel, parents, and community leaders in the improvement of their roles as they relate to the well-being of tomorrow's adult.

In structure and scope the text is divided into three principal parts, each of which concerns a different environmental context. First, the ways in which family, community, and peer groups exert influences that retard or advance positive attitudes, self-concept, aspiration, and other requisites of achievement are considered. In response to new demands and expectations, the changing function of school staff and the institution is discussed. Finally, a focus on the classroom involves programs of curricular innovation, new understandings about the teaching-learning process, and workable techniques of evaluation. Admittedly the emphasis of the entire book is on children of poverty, the slow learners, the disadvantaged—those for whom the prospect of mental health and achievement is least likely.

E. Paul Torrance
Robert D. Strom

Minneapolis, Minnesota
Columbus, Ohio
August 1965

CONTENTS

Part One Home and Community: Influence and Responsibility

Lyndon B. Johnson, in his declaration of war on poverty, stated that "our national goal is to provide every citizen with the opportunity to advance his welfare to the limit of his capacities." Much progress has been made toward reaching this goal. Yet the domestic enemy of poverty still holds captive one-fifth of our nation. In those homes with an annual income of less than 3000 dollars live eleven million children to whom the gates of opportunity have been closed—victims of an environmental trap that threatens to impose on them a lifetime devoid of dignity. This element of society represents our greatest loss in achievement and mental health as shown by a high incidence of school dropouts, youth crimes, and unemployment.

The first part of this book examines environmental influences of the home, community, and peer groups which act to retard personal advance. Each of the writers has attempted to map strategies for overcoming poor health and failure, not only in the culture of poverty but everywhere boys and girls may live.

The role of parents in fostering child growth has always been considered important, even though it was assumed that intelligence is fixed and development determined by genes. This fixed-intelligence concept, which resulted in educators overlooking the need for preschool experience, has recently been challenged by those who contend that the difference between a favorable and an underprivileged environment may affect intellectual development ten I.Q. points over the first four years. Further, a cumulative effect of about twenty I.Q. points has been suggested during the first seventeen years of life, when contrasting deprived and abundant backgrounds as they exist in America today.

1

After investigating home influences that facilitate and retard educational progress, Hess maintains that inadequacy in the cognitive features of early mother-child exchange tends to foster later alienation from the educative processes and other basic institutions of society. Mothers of low-income groups appear less able than middle-class mothers to prepare children for school because their patterns of communication do not include such elements as sharing information, conveying concepts, and programming simple tasks. Strom reports that frequent absence of the male parent tends to exacerbate the problem of interaction, which, in constricting a child's life space, results in a cumulative deficit of the language component.

Pupil attitude toward learning and school differs depending on home influence. In his studies Hess found that most middle-class children view school as a place of learning, whereas low-income pupils usually approach the academic environment unoriented toward learning but attuned to a need for getting along with the institution. To children of the poor, school experience is defined more as a problem of adapting physical behavior than of emphasizing mental activity. In corroborating the relationship of parental attitude to student achievement, Bowman's findings show, when controlling for intellect and social class, the major difference between pupils who drop out and those who remain to graduate is parental attitude toward school. Even when lower-class parents have an affinity toward education, Strom suggests they may not know how to give the support that is the logical concomitant of this attitude.

It appears we must discover ways to govern the encounters children have with their environment during the early years in order that they might be better prepared for expectations and demands of school. To Hess it seems likely that programs can be developed wherein mothers of educationally disadvantaged homes can become adept in teaching preschoolers the basic cognitive skills needed upon entrance to first grade. A successful corollary to this approach calls for school systems to introduce compensations in the form of prekindergarten enrichment programs designed to include a dimension of experiences that are comparable to the background usually brought to school by children from middle-class families. Ostensibly these programs prepare children for a more adequate chance to compete in later academic situations.

Calling attention to the strong relationship between academic achievement and self-image, Bowman points out that the mechanism through which parental influence is mediated seems to be pupil self-concept. Further, the most effective method now known to alter pupil self-concept is training parents for their role. It is evident in pupil self-view that parent influence is more important than the school and can be positively modified by training. Greater emphasis is also urged in helping the adult world convey important nonintellectual factors such as aspiration and drive to succeed, which in some cases are better predictors of success than scholastic measures.

Strom invites the school to utilize any positive features that emerge from life in the circumstance of poverty. Numerous strengths, presently rendered nonfunctional in the classroom, have potential use for instruction. Also there is a real danger in constantly describing children of the poor as culturally handicapped, deprived, and disadvantaged in that, although the referent is their environmental limitation, it tends to transfer to an image of less potential. And if teachers cannot be optimistic regarding the prospect of such children, how can a transfer of positive aspiration occur?

Responsibility for providing an environment conducive to personal growth is not exclusive to the family. In the larger context every community is charged with offering whatever support and services are necessary to ensure a state of well-being for its membership. Usually this job is well done; nearly a dozen statistical measures confirm the fact that on the average our current edition of youth faces a brighter future than any preceding generation. But for those 700,000 who each year drop out of school, a different prospect is forecast. Unemployment among out-of-school teenagers has risen 50 per cent in the last six years, 20 per cent in the past twelve months, while our country's total employment rate is at its highest peak since World War II. These figures suggest the comparative suddenness with which this crisis has developed.

Perhaps the most significant factor has been that machines, which at the turn of this century did 6 per cent of our work, now do 96 per cent. To be sure, machines are cheaper than people; they reduce human relations by reducing personnel; they improve business procedures with almost instant feedback of information; they increase efficiency because distance is not a barrier to control and coordinate. But they also displace some 4000 jobs every week in this country.

In describing the pressures that confront man in an automated society

Braceland maintains that adaptability is the key to mental health. Most often the drama of emotional upset is played in those lives where there is inability to encounter change and stress. Already most job specifications require that new workers possess a high-school diploma since it is generally believed that completors of secondary education more likely will be able to acclimate to the changing demands characteristic of a progressing economy. Employers are faced with this gamble: Can a dropout who has not met the educational demands of the school be expected to meet similar educational demands of a company by updating his skills when the need may arise? More often than not, reports Brown, the risk is not taken. There is no doubt about it—high-school graduation is a necessity. Although this is not a new idea, under the circumstance it becomes a new imperative, a communal responsibility.

Since a community by its style of sanction can reinforce or neutralize the orientation of youth toward higher education, Braceland believes that every institution should encourage the growth and development of all its patrons. This is especially important where children come from environments in which academic aspirations are viewed with disfavor. To overcome the negative influence of inappropriate adult models, Farnsworth argues it is necessary to create channels of communication within each community so that children can come into contact with older people of integrity who may serve as worthy prototypes for emulation.

Community volunteer groups could be more influential as a resource of guidance for the young, writes Torrance, were they to utilize their latent power. The favored role of these organizations is shown by research indicating youngsters more readily confide in nonacademic teachers than in public-school staff. Largely this preference relates to an atmosphere of learning wherein creative-thinking abilities are encouraged, unconventional response is tolerated, and activity is not subject to constant evaluation. Strom observes that since youth look to their peers for behavioral cues, voluntary organizations might inculcate desirable habits and attitudes through programs which utilize exemplary boys to teach their age mates. Depending much on experience with associates, one can be made to feel more or less capable, more or less worthy, more or less acceptable.

A combination of informed community action and attitude inheres in the New Haven approach reported by Brown. Designed to attack social problems in neighborhoods of low income, the program concentrates on mental health and achievement of all age groups from pre-kindergarten experience through job training for unskilled adults. Called by Secretary of Labor Wirtz "A model for community development," New Haven's effort served as a guide in drafting President Johnson's Economic Opportunity Act of 1964 (H.R. 11377). This legislation, which in its first year cost an estimated 962.5 million dollars, seeks to attack environmental conditions in the community that limit personal growth. The rationale for national, state, and local involvement stems from the observation of our late President John F. Kennedy: "If a free society cannot help the many who are poor, it cannot save the few who are rich."

How the other half lives has long been a common subject for discussion. Though the question remains, the reference group now is one of age rather than economics. That is, we as adults are becoming more interested in how the other half of our people live, those constituting the "teenage subculture." Recent growth in proportion of young people in the population is not exclusive to the United States; indeed two-thirds of Latin America's population is under 21 years of age. In nations other than our own, however, more cultural uniformity and a slower rate of progress have allowed maintenance of close adult-adolescent relationships. In contrast, the rapidity of change in America, in rendering child life today so much different from a few years ago, tends to lessen the experiences young and old have had in common—this separates persons of different generations.

It is apparent that children in the future will learn more from one another than from adults. What is not so obvious, writes Jones, are the ways in which peer groups influence patterns of attitude and behavior. Were such knowledge available there would be little cause for educator consternation since teaching could effectively proceed by using peer pressures as the sanctioning agent for youth behavior rather than the extrinsic, less acceptable adult authority. Anticipating the need for insight regarding cohesive features of peer organization, Williams offers a definitive treatment of group structure with special attention given role-conduct expectations. Another aid comes from Jones who, in underscoring academic dimensions in which associates most influence behavior, sheds light on the areas wherein adults might best focus their attempts to penetrate teen spheres.

To generate popular motivation for academic excellence requires an understanding of goal orientation among teenagers. That athletes are more esteemed than scholars is to be expected, Coleman explains, since victory on the field is communal, involving and rewarding the entire group. On the other hand, classroom wins are personal and often gained at the expense of one's fellows. Consequently, many would-be academicians choose to excel in the activities where peer reward is forthcoming rather than run the risk of exclusion for being a "curve raiser." In proposing academic contests among schools, Coleman hopes to arouse group encouragement of individual achievement. The idea of using groups to support individual growth may have implications for work with juvenile delinquents. Cohesion is very strong among gangs and cliques of disadvantaged children, perhaps because of communal victory. That is, the efforts of each member can jeopardize or enhance the welfare of his entire company; hence strong attachment and unswerving loyalty.

Undoubtedly youth aggregations can be directed to sponsor aspects of mental health that heretofore have been impossible. A case in point might be to reverse the sanction opposing intuitive and affective behavior by male youngsters. Although Jackson, Getzels, and Xydis admit it is impossible to assess the extent to which creative behavior is lessened by arbitrary determination of sex roles, few psychologists would deny the amount as influential. Perhaps by manipulating adolescent support and encouragement of creative activity, such behavior may flourish.

One thing is certain. Adolescents should be able to profit from and enjoy their peer experiences. Whether this is true will depend on the setting provided by each community and home. If the setting is wholesome, youth will demand of their fellows a good life with desires and aggression both directed into acceptable channels. Where inadequate parental support and poor community models exist, however, peer groups are likely to impede rather than facilitate personal development. Plato said it well in his ever-contemporary adage: "What is honored in a country will be cultivated there."

R. D. S.

1 *Family Role in the Mental Health of School Children*

Paul H. Bowman

Popular and professional journals contain many articles on the obligations of the family to the child and to the school, the kinds of problems that arise, and what ought to be done about them. Generally, the ideas presented in these discussions sound very familiar, and I presume they are ideas on which most people are fairly well agreed. For instance, most will agree that much of the child's personality and his stock of attitudes and patterns of behavior are determined very early in his life, and that his parents are the major determinants in the formation of these permanent directions of the child's life. We might generally agree that when a child has parents who are understanding, who give him support and freedom within limits, but who also exercise positive guidance through precept and example, this child has a greater chance for mental health and school achievement than when these parental attributes are absent.

But when this is once said, all we really have is an assumption based on our personal experience, observation, and opinion. Is it supported by any specific evidence? Over the past half-century clinical psychologists have accumulated considerable evidence that would support the foregoing theoretical assumptions, and these bits of new evidence have been utilized by theorists to expand and particularize their theories. Research evidence in the area of parent-child relationships, however, has been very limited and is appearing only rather lately. A brief review of a few selected studies is important to our consideration of school mental health and achievement.

A number of earlier studies showed a positive correlation between intelligence and various measures of academic and life success. This was to be expected; children with more intellectual skills and capacities are likely to accomplish more on academic tasks and jobs that require such skills. Some studies also showed a positive correlation between intelligence and social adjustment. This information was received with surprise by some, but it should not be surprising that those with superior skills who are achieving academic success and the approval of their world are also more happy, contented, and emotionally satisfied. This also is to be expected.

Later studies began to show that among children of the same level of intelligence there could be—and were—great differences in their level of school achievement, so there had to be factors of major importance other than intelligence affecting the outcome of educational efforts. Anne Roe (1953) found in her study of American scientists that, above a certain level, intelligence is a poor predictor of success. In a study of gifted children Terman and Oden (1947) also showed that social adjustment and drive to achieve significantly differentiated the most and least successful of his group. These studies seem to indicate that adjustment of mental health is a major factor in achieving academic and social success in childhood and adult life.

Other studies have attempted to identify the sources or origins of these nonintellectual factors in success and adjustment. Rosen and Andrade (1959) found that high motivation for achievement was related to early training by parents in doing things well and in doing things without help. Some other studies indicate that "drives to achievement" can be developed later in life through other social pressures, but that motivations developed this way are less powerful than those developed earlier in the family structure (McClelland, 1955; McClelland, Baldwin, Bronfenbrenner, and Strodtbeck, 1958). Several of our own studies give further support to the importance of parental influence on mental health and achievement. In a study of high-school dropouts (Bowman and Matthews, 1958) it was discovered that, when intelligence and social class were controlled, the major factor that distinguished the dropout from the stay-in was the attitude of the parents to education. Most of the parents of the dropouts had no objection to their child's plan of leaving school, whereas most of the parents of the stay-ins put great value on education themselves and insisted that their children finish high school.

Another study was concerned with the very bright students in high school, and compared the high achievers with the low achievers (Pierce and Bowman, 1960). It was found that these family factors were characteristic of the high-achieving students: they more often named their parents as having been significant influences in their lives; the parents themselves were better educated, held higher aspirations for their children, regarded their children as more responsible and independent; and they encouraged more verbalization among their children.

Very recently researchers at Michigan State University have reported findings that give considerable emphasis to the importance of parents in the mental health and achievement of children, and that also begin to indicate the mechanism through which their influence is mediated (Brookover, Shailer, and Patterson, 1964). They discovered a strong relationship between academic achievement and the self-concept children have of their own ability. They also found that as self-concepts of ability changed there tended to be corresponding changes in grade-point averages. These findings are consistent with and lend support to the theoretical position that social behavior is a function of the self-concept that people hold of themselves.

These investigators went one step further and measured the effectiveness of three different methods of changing the self-concepts of students, namely, through (1) formal, large-group information sessions, (2) group and individual counseling, and (3) training parents on how to improve the self-concepts of their children. The first two methods produced no significant changes in the children, but by training parents in their role significant changes were produced in the self-concepts of their children in a one-year period and this change was reflected in significant changes in the children's grade-point averages for the same period. This seems to indicate that parents are the primary influence on self-concepts of children, more important than teachers or counselors, and that the parental influence can be positively modified by proper training.

Evidence seems to be accumulating that personal and social factors, as well as intelligence, are inextricably involved in the teaching-learning process, that the most critical of these is probably the self-concept, and that the strongest influence on the self-concept is that of the parents.

COMMUNICATION BETWEEN TEACHERS AND PARENTS

It seems a safe assumption to say that most parents are genuinely interested in their children and concerned about the best way to exercise their parental responsibilities. It is also safe to say that most teachers have a genuine personal investment in their elementary-school pupils. Both parents and teacher see the child almost every day and put in much time and energy aiding the education and development of a particular child. Both family and school invest thousands of dollars in each child.

In most situations of joint responsibility for human well-being much effort is spent in communication and joint planning between the parties sharing that responsibility. If two doctors are simultaneously treating the same child they will likely spend as much time in consultation as they do in treating the child. If two agencies are treating the same family they will usually spend much time in joint planning. In a child-guidance clinic staff conferences on each case are held regularly to evaluate progress and plan treatment. But communication between parents and teachers is usually limited to five or six report cards a year plus occasional notes perhaps. It is rather difficult to understand why two or three persons genuinely concerned with the same child over long periods of time have so little to do with each other.

I have had a number of personal opportunities to see both sides of this issue, as a parent and leader of parent groups, as a consultant and teacher of teachers, and as a therapist with children and parents. It is my opinion that behind this lack of communication is a considerable amount of fear, mistrust, and even hostility for one another. I am sure that this opinion will be challenged by many readers and there will always be instances of good relationships that can be cited. But it has been my observation in many different communities in different states that when teachers or parents are in their own groups and are together long enough to break down their reserve, they are very likely to be critical and start blaming the other for the shortcomings they see in the child. Teachers often say, "I have another Jones kid this year and everyone of them has been a mess, but there is nothing you can do with those parents"; or "I never hear a word from my parents; you would think they would show some concern for their children in school"; or "the PTA is just a bunch of busybodies or status seekers who want to run the school." On the other side parents often remark, "The teacher never gives any individual attention or help to a child"; or "I can't blame the kids for not wanting to go to school to those teachers"; or "I wouldn't dare to talk to the teacher or principal about Johnny because I know they would resent it and then take it out on Johnny in school." This last feeling is much more common than is supposed.

Such comments are indicative of hostility, obvious or covert, and there must be reasons behind them. At one point I felt that this must be due largely to poor information and little opportunity for contact. To test this assumption we formed a two-week summer workshop composed of teachers and parents in equal numbers. The result was failure; by the beginning of the second week the parents were complaining that the teachers were cliquish and talked a jargon of their own, that they were concerned with curricula and not children, and that they refused to get to know the parents. Teachers said they had nothing in common with parents, and felt that parents were only being critical. This led to rather open hostility that was never bridged in the group, and these were people chosen because of their interest in better understanding between parents and teachers.

Obviously more is involved than simply poor information or lack of communication. When fear and hostility are present to this extent, both parties probably feel inadequate about their own ability to fulfill their difficult task. I believe, too, that each feels exposed and vulnerable to the other. The teacher feels subject to unfair and unreasoning criticism from people in the community, particularly from those persons who are powerful or quite vocal and who frequently seek unrealistic treatment of their children. Parents also feel vulnerable. They feel that the school is a closed system to which they are outsiders, that to be good parents they are expected to stay at home and not bother the school, and that if they take a complaint to the school their child may suffer some discriminatory action. Both attitudes are probably created by the same cause, that is, by the relatively few extreme persons, both parents and teachers, who are misfits themselves and who make life difficult for all others around them. This situation will probably continue until the schools find a way to police their own ranks more adequately, and until communities find ways to deal with irresponsible parents.

INCREASING TEACHER-PARENT COOPERATION

Assuming mutuality of interest in the child by parents and teacher, what can be done to increase cooperative effort? I propose here a simple statement of these roles as a basis for more detailed discussion, namely, that the responsibility of parents is to send the child to school interested in and ready for learning, and that the school's task is to help him master the tools of learning. Let us now make these role definitions more specific.

Consider first the parents. The parent role concerns developing interest and motivation and guiding the formation of the self-concept, hopefully in a positive direction. The parent would not be considered a supervisor of homework, and would not usually be involved in helping on subject matter except at the request of the teacher for help on particular problems that a child may have.

There are specific things that parents can and should do. The first of these is developing curiosity or the questioning attitude in their child. This can be aided by asking questions at times when the child is observing an event or having a new experience, and by responding to the child's questions with other questions rather than answers. For example, when a child asks why windows frost over on a cold day, a parent might easily give a one-sentence answer. However, he could more effectively encourage curiosity by asking, "What is that on the window? Where did it come from? What made it settle on the window?" A child's curiosity is often stimulated by being exposed to new experiences, and parents can usually use the family vacation or the Sunday drive to include some stops, such as museums, historical markers, or watching ants build their homes. Curiosity is the basis of learning, and it is an attitude that can be transmitted from parent to child.

Second, parents can make their own values much more explicit to children. Children usually will pick up their parents' real values whether they are verbally taught or not, but usually they will not know the reasons for them. If parents can make explicit to their children the values they hold and the reasons for which they hold them, then children in later life can make more intelligent choices of their own. A child may know that his parents do not approve of smoking, but is it because it is sinful, expensive, or a health or fire hazard? Values play such an important role in personal development that help should be given where possible in their development.

Third, parents can enhance self-concepts and confidence by guiding children to successful accomplishments in whatever activities the child chooses. It is a delicate operation to foster completion of tasks without either driving the child or taking away his freedom to fail, but it can be learned. Suppose a boy wants to make a birdhouse; he should do everything by himself that he possibly can so it will be his product; on the other hand he should not be allowed to fail for not having tools or a plan. If there is sawing to do, the boy should do the sawing and the father should hold the board if necessary, not vice versa. The boy should decide how he wants it built, but the father should make suggestions of various ways. Strangely enough, an important part of developing confidence and success is this freedom to fail; there is much less opportunity for growth if the father always steps in to complete unfinished tasks. A boy may well build a birdhouse that no bird will have, but with help he can learn why the birds do not use it. The father himself may not know, but he can direct the boy to a book or a neighbor.

Fourth, a major task of parents is to help the child develop individuality. From school and from peers the pressure on a child to conform is strong. The spark of individuality or creativity is very precious, and it is mostly through the family that it is protected and encouraged. As a parent I have found this to be one of my most urgent responsibilities.

Finally, parents need to provide the atmosphere of psychological safety and support which makes it possible to live amid tensions from many sources. This is an indivisible base of all growth and learning.

THE SCHOOL'S RESPONSIBILITY TO PARENTS

This book is directed to professional educators, and therefore this chapter should include a discussion of the school's responsibilities to parents. Since both are concerned with the child, and since it is evident that the parent holds such an influential role in the learning process, does the school itself have any obligation to the parent?

The school through its own program and personnel can try to enhance the self-concepts of children by building success experiences into the classroom, but experimental evidence indicates that they could be more successful perhaps by trying to bring parents into a real partnership in the educational enterprise.

I think it must be recognized that unless the school takes the initiative in establishing the partnership, nothing will be done. The school is a central community institution with professional personnel and tax money, and the initiative for action must rest with an organized group. It is useless to expect parents to take this step. I know of no examples where parents have been made a real part of the school program. What might be done?

First, there must be a real and continuing two-way exchange of information about the child. The task of the school might be done more effectively if it systematically sought from every parent his store of information about the child, his strengths and weaknesses, his friends, his ambitions, his hurts and joys. This might be obtained through home visits, where additional insights could be gained into the child's world, or by school conferences. Also, if the school communicated to the parents the meaningful information it had about the child, some parents could more adequately fulfill their own role. Then too the school might undertake actual training programs for parents on how to develop curiosity and self-concepts at home (Brookover, Shailer, and Patterson, 1964), and such meetings would be far more meaningful than social visits to the classroom once a year.

Second, the school needs to organize definite and easy routes of communication between home and school. This is both an attitudinal and a mechanical problem. Parents must be convinced that the school wants their communication, but also the school must make clear the time, the place, and the means by which it can take place. Pediatricians frequently advise their patients when and where to phone them, and what kinds of problems can be handled by a phone call. Parents ought to know how and when to reach the teacher. They ought to know also some other person to talk to in the school when there are problems with the teacher which they feel they cannot discuss directly with her. There may be occasions when the school would seek systematic information from parents about their opinions on school policies or practices, and at other times it would be important to interpret new programs to parents.

Some might say that suggestions such as these might be realized in a middle-class neighborhood, but would be impossible in a lower-class area. There is some experience with experimental programs for parents in both kinds of areas; it has been found that there are more barriers in the underprivileged areas, such as more working mothers, fewer two-parent homes, more suspicion of the school, but no less concern was found for children. In one attempt to interview parents in all schools of a community, we found somewhat less participation in underprivileged areas, but still 50 per cent of these parents participated in the program after only one announcement.

It is the contention of this essay that the family has the central role in fostering the mental health of school children, and that the school, if it could utilize the parent resources as a partner in the educational enterprise, could greatly increase its effectiveness in both social and academic achievement.

2 Maternal Teaching Styles and Educational Retardation

Robert D. Hess

The view I wish to present is that the dropout syndrome originates at the preschool level in the nature of the communicative and interactive modes that develop between mother and child. The affective, regulatory, and disciplinary aspects of mother-child interaction are traditional topics for research and theory, but the importance of the cognitive components of these early experiences has not been fully recognized. The argument of this chapter is that inadequacy in the cognitive features of early mother-child exchange fosters later alienation of the child and adolescent from the educative processes and other basic sectors and institutions of society.[1]

Within the last year I have had two experiences that illustrate vividly the problems arising from educational inadequacy, particularly those of adults in urban areas. Last spring I started working with a community group attempting to develop a retraining program for adults in an economically depressed section of Chicago. In preparing our proposal we inquired of the appropriate agencies about the success of established training programs for adults. We discovered that one of the difficulties these programs encounter is a frequent failure of applicants to pass qualifying exams for the program; of twenty persons who apply, about three pass the tests that qualify them to enter available courses of training.

The problem of semiliteracy in adults in the United States, although usually ignored, is not new. Our method of dealing with adult illiteracy has been through education of children in the public schools so that illiteracy will gradually disappear from our society. But our efforts to raise the general level of education of populations in economically depressed areas of this country are inadequate. Although it is difficult to

This is a revised version of a presentation to the Invitational Meeting on Secondary School Curriculum for Potential Dropouts, Washington, D. C., November 17–20, 1963.

[1] The various circumstances involved in alienation of youth are described in a paper by Havighurst and Stiles, 1961. In this essay I am adopting their definition of the term.

15

obtain firm data (primarily through the reluctance of school boards to release achievement-test results and other performance indices on schools located in culturally deprived areas), there is reason to believe that many, if not most, of our high-school students in economically disadvantaged areas are semiliterate when they drop out or graduate from high school. Moreover, given current population and migration trends, the average level of functioning education in our major cities may be decreasing. The dropout syndrome is part of a larger, critical problem of education in the urban context.

The second experience that illustrates another dimension of this total educational issue was a series of conversations with teachers and principals in several schools in three of our large cities. These professionals were aware of the extent of illiteracy at adult levels in depressed urban areas, but they were more concerned about a situation at the other end of the age range—one not so well known. They agreed that in some areas of the large cities one-half to two-thirds of the children are educationally retarded when they enter the first grade. That is, on opening day in many schools as few as one-third of the first-grade class may be ready to start a typical first-grade curriculum.

What is behind the circumstances that prevent vast numbers of young people in working-class areas of urban regions from taking advantage of opportunities offered by the institutions of the city and community? What are the implications of this situation in view of skills that youth must develop to be fitted for occupational and other roles in our society?

It is my thesis that it is necessary to examine the early experiences of urban youth and to study the origins of attitudes that create educational retardation if we are to be effective in an intervention program. The problems of junior-high-school and high-school students are fairly well known. We have much less information about the conditions that operate to produce them and we do not have adequate information about the skills that are lacking when children come to kindergarten and first grade. In the hope of finding some answers to these questions, we began a project at the University of Chicago which inquires into the origins of motivational attitudes and behavior leading to dropout and other educational failure.

Orientation for this research goes back to the well-documented relation between social class and both academic performance and intelligence, which consistently shows test scores to be relatively low in working-class groups, especially in that socioeconomic level we now term "culturally deprived." This relative deficit in scholastic competence and educability is the essential problem facing the schools in metropolitan areas of the United States.

The question our study presents is this: In what way does social-class experience affect mental development? What happens in the cultural environment that produces behavior which by the seventh, eighth, or ninth grades results in educational retardation of two to three years? Part of the theory for the project comes from Basil Bernstein (1961) of the University of London, who takes the position that the effect of cultural disadvantage is understandable if we consider social-class experience as a set of conditions or variables involving a wide variety of effects that impinge on the young child. To deal with the problems of social class and learning, we need to understand what occurs in the interchange between the child and his cultural setting. It is essential to break these experiences down to small bits—to their basic component parts—and to analyze social class and cognitive deprivation in specific and manageable terms.

In this context our hypothesis is that in cultural deprivation the pattern of communication that develops between mother and child affects the child's cognitive equipment and handicaps him when he begins his school program. This is not so much a theory of deficit as an argument that there are cognitive patterns of responsive behavior and ways of interpreting stimuli from the external world that these children learn in interaction with their families. These patterns are not adaptive or functional for academic learning and may prevent the child from taking advantage of cognitive experiences available in a classroom.

In Bernstein's view, language structures and conditions what the child learns and how he learns, setting limits within which future learning may take place. He identifies two forms of communication codes or styles of verbal behavior: *restrictive* and *elaborate*.[2] Restrictive codes are stereotyped, limited, and condensed, lacking in specificity and the exactness needed for precise conceptualization and differentiation. Sentences are short, simple, often unfinished; there is little use of subordinate clauses for elaborating the content of the sentence; it is a language of implicit meaning, easily understood and commonly shared. It is the language form often used in impersonal situations when the intent is to promote solidarity or reduce tension. Restrictive codes are nonspecific clichés, statements, or observations about events, made in general terms that will be readily understood. The basic quality of this mode is to limit the range and detail of concept and information involved. Elaborate codes, however, are those in which communication is individualized and the message is specific to a particular situation topic and person. It is more particular, more differentiated, and more precise. It permits expression of a wider and more complex range of thought, tending toward discrimination among cognitive and affective content.

---

[2] Bernstein has used different terms for these two communication modes. In his chapter in Halsey et al., he calls them "public" (restrictive) and "formal" (elaborate). The terms used in this summary come from more recent papers.

Let us consider two possible examples of mother-child communication using these two types of codes. Assume that the emotional climate of two homes is approximately the same; the significant difference is in style of communication. A child is playing in the kitchen with some pots and pans when the telephone rings. In one home the mother says, "Be quiet," or "Shut up," or any one of several other short, peremptory commands, and she answers the phone while the child sits still on the floor. In the other home the mother says, "I'd rather you kept quiet while I answer the phone, dear." The question our study poses is thus: What inner response is elicited in the child, what is the effect on his developing cognitive network of concepts and meaning in each of these two situations. In one instance the child is not asked for any kind of mental response. He is simply told to do something; he is not called on to reflect or make mental discriminations. In the other example the child is required to follow two or three ideas. He is asked to relate his behavior to a time dimension; he must think of his behavior in relation to what happens to another person, and he is asked to attend to how the mother thinks and feels. He has to perform a more complicated task to follow the communication of his mother in that his relationship to her is mediated in part through concepts and shared ideas; his mind is stimulated or exercised (in an elementary fashion) by a more elaborate and complex verbal communication initiated by the mother. As objects of these two divergent communication styles, repeated in various ways in similar situations and circumstances during the preschool years, these two imaginary children would be expected to develop significantly different verbal facility and cognitive equipment by the time they entered the public-school system.

The orientation of our project is to view the child as an organism that receives a great deal of information of many kinds, much more than he can accommodate. Even as adults we respond to only a small part of the total stimulation we receive in a typically active working moment. What the child responds to, how he interprets stimuli, and how he reacts are learned in interaction with the environment. He is taught what to attend to, how to interpret messages, and how to respond. These patterns of cognitive response are socialized in early experience in the home, and become the basis on which further cognitive development proceeds.

Operating within this basic rationale, our project attacked this problem: *If children from working-class homes come to school unprepared to do the level of work the classroom demands, and if middle-class children generally come to school adequately prepared, what facilitating experiences are present in middle-class homes that typically do not occur in the working-class homes?*

To study this problem we have selected 160 mothers and their 4-year-old children: 40 from upper middle-class backgrounds, 40 working-class mothers from skilled occupational levels, 40 from unskilled occupational levels, and 40 mothers on public assistance. All families are intact, except those on public aid.[3] To enable us to examine what it is (in addition to the information that the mother passes to the child) that affects learning, we are studying these mothers along several dimensions: (1) the mother's self-concept and her view of herself in relation to the community and to the school; (2) the attitudes the mother has developed toward the school as an institution and toward learning as an experience; (3) the cognitive aspects of communication process between mother and child; and (4) the affective aspects of interaction.

It is in terms of self-concept and motivational structure that we find some of the greatest differences among the mothers of our research group. The aspiration levels that mothers have for their children vary, of course, within the social classes as well as among social classes. It is not at all uncommon, however, for a working-class mother to respond to the question "What would you like Johnny to do when he grows up?" with the comment: "I want him to be a doctor." Then if the interviewer asks, "What do you think he'll really do?" she is likely to offer a completely different choice: "Oh, maybe he'll end up working in a steel mill." Or if she is asked about her daughter, she will say, "I want her to be a teacher," and later say she expects her to be a clerk in a dime store. There is often a large gap between what they feel is a desirable occupation level and what they think their children are going to do.

Think of this view of the world in terms of its effect on the self-concepts of mother and child. In a society that offers a wide range of opportunities, the mother is convinced that the child is not going to reach desirable goals, through lack of opportunity, lack of schooling, or lack of ability. If we ask these mothers about their own educational and occupational experience, we obtain a similar response—less preparation than needed, much higher aspirations than can be achieved.

We find also that in economically depressed sections of the city the mother's interaction with the community tends to isolate her from the world in which she lives so that her view may become one of "family against the world." Her interaction with the school, with other agencies, particularly agencies that have to do with public welfare, reveals a great deal of ambivalence. Anyone who has worked with families who have been subject to the various regulations of public housing, of public-

[3] These mothers are all Negroes, so selected because of the significant representation of Negroes in economically depressed areas of Chicago. Obviously, cultural deprivation in the United States occurs in several different national and racial groups, including Indians, Mexicans, Puerto Ricans, and whites. An added advantage is that this will provide one of the few research opportunities to study social-class differences in maternal behavior and cognitive development among Negroes.

assistance programs, or of other programs that subject their clients to suspicious scrutiny can easily observe the negative effect this treatment has on dignity and self-confidence. Our research interest is in the resulting impact on the child's sense of confidence and competence as he approaches public school.

Another area, that of achievement motivation and the acquisition of attitudes toward school, approaches the socialization of educability from another vector. One technique we used was to ask the mother to tell us what she would say to her child as she sent him away on the first day of school. We got quite different responses within and between classes. The typical pattern in a working-class home was something like this: "I tell him to do what the teacher says, not to get into trouble, not get into any fights, be sure to come home after school, and don't get lost." This is a view of the school as raising issues of dealing with authority and with peers, rather than presenting educational content. There are occasional references to learning but, if so, they are presented almost inadvertently. Such a response contrasts with the upper-middle-class families where the mother is more likely to say: "Well, the teacher is sort of like your mother, you learn from her; if you have any problems, go to her; you are going to learn to read and write." This approach views experience in school in terms of the child's learning experience.

We also asked the subjects to tell a story about a picture showing a teacher and mother in conference. In our preliminary data the working-class mothers most often say that the mother has been called in by the school over some disciplinary problem; the upper-middle-class mother more frequently sees the conference as one in which the mother is coming to consult with the teacher about a learning problem.

The major difference between these two types of response is in the view of the school as an institution with which the child must cope, as contrasted with a view of the school as a place for learning. The lower-class child approaches school not oriented toward learning but attuned to the need to get along with the institution. The experience is defined to him as a problem of adapting to the teacher and to the peer situation. This presents a misconception of the school's purpose with a heavy emphasis on conformity and physical behavior, rather than mental activity.

The most critical part of our project is a detailed study of the cognitive exchange between mother and child—how the mother teaches the child; as a secondary point we shall study the ways these teaching styles may be related to the child's school performance. In our project the mothers are brought to the University Nursery School where they are taught three simple tasks by our staff. One is to sort some plastic toys (cars, spoons, and chairs) by color and function; another is to sort some varying shaped and colored blocks by size and marking; and the third is to draw designs on an etch-a-sketch toy, which is a small screen with two knobs. Underneath the screen is a lever which draws a line on the screen and which can be operated by moving the knobs. One knob handle controls the vertical movement; the other controls the horizontal movement. The mother is instructed to operate one knob and the child the other. Together they are to make a series of designs which increase in complexity. We first teach the mother how to do each of these tasks; then we ask her to teach or work with her child. Our object is to observe the interaction between her and the child in this teaching situation. What is her teaching style and how does it affect the cognitive development of her child?

The variation in styles of maternal teaching can be illustrated by one of the tasks we used in the pilot phase of the study. We had a jigsaw puzzle with fish of various size and color. The mother was asked to teach her child how to put the puzzle together. Mothers showed a great deal of variation in their approach to teaching their children this problem. One mother, for example, took the puzzle and said to her child: "This is a jigsaw puzzle. You've never seen one before. We take the pieces out and then put them back together. See where all the pieces are and look at the colors, look at the shape so you'll know where they go." She had defined the task. She had told the child how to proceed. Then she spilled out the pieces, gave the equipment to the child and was able to guide him, by verbal direction, to respond to visual clues needed to solve the problem. Another mother, equally supportive of her child (according to our interviewers who saw her in her home), took the puzzle and dumped it out on the table in front of the child without a word and then said: "Now you do it." Then she watched and as the child would pick up a piece and try to put it in place, the mother would say, "Turn it around; turn it around." Thirty-five times she repeated the instruction: "Turn it around." Finally, in frustration and defeat, the child said to her, "You do it."

Although this mother was trying to help the child, she did not know how to teach, she was unable to convey the concepts needed to solve this simple problem. It is apparent that the ability to communicate concepts, to share information, and to program a simple task is found least often in the low-income family situation. This is not, however, the only important outcome of a situation of this kind. Imagine the child in repeated interaction with his mother coming upon situations which he tries to solve but, through lack of maternal assistance, finds it impossible. The reaction of defeat ("You do it") is likely to recur and be magnified many times, and develop in the child an orientation, toward both the world and toward certain kinds of problems, that sees difficulties as not solvable. Compare his response with that of the first child in our example who knew no more about the puzzle to begin with, but who through experience realized that with some guidance there was a way to reach a solution. Upon this kind of motivational base attitudes toward new learning may very well emerge.[4]

Difficulty arises when the mother is not able to transmit to the child the kinds of things prerequisite to success even at this very early level. If the young child experiences success in mental tasks in the home so that there is positive reinforcement, some reward for learning, his natural curiosity can then take him through most of the early stages.

From our experience it seems likely that many mothers can be taught to develop these cognitive facilities in their children. We are now in the planning stage of a program to prepare mothers in educationally disadvantaged homes to teach preschool children the basic cognitive skills they need for the first-grade curriculum.

The next area we have been exploring in these interaction situations is the role of emotional support and achievement pressure in the teaching process. Our learning situations thus include: (1) the amount of information the mother can transmit; (2) the amount of support she gives the child in the learning situation; and (3) the pressure she puts on the child to achieve. The way a mother uses information, support, and pressure not only reveals her teaching style but may have systematic effects on the child's approach to learning and problem solving. That is, it seems likely that if a mother offers support to the child in learning situations but gives little information about how to solve problems and little pressure to complete tasks or achieve, the child will respond with a casual attitude toward learning and achievement; a mother who puts a great deal of pressure on a child to achieve and perform, but who is unable to supply the information necessary for successful learning, may well induce disappointment and frustration in the child and inhibit curiosity; the mother who offers information and pressure without effectively supporting the child may arouse undue anxiety in learning and performance situations. The focus of our study is to examine the effects of these various maternal teaching styles on the educability of the child, both with respect to his cognitive ability and with regard to his motivation for learning.

One important requisite is the need to involve the community and home in a task of this kind. The problem of strategy on a long-range basis should be to shift as much responsibility and participation to the community level as possible. The participation of community organiza-

---

[4] We have been surprised at the resources of motivation and energy these mothers display. They try—they try very hard, indeed. We thought that an abstract task like sorting blocks might bore mother and child. On the contrary, we have seen 4-year-olds stay with a task for twenty minutes, with the mother concentrating on her efforts to help and to teach.

tions and institutions, particularly of the family and mothers, in this sort of program offers an opportunity to improve communication between school and mother, and to give the mother a different concept of the school and what the school can do. It may also give her a new view of how she may work with the school to provide for the child the preconditions for successful learning. This kind of coordinated effort in urban areas eventually may make school-dropout conferences unnecessary.

3 The Dropout Problem in Relation to Family Affect and Effect

Robert D. Strom

"The most vivid truth of our age," Margaret Mead (1959) has suggested, "is that no one will live all his life in the world into which he was born, and no one will die in the world in which he worked during his maturity." Rapid change appears to be the mode for our time, with all facets of community life subject to adaptation. Serving to lessen or undermine the cohesion of society's primary unit, the family, has been a passing of home industry, the frequent employment of both parents, the invention of the automobile, and the development of commercial amusements.

In spite of universal exposure to these changes, our society today comprises more divergent family types than ever before. Differing by section of the country, communities within cities, ethnic and religious groups, economic and social classes, and vocations, families vary according to life cycle, number and role of family members, locus of authority, and life style. Both in apparent variety and essential unity, the American family needs to be viewed in a perspective of ongoing transition from an old rural institution form to a democratic companionship type of relation geared to an urban environment with a shift of emphasis from rigid stability to adaptability (Burgess, 1957).

JUXTAPOSITION OF DROPOUT EFFECT—1900–1963

Just as family operation has altered during recent times, the effect of school dropout on families has changed. Early in this century, when a youngster quit school his decision had a negligible effect on the home. Indeed in some cases the family encouraged such a decision. Because 90 per cent of the working population were persons whose secondary education was incomplete, there was no stigma attached to leaving school before graduation.

Reprinted from *Journal of Home Economics*, 56, May 1964, 299–304.

Nor was a dropout's family held in disdain by neighbors, for they viewed a youngster's preference of work to school not as a shameful choice but as a legitimate alternative. Moreover, there was no public cause for concern about whether a dropout would constitute a social liability since the transition from education to employment was a smooth one with over half the available jobs requiring few if any skills and little or no academic preparation.

Drastic changes in the economy and occupational structure, however, have served to diminish job prospects for today's dropout. No longer are a third of our people employed on farms, as was true in 1900. Today only 10 per cent are so employed and it is predicted the ratio will decline to 5 per cent by 1970. No longer are most available jobs for the unskilled. Today these jobs constitute only 17 per cent of the positions in our labor market, and it is predicted this percentage, too, will decline to 5 per cent by 1970. Indeed the number of unskilled jobs in our economy is less today than it was fifteen years ago despite the fact that the work force has increased by several millions in that period.

The problem is not that there are more dropouts today but that there is a smaller demand for them than ever before. There no longer is the absorptive quality in the work force to take care of mistakes made in the educational system.

NO ROOM AT THE BOTTOM

Accompanying the decrease in job opportunity for less-educated persons is an unprecedented growth in the number of young people entering the labor market. During this decade the number of workers under age 25 will increase by at least 45 per cent. Since most of this influx is composed of men and women who have twelve or more years of formal schooling, it is understandable that the approximately 700,000 dropouts each year are last in line to secure an ever-diminishing number of low-level jobs for which they might be suited. For the first time there is "no room at the bottom."

At this juncture, communal concern becomes more than just a regard for wasted talent. The dropout's problem makes him a public liability; his lack of funds becomes a public debt rendering a severe financial burden on the community in which he resides.

For example, some 270,000 persons are on public assistance in Cook County, Illinois. Fifty per cent of the Chicago-area reliefers cannot read at the eighth-grade level; over half of them are under 32 years of age. Because of their youth the latter group may be expected to reproduce young who, in turn, will drop out. According to Raymond M. Hilliard, director of public aid for Cook County, grants totaling approximately 15-million dollars a month are made to these people. It is estimated that

Illinois will have an annual welfare budget of 1-billion dollars by 1970 unless the present trend of unemployment is reversed.

THE CULTURE OF POVERTY

It would appear that leaving school before graduation has a deleterious effect on the dropout and his family, for without economic efficiency he lacks a vital requisite for community respect. It follows that parents of dropouts may view their youngsters' decisions with disappointment, distress, or anger. None of these emotional reactions is exclusive to a particular stratum of society. It is not always the middle-class parent who is disappointed nor is it always the lower-class parent who doesn't seem to care. Because this is true it would profit us to examine the reciprocal of dropout effect on the family and concern ourselves with the family effect on dropout.

In considering the lower class, one finds that novelists and urban sociologists have been preoccupied with an image of the slum as a place where the violent contrasts of city life find their sharpest expression. Slums are seen both as urban jungles in which lawlessness prevails and, because of their association with tight little immigrant colonies, as the last stronghold of traditional, intimate social life in the impersonal city (Stein, 1960). These two images—the slum as jungle and the slum as ghetto—still dominate both the sociological and literary approaches to this subcommunity. Which approach is more correct is subject for conjecture.

CONDITIONS MAY FOSTER DROPOUT

One can say with certainty, however, that within the neighborhood where the so-called "culture of poverty" exists, there are familial tendencies which induce conditions that foster dropout.

Here one finds a high proportion of disrupted and broken homes in which the father often is absent and the distance in the parental relationship results in dilution of affection for the young. Ten to 15 per cent of the fathers in white slum families are seldom home evenings while 50 per cent among the Negro fathers are seldom home. Where no father is present in the evening, there is usually no organized meal, no organized opportunity for language exchange, no real interaction. The common result is a cumulative deficit in the language component of a youngster's development. This becomes most obvious by the eighth grade, where in the area of reading such children are usually two years behind.

Then, too, there is a dearth of family activity outside the home. For many youngsters this means they have never been to the country, to another city, or even out of their neighborhood.

Recognizing the inadequacy of the life space in which such children function, some educators have attempted to compensate for cultural deprivation by initiating preschool or early-school enrichment programs designed to include a dimension of experiences which are comparable to the background usually brought to school by children from middle-class families. Ostensibly this exposure will allow the child from a poor neighborhood a more adequate chance to compete in school (Deutsch, 1962).

STRENGTHS EMERGE FROM SLUMS

If, in fact, competition is a virtue of school programming, it is unfortunate that we eliminate the competitive potential of youngsters from slum areas. We do this by failing to recognize certain strengths emerging from their background. When these strengths are declared off limits they become nonfunctional and the child is forced to compete at a disadvantage by using strengths characteristic of middle class. For example, youngsters of poverty often have a richness of language expression which is unacceptable in the classroom. Though high in verbal output, such a child usually has poor command of syntax and verb form so that he is unable to say what he would like to say inasmuch as class rules demand that proper expression be used.

Students from slums have a remarkable degree of independence and seldom need continued adult approval for their actions. As a result they might well be given responsibilities in the classroom; but under the current system anyone with poor grades is denied such an opportunity.

Studies in New York City have shown some pupils from poor areas to be more cooperative than their peers from better neighborhoods; for having always been at the bottom, they less often seek a scapegoat.

It also has been shown these children have a lengthy interest span for that which is familiar to them. Lamentably, most of the materials in textbooks do not represent the type of life to which they have been exposed; so their attention span is considered, unfairly, as shorter than that of middle-class youngsters. It is hoped that some of the strengths of children from the culture of poverty may become functional in the school if our aim to encourage and enhance self-esteem is to be realized (Mitchell, 1963).

TEACHERS EXPECT LITTLE

Finally, parents in the culture of poverty have an adverse effect on the schooling of their young as a result of the social image they represent to the community. A recent statement by John Neimeyer (1963), president of Bank Street College, New York, asserts that a major reason for low achievement among children in poor neighborhoods is the low expectation held by the teachers as to their learning capacity. Instructors often perceive a youngster in this element who misunderstands directions as one who is challenging school authority. An inadequate tax base assures the schools in low-income districts of substandard teacher salaries so that, for the most part, tired or inexperienced teachers are attracted.

In fairness, one should say that the parents in low-income areas may be naïve but they do have deep hope that, through the school, their children will achieve a better life than they themselves have had, even though these parents may not know how to give the support which is the logical concomitant of this attitude. In terms of fundamental motivation which can serve to aid learning, what more can a school ask?

MIDDLE-CLASS AFFECT

The magnitude of problems in the culture of poverty ought not to prompt one to assume that the desired parent-student relationship exists in the middle class. Looking at the social structure of the common suburb one finds a paradox. On the one hand, it arranges matters so that the daily life of the individual, no matter what his age or sex, is divided into many compelling tasks that leave little or no time for freely chosen activities. Like modern industrial employment, which it fundamentally resembles, the suburb is fanatically devoted to the rhythm of keeping busy with even the playtime of children subject to routine. Many families find that the separate schedules of the various members leave no time for intimate moments with one another.

On the other hand, while people are so desperately busy, they do not know or have forgotten how to perform some of the most elemental tasks. Most glaring evidence of this is the crisis over child rearing, where anxious mothers, uncertain how to raise their children, turn to scientific experts to find out whether their children are normal or, even more important, what the standards of normality might be.

For many parents in this middle-class segment of society who live through their children as extensions of themselves, somehow hoping to accomplish through their progeny what was not possible in their own lives, the concept of preparation for college becomes a paramount concern from the day the child enters kindergarten to the senior prom.

Realizing that promotions, honors, awards, and scholarships are contingent upon marks, many parents early choose grades rather than growth as a goal for their child in school. The student, if successfully indoctrinated, relocates his interest from subject to grade. That this occurs is obvious to any who have taught in middle-class neighborhoods where report cards are used by parents as status symbols. A premium is put on marks; parents often bribe, cajole, or threaten a child to obtain them.

Underlying the pressure imposed on the child is an assumption that most, if not all, can have high grades if they just work hard enough.

This often results in a student's making lower marks than his industry would normally permit him to make, simply because his concern impedes effective concentration. Some pupils whose school work has become grade-oriented are unduly disappointed as they perceive failure to get a grade as complete failure and hence lose even that which is within their reach. Although one cannot accurately assess the degree to which preoccupation with grades retards learning, few psychologists would deny the amount as influential.

All of us should be acquainted with the unnecessary anxiety, disappointment, and parental disfavor accompanying report time for some youngsters. By the nature of grading systems, the weaker student is forced to endure failure over and over again. Aside from the questionable desirability of such negative motivation, the blighting effects of constant frustration upon personality development should be a matter of grave concern.

THE SCHOOL AS PARENT SURROGATE

Attention has been given to the effect of low- and middle-class families on dropout. But what of the family with which we are most familiar —the school? As parent surrogate operating under *loco parentis*—in place of parents as agents or substitutes—how does it affect the dropout? In some ways the effect has been to stimulate enrichment and remedial programs but by and large it has been negligible or negative.

Before the potential dropout can realize his appropriate educational opportunity, certain views must undergo alteration. Popular acceptance is needed for a concept that allows quality to occur within a framework of quantity. Presently quality is viewed solely as academic rigor and as such necessarily is confined to those whose intellectual prowess has been demonstrated. Adherence to this limited view of quality finds expression in schools around the country which perpetuate a restricted, formalized curriculum that was appropriate in the nineteenth century when only the so-called "cultured few" were represented in secondary schools. When one prescribed then that "everybody" should study certain subjects, everybody meant anybody who was somebody, but today the term everybody is coming to mean "everyone."

It is obvious that actual curricular change has not kept pace with changes in educational objectives as our schools have ostensibly moved from serving a select clientele to the future body politic. In some cases educators have shown a remarkable ability to resist new knowledge and research findings. This has been especially true in the area of individual differences, where resistance to innovations of proven value would seem to indicate a belief that it might be easier for youngsters to modify their needs than for the school to change its requirements.

Every year a significant number of basically sound young Americans discover that they are not really wanted, and that neither their teacher nor their curricular experiences seem to pay any attention to who they are, to what they have and what they have not, to what they can do and what they cannot do, but instead impose upon them a nonsensical experience which goes under the name of education.

At his news conference of August 1, 1963, the late President Kennedy asked all American parents to urge their children to go back to school in September and to assist them in every way to stay there. This cure is both inadequate and irrelevant to the real problem of the dropout. Students are not leaving school because they are too shortsighted to realize that more education would benefit them, but because they are learning nothing of value or nothing they perceive as valuable.

The assumption that the cause of dropout lies within the person himself has been challenged by only a few educators who have recognized that in some cases high incidence of dropout may be a symptom of the school's chronic disorder. There is need for each school faculty to examine its own program and procedures, to ascertain whether the institution itself engenders any factors that might tend to encourage dropout. Special attention might be directed toward constructively challenging any fallacious assumptions that operate to reject or squeeze out a segment of those leaving school. The most prominent areas tending to eliminate pupils show up in the following questions:

Do set standards exist for all students on the assumption that equality of education may be realized through an identical course of study?

Does the evaluation system measure individual progress or communal improvement?

If individuality is excluded as a criterion for marking in deference to a curve measure, can we purport that grades represent individual growth or achievement?

Does scholastic eligibility squeeze out some by denying them the privilege of participation in athletics, newspaper club, and other extracurricular activities because their grades are not in accord with a requisite?

Does this not inadvertently affect holding power and student interest by taking from such students the one thing they relate to in school?

Is discipline a squeeze out?

Is there a social squeeze out by fraternities, sororities, or peer groups in student affairs which can induce dropout by exclusion?

What can be done to modify those factors that might squeeze out some pupils?

Questions such as these are incumbent upon any staff that seriously hopes to diminish the problem.

Curriculum change is not always an easy venture, for there will be those who prefer to introduce noise rather than improvement. The current debate about curriculum seldom demands that the major points of view confront one another. As a result, college intellectuals attack popular education in their journals; administrators defend their programs to the school board; and students of curriculum report their research in uncongenial verbiage.

Part of this disconnection relates to the fact that we suffer from an odd claustrophobia of occupation and groups in American life: the sense of isolation and insulation that seals off historians from journalists, jazz from long hair, Catholics from Mormons, Republicans from Democrats, and television repairmen from everybody. There is need for concern that a discipline like education, purporting to communicate to all, be able to communicate among its own (Henry, 1963).

Arthur Koestler (1941), in a provocative book entitled *Darkness at Noon*, has the chief character, Citizen Rubashov, state the following dilemma of one who has fallen victim to his own political party:

The party denied the free will by the individual and at the same time expected his willing self sacrifice. It denied the capacity to choose between two alternatives—and at the same time demanded that he should constantly choose the right one. It denied his power to distinguish good and evil—and at the same time spoke pathetically of guilt and treachery.

Perhaps analogy is not amiss at this point. Do we not overwork the language or doctrine of individual differences and yet seldom employ this practice in teaching and evaluating children? Do we not insist that children remain in school because it is good for them when, in fact, for those whose history of failures is constant this is socially sadistic? Do we not tell the student he ought to choose what's right and yet limit his right of choice by giving him no alternative within the curriculum? Is tyranny a word for events on foreign soil or does it include the practices of some public schools? Until potential dropouts are individually helped to succeed, schools will collectively fail.

4 Emotional Problems of Contemporary Life

Francis J. Braceland

CURRENT PROBLEMS

What do people worry about? Is it nuclear warfare or atomic extinction? Are they concerned with international tensions and the brinkmanship of some nations? Apparently not; according to a national survey (Gurin, Veroff, and Feld, 1960), the anxious atmosphere of a troubled world does not seem to concern them unduly. At least, this is what they report. People claim to be more concerned about mundane things, about affairs much closer to home. One reason for this could be that each of us in adult life is vitally concerned with the realities of the immediate environment, and the extent to which sources of worry affect us decreases in proportion to their remoteness.

The survey also hints that these more practical attitudes which we exhibit might reflect a retreat from the worrisome and frightening realities of a larger world, a sense of helplessness in events the individual feels are beyond his ability to control; or it may be an undue concern with self and renunciation of social responsibility.

For myself, I am not convinced at all that people are as unconcerned as they say they are about the possibilities of worldwide conflagration and the dangers of the armament race. Their fears heat up when the newspaper headlines about Vietnam or Berlin become black and large, and they cool off and are put out of mind as quickly as is possible when things settle down.

It is true that we are normally and naturally concerned about everyday worries, but it is also known that there is a phenomenon called "displacement" and by means of it we can change the focus of our wor-

This chapter is a revised version of an article that originally appeared in *Contemporary Emotional Problems*, published by the Connecticut Mutual Life Insurance Company, Hartford, Connecticut, 1963, pp. 12–19.

ries from more difficult, disagreeable, and painful problems to much smaller and more harmless ones, and by accenting the latter forget the larger issues.

Dr. Spock says American children are being made anxious by the cold war. Between 25 and 50 per cent of them are fearful of nuclear fall-out and of separation from family in disaster and death. Adolescents, he says, are bitter about the uncertainty of the future and the futility of striving and working hard in emulation of their fathers.

I have no way of knowing about the children of whom he speaks, but I can attest to the unrest among adolescents who see little reason for following the ideals we hold before them or the methods of hard work which we hold out to them to attain these ideals. Some of them have convinced themselves that we adults are handing on to them a "messy world."

APATHY AS DEFENSE

It may be that the feeling of helplessness in the face of the possibility of worldwide catastrophe may underlie some of what looks like popular unconcern. This is a defensive reaction, for one cannot remain in a state of constant fear and stay well. Admiral Byrd (1959) in his remarkable description of his solo stay in the Antarctic says:

The tolerable quality of a dangerous existence is the fact that the human mind cannot remain continuously sensitive to anything. Repetitious, dulling impact sees to that.

The threat alone of sudden death can scare a man for only so long; then he dismisses it as he would a mealy mouthed beggar. . . . Fright and pain are the most transitory emotions; they are easily forgotten.

There is always some remnant to plague us, however, and Admiral Byrd recognizes it when he says: "It is one thing to instruct the mind and another to make it obey." All of us have experienced this phenomenon as we have told ourselves in time of danger that there is really nothing to be scared of, but it seems hard to convince our bodies that this is true.

NEW AGE OF CHANGE

Although all things human are prone to change—and change has been a constant accompaniment of history and the lives of men—the present order of change is completely different from anything ever seen before and anything our ancestors ever experienced or knew. Presently we are changing from one epoch to another. The changes are deep, pervasive, and inevitable. We have moved out of an electromechanical age into an electronic age. The psychiatrist is vitally interested in this rapid change, for it is certain to occasion stress upon many of us, and the reactions of stress upon men, particularly when pathological, are the psychiatrist's main concern.

We have mentioned a number of times that disease has changed and the practice of medicine has changed even in this past decade. Certainly the type of patient the psychiatrist sees has changed markedly. Dr. Dubos (1959) states:

Any change in the environment demands new adaptive reactions and disease is the consequence of inadequacies in these adaptive responses. The more rapid and profound the environmental changes, the larger the number of individuals who cannot adapt to them rapidly enough to maintain an adequate state of fitness and who, therefore, develop some type of organic or psychotic disease.

Hippocrates once wrote: "It is changes that are chiefly responsible for diseases—especially the great changes, the violent alterations both in seasons and in other things. . . . The chief causes of disease are the most violent changes in what concerns our constitution and habits."

There are fascinating things written about change and its influence on disease, physical and mental. I do not want to go too far afield regarding them but a few quotations from Dubos will serve to fix these phenomena in our minds. He notes that the pattern of disease changes with each phase of civilization and that these changes are brought about by new environmental and technological factors and the profound disturbances that culture and ethics exert on the individual. "Science," he says, "provides methods of control for the problems inherited from past generations but it cannot prepare specific solutions for the specific problems of tomorrow, because it does not know what these problems will be. Physicians and public health officials, like soldiers, are always equipped to fight the last war."

It is in this area of change and stress that the drama of emotional upset is frequently played, for some people simply cannot adapt to changing situations. Rigidity and lack of malleability prevent them from adapting to new conditions and situations and this is particularly true of some people in the middle and older age groups. Because of the rapidity of change and the rigidity of the individuals, these persons fall by the wayside and sometimes become depressed and withdrawn.

LIFE IN SUBURBIA

One or two changes in external environment might be commented on briefly at this point. There are a number of population shifts in the country at present but one that might interest us here is the trek to suburbia.

Men who formerly worked ten hours a day now work only eight

hours and spend the extra two trying to get through workbound and homebound traffic. Also, they take work home in brief cases, and it is doubtful that the working hours of some businessmen have really been shortened. Although there are better living conditions for children in suburbia, the sociologists tell us husbands' and wives' worlds become further apart, both geographically and socially. Children see their fathers less and this is hard on boys. The situation may lead to boys coming almost completely under the direction of women at home and in the schools.

Many fathers, aware of the demands of home and job, feel unsure of themselves in their relations with their families. The need to attain status in their work is pressing and the competition is keen. They are also vaguely aware of the fact that they are neglecting their children but can make only sporadic attempts to make up for it. Wives, frequently seeing themselves cast in secondary roles in the present culture, are often anxious and depressive. This is particularly true of those in comfortable circumstances. They have a feeling of lack of fulfillment and they are much more willing to admit their unrest than are men. This situation obtains nationally and we shall consider it later as we talk of the mental hygiene of the later years.

CRUCIAL TEEN YEARS

It is a curious thing, Dr. Kingsley Davis tells us, this present mixture of extreme permissiveness and intense concern on the part of American parents. We let children do anything they want and worry about everything they do. Most children survive it, but some come through emotionally distressed.

The main interest of the youngsters at times seems to be conforming to the standards, or lack of them, set by their companions or their peer groups. Then Dr. Davis makes one remark that all of us will recognize, whether we come from suburbia or not: "There is an anti-learning and an anti-effort bias in these groups and intellectual endeavor is identified with an alien and inimical adult world."

By its very nature adolescence will be rugged for all concerned. If the adolescent does not have some unrest as he passes through this difficult period, one should inquire about him. Inconsistent and unpredictable, then pleasant and delightful; surly and moody, then kindly, gentle, and loving—all of these are moods one can expect in this period. Idealistic at one time, cynical at another; lazy, then a virtual busy-bee—although not necessarily busy about things that parents and teachers are anxious to have him do. At one moment confiding, at another withdrawn, the adolescent is on his way to being an adult and it is a difficult path. Holding on to parents with one hand lest he make a misstep, angrily demanding his freedom on the other, he becomes veritably "a stranger in the house," much to the dismay of all concerned.

All manner of new urges arise within him; his moods swing; parents vacillate, at one time angry, at another indulgent; he is trying to find out what life is about and to establish his identity. He needs strong parents, who do not panic; he needs limits set for him, subtly, not by an iron hand. When he is ready, he will need some reasonable degree of emancipation and parents must not be reluctant to grant it. He cannot be kept in childish dependence, nor can he be pushed into a vocation that "mommy" wishes for him.

Please note that we do not advocate a softness or overpermissiveness; this has never been a tenet of psychiatry, although some people have concluded that it is. The adolescent must be allowed to grow, but he must be guided wisely while he is growing.

JOB IS MAIN WORRY

To return to our consideration of jobs, husbands and wives, and suburbia, it has been established by professional inquiries that managers, farmers, and salesmen worry most about their jobs. The wives of professional men and some salesmen complain that their husbands' occupations interfere with their marriages. What is rarely recognized, however, is that many times emotional upsets which cause family disruptions are due to emotional problems deep within the individual's own psychological make-up rather than in the job or in external surroundings.

Furthermore, people sometimes flee from one unhappy situation, only to find in their new environment that they have created another. The same thing is true in industrial relations. By far the largest proportion of discharges in industry is due to interpersonal difficulties rather than technical incompetence.

There are many emotional problems connected with getting and holding a job in this present culture. We have already mentioned the need for attaining status. It is probable that this is a more important requirement for men than is higher wages. This is understandable and healthy, if it is kept within bounds. Every normal human being wants to be thought well of and to have a place in everyday affairs.

Man has an inherent dignity; he does not want to be "pushed around," slighted, or considered insignificant. It is when these feelings get out of bounds and unwonted ambition intrudes itself that there is trouble ahead. A healthy respect for one's own dignity and the dignity of others is necessary spiritually and is also a social, cultural, and interpersonal lubricant in industrial relations.

It is probable that this is a good place to insert the observation that man does not prosper and grow under extreme conditions of hardship and adversity, but a certain amount of adversity, stress, and strain does help his character to develop. He functions best when he is under some pressure; a life sheltered altogether from adversity loses its ability to cope with ordinary problems when they do arise.

It is axiomatic, too, that a person is able to handle problems infinitely better if he can view them objectively, lets reason help him, and does not get tied up so completely emotionally with them that his vision is unclear. If we were more objective, we soon would see that a large number of our emotional problems originate within ourselves.

The greater the degree of self-awareness and the greater the willingness to admit weaknesses and the fact that problems do exist, the more chance one has of solving them. Perhaps then one might be compared to those men in the Byrd (1938) expedition of whom he said: "The ones who survive with a measure of happiness are those who can live profoundly off their own intellectual resources, as hibernating animals live off their fat." More of us need to live off our own resources.

HELP IS AVAILABLE

If a person does need help, where does he usually go for it? Most people queried stated that they take their problems to their clergymen (42 per cent) or to their family doctors (29 per cent).

Most people felt also that they really received help when they sought it. Only 18 per cent went to psychiatrists first with their problems, and this is as it should be. Clergymen and family doctors, as we have said before, are the first lines of defense against mental and emotional disorder. We may reasonably assume that, when the difficulty is deep and beyond their purview, the person seeking help will be placed in proper hands.

AUTOMATION

We should make one brief observation about a growing source of emotional concern before proceeding further. For many people there is a fear brought on by the prospects of automation. But we must be careful of the tyranny of terms. Words such as automation are like those of schizophrenia and epilepsy; they contain within them a built-in fear.

Actually, automation began long ago with the invention of the sewing machine, the steamboat, and various other machines, and we went through a long period of technological change called the industrial revolution. That revolution changed man's health and welfare more than anything since the introduction of hand tools in agriculture. Now we seem to be entering a period which a British author (Raffle, 1963) states may alter man's way of life as profoundly as the introduction of mechanical power into manufacturing.

It is probable that automation will proceed slowly and that the worker's physical and mental health will not be harmed by it. The chief impact it will make undoubtedly will be social. The question whether it will cramp individual creativity and sanctify materialism, as has sometimes been alleged, I do not know, but in my opinion it will not. It is probably wise to remember that in the long run it is man who will bring about automation and who will make the machines, and he still will remain superior to them.

We cannot and should not try to stop automation any more than we should have tried to prevent the invention of the sewing machine or the progress of the industrial revolution. Both brought many benefits to people in general and raised the standard of living. Automation will bring even more benefits and what is needed now is knowledge to prevent any social abuses that might come in automation's wake.

There will be problems, of course, but problems are for solving and our task is to welcome this new advance, for it probably holds a key to a higher standard of living at home and a help to others abroad.

PREPARE FOR OLD AGE

Although it sounds fatuous, nevertheless it is true that the best preparation for meeting the problems of declining years is sound mental hygiene in early life. The dictum of Cephalus in Plato's philosophy of old age is still applicable today. "The truth is, Socrates," he says,

that these regrets and also the complaints about relations are to be attributed to the same cause, which is not old age, but men's characters and tempers; for he who is of calm and happy nature will hardly feel the pressure of age; but to him who is of an opposite disposition, youth and age are equally a burden.

Though the physician cannot change the nation's retirement laws, cultural patterns, or the economic situation of the country, he can be of assistance in advising those who are interested in the welfare of the elderly and, incidentally, it is an error to lump all of these persons into one group willy-nilly. These people are individuals, with all that designation implies—some are rich and some are poor, some are sick and some are well, and each person and his problems should be considered separately. What is it that separates some older persons from their fellows and closes them off from the stream of everyday life? For the most part it seems to be a loss of communication with their surroundings. Beset with problems, they frequently neglect to keep up with the times. As they dislocate themselves in time, their standards and symbols lose meaning and there is a pathetic clinging to values to which these symbols were once appropriate. The first rule of mental hygiene in aging, therefore, is keeping open the channels of communication. It is insurance against getting lost and out of contact with younger age groups and with daily happenings. Also, one might heed the admonition of the psalmist: "A joyful mind maketh age flourishing; a sorrowful spirit drieth up the bones."

The watchword, then, is that everyone must have some interest, some responsibility, some task, some spiritual, cultural, artistic, or occupational interest that will keep him within the currents of contemporary life and make him feel useful and a part of things. Without this the person may be inclined to just sit. The consuming interest, of course, must be geared to the person's physical, cultural, and educational status. This interest rarely can be started at the age of 65. It should be begun in early life, at that time in which we noted young wives begin to become discontented with their position in the scheme of things. A consuming educational or cultural interest, developed then, is insurance against boredom and is an excellent preparation for later years.

It is useless for harried husbands to point out that their mothers and grandmothers found interest enough in their household chores, for the situation in which women find themselves today is entirely different. The present-day cultural surroundings have changed completely.

KEY IS AWARENESS

Careful stock taking of ourselves may impress on us the fact that the image we think we project to others is not at all the one that actually is seen by our family and friends. The mirror in which we see our reflection may be distorted, like one of the mirrors in the "Fun House" in amusement parks. Thus we may be deceiving ourselves and this may account for some of the problems that arise in our dealings with others. The image that we think of as kindness and thoughtfulness may be seen by outside viewers as gruffness, unpleasantness, or even destructiveness. A horrible thought, but a possibility nonetheless. We may have to do some rearranging of ourselves rather than changing our external surroundings.

My first piece of advice is an admonition from Fenelon in his Farewell to Telemachus:

Above all be on guard against your temper; it is one enemy that you will carry everywhere with you until death; it will enter into your counsels and deceive you if you listen to it. Temper makes us miss opportunities of the greatest importance: it gives the inclinations of a child to the prejudice of greatest interest. It makes us decide the greatest matters by the smallest reasons—it will obscure talents, lower courage, rend a man uneven, vile and insupportable—mistrust that enemy!

This is excellent advice for everyday use.

In closing I would like to decry again those ideas which hold that life should be free of anxiety and that everyone should be tranquil. I believe that we are on the eve of a remarkable future, an awakening of the intellect and the spirit, and it would be disastrous if it found us somnolent and uninterested. We might well keep in mind Montaigne's observation:

"The good fortune of our life dependeth on the tranquilities and contentment of a well borne mind and of the resolution and assurance of a well ordered soul." In other words, it is definite and certain that the fountain of tranquility really resides within ourselves, not in stimulants or tranquilizing drugs.

5 *Motivation for Learning: Community Responsibility*

Dana L. Farnsworth

One of the most encouraging signs of the present era is the preoccupation of Americans with their educational system. That this preoccupation is almost a national obsession is a healthy sign, for no one can ever become completely educated. Continued search for fuller understanding is essential to continued vigor. In a democracy, widespread education seems particularly appropriate provided that it aids the citizens to shape, evaluate, and constantly improve their society and does not train them to serve their nation without evaluation of its aims. Education can lead either to freedom or to subservience to arbitrary power. If America is to remain free while competing with nations that demand unquestioning subservience, her citizens must hold in high esteem the kind of education that promotes the freedom, strength, and versatility of the individual. Widespread education of this type can make it possible for America to compete with her ideological rivals at the point of her greatest strength and their greatest weakness. She need not repeatedly let her rivals set the conditions for a test of strength.

UNDERLYING ASSUMPTIONS

A very few assumptions underlie my discussion of community responsibility for the motivation of learning: first, children inevitably learn something, no matter what kind of instruction they have (in other words, learning is undiscriminating at first); second, students prefer to learn what brings them satisfaction and esteem, not what fails to bring rewards; and third, young people find imitation of acceptable behavior basically more satisfying than indulgence in antisocial activity. If these assumptions are true, and I believe they are, it is well to let them illumi-

Reprinted by permission of Melvin R. Karpas (Ed.), *Rhode Island College Journal*, 1, March 1960.

nate the connection between the attitudes and standards of behavior of the older members of our society and the attitudes and standards of behavior of the students in our schools. This may at times be embarrassing. To these three assumptions I should like to add one more; namely, that the primary purpose of our schools is to develop to the greatest extent possible the intellectual potentialities of every pupil without losing sight of secondary goals that safeguard the main educational endeavor. In other words, schools cannot provide everything that is needed for the optimum development of the child, but they can plan their activities in such a way as to demonstrate that education involves far more than the mere acquisition of knowledge.

I shall try to relate some ways in which all the citizens of a given community may encourage the kind of learning that enables a society to hold together and at the same time respects the particular needs of every individual in that society. For every member of the group to live up to his inner potentialities would be self-defeating, because many young persons could develop into excellent criminals or rascals. It is the *best* potential that must be developed. The final goal of education is far beyond mere learning for learning's sake. As John Gardner (1958) has stated so eloquently, "What we must reach for is a conception of perpetual self-discovery, perpetual reshaping to realize one's goals, to realize one's best self, to be the best person one could be." And he goes on to say that this involves not only the intellect but emotions, character, and personality.

The time has come when planning for our schools and colleges is the responsibility of everyone, not just of school administrators and teachers. When a particular community is able, by virtue of many thoughtful discussions, to decide what it wants from its schools, paying for the planned program becomes a secondary problem. I shall discuss some of the general goals which I consider desirable and some specific ways in which the community may set about reaching them.

Fortunately there are many favorable factors to work with even in the early stages of making the most of human potentialities. Soon after a child is born, he develops characteristics that are necessary for his optimum growth and development. He enjoys learning for its own sake. His sheer joy in exploration and understanding are obvious unless in his eagerness and enthusiasm he encounters conditions that cause pain and grief. The child is a natural research worker, pushing with ever more determination into the unknown, relating disparate objects and concepts to one another. So greatly does he enjoy sharing what he learns with his playmates and parents that he teaches almost automatically.

As the child grows older he may come to appreciate the natural things around him—birds, plants, animals, and the changing seasons—

but he soon discovers that while interest in such things brings him inner satisfaction, it does not reward him with nearly as much prestige within the group as does participation in activities that all the other children engage in. He finds that all too often his fantasy life, his flights into poetic expression, his early artistic endeavors are frowned upon and discouraged because they are not "useful." In hundreds of ways he is shown that learning is to be regarded as drudgery and hard, boring work. Only the fortunate few have opportunity to observe at first hand that people actually take pleasure in reading books, in meaningful conversation, in quiet contemplation without external stimulation and excitement. Since all children tend to emulate what they see and experience, it is much to be regretted that so many children learn that their parents and friends do not or cannot enjoy reading, that school work and other forms of learning are considered unpleasant, and that family life involves constant search for excitement without opportunity for reflection or development of an inner life. As an old-time teacher in West Virginia stated in his autobiography, "it takes a kind of genius to want that which it does not know to want" (Patterson, 1940).

Any student of human behavior is aware that people usually have a strong desire to gain the esteem of those whom they admire. This is especially noticeable in children who have not had excessively traumatic experiences; but it is apparent also in children with severe psychopathological disorders who have found someone they can trust. However distorted their attempts may appear, the disturbed children also want to please. The problem faced by man in developing his own potentialities to the fullest can be accurately stated in terms of his aspirations. What people want they will usually work hard to get, even at great sacrifice. Not until large numbers of our people have acquired a concept of excellence and what it connotes will there be more general striving toward this goal.

Professor Galbraith (1958), in his book *The Affluent Society*, has brilliantly described the bankruptcy of the idea that our welfare depends upon piling up material goods. He shows with equal clarity that the basic demand on the America of the future will be for its resources of ability, intelligence, and education. As he says, if our hope for survival, security, and contentment lies in guiding resources to the most urgent ends, we must give increasing thought to making those ends evident in a very personal way to all our citizens.

The effectiveness of the education provided in our schools depends in large measure on the basic attitudes in our homes. Awareness of fundamental human attributes, both self-knowledge and understanding of others, is woefully lacking in many persons who have great influence in the community. Even more regrettable is the apparently generalized disregard or lack of comprehension of the ways in which attitudes are transmitted from one generation to another. The individuals in our society who *are* aware of the methods of attitude transmission are almost hopelessly outnumbered by people who inculcate hostility to properly constituted authority, indifference toward learning, and false standards. If the human potentialities of America are to be realized, a vast change must take place in the judgment of our people concerning worthwhile goals.

SOME BASIC FACTORS IN FAMILY LIFE

Suppose we start with the home. What are the basic factors in family life that will encourage each child to utilize his best qualities to the fullest? During the long period of childhood, needs are very intense and prompt satisfaction of them is of major importance to immediate comfort and future development. If a child encounters essentially friendly and accepting attitudes in the people around him during his years of helpless dependency, he has a reasonably good chance of growing up with basic attitudes of trust and a sort of optimism that enables him to make satisfying contacts with his fellows as he goes along. Every child needs affection, the feeling of belonging and being wanted, respect as an individual in his own right, a favorable setting for growth and the development of security, freedom from excessive domination, firm discipline from a respected source, and privacy enough to allow his active imagination to develop. He usually reacts more favorably to judicious praise than to indiscriminate fault finding; and he needs to feel that what he does has meaning. Recent students of child-rearing practices have found that most of these needs are met almost automatically when the mother and all other members of the family have a warm relationship with the child.

Some parents treat their children as if they were extensions of themselves: they want their offspring to have what they lacked themselves; they try to shield their children from the hardships they had to face in their own early years; and they tend to adhere strongly to the tradition that any boy who does not surpass his father's achievements is not an unqualified success. Other parents look upon their children as distinct persons from the very beginning. These parents respect their individuality, cultivate their particular strengths, compensate for their personal sensitivities, and feel responsible for providing the best possible conditions in which their children may grow as fast and as long as their natures permit.

As I see the situation, widespread education for family living is the best possible means of establishing conditions under which excellence will be encouraged and prized. Whose responsibility is it to provide such education? If becoming a parent does not automatically confer the knowledge and skills needed for bringing up children properly, who should organize the sound knowledge already available and make it accessible to young people who are about to establish their own families? In my opinion this responsibility should be assumed by our schools, but only with the understanding that many other institutions, particularly the churches, should carry equal though different responsibilities. It is only in our educational institutions that the desirable theoretical knowledge can readily be gathered, criticized, and organized into transmissible form. Those students in our institutions of learning who are preparing to help people relate themselves satisfactorily to one another and to resolve the life crises that arise from time to time are in the most favorable position to transmit the needed information. Some of it can be taught directly in courses about marriage and family living, but most of it will have to be transmitted indirectly, often during discussion of issues pertinent to a particular discipline.

If all prospective teachers, lawyers, clergymen, and physicians thoroughly understood the essentials of personality development and the conditions that best foster family solidarity, their knowledge would spread outward to their colleagues in other fields and upward to the older members of their own professions. The community would then have more effective critics of those city planners whose designs show greater preoccupation with the needs of physical than of personality development; more people would understand the effectiveness of discipline, as compared with revengeful punishment, in the regulation of behavior; and there would be greater awareness of the amount of harm one rude and overbearing representative of the state can do in undermining respect for properly constituted authority. As Eric Hoffer has said, "Rudeness is a weak man's imitation of strength."

Emotional immaturity is not confined to offenders against society or to those with emotional illness. It is prevalent among people who are intelligent, well educated by formal standards, religious in intent and belief, and among persons who occupy positions of great responsibility and influence. It is obvious to any serious observer that many persons influential in the professions, in business, and in government lack understanding of themselves, of the effects of their actions on others, and particularly of the needs of young, developing personalities.

Is it possible to develop in large numbers of our people the knowledge and insight necessary to counteract the causes of severe and incapacitating emotional illness and social conflict at their points of origin? For some reason many persons react to this question with great vigor—some with anger, others with anxiety, and still others with quite arbitrary insistence that concepts of prevention in such matters are unsound. Certainly something far more subtle than knowledge alone is involved in the development of maturity and integrity. Who is in a better position to explore such matters than the educational institutions that train professional men and women?

A look at some of the distressing attitudes now prevalent will show where major opportunities for improvement lie. Our propensity for excessive competition stems from overvaluation of material goods. Competition for one's proper share is desirable; attempts to get so much of any particular commodity that others with rightful claims do not get enough is provocation for extreme retaliation. A balance between legitimate acquisition and rapacity can be achieved only when the great majority of people show concern for others and when people who pay no heed to the welfare of any but themselves are restrained by vigorously enforced laws.

Attitudes toward authority are of vital importance in determining how a community or society can effectively bring to bear pressures for excellence. As Sir Richard Livingstone has so clearly depicted, people who do not know the meaning and necessity of law do not long enjoy liberty. Need for the restraints that make our freedom possible becomes obscured when the agents of society lack those characteristics that enable human beings to relate themselves to one another with a minimum of friction and hostility. Officials who are discourteous and insulting to people who are for the moment helpless, community leaders who exhibit primitive and vengeful attitudes toward wrongdoers, and individuals who equate understanding with softness all contribute to the harsh and excessively competitive attitudes with which many people constantly threaten our democratic form of society. High standards of behavior can be fostered without depriving people of the dignity and respect which are their birthright.

The way in which pressures for excellence are exerted has an enormous effect on the type of reaction these forces elicit from young people. Every institution has its own methods of encouraging high standards. The most effective pressures toward excellence with which I am familiar are exerted in an educational institution that has no grading system and no fixed rewards for achievement. Instead of these, it has exceedingly numerous channels of communication between all its members which permit immediate evaluation by students and staff of behavior that is not as appropriate or adequate as circumstances require. Consequently, students and staff regard each other as colleagues rather than opponents and their attitude supports and is consistent with the goals of the institution as a whole. The point of view of this group is in sharp contrast to that found in many educational institutions where students hold that it is smart to get away with as little work and as much deception as possible. In institutions of this latter type, official goals and faculty efforts are largely undermined by a climate of student opinion that discourages excellence.

The prevailing attitude of vast portions of our society today seems to be similarly insensitive, and even actively hostile, to excellence.

The troubled young people who create serious social difficulties today are for the most part those who have not been able to identify themselves with individuals or groups whose ideals and actions are consistent with a strong, decent social order. It is unfortunate that the social and cultural influences spread by many of our agents of mass communication encourage emulation of persons of very dubious quality. The full power of these degrading influences is neither appreciated nor understood. We cannot expect young people to adopt standards of taste and behavior consistently higher than those of the adults who are their models. Our real task as educators, therefore, is to create satisfactory channels of communication within the community so that young boys and girls may come into contact with older people of integrity who may serve as worthy models.

The moment we attempt to raise basic standards, it becomes apparent that we have to deal with much more than apathy and inertia. Many people adhere to mediocrity and low tastes because they are profitable. H. L. Mencken has said that no man ever went broke underestimating the tastes of the American public. Occasional efforts are made to counteract the influences that debase our standards of integrity. A few public-spirited and courageous policy makers have found that both news and radio and television programs of high quality are widely enjoyed. It is the duty of every responsible citizen to support the efforts of all who dare to insist that whatever is offered to the public shall be of high quality. Only when there is generalized appreciation of the value of such insistence can excellence become profitable.

Not long ago, during an examination of candidates for medical internships at the Massachusetts General Hospital, a fourth-year medical student was asked to mention some personal assets that he could bring to the practice of medicine. His reply embodies the central theme of my present discussion: "In our family we were taught that learning is enjoyable." The significance of his answer is reinforced by more formalized data already available. These indicate that the proportion of the sons and daughters of professional people—ministers, teachers, lawyers, and physicians—that goes to college and is successful there is greater than the proportion of children from nonprofessional backgrounds who do likewise. At first this fact may seem too obvious to merit discussion, but such an evaluation of it illustrates our tragic lack of foresightedness. We need increasing numbers and a larger percentage of highly educated, skilled people in the kind of society we are creating. We cannot afford the waste of allowing potentially fine-quality children to develop under the influence of inferior or even degrading stimuli without exposure to the challenge of high standards. In some fashion we must develop an all-pervasive climate of opinion that excellence is desirable, necessary, and even enjoyable. This cannot be done until we cease to reward the shallow, the spectacular, and the insincere, and establish as our ideal prototypes those men and women whose constructive and enduring achievement has made them preeminent.

As citizens we are in somewhat the same position as the customers of many of the large chains of restaurants that have definite standards for preparation of food, methods of serving, even for architecture. When a prospective customer sees one of these buildings with its characteristic sign, he knows he can count on obtaining a satisfactory meal; but he also knows that he is not likely to obtain an excellent one. He can relax in the anticipation of controlled mediocrity.

Our country's predicament resembles that of the man who has worked very hard throughout his life, overcome severe poverty in his youth and early manhood, and finally reached a state of complete financial security with all his original goals and aspirations attained. He tells himself that he should be happy, but he does not feel happy. In fact, he feels miserable because he has organized his life so exclusively for *getting* that he has no capacity for *being*. The green leaves of expectation have turned to brown dust in his hands. He can derive pleasure only from acquisition. He tries to cure his despondency by gaining possession of more material goods, but happiness and satisfaction continue to elude him. He becomes a prey for all kinds of impractical and often unwise schemes designed by the unscrupulous for the unwary.

VESTED INTERESTS IN MEDIOCRITY

Who are the people with a vested interest in mediocrity? If we are to learn how to exert pressures for excellence in our complex society we may have to discover the answer to this question, but in doing so we should avoid pitting one group of our citizens against another in a test of strength. Goethe once said that opinions divide but sentiments unite. As we search out the underlying causes of our intellectual apathy and moral disintegration we cannot afford to fall into the habit of hunting for scapegoats. Although it is more difficult, we would do well to take the less dramatic approach which consists in elevating the taste and standards of large numbers of our people so that widespread preference for higher standards may render degrading activity unprofitable.

As we observe that a steadily increasing proportion of the material broadcast by radio and television is banal and discourteous, it becomes increasingly clear that educators must enlist effective support for the small number of courageous producers who demonstrate that programs can simultaneously be enjoyable, satisfying, and intellectually interesting. Instead of shrugging our shoulders at the stupidity and insincerity of certain politicians, it would be beneficial to provide warm support for the much larger number who genuinely want to find appropriate solutions for the social problems that vex our communities. Because an unprincipled minority manages to make its antics very entertaining and dramatic, we need to develop unusually effective methods of showing adequate appreciation of the vast amount of constructive and sound activity carried on by our political, cultural, and social leaders.

In any direction in which we choose to look, we can see people who fail to utilize their capabilities to the fullest. Many of these people work extremely hard at what they do. It is not the amount of their activity that is deficient, but rather their awareness of relative values. Most people do not seem to know what our community goals are or how to draw a group together in an effort to decide what goals to strive for. Most Americans seem to proceed on the principle that speed and energy will somehow take the place of or be transformed into thoughtfulness and integrity. It seems as though many people consider that the highest virtue is to accumulate material goods or services, or to attain what they fondly think of as economic security.

A major goal of all teachers is to instill in their students a love of learning. Once a student wants to know as much as possible about a subject, the teacher's responsibility changes. It is, therefore, no longer the teacher's function merely to ascertain that a given amount of factual material has been learned. When this point has been reached, the teacher's task is to open up new vistas for the student and while doing so to broaden his own interests. Under these conditions, teaching becomes a pleasing, satisfying, and stimulating activity. Our most respected citizens can contribute nothing more valuable to the education of the community than motivation of the children toward learning.

APPRAISAL OF EDUCATIONAL PROCEDURES

A society that holds education in high esteem is critical of methods of teaching and learning. The more education is valued, the more it is subjected to criticism. As the educational process becomes increasingly effective, a steadily increasing proportion of the community is prepared to appraise educational procedures with clarity and precision. Since criticism can be both constructive and destructive, community leaders need to have recognized criteria with which to evaluate it. All too often, the loudest denunciations come from people who know little about the work of schools or the problems encountered by teachers and school administrators. It is usually necessary, however, to listen to even the extreme critics because some of their comments may be constructive. As one of my students has said, "We must learn to talk to one another without getting mad." Self-control often brings desirable awards. At present, the popular scapegoats for the shortcomings of our educational system seem to be schools of education, John Dewey and progressive education, and Sigmund Freud. Those who attack schools of education are particularly fond of assailing "life-adjustment classes," but the very form of their assaults shows that most of these denunciators do not know what they are talking about. Anyone who attempts to aid in the solution of great human and social problems must be prepared to be blamed for creating the very conditions he seeks to improve.

Often when honest critics of our schools voice their opinions, they are joined by other critics who have an ax to grind. Some of these dissemblers wish to have taxes reduced regardless of consequences, others want different kinds of schools for different kinds of people or disproportionately strong emphasis on special subjects, and a few become agitated if certain concepts are so much as mentioned within the precincts of a school. Consequently it becomes the duty of community leaders to inquire into the motives of school critics, as well as into the merits of their arguments. In dealing with intemperate and unwise criticism, no weapon is more effective than clear comprehension—providing, of course, that a large enough proportion of the community *does* comprehend. Many of our current institutions, notably the mass-communication media, seem to attribute great value to majority opinion regardless of whether or not that opinion has merit. If our schools were to be run on the same principle, we should soon be in real trouble. But if we provide education that does not satisfy the needs of the majority we shall also be in trouble.

CRUCIAL QUESTION

This brings us to the crucial question—how can school curriculum planners develop educational programs that will arouse the interest of the majority and at the same time command the respect of influential members of the community who are in a position to mold public opinion? To answer this question, I believe that we must examine the attitudes of the general population and of those who are in positions of leadership. When the goals of the schools are consistent with community ideals it should be possible to devise satisfactory educational programs. Widespread awareness within each neighborhood of what the schools are trying to do and of the difficulties they face is essential for this purpose.

Certain undesirable reactions frequently prevent the development of satisfactory rapport between schools, community leaders, and parents. When a child fails in his work or is not promoted according to schedule, a scapegoat is often sought. "It was the teacher's fault." "He should have developed more interest in the subject." "He didn't make the assignments clear." "He expected too much of the children." "He grades on a curve and, therefore, someone has to fail whether he deserves it or not." "He didn't say what was expected." When a child's progress falls short of the hopes of his family, it is not uncommon for the parents to demand that members of the school board or other prominent people subject the teacher or school principal to pressures that will lead to a change of grades. It is obvious that community opinion should stand firm against subversion of this sort.

Fortunately there are always a number of parents who react very sensibly when their children do not live up to expectations. They accept the failure, but try to discover its real causes so that it need not be repeated in the future. They ask such questions as: "Are any handicaps present which can be removed or modified?" "Is there any health impairment?" "How can better study habits be encouraged?" "How can we help our child without taking away his initiative or doing his work for him?" "Could we provide better working conditions for him at home?" Some failure is the lot of every human being and early shortcomings may be made constructive if the child receives appropriate support and understanding.

"WHO RUNS OUR SCHOOLS?"

Considerable light is thrown on the subject of our discussion by a book entitled *Who Runs Our Schools?*, in which Dr. Neal Gross (1958) describes a study conducted in Massachusetts. He reports that crucial unsolved problems center around the activities of the school-board members, the quality of leadership provided by school superintendents, the ability of school-board members and superintendents to resist unsuitable pressures, and the question of obtaining adequate financial support.

The quality and motives of school-board members play a decisive role in determining whether motivation to learning shall grow stronger or weaker within a given community. Some board members regard their positions as political-patronage posts; others busy themselves with details that belong to the superintendent, principals, and teachers; a few have very hazy notions of what their responsibilities are. In the Massachusetts study nearly 20 per cent of superintendents reported that their school boards were major obstacles to the professional conduct of their schools, a fact which implies that 80 per cent of school boards do a creditable piece of work. In the last analysis the credit or blame for the behavior of school boards falls on those who elect or appoint them. Here the responsibility of the community is clear: the most capable, interested, judicial, high-minded citizens who are available should be selected to determine the policies of our educational institutions.

In the Massachusetts study it was also noted that the quality of educational leadership provided by many superintendents was not as good as it should be. Too few were skilled in the building of good public relations, and many lacked the ability to make parents understand the significance of good and bad school procedures, or to establish strong bonds between the schools and the community. Continued resistance to improper pressures is possible only if the character of these pressures is recognized by a large proportion of the community. Proper financial support cannot be obtained unless there is widespread understanding of what good schools can contribute to the public welfare. Participation of many public agencies in discussion of the financial problems of schools provides perspective for the making of wise decisions. In the end it is the citizens who must determine whether comprehensive education of children is as important as accumulation of nonessential material goods. The outlook of a community determines the quality of its schools.

"THE AMERICAN HIGH SCHOOL TODAY"

The report by Dr. James B. Conant (1959) on *The American High School Today* should be required reading for all school-board members as well as for everyone who participates in the planning of secondary-school instruction. The logic and simplicity of Dr. Conant's twenty-one recommendations are so sound and disarming as to be almost revolutionary. Any one of his recommendations immediately evokes fervent discussion among people interested in education. The salient feature of his suggestions is that they favor equality of opportunity, not merely equality of treatment. In other words, Dr. Conant emphasizes the great variety of individual differences encountered in any school system and the need to adjust instruction to the particular requirements of individuals who differ notably from the average. He feels that it is particularly important to develop counseling programs, to group students by ability so that gifted pupils may be challenged to use their capabilities to good purpose, and to provide prolonged and consistent training in science, mathematics, and foreign languages. For community leaders perusal of his book should be obligatory.

CONCLUSION

In conclusion, let me review briefly what I have been saying. It seems obvious that the attitudes of the community can reinforce the work of teachers and school administrators or can virtually neutralize them. The motivation of young people for learning is certain to be weakened if high standards of work are not valued by classmates, parents, and the community at large.

If it wants good education for its children, the community is clearly obligated to provide comfortable school buildings that can be adapted to the changing requirements of classroom procedures, audio-visual aids and other equipment that make enrichment of the curriculum possible, and recreational facilities that will foster constructive release of the enormous energy of growing children.

It should staff its schools with the best teachers available, pay them well, and insist on a type of school program that will permit them to grow professionally and protect them from a wide assortment of miscellaneous duties that are not an integral part of the teaching process.

It should strive to develop respect for learning in all fields, academic or applied, which will encourage students and teachers to improve themselves and work toward excellence.

It should encourage the development of tolerance for differences of opinion about educational plans and programs because opportunity for friendly friction between independent minds stimulates learning.

It should attempt to understand both the ideas and the motives of those who attack our schools so that what is positive in their ideas may be put to use while unacceptable motives may be exposed to public scrutiny.

It should aid in the development of community advisory councils to study the work of the educational system, interpret existing schools to the mass of citizens, and give advice during times of stress. Council members should be chosen from the most capable citizens available, should not receive compensation, and should have power only in the sense of being able to clarify complex educational issues and interpret them to the community. Many community organizations, such as service clubs and the League of Women Voters, might well reinforce the efforts of parent-teacher associations to further the effectiveness of school programs.

Finally, the community should help make every one of its citizens aware of the ways in which values are transmitted from one generation to another. It can do this in no more effective manner than by strengthening family life in every possible way. Children can hardly be expected to raise their standards of thought and behavior unless their parents, teachers, ministers, and other community leaders demonstrate by example that there are higher levels of activity and thought.

Whether we succeed in surviving the present apparently endless series of local and national crises depends in no small measure on the attitude developed by our people toward learning. We may continue to try to avoid facing basic issues, or we may come to our senses and decide that life can and does have real meaning and purpose. It will be impossible to look beyond our immediate turmoil, however, unless a large proportion of our people become intolerant of the conditions that lead to mediocrity and lowering of ideals. The creation of this particular type of intolerance is one of the major opportunities that confronts our educational institutions at the present time.

6 An Enlarged Context for Education: The Community

Milton Brown

Former Secretary of Labor Arthur J. Goldberg said in a speech delivered in 1962 that "one of the great imperatives facing the nation is to find solutions for the job problems of a million unemployed, out-of-school youth, and to plan for the unprecedented surge of young people over the labor market horizon in the next few years." That the great imperative remains with us was shown recently by the *Wall Street Journal* in an editorial entitled "Teen-Age Woes" by John W. Grimes. He reported on the plight of 18-year-old Joe Young who decided in June that he would end his formal education and seek a permanent job. This simple decision automatically turned Joe into a statistic of national economic impact and part of a problem of intensifying national concern.

According to present expectations there is about one chance in six that Joe, lacking needed skills or training, will wind up in the rising ranks of the teenage unemployed. And although Joe Young is an imaginary figure, he may represent a very real phenomenon, for, like him, hundreds of thousands of unskilled youngsters probably made the same school-leaving decision in June. Scanning the want ads, our Mr. Young will find strong employer demand for IBM punch-card machine operators, electronics trainees, clerk-typists, service technicians for office equipment, and other skilled help. But Joe, with an average high-school education, will find that employers prefer the person with a bit of college training, or the high-school mathematics whiz, or his classmates who took certain technical courses.

The jobs requiring less skill, Joe will find, are harder to come by nowadays. The elevator operator's job he thought of as a last resort is gone; the lift is automatic now. The warehouse helper's job he heard about earlier has vanished; fork-lift trucks do the work. There are plenty of construction jobs around town, but the builders are not hiring ditch-diggers and other common laborers; heavy machinery run by trained men fills the need.

"There used to be a place for the unskilled youngster in the old work force," remarked Labor Secretary Wirtz, "but machines are now taking over the unskilled jobs." Recently Mr. Wirtz addressed an open letter to high-school students debating whether to return to school next fall. "Your decision to go back and finish up," he said, "may very possibly be the difference between your life meaning something instead of being spent fighting the fear—and the fact—of unemployment."

How are young people who drop out of school without having developed any skills or specific interests to find a useful place in society? There are those who would place all the blame for "dropouts" on the doorsteps of the school authorities. The idea that any one agency or any single institution can help these young people "find their way" or "secure a job" is erroneous for it fails to consider fully either the nature of this problem or the highly individualized basis for each youth's failure to conform. In my opinion all community agencies, voluntary and public, have a role to play. The important task, therefore, is how to channel all the resources of our communities to help these young people develop an image of themselves as worthwhile citizens and then take their place in society as such.

I propose to relate three experiences in dealing with school dropouts and their families. Two of these examples have been provided by settlement-house experiences. The third example has to do with the Youth Employment Program which operates under the direction of the Manpower Director of Community Progress, Inc., in New Haven, Connecticut.

Example 1. *Study Den Program—Hudson Guild Settlement House, New York, New York*

The Hudson Guild is a settlement located in the Chelsea section of New York City. A foundation grant, supplemented by a small addition from the Guild's general operating budget, has made the program possible. Since it began in 1957 many children and teenagers have been helped not only to maintain a passing academic record in school but in most cases their interest in school work has increased to a very marked degree and it is the firm belief of the agency that they were thereby prevented from becoming school dropouts.

The program was initiated at the request of the group-work staff and of many youngsters and their parents because the youngsters had no place to study because of the crowded conditions in which they live, or because their home environment actually discouraged a desire to learn. The program was expanded into a remedial tutoring service when it became apparent that having a place to study was not in itself enough to maintain many of the children in school.

During the five years the program has been in operation a total of

325 children have been enrolled and helped. Their ages ranged from 8 to 18 and they came from a variety of schools in the area, including secondary, junior high, and senior high schools. The program has had the complete cooperation of teachers, principals, and assistant superintendents in the district who have found it a helpful adjunct to their own educational programs.

In setting up the program many useful lines of communication were established between the schools in the area and the program. Where formerly the youngsters themselves needed sufficient motivation to seek out this help, referrals are now made by the schools themselves. Parents often bring their children in, however, or in some instances one child refers another. When a referral is made by the school, much pertinent information on the student accompanies it. When students have come in without referral, the program sends a letter to the school, requesting an outline of the nature of the student's deficiencies, his intelligence quotient, his reading and mathematics level, and information on any behavioral problems the student may have. The program has tried to keep track of the students who have been helped, to see what kind of positive results this program can produce. Most of the children who were helped at one time or another in the Study Den Program have stayed in school and maintained passing work. The coordinator of the program is of the opinion that many of these students would have become dropouts if it had not been for the Study Den Program.

Students of many different ages and grades have been helped. The program was completely integrated ethnically. Subjects in which the students were tutored included: elementary, junior-high-school, and high-school mathematics; reading on all levels; history; high-school English; physics; French; accounting; social studies; physiology; chemistry; Pitman shorthand; and economics. Special care was taken with Spanish-speaking children, whose English-reading levels were low. It was found that the majority of these children, once their reading levels had been raised, were able to maintain passing grades in all other courses.

Students were tutored individually and in groups by volunteer tutors. The tutors were supervised by a paid part-time coordinator. The coordinator of the program interviewed all students registered in the program and made specific recommendations to the tutor on areas of weakness. The coordinator held weekly conferences with the tutors on each student's progress.

Intelligence tests were administered where necessary, and under certain conditions, when trouble persisted that could not be traced to academic deficiencies, the child was referred to the Hudson Guild Psychiatric Counseling Service for further testing.

The tutor used audio-visual aids, maps, flash cards, and blackboards to aid him in helping the students. A group technique involving three to four children met several times a week. Groups were led by a teacher with graduate training in remedial reading. Tape recordings were used to aid and pace the children in their reading exercises. This group method was found very helpful in achieving higher reading levels.

For all who attended positive results were recorded, both tangible and intangible—intangible in the sense that they were not really measurable by any statistical yardstick, such as increase in a feeling of self-worth, improved family relationships, and better adjustment in other areas such as the community center. In results that can be measured statistically, most of those who entered the program showed marked academic growth. In reading ability the growth was one to three years, and one to two years in mathematics. During the five years that this program has been in existence, very few of those who registered dropped out before their deficiencies had been corrected. Last year (1962) a total of 75 were served. Of this number only four dropped out. This average can be applied to the total program.

If the budget permits it is hoped that the Study Den can be expanded so that all those who need help can be accommodated. Many children who have been worked with on remedial reading are in need of psychiatric treatment. Hudson Guild would like to build into the program a team approach to the students' total problems whereby conferences would be held with the parent, teacher, coordinator, and a case worker so that a complete program could be worked out, including case work and psychiatric service where necessary for both the family and the child. Utilizing this team-consultation technique, all interested parties could be brought together for the benefit of the student's total growth. Overall budgetary needs will determine whether this project can be carried on, because the expanded program requires a substantial investment of professional time.

Example 2. Stimulating Scholastic Achievement in Teenagers in a Socioeconomically Deprived Neighborhood—Baden Street Settlement, Rochester, New York

The Baden Street Settlement is located in one of the oldest sections of Rochester. It is surrounded by a high-rise, low-income, public-housing project on one side and varying stages of urban redevelopment on the other.

Most of the residents live under the frustration of unemployment, for jobs are hard to find and money is scarce. So instead of having money left at the end of the month, they have none at all. Their faces are etched with disappointment and despair. Their eyes reflect disillusionment and discontent. This attitude of futility has filtered down to the teenagers. They exhibit the same frustrations as the adults, but in different ways.

Some attend school more regularly than others, perhaps in part to escape from the harsh realities and drawbacks of their homes. Others stay home because they are ashamed. Daily life seems to hold few hopes, and the future holds nothing. Few have thought of college and its importance.

The Baden Street Settlement bases its program of scholastic encouragement on the premise that the teenagers in its neighborhood are as educable as any others. The problems to be faced are how can teenagers who place no emphasis on education be encouraged to participate in a program designed to overcome educational apathy, and how can parents, who are not academically oriented, be expected to help both financially and morally? In analyzing total needs it was decided by the agency to emphasize tutoring and stress the importance of college. The agency made available a large meeting room with a small room adjacent to it as the new tutorial room and office. One neighborhood group helped to refurnish and refurbish this facility. Another group supplied pictures, books, magazines, and curtains.

The big problem then faced by the staff was how to go about getting those who wanted to attend into the program and how to cope with those who wanted not to attend but rather to harass and ridicule those who did. It was decided that the general program should be closed for a half hour. All members then were "encouraged" to visit the Tutorial Room, to browse around, look at the magazines, ask questions about school, and so on. It soon became apparent that many teenagers were eager to get help with school work. Few had adequate places to study at home. Most had poor study habits.

Conferences were held with school advisors to explain the program and secure their cooperation. Tutors were recruited from all walks of life. All had one overriding concern—the interests of their students. The relationship factor was stressed. While helping the student with a particular subject was important, so also was the realization by the teenager that someone was interested in him. No more than two teenagers were assigned to a tutor so that a more intensive helping relationship could be developed.

The agency stressed the importance of college. The staff used a bulletin board to display information about colleges and this was kept current and changed weekly. All of the agency clubs were encouraged to have from time to time informal talks about finishing high school and going on to college. Speakers like the mayor and superintendent of schools were secured and urged to speak about "What after graduation? How will you prepare yourself for tomorrow?"

Visits were arranged for many of the teenagers to Syracuse University and other local colleges on days when there were social activities as well as opportunities to visit classes in order to gain an overall impression of college life. When it was felt that students were sufficiently prepared, an "overnight" was arranged at the University of Rochester with the sororities and fraternities. This projected visit posed all sorts of problems. To visit a "strange" world with a "strange" way of life was threatening enough but to actually stay overnight was considered a really traumatic experience. The seniors who faced it came up with every excuse imaginable as to why they could not stay overnight. Many complained of the lack of proper clothes. The group worker assured them that the average habitue of Greenwich Village is well dressed compared to the average college student.

The university groups who were to receive these high-school seniors had been thoroughly briefed about their responsibility and had met each senior at the Settlement prior to departure. The weekend program consisted of eating in the cafeteria, attendance at a basketball game and student play, an informal meeting at the student union for snacks, and a return to the dorms for a bull session. Saturday was spent in attending classes with departure for home scheduled for noon.

All of the children were impressed with the visit. They were surprised at the many and devious ways the college students had devised to save and make money. They were also impressed by how easily and warmly they were accepted. This was the forerunner of other programs designed to motivate an interest in college.

In an attempt to deal with some of the very real financial problems encountered, the Baden Street Settlement in conjunction with the Junior Chamber of Commerce embarked on a job-placement and counseling program. The function of the Junior Chamber was to find after-school, weekend, or temporary employment. Staff were to select, counsel, and advise students as to their responsibility to their employers.

The tutorial program was expanded. A scholarship program was set up. The college-encouragement program became so large that a special college counselor was assigned to investigate colleges that fitted the needs of the applicants and to confer with students as to the various college requirements.

The agency concludes that this program has been instrumental in encouraging students to attend college and also to decrease the potential number of dropouts.

Example 3. *Early Prevention of Dropout and Youth Employment Programming, Community Progress, Incorporated, New Haven, Connecticut*

Community Progress, Incorporated, is a program devised as a cooperative, coordinated, integrated attack on social problems that affect New Haven. Major points of intervention are concentrated on education and employment with efforts focused on six low-income districts wherein

60 per cent of the city's population resides. While employment developments are handled by CPI, the educational scheme operates under New Haven's Board of Education and is financed by Ford Foundation funds.

Curricular designs to prevent dropout begin with programs in early elementary education. First of all, there is a prekindergarten to help those children who need to attain a higher level of readiness for formal schooling. While these disadvantaged boys and girls meet two hours a day for three days a week, their mothers attend seminars on child development and home management. A higher-horizons approach utilizing community resources is employed to help those culturally deprived children in grades one through six.

Rising concern about dropout in the central part of the city has resulted in attempts to improve teacher effectiveness. Some twenty certified instructors have entered inner-city schools as classroom aids. Helping instructors will serve to enhance the concept of teachers in these schools by reducing teacher failure and dissatisfaction, thereby reducing staff turnover. This modified team-teaching approach will hopefully upgrade the instructional program by helping slow learners and poorly motivated pupils. Inner-city concern also prompted a new concept of summer school begun in 1963 affording students in grades four to ten an opportunity for learning in an informal atmosphere without report cards or marks. Makeup work can be taken during this time; curricular innovations are tried; and new teacher techniques are employed.

Although prevention is a primary interest in the dropout situation, consideration also has been given to the problems of those who have actually quit school before graduation. The community cannot afford to neglect young workers for their proportion in the labor force is steadily increasing. Yet they will have fewer and fewer employment opportunities unless their level of job skills is raised and unless more employers are willing to cooperate in developing jobs that have a future for young people. Therefore CPI has initiated an action approach to providing jobs.

A number of working committees have been chosen to stimulate youth employment. Committee membership is composed of representatives from the State Department of Education, the New Haven Board of Education, the State Employment Service, labor unions, representatives from participating companies, and CPI. Companies with available positions assign a specialist to the committee who describes the precise nature of the opening. A training program is agreed upon regarding the curriculum content, hours of training, testing techniques, recruitment, selection of instructors, and job standards. After criteria and standards have been decided on, the New Haven Office of the Connecticut State Employment Service launches a recruitment drive in which candidates are examined. Selected trainees begin their training program assured of a position upon graduation from the course. The training expense is financed by a Manpower Development and Training Act grant and only such remedial academic school work as is necessary for job function goes into courses. Finally, a research committee does follow-up studies on trainees who have graduated and entered the labor force.

At the outset of the program a decision was made to move first in the technical skills as this clearly represented the best opportunity area for new jobs both in terms of present and future labor-market conditions. Following a series of meetings with prominent employers in the New Haven area, Olin Mathieson and AVCO agreed to participate in three training programs involving courses for industrial draftsmen, x-ray technicians, and industrial-laboratory technicians. Again the MDTA grant paid for the training program which began in March 1963 for 50 trainees. By mid-April, 11 trainees for industrial x-ray technician jobs at AVCO completed their course and started work at approximately 100 dollars per week. Three of these successful trainees were school dropouts; five were Negroes; two were former welfare clients; all were unemployed.

In the service trades the labor specialist at CPI has worked closely with the Department of Labor, the State Department of Education, and the director of the Culinary Institute in New Haven to plan for three programs including a course for chefs (17 trainees) and two courses for formal waiters (14 trainees in each). As in the AVCO and Olin Mathieson programs, the culinary experiment has demonstrated that unemployment among youth can be significantly reduced; 23 of the trainees were high-school dropouts and 17 were Negroes. In June 1963 a similar training venture at the Institute began for 45 more trainees. This program and subsequent ones have proved successful.

With assurance that more Labor Department funds for specific training programs will be available during the current fiscal year, the Manpower Director and Labor Specialist at CPI met with at least a dozen area employers in industry, retail business, public utilities, hospitals and various service trades to work for educational programs with job commitments built in.

CONCLUSION

In sum, programs like the Study Den Project of New York City where youngsters obtain help in academic study, the Baden Street Settlement in Rochester, New York, where opportunities are provided for teenagers to realize the possibilities of education, and the Community Progress program of New Haven where prevention of dropout and youth-employment programming are underway may not be a final answer in resolving social problems caused by incomplete education. Yet they do represent significant and successful efforts on the part of interested communities to upgrade the potential of youth by affording an increase in their training. Perhaps the effect of such efforts is best described in the words of Superintendent Paquin of New Haven Schools, "We are not where we are going to be, we are not where we should be, but certainly we are not where we were." Applying this statement to the dropout problem in American cities generally, "where we were" was a point in time from which there was probably nowhere to go but up.

7 *Raising Aspirations of Youth: Implications for Community Organizations*

Daniel Schreiber

Ah, but a man's reach should exceed his grasp, or what's a heaven for?
—R. Browning

There is growing concern today for an increasing number of young people whose lack of self-esteem threatens their future. Though adults are expressing a desire to help, most efforts so far have been curtailed by the youngsters' apparent paralysis of will, reluctance to strive, and lack of aspiration. In a time of accelerated societal demands for longer and better educational preparation it is essential that we probe the causative factors that give rise to the immobile stance of some young people. Particularly important is an examination of the forces extrinsic to the child that influence his aspirations. Some of these forces are the home, the school, his peers, and the community.

EXTRINSIC DETERMINANTS OF ASPIRATION

Familial influence on aspiration is well known, for in the home are developed attitude sets toward personal growth or limitation. Unfortunately, in some families in which the educational experience of parents has been less than satisfying, there is a tendency to delimit advantages of learning. Reading and writing skills are seen as demands that the student must fulfill in order to meet the requirements of society. The extent to which a student is willing to meet these demands often depends on the attitude toward the dominant society that he has absorbed in his home. A feeling on the part of some students involved in San Francisco's Special Reading Laboratory that learning to read well, or to read at all, is worthless can be traced to families in which there is constant repetition of the theme that no matter how well a student does he will never be allowed by society to practice his skills. That such an environment tends to diminish the aspiration level of its young is obvious.[1]

Reprinted by permission of *The Catholic Educational Review*, May 1964.

[1] Raising the aspiration level of minority groups represents a related and even more acute problem. Not only does ego deflation occur when a child of discrimination perceives the status position of his ethnic or racial group, but one of the most damaging effects resulting from

63

Equally disappointing, however, is the increasing number of homes in which parents set unrealistically high aspirations for children. Viewing sons and daughters as extensions of themselves, such parents seek to accomplish in the lives of the children the goals that eluded them during their own youth. Often the concept of preparation for college becomes a paramount concern from the day a child enters kindergarten. Anticipating grades as the criterion for success, parents frequently bribe, cajole, and threaten children to obtain enviable records. Although parental concern regarding the future of their progeny is commendable, there are far too many parents who evidence a total lack of regard for such factors as: Does the child's potential indicate college material? What are his curricular and vocational interests? Are present achievement expectations by his parents in line with the pupil's capacity of performance?

SCHOOL INFLUENCES

Schools all too often reinforce unrealistic expectations of the home. Allegiance to the normalization concept leads some educators to an expectancy of how children should think, speak, and feel according to standards of a given age or grade. More often than not, norms become the minimal level of achievement urged for all class members. To be sure, test scores do not cause all teachers to prejudge the success or failure of their students; but, guided by norms, many instructors classify children before involvement with them. Although the aspiration for pupils as held by teachers is not a subject for discussion here, the increasing impersonality of schools cannot be dismissed as a factor.

One thing appears certain—if we are to keep all students in schools, then all required courses must be designed and taught to meet all ability levels. Unless we can come nearer to this objective in practice, we will continue to have "built-in" standards of performance that will force some students out of school. It is precisely in the basic courses of reading, language arts, mathematics, and social studies that antipathy or enthusiasm is nurtured, success or defeat is sealed, dropout or retention is determined.

PEER INFLUENCES

Peer pressures obviously have an effect on individual achievement. There are at present myriad studies underway that purport to investigate the ways in which youngsters determine or govern aspirations, behavior, and, in some measure, the progress of their age mates. Underlying these

---

prejudice on this victimized group is that it provides an all-embracing rationalization for personal shortcomings, lack of striving, and antisocial behavior.

research efforts is a hope that we can use peer groups to influence and instruct their membership with even more efficiency than is now possible with the use of adult-directed teaching. Especially is this true in the area of attitude development.

The rationale prompting this new interest in adolescent interaction comes largely from cultural anthropology where predictions are being made that the amount and nature of the ways children learn from each other will increase. It is likely that the rate of instructional change will be so great that children being born at this time will find few patterns of behavior of the present adult population that will stand them in good stead when they reach maturity. Hence children may be forced to turn more and more to each other in working out effective and satisfying patterns of action. It seems proper therefore to work toward increased knowledge of the conditions under which peer groups can both influence and reinforce the development of realistic aspirations for their individual members.

Community Influences

Communities have a stake in the development of responsible goals for our future citizens. Inasmuch as personal responsibility is a vital element of emotional strength, it is unfortunate that communities have not given more attention to the role of young people in building and maintaining the community in which they reside. Psychologically, all beings need identity; they want to fulfill a purpose, to contribute, to be recognized, and to be needed. In the United States, almost as if by design, we have denied our adolescents the fulfillment of such needs. Improvement of economic conditions has blessed us with mass affluence, but ironically we have been cursed with an inability to maintain the identity of the teenager. In earlier times he filled a need, found his place fighting our wars, chored his own farm, and married into responsibility. In other words, he played a role for which he received his applause.

By sharp contrast, the teenager today is asked to hibernate until adulthood in a state of limbo we now term adolescence. He is no longer a child yet not adult, uncommitted to any specific occupation or task. He is not made responsible for anything, contributes little to anyone or anything, and as a result, in some instances, stumbles into misadventurous directions seeking a meaning of himself; burns his excess energies in ways that inflame his home and community, rejects and resents the authority that would restrain him; rants, rebels, and cries out to a neurotic wilderness that "there is nothing to do," "no one understands me," "what do we do for kicks?"

The young person of today has rocket energies and seeks ways in which to test his strength and determine his limitations. Though knowledge is gained at an earlier age, and adult activities are initiated earlier than ever before, responsibilities are deferred to an ever-later period. While urging the teenager to grow up, we hold him back by assigning counterfeit responsibilities, telling him these are more useful than the real thing. Then suddenly we let the barriers down and demand immediate and successful adult behavior. We seldom get it. Communities must begin to distribute realistic responsibility to their young if we have any expectation of developing civic-minded aspirations.

SOME OUTCOMES OF IMPOSED ASPIRATIONS

At this juncture it is appropriate to interject the query of what happens when a child is pressured to adopt aspirations for self that have been set by others. Some become overstrivers and announce goals far beyond their past attainment. They are uncertain about what they can really expect of themselves. They cannot admit inadequacy, or discriminate the reasonable from the unreasonable. Lacking confidence, they reduce their anxiety by aiming beyond what they can hope to achieve. It is as though they were to say: "My attainments aren't much but at least my goals are worthy of praise." And failing to reach lofty goals hardly counts as failure. Thus, if they succeed, their pleasure is great; if they fail, their self-respect does not suffer. Sears (1941) found overstrivers to be apprehensive, inflexible in thinking, and poorly adjusted socially. Not knowing what they can do or how others will regard them necessarily implies a lack of self-respect. There are others for whom long-continued difficulties lead to hopelessness and withdrawal. These children set goals cautiously, often much below previous achievements, for they have learned that it is better not even to try since repeated experience has produced nothing but failure when they have been compared to their peers in achievement.

It is important to recognize that goal setting reflects personality. A steady but realistic raising of aims is usual among self-confident children who are assured in their performance. They may show pleasure and strong effort but in a realistic fashion which places socially and self-approved limits on their achievement. They do not react with feelings of failure or poor performance on material that is clearly too difficult for them, nor do they gloat over good performance on easy material. In contrast the overstriver lacks a clear self-concept, hence is insecure, apprehensive, and inflexible. Those who withdraw appear self-conscious, dissatisfied with themselves, and eager to take an easy way out. It is interesting to note that the assured pupil strives in response to criticism, whereas the worried, sensitive pupil seems to respond better to praise.

With this cursory appraisal as a base, let us view several general principles presently operative that appear to raise the aspirations of youth.

Areas of concern which follow have particular relevance to the unique role of voluntary organizations.

GUIDELINES FOR RAISING ASPIRATIONS

Realistic aspirations can be developed in an environment of responsibility. When youngsters are given tasks of positive consequence in which they can witness firsthand the outcomes of responsible service to the community, the elements of personal satisfaction and aspiration are generated. Although some schools deny responsibility to those who most need it, it need not be true in the programs of voluntary organizations where service can involve work on fund-raising activities for hospitals, charity · organizations, institutions for the aged; participation in civil-defense and other safety programs; community conservation and holiday activities; helping in religious and political programs, such as "Get Out the Vote" campaigns, United Nations Day, Brotherhood Week, Religion in American Life, and similar affairs.

Especially important is the concept of work experiences for those youngsters who come from the "under class." Very often such children who live in the center of our large cities are not exposed to the dignity of labor, personal responsibility, or the satisfaction of a job well done. Their living circumstances do not include chores at home for in the central city there are no corner stores to work in, no grass to mow, no snow to shovel, no leaves to rake. Then too, in some instances, with unemployed parents, teenagers fail to see the benefits of labor.

Realistic aspirations are a product of guidance. Voluntary organizations such as the Boys Clubs of America find themselves in a rather favored role today in the guidance of youth. Torrance (1965) and others have found that youngsters confide more readily in the instructors from such organizations than they do in their public-school teachers. Many teenagers report that youth leaders of voluntary organizations are more accessible, less dictative, and closer in touch with the real problems confronting adolescents. This view is corroborated by an article in the *Washington Post* (Hogan, 1964) entitled "The Silent Teens: Parents Wonder Why They Won't Talk." When approached with the complaint of parents that communication with children has been disrupted, high-school pupils reply thus:

They're removed from our world, pretty much. Oh, I know they always say they were young once, too, but we don't believe it.

Most kids would rather talk to their friends than their parents, because friends are more aware of the situation and more understanding.

Language presents problems—words and slang change so fast. I know Mom tries but sometimes she can't understand so I just say "forget it."

In a piece entitled, "Adolescent Medicine: New Prescription for a Neglected Age," Dr. Felix Heald (Brandel and Hogan, 1964), Chief, Adolescent Medical Clinic, Washington, D.C., Children's Hospital, explodes some of the myths about growing pains and amount of sleep needed for adolescence. The one area in which adults must manifest more interest, said Dr. Heald, is not in advising, but listening to teenagers regarding their concerns and problems. Listening is a legitimate role for all those who would seek to counsel youngsters and give direction to their aspirations. The implication for youth leaders is obvious and hopefully through initiating parent clubs a combination of primary forces can enhance the chance of raising aspiration levels.

Any personal ambition involves a goal for which to strive. The establishment of career clubs often meets this need for many youths whose decision on a vocation or the future itself has been indeterminate. In addition to discussion about the opportunities and possibilities in the world of work, such an organization can provide vocational exploration by arranging tours through factories, banks, stores, and other places of business. This orientation can include a discussion of comparative salaries, working conditions, necessary skills and types of preparation needed.

When deficiency in the basic skills precludes any realization of vocational aspiration, it is helpful to organize tutorial efforts. Though desire to help is important, competence to help appears an equal requisite. Close contact should be kept with the public schools involving tutorial assistance so that efforts support rather than oppose one another. It is pertinent to mention that Mobilization for Youth in New York City has found that success is more likely if the tutor is one of the youngster's peers whose prowess in the subject has been demonstrated.

Perhaps the clearest guide to the tutor in adjusting level of difficulty is "Keep tasks within reach of the pupil." Reaching does, and should, involve effort. To maintain self-confidence, however, the pupil should be able to complete most of his undertakings. No harm is done if periodically he is challenged to try for some goals that he has only a small chance of reaching. Reaching an unlikely goal once in five tries can strengthen willingness to try if the one success is satisfying and if the learner understands then that his failures are not to his discredit. The reformer, inventor, politician, and athlete, artist, teacher—all of them must try many times to be rewarded with one triumph. A humane experience with education can teach one to accept the failures that are the inevitable price of daring.

Aspirations are more readily raised where example and peer approval are present. Since the school cannot provide appropriate real-life experiences as the family once did, nor specific adult models to be emulated as the parents once offered, youth cleave to one another and seek exemplary behavior within their peer groups. In this context voluntary organizations can be very effective through programs that foster leadership in sports, self-government, and personal development, by utilizing exemplary boys to teach their age mates.

How children feel about themselves and about their world is important because the concept of self is manifest in a wide range, if not the entire range, of their behavior. Depending much on experience with his fellows, an individual can be made to feel more or less capable, more or less worthy, more or less acceptable. Only as he feels worthy will he behave in worthy ways, will he continue to strive for those goals in life that are within his reach, if not his grasp.

In conclusion, the human being who has resigned himself to a life devoid of striving aspiration and ambition for personal achievement has resigned himself to the death of attributes that are distinctive elements of human life. Many youngsters in our land will forfeit their future unless their expectation of self can be brought to a point compatible with the demands made of citizens in an industrial society. The tragedy of a life without aspiration is shown clearly in a recent novel called *Where the Boys Are* by Glendon Swarthout (1960). This is a story whose plot is based on that strange phenomenon of American college kids—their annual spring vacation—swarming, by thousands, down to the broad beaches of Fort Lauderdale, Florida.

What follows is adapted from a speech, in effect a soliloquy, spoken by Basil, who is one of "the boys," during a long evening with his girl in a deserted section of the beach. I quote this because somehow it reflects the essence of all I have been trying to say. But it does so in the language of our new times and of a troubled new generation. Basil speaks:

This is the bad news for kids today: We are undramatic. We have been rooked out of every generation's birthright, which is conflict. The twenties had a reputation to build . . . The thirties an economic struggle . . . The forties a World War . . . But we have no damn contrast. We have pimples but no suffering . . . money but no wealth . . . delinquency but no evil . . . television but no insight.

We have roll without rock . . . tolerance without love . . . sex without delight . . . death without sting.

We have sweatsox instead of sweat . . . we have IQ's instead of intellects— in short, we have everything to live for but the one thing without which human beings cannot live—something for which to DIE slightly—not mortally but sufficiently—and we need it so pathetically and crucially that I am sorry for us to the coldest shadows of my soul!

We have it within our power to effect a change in this somber picture. Not a new alternative but, under the circumstance, a new imperative is the judgment that "It is easier to build a boy than to mend a man."

8 Are There Open Tops in the Cages?: Using Educational Resources

E. Paul Torrance

The dropout problem in high school and college has always been a serious one. In recent years it has become even more serious—or at least we recognize it as being more serious. Almost one-half (about 46 per cent) of all children in the United States drop out of high school before graduation. Many very talented young people choose not to enter college and we carefully screen those who do. Even where high admission standards are maintained, over one-half of those who enter college drop out. Nationwide, the dropout rate in college is reported to be about 60 per cent (Boroff, 1960). Adults who have talked with these youngsters honestly and frankly know that many of them feel that "they are in a cage," that they "are trapped" as long as they remain in the educational situation. They see dropping out as the only way of escaping from this "trap" or "cage."

One mother described her 13-year-old son's predicament in just these words. She wrote:

> He speaks of wanting to go to an "electric college" but says he'll probably quit school when he's 16. I feel that he is in a steel box—I think he feels he is too and thinks the only way to be free is by quitting. Where is the spirit of educating and using talent? How can doors be opened, can you tell me? Can you advise or suggest *anything* that could help? *Please,* don't be too busy to care or answer me. . . .

Educators and others who work with youth need to feel the urgency which this mother expressed so eloquently. There is indeed an urgent need to stop, appraise, and discover how we can better utilize our educa-

Paper prepared for Annual Meeting of Home Economics Section, American Vocational Association Convention, Milwaukee, Wisconsin, December 6, 1962.

tional resources. Professional training and experience have given us many tested and established procedures for "appraising and utilizing educational resources." I would like to suggest that we approach this problem by thinking of ways by which we can appraise and utilize our *creative* resources. I would like to suggest that we first appraise and try to discover better ways of using *our own creative resources.* Next, I would like to suggest that we do the same in relation to *our students, our fellow staff members,* and *our administrators.* Even with no suggestions from me, I am sure that you would find such an undertaking exciting and richly rewarding. It is my task, however, to suggest ways for accomplishing this task.

To succeed in any measure, however, I know that I must somehow limit the task. During the past five years, my staff and I have engaged in a program of research concerned with the identification, development, and utilization of creative talent. The results of this work are reflected in something over forty publications in open sources, an even larger number of mimeographed reports, and many uncompleted reports. Perhaps the best known of these efforts is my book, *Guiding Creative Talent.* In this volume I have tried to show how various creative talents can be identified both in test and nontest ways, how these talents develop in our culture, and how I believe we can contribute to the development of this kind of talent. As I have engaged in this research, there have been times when my heart has bled for the plight of some tremendously creative children, young people, and adults. These are people who are able to produce a large number of ideas, exhibit a high degree of flexibility in their responses, produce ideas that are unusual or off the beaten track, or are able to develop these ideas in detail. We call these qualities fluency, flexibility, originality, and elaboration. We believe that they are capable of a high degree of creative achievement. Although many of these individuals feel that they are in cages, and frequently their parents, teachers, and counselors agree, I am convinced that almost always there are "open tops in these cages."

I think the critical incident that brought me to this realization was a simple story written by a sixth-grade Indian girl about a flying monkey. (These imaginative stories about flying monkeys have been tremendously revealing to me about the way boys and girls see pressures to conformity, especially pressures against high achievement.) Most of these stories tell how in some way the monkey has to give up his flying, cut off his wings, conceal the fact that he has wings, or is destroyed.

Thus I found tremendously refreshing a group of these stories written by a sixth-grade class in a small Oklahoma town. The following is the story written by Janet Red Eagle:

Once there were some monkeys sitting in a group. They were all alike except three. They were very different because they could fly.

One day some men from a park zoo were looking for some monkeys, because theirs had died. They came upon the three that flew. (They were off all by themselves.) Of course, the men didn't know that they could fly. So they took them in a cage. When they got to the zoo, they put them in a cage that didn't have any top to it. They were in the sun one day and one monkey said to the other, "I wish we could get out of here." "Then why don't we fly out of here," said the other.

They started to fly out. When they got about a half mile, the men came to feed them. When they couldn't find the three monkeys, they saw them flying away and one said, "If we would have put them in a cage with a top, we would have had a good thing here in the zoo."

There are many interpretations that can be placed on this fascinating tale. Some might say that we do not recognize and appreciate creative talent when we have it in our classes and schools. Later, when it is expressed in the form of outstanding creative achievements, we recognize that we could have exploited it and are regretful. Others will use it to support their argument that it is unnecessary and unfruitful to attempt to identify creative talent. Another obvious interpretation is that there are open tops in the cages of many creative people, but they do not look for them and they need help in seeing them. I would like to discuss all three of these possible interpretations as approaches to appraising and utilizing creative resources.

IS IDENTIFICATION NECESSARY?

First, I would like to discuss the interpretation that identification is unnecessary. Many have long argued that it is unnecessary and unfruitful to attempt to identify creative talent. They contend that if an individual possesses a real spark of creativity, it will somehow flourish and manifest itself miraculously in spite of neglect and repressive or coercive forces that inhibit it. They maintain that creative persons have always met opposition, ridicule, and scorn and that they always will. Thus no matter how innately creative they might be, this talent is of no social importance unless the individual is able to prevail against these forces. My own observations have convinced me that this is a dangerous fallacy. In our longitudinal studies we see children in the process of sacrificing needlessly what promised to be great creative talents. It is true that some of them will sacrifice their creativity only for a time and will regain it when they learn better how to cope with coercive pressures. The truly creative person, some say, may be the first to give in but the last to give up. I am afraid, however, that some never regain the creativity they showed so richly in the third grade. Instead, they choose the path of delinquency, mental illness—or at best a life of mediocrity and unrealized possibilities.

There are others who have contended that the best way to identify individuals who will make creative contributions is by tests of intelligence or scholastic aptitude. Still others would identify them on the basis of teacher's grades or measures of scholastic achievement. I believe that the history of creative achievement proves all of these arguments to be false —or at best to have serious weaknesses. I would also argue that under existing conditions there is a conflict between scholarly achievement as usually defined and measured and creative achievement. Throughout history there have been outstanding creative and inventive people whose scholastic performance has been very poor.

Some have objected, "Measures of I.Q. or scholastic aptitude also identify creative individuals. Measures of creativity and measures of I.Q. are inseparable and measure the same thing." This contention is simply not true. For the past seventy years, investigators have consistently found little or no correlation between these two types of measures. In the upper ranges of intelligence, there is practically *no* relationship between these two kinds of measures. Within a group varying widely in intelligence, there will be *low but statistically significant* correlations. Within a group low in intelligence, there will be relatively high correlations. The abilities measured by tests of intelligence and scholastic aptitude emphasize logical reasoning, memory, and convergence. Tests of creative thinking emphasize divergent kinds of thinking (ideational fluency, flexibility, originality, and elaboration), sensitivity to defects and missing elements, and ability to redefine and restructure. Traditional measures of intelligence emphasize conformity and getting the "correct" answer. Measures of creative-thinking abilities call for the unconventional response, breaking away from the beaten, safe pathway. The type of response required is also different, especially the group forms of intelligence tests in the multiple-choice format.

Tests of the creative-thinking abilities, of course, have many uses other than for identification. Our own major interest in developing such instruments has been to be able to study the development of the creative-thinking abilities, to discover what conditions facilitate or inhibit their development, and to evaluate the effects of various teaching methods and guidance procedures on the development of the creative-thinking abilities. Lest it appear that I am disparaging the value of appraising creative talent and creative achievement, I might pause to say that we can cite from our own studies many exciting examples of how a knowledge of a child's performance on tests of creative thinking caused "open tops of cages" to be discovered or uplifted for particular children.

On the other hand, it is possible to identify creative individuals without tests. Most teachers, however, have to redefine their concepts and values before they can do this successfully. Recently I asked two teachers of gifted sixth graders to give me the names of the five most and the five least curious children in their classrooms. To help them in this redefinition process, we used Wallace and Ethel Maw's (1961) criteria of curiosity. Both of them commented that they had never before thought of their pupils in this way and admitted that they were forced to place in the low group some of the children whom they valued most as pupils because they were so good in arithmetic computation, spelling, and the like. Quite interestingly we obtained excellent differentiations on all of our measures of creativity between the two groups of children nominated as most and least curious.

I first started thinking of this redefinition process and its meaning after we had administered our first battery of creative-thinking tests in our first school. A third-grade teacher commented afterward that the study had helped the whole school whether our research revealed anything or not. She said, "You have changed the entire way we look at behavior. For example, we no longer think of children as being naughty but as creating ideas for being naughty." As I began to think about the matter, I began to see what a difference it makes in the way teachers treat children, whether they see them as *being* naughty or as *creating* ideas for being naughty.

Its meaning became even clearer to me through the experience of an acquaintance who teaches in the industrial-arts field in college. He caught one of his students cheating on an examination. The methods the student used in cheating, however, were so clever and ingenious that the instructor recognized that he was dealing with an exceptionally talented individual. Suddenly he realized that his assignments had called only for reproductive thinking and that he had done nothing to challenge this unusual talent. Instead of giving this cheater an automatic failing grade or expelling him from the class, he began thinking up more and more difficult problems calling for creative problem-solving. The boy worked as he never worked before. At the end of the course, his achievement was so far ahead of everyone else in the class that the instructor felt compelled to award him a grade of "A." Here you see an example of how the identification of this student's unusual talent required a modification of the teacher's usual definition of desirable behavior. Many people condemn this teacher's behavior. Although I do not condone cheating, the values that I place on freeing students to achieve their potentialities will not permit me to condemn him. Instead, I must praise him.

WHY CAN'T CREATIVE PERSONS SEE THE "OPEN TOPS IN THE CAGES"?

Now that we have seen how the appraisal of creative talents may be used—not to exploit an individual but to help him achieve in school and not drop out—let us examine a problem arising from another interpretation of our tale about flying monkeys. Why are creative persons unable to see the open tops of their cages? We know that one of the marks of the creative person is his ability to see where others cannot see. Why is he unable to see his way out of some of the predicaments in which he finds himself? Most of the successful ones are. Even some of our dropouts might be credited with seeing the "open tops of their cages." They are willing to take their chances without the benefits of diplomas and degrees. They are so absorbed in developing some idea and believe so strongly in this idea that they are willing to take their chances. The trouble is that many of them become bogged down later and are unable to achieve their aims and potentialities.

One of the very troubles, of course, is their absorption in ideas, in experimenting, in testing some hypothesis, so that they are unable to focus their energies on their own personal problems and thus become overwhelmed by them. This is the reason why counselors, teachers, and deans have so much difficulty in activating the creative person's creativity in solving personal and school problems that threaten his success.

WHAT CAN WE DO?

I hope that from these ideas you may be able to remove some of the blocks in your own mind about appraising and utilizing the creative resources of students. (I would include, however, the creative resources that you and your professional colleagues possess, but our more direct concern will be with students.) Let us look constructively at the problem of what we can do.

Provide a Curriculum That Gives Opportunities for Creative Achievement

Even though there are many "open tops in their cages" that creative individuals do not use, I think we ought to accept responsibility for creating more "open tops" by providing a curriculum that gives opportunities for creative kinds of achievement and for learning through creative ways. In other words, create more "open tops in the cages." This is essentially what the industrial-arts teacher did when he realized that his cheating student possessed a high level of creative talent.

There are many ways in which this can be done. It can be done, as the industrial-arts teacher in my example did it, by making assignments that call for this kind of performance. It can be done daily by the kinds of questions we ask in class or by the kinds of problems that we set for class discussion. In a recent study in Wisconsin, arrangements were made for one pupil each day to make a record of all of the questions asked by the teacher in junior-high-school social-studies classes. When these questions were analyzed over a period of time for several teachers and classes, it was found that 90 per cent of the questions called only for recall. Few questions called for thinking of any kind—creative thinking, critical thinking, convergent thinking, evaluative thinking, and so on. Although the situation may not be this bad in your class, the chances are that there is room for improvement in asking questions, using problems and materials that require creative problem-solving, and making other changes in the curriculum that supply more open tops for the creativity of your students.

Rewarding Creative Behavior

Long ago, Plato said, "What is honored in a country will be cultivated there." Educational research has indicated repeatedly that individuals tend to develop along whatever lines they find rewarding. It is my firm belief that every educator from nursery school through graduate school should be ever on the alert to notice new ideas and to encourage creative behavior. Every educator should consider this as important, or more important, than teaching information. Furthermore, creative thinking can lead to the acquisition of information, certainly to the motivation of its acquisition.

Recent experiments of our own in creative writing and in problems requiring inventiveness have shown that we obtain the kind of creative thinking we reward. If we reward originality, responses will become more original. If we reward fluency, a larger number of ideas will be produced. If we reward elaboration, more detailed and more elaborate products will result.

There are, as I see it, two major obstacles to valuing creative thinking. The first is the difficulty of recognizing and appreciating the student's creative productions. It is hard for a conventional teacher to see and appreciate the contribution of an unconventional or an unloved and unlovely student. Recent research by Getzels and Jackson (1962) and by my own staff (Torrance, 1962a) give eloquent witness of this fact. In spite of average differences in I.Q. as high as 26 points, we have found that highly creative but less intelligent students achieve as well as the highly intelligent but less creative ones. Teachers, however, rate the highly intelligent ones as more desirable students, more ambitious and hard-working, less unruly, and more friendly. Teachers also say that they know and understand the highly intelligent pupils better than the highly creative ones.

A second obstacle to valuing creativity is our tendency to overrate the finished product—the completed poem, the masterpiece of music or art, the organized behavior of the championship team. We are too easily deceived by the comparative perfection and smoothness of these master-pieces and evaluate them as if they were the immediate deliveries of a creative act.

We reward or punish creative behavior, as the case may be, in many ways other than by the way we grade. (I should add, however, that I think our testing and evaluation procedures should be revised to include the evaluation of creative kinds of achievement.) I would like to offer five very simple but potentially rather powerful suggestions.

1. *Be respectful of unusual questions.* Nothing is more rewarding to the person who asks a question than to find an answer to his question. Questions reflect a "mind hunger" and this hunger must be satisfied lest the mind be starved. Although the need should be met immedi-ately, there is much that teachers can do to enrich the period between the question and the answer. In general, they should tell students only what they cannot learn for themselves. This means that students need to be taught the skills of inquiry and research. They need to learn how to sustain a question, to play with it, toss it back and forth, refine it, and accept the questioning mood without the need for ready-made answers from the teacher.

2. *Be respectful of the unusual ideas of students.* Students who are stimu-lated by creative approaches will see many relationships and signif-icances that their teachers miss. They will present ideas and solutions that their teachers will not be able to evaluate. Thus it is extremely difficult for teachers properly to reward such thinking and it is usually the more creatively talented students who suffer most from such un-rewarded effort.

3. *Show students that their ideas have value.* In showing students that their ideas have value, the trouble is that many teachers do not believe that students are capable of thinking of ideas that have value. Such teachers obviously will not be able to reward creative thinking in stu-dents. I would suggest that teachers who do not genuinely believe that the ideas of their students have value be on the alert for a few days to recognize new ideas among students. They can be shown that their ideas have value, if teachers listen to their ideas, consider them, test them, use them, communicate them to proper individuals or groups, give students the credit for them, and the like. We need to give more attention to the lure of discovery and the role of curiosity

and interest in motivating learning. Teachers would do well to look at the long list of teenagers who have made history with their creative achievements in science and invention.

4. *Provide opportunities for self-initiated learning and give credit for it.* An old principle of learning is: "Excite and direct the self-activities of the learner and tell him nothing that he can learn for himself." Almost all children have strong curiosity and exploratory tendencies. The problem of high-school and college teachers is to keep these tendencies alive or reawaken them. Overly detailed supervision, too much reliance on prescribed curricula, failure to appraise and give credit for growth resulting from the student's own initiative, and attempts to teach too many subjects and cover too much material may seriously interfere with such attempts.

5. *Provide for periods of nonevaluated practice or discovery.* There is a need for periods when students can learn and discover without threats of immediate evaluation. External evaluation is always a threat and creates a need for defensiveness. This makes some portion of the individual's experiencing or sensing denied to awareness (Rogers, 1954). Thus there is lacking the openness that is so necessary in the production of new ideas.

We need to invent devices that will make it possible for students to formulate an inaccurate or even a wild idea without ruining their careers or their chances of succeeding in a course. In industry, Maier and Hayes (1962) found "that superiors want subordinates to submit creative ideas, but subordinates are reluctant to do so because the result may be an unfavorable reaction from the superior" (p. 41). "One criticism that a subordinate feels is unjust," Maier and Hayes remark, "is enough to cancel the effect of ten praises, and it suppresses similar acts of initiative in the future."

MAKING CREATIVE INDIVIDUALS FEEL YOU ARE ON THEIR SIDE

I could recite dozens of suggestions about how to create more favorable conditions for creative growth and thereby find more open tops in your own cages and help others find them in theirs. I would like to add one more idea capable of transforming your relationships with creative students and staff members: *the necessity for making creative individuals feel confident that you are on their side.* This is always important in helping people find the "tops in their cages." It is illustrated beautifully in Whitehorn's (1959) study of the kind of psychiatrist who is most successful in working with schizophrenics. Psychiatrists most successful in helping schizophrenics had vocational interest patterns most like those of lawyers and certified public accountants and least like those of printers and mathematics and physical-science teachers. The interest patterns of those least successful in working with schizophrenics were just the opposite. I think we all recognize that one of the functions of the lawyer is to help his clients find loopholes in the laws, or to help keep the restrictive regulations of society from binding human activity so tightly and rigidly as to thwart reasonable human activities and desires. In other words, they help their clients find the "tops of their cages" or at least the holes in them. The client feels that his lawyer is "on his side," that he is "for him." The psychiatrist whose attitudes are like those of the printer sees things as "black or white," "right or wrong," and is likely to view the schizophrenic as a person with a wayward mind that needs to be corrected and held within strict bounds.

In fashioning your relationship to the highly creative student or staff member, I would suggest that you adopt attitudes more like those of the lawyer than of the printer. I would like to suggest seven ways in which you can play this important role for such persons.

Provide a Model of Creative Behavior

Perhaps one of the most fundamental roles any adult can play in helping creative individuals is to provide a model of creative behavior in whatever way is appropriate to him. This does not mean that he must possess outstanding abilities in art, music, writing, science, or invention. It is far more important that he maintain his curiosity, his openness and aliveness, his excitement in learning and thinking, his courage and independence in thinking. If he does this he will provide a model whereby others will learn how to behave in creative ways. If he has learned to maintain his creativity without being obnoxious, he should be especially helpful to the highly creative individual who has difficulty in getting along with the group.

Provide a "Refuge"

Society in general is downright savage toward creative individuals. From recent studies (Getzels and Jackson, 1962), we know that highly creative adolescents are estranged from their teachers and peers. Thus the highly creative person needs encouragement. He needs help in "becoming reconciled and in being made cheerful over the world's stubborn satisfaction in its own follies." The adult must recognize, however, that the estrangement exists and that he will have to create a relationship in which creative individuals feel safe.

Be a Sponsor or Patron

Someone has observed that almost always wherever independence and creativity occur and persist, there is some individual or agent who plays the role of sponsor or patron. This role is played by someone who is not a member of the peer group, but who possesses prestige and power in the same social system. He does several things. Regardless of his own views, the sponsor encourages and supports the other in expressing and testing his ideas and in thinking things through for himself. He protects the individual from reactions of his peers long enough for him to try out some of his ideas and modify them. He can keep the structure of the situation open enough so that originality *can* occur.

Help Him Understand His Divergence

A high degree of sensitivity, a capacity to be disturbed, and divergent thinking are essentials of the creative personality. Frequently, creative young people are puzzled by their own behavior. They desperately need to understand themselves, particularly their divergence, the ways in which they are different from others. There are crucial times in the lives of creative persons when being understood is all that is needed to help them cope with the crisis and maintain their creativity.

Let Him Communicate His Ideas

The highly creative person has an unusually strong urge to explore and to create. When he thinks up ideas, or tests them, and modifies them, he has an unusually strong desire to communicate his ideas and tell others what he has discovered. Yet both peers and teachers named some of the most creative pupils in our studies as ones who do not speak out their ideas. When we see what happens when they do speak out their ideas, there is little wonder that they are reluctant to communicate them. Frequently their ideas are so far ahead of those of their classmates and even their teachers that they have given up hopes of communicating.

If you are to perform this function, you must have a genuine respect for the questions and ideas of young people in order to sustain the highly creative student or staff member so that he will continue to think.

See That His Creative Talent Is Recognized

Information from many sources indicates that much creative talent goes unrecognized. In our own studies at all educational levels, about 70 per cent of those in the upper 20 per cent on tests of creative thinking would be eliminated if only an intelligence or scholastic aptitude test had been used.

Of all of Elizabeth Drews' (Drews, 1961) three gifted groups of high-school students (social leaders, creative intellectuals, and studious achievers), the lowest teacher grades were achieved by the creative intellectuals. When the others were studying for examinations, they would be reading a book on philosophy or a college textbook, activities with almost no payoff in the teacher's grade book. Thus on difficult standard-ized achievement tests the creative intellectuals surpassed the other groups as a result of their wide reading and uncredited self-initiated learning.

Frequently the top can be lifted from a highly creative individual's cage by having someone call attention to his talent at the opportune time and place to a person who can create the proper kind of opportunity for the utilization of his talent. Such talent may be overlooked, if judgments are made only on the basis of course grades.

Help Parents Understand the Creative Student

One of the most tragic cases that I have witnessed among university students of the creatively gifted category was one whose parents failed to understand him. Frequently destructive or incapacitating hostility is the result of this failure. When teachers fail to understand highly creative individuals, refusal to learn, delinquency, or withdrawal may be a con-sequence. In some cases, the quiet and unobtrusive intervention of a responsible person offers about the only possibility whereby teachers and parents may come to understand them and thus salvage outstanding talent.

CONCLUSION

I am sure that no one is so naïve as to believe that you can assume the roles which I have suggested without some risk, some danger. Your colleagues, even your administrators, and perhaps even your students, may criticize you in your efforts to appraise and utilize the creative resources which you, your colleagues, and your students possess. Thus, as a closing caution, which I hope you will not take too seriously, I shall quote another imaginative story by a child, a story of "The Lion That Doesn't Roar":

The Great Fearless Lion, Majella, had been caught and put in a cage. He went to a zoo. Majella didn't like this, so he tried to get out. The only time he could get out was when the cage keeper brought his dinner, a big bloody steak. One day he tried to get out. He got out and scared everybody around. The zoo people caught him and put him back in his cage. He got out three more times. He didn't really scare people but his roar did. One day the keeper put some stuff in the lion's dinner. It was a drug. It put him to sleep after his dinner for an hour or two. Every time he got out he scared someone. The cage keeper finally put a lot of alum in his dinner and he couldn't roar. He cried and cried and cried all night. He went to 101 doctors. They said he would never roar again.

I shall let you place whatever interpretation you wish upon this tale. We do have to recognize that creative behavior can be very threatening to many people, and when people are threatened they act with hostility.

You might say that the story shows that one should not roar so loud and that he should be more unobtrusive about finding opportunities to be himself. Or, if you want a simple interpretation, I might suggest the following: "Go ahead and roar about the open top in your cage but don't let anyone give you any alum!"

9 *Adolescent Subculture and Academic Achievement*

James S. Coleman

Industrial society has spawned a peculiar phenomenon, most evident in America but emerging also in other Western societies: adolescent sub-cultures, with values and activities quite distinct from those of the adult society—subcultures whose members have most of their important associations within the youth group and few with adult society. Industriali-zation, and the rapidity of change itself, has taken out of the hands of the parent the task of training his child, made the parent's skills obsolescent, and put him out of touch with the times—unable to understand, much less inculcate, the standards of a social order which has changed since he was young.

By extending the period of training necessary for a child and by en-compassing nearly the whole population, industrial society has made of high school a social system of adolescents. It includes, in the United States, almost all adolescents and more and more of the activities of the adolescent himself. A typical example is provided by an excerpt from a high-school newspaper in an upper-middle-class suburban school:

SOPHOMORE DANCING
FEATURES CHA CHA

Sophomores, this is your chance to learn how to dance! The first day of sophomore dancing is Nov. 14 and it will begin at 8:30 A.M. in the Boys' Gym . . . .

No one is required to take dancing, but it is highly recommended for both boys and girls . . . .

If you don't attend at this time, except in case of absence from school,

The research discussed in this paper was carried out under a grant from the United States Office of Education; a full report is contained in "Social Climates and Social Structures in High Schools," a report to the Office of Education. The paper was presented at the Fourth World Congress of Sociology, Milan, Italy, September 1959.

Reprinted by permission of *The American Journal of Sociology,* 65, January 1960, 337–347.

you may not attend at any other time. Absence excuses should be shown to Miss . . . . . . or Mr. . . . .

In effect, then, what our society has done is to set apart, in an institution of their own, adolescents for whom home is little more than a dormitory and whose world is made up of activities peculiar to their fellows. They have been given as well many of the instruments which can make them a functioning community: cars, freedom in dating, continual contact with the opposite sex, money, and entertainment, like popular music and movies, designed especially for them. The international spread of "rock-and-roll" and of so-called American patterns of adolescent behavior is a consequence, I would suggest, of these economic changes which have set adolescents off in a world of their own.

Yet the fact that such a subsystem has sprung up in society has not been systematically recognized in the organization of secondary education. The theory and practice of education remains focused on *individuals;* teachers exhort individuals to concentrate their energies in scholarly directions, while the community of adolescents diverts these energies into other channels. The premise of the present research is that, if educational goals are to be realized in modern society, a fundamentally different approach to secondary education is necessary. Adults are in control of the institutions they have established for secondary education; traditionally these institutions have been used to mold children as individuals toward ends which adults dictate. The fundamental change that must occur is to shift the focus: to mold social communities as communities, so that the norms of the communities themselves reinforce educational goals rather than inhibit them, as is at present the case.

The research being reported is an attempt to examine the status systems of the adolescent communities in ten high schools and to see the effects of these status systems upon the individuals within them. The ten high schools are all in the Midwest. They include five schools in small towns (labeled 0–4 in the figures that follow), one in a working-class suburb (6), one in a well-to-do suburb (9), and three schools in cities of varying sizes (5, 7, and 8). All but No. 5, a Catholic boys' school, are coeducational, and all but it are public schools.

The intention was to study schools that had quite different status systems, but the similarities were far more striking than the differences. In a questionnaire all boys were asked: "How would you most like to be remembered in school: as an athletic star, a brilliant student, or most popular?" The results of the responses for each school are shown in Figure 1,[1] where the left corner of the triangle represents 100 per cent

[1] I am grateful to James A. Davis and Jacob Feldman of the University of Chicago for suggesting such graphs for presenting responses to trichotomous items in a population.

saying "star athlete"; the top corner represents 100 per cent saying "brilliant student"; and the right corner represents 100 per cent saying "most popular." Each school is represented as a point whose location relative to the three corners shows the proportion giving each response.

The schools are remarkably grouped somewhat off-center, showing a greater tendency to say "star athlete" than either of the other choices. From each school's point is a broken arrow connecting the school as a whole with its members who were named by their fellows as being "members of the leading crowd." In almost every case, the leading crowd tends in the direction of the athlete—in all cases *away* from the ideal of the brilliant student. Again, for the leading crowds as well as for the students as a whole, the uniformity is remarkably great; not so great in the absolute positions of the leading crowds but in the direction they deviate from the student bodies.

This trend toward the ideal of the athletic star on the part of the leading crowds is due in part to the fact that the leading crowds include a great number of athletes. Boys were asked in a questionnaire to name the best athlete in their grade, the best student, and the boy most popular

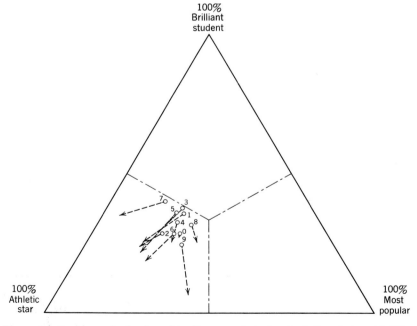

Figure 1. *Positions of schools and leading crowds in boys' relative choice of brilliant student, athletic star, and most popular.*

with girls. In every school, without exception the boys named as best athletes were named more often—on the average over twice as often—as members of the leading crowd than were those named as best students. Similarly, the boy most popular with girls was named as belonging to the leading crowd more often than the best student, though in all schools but the well-to-do suburb and the smallest rural town (schools 9 and 0 on Figure 1) less often than the best athlete.

These and other data indicate the importance of athletic achievement as an avenue for gaining status in the schools. Indeed, in the predominantly middle-class schools, it is by far the most effective achievement for gaining a working-class boy entrée into the leading crowd.

Similarly, each girl was asked how she would like to be remembered: as a brilliant student, a leader in extracurricular activities, or most popular. The various schools are located on Figure 2, together with arrows connecting them to their leading crowd. The girls tend slightly less, on the average, than the boys to want to be remembered as brilliant students. Although the alternatives are different, and thus cannot be directly compared, a great deal of other evidence indicates that the girls—although better students in every school—do not want to be considered "brilliant

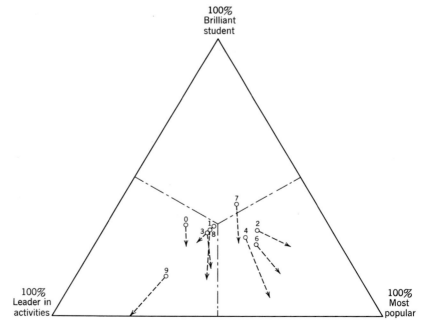

Figure 2. *Positions of schools and leading crowds in girls' relative choice of brilliant student, activities leader, and most popular.*

students." They have good reason not to, for the girl in each grade in each of the schools who was most often named as best student has fewer friends and is less often in the leading crowd than is the boy most often named as best student.

There is, however, diversity among the schools in the attractiveness of the images of "activities leader" and "popular girl" (Figure 2). In five (9, 0, 3, 8, and 1), the leader in activities is more often chosen as an ideal than is the popular girl; in four (7, 6, 2, and 4) the most popular girl is the more attractive of the two. These differences correspond somewhat to class background differences among the schools: 2, 4, 6, and 7, where the activities leader is least attractive, have the highest proportion of students with working-class backgrounds. School 9 is by far the most upper-middle-class one and by far the most activities-oriented.

The differences among the schools correspond as well to differences among the leading crowds: in schools 2, 4, and 6, where the girls as a whole are most oriented to being popular, the leading crowds are even more so; in the school where the girls are most oriented to the ideal of the activities leader, No. 9, the leading crowd goes even further in that direction.[2] In other words, it is as if a pull is exerted by the leading crowd, bringing the rest of the students toward one or the other of the polar extremes. In all cases, the leading crowd pulls away from the brilliant-student ideal.

Although these schools vary far less than one might wish when examining the effects of status systems, there are differences. All students were asked in a questionnaire: "What does it take to get into the leading crowd?" On the basis of the answers, the relative importance of various activities can be determined. Consider only a single activity, academic achievement. Its importance for status among the adolescents in each school can be measured simply by the proportion of responses that specify "good grades," or "brains" as adolescents often put it, as a means of entrée into the leading crowd. In all the schools, academic achievement was of less importance than other matters, such as being an athletic star among the boys, being a cheerleader or being good-looking among the girls, or other attributes. Other measures which were obtained of the importance of academic achievement in the adolescent status system correlate highly with this one.[3]

[2] This result could logically be a statistical artifact because the leaders were included among students as a whole and thus would boost the result in the direction they tend. However, it is not a statistical artifact, for the leading crowds are a small part of the total student body. When they are taken out for computing the position of the rest of the girls in each school, schools 2, 4, 6, and 7 are still the most popularity-oriented, and school 9 the most activities-oriented.

[3] Parenthetically, it might be noted that these measures correlate imperfectly with the proportion of boys or girls who want to be remembered as brilliant students. These responses depend

If, then, it is true that the status system of adolescents *does* affect educational goals, those schools that differ in the importance of academic achievement in the adolescent status system should differ in numerous other ways that are directly related to educational goals. Only one of those, which illustrates well the differing pressures on students in the various schools, will be reported here.

In every social context certain activities are highly rewarded, while others are not. Those activities that are rewarded are the activities for which there is strong competition—activities in which everyone with some ability will compete. In such activities the persons who achieve most should be those with most potential ability. In contrast, in unrewarded activities, those who have most ability may not be motivated to compete; consequently the persons who achieve most will be persons of lesser ability. Thus in a high school where basketball is important, nearly every boy who might be a good basketball player will go out for the sport, and, as a result, basketball stars are likely to be the boys with the most ability. If in the same school volleyball does not bring the same status, few boys will go out for it, and those who end up as members of the team will not be the boys with most potential ability.

Similarly, with academic achievement: in a school where such achievement brings few social rewards, those who "go out" for scholarly achievement will be few. The high performers, those who receive good grades, will not be the boys whose ability is greatest but a more mediocre few. Thus the "intellectuals" of such a society, those defined by themselves and others as the best students, will not in fact be those with most intellectual ability. The latter, knowing where the social rewards lie, will be off cultivating other fields that bring social rewards.

To examine the effect of varying social pressures in the schools, academic achievement, as measured by grades in school, was related to I.Q. Since the I.Q. tests differ from school to school, and since each school had its own mean I.Q. and its own variation around it, the ability of high performers (boys who made A or A— average)[4] was measured by the number of standard deviations of their average I.Q.'s above the mean. In this

---

on the relative attractiveness of other ideals, which varies from school to school, and upon other factors unrelated to the status system.

[4] In each school but 3 and 8, those making *A* and *A*— constituted from 6 to 8 per cent of the student body. In order to provide a correct test of the hypothesis, it is necessary to have the same fraction of the student body in each case (since I.Q.'s of this group are being measured in terms of number of standard deviations above the student body). To adjust these groups, enough 6's were added (each being assigned the average I.Q. of the total group of 6's) to bring the proportion up to 6 per cent (from 3 per cent in school 3, from 4 per cent in school 8).

way, it is possible to see where the high performers' ability lay, relative to the distribution of abilities in their school.[5]

The variations were great: in a small-town school, No. 1, the boys who made an A or A— average had I.Q.'s 1.53 standard deviations above the school average; in another small-town school, No. 0, their I.Q.'s were only about a third this distance above the mean, .59. Given this variation,

---

[5] The I.Q. tests used in the different schools were: (*0*) California Mental Maturity (taken seventh, eighth, or ninth grade); (*1*) California Mental Maturity (taken eighth grade); (*2*) SRA Primary Mental Abilities (taken tenth grade); (*3*) California Mental Maturity (taken ninth grade; seniors took SRA PMA, which was tabulated as a percentile, and they have been omitted from analysis reported above); (*4*) Otis (ninth and tenth grades; taken eighth grade); Kuhlman Finch (eleventh and twelfth grades, taken eighth grade); (*5*) Otis (taken ninth grade); (*6*) California Mental Maturity (taken eighth grade); (*7*) California Mental Maturity (taken eighth grade); (*8*) Otis (taken ninth or tenth grade); and (*9*) Otis (taken eighth grade).

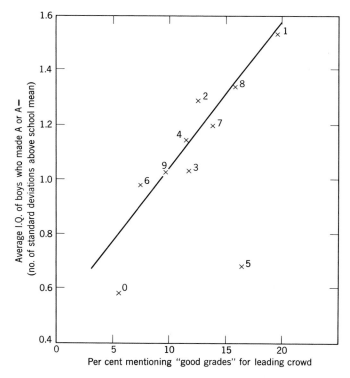

Figure 3. *I.Q.'s of high-achieving boys by importance of good grades among other boys.*

the question can be asked: Do these variations in ability of the high performers correspond to variations in the social rewards for, or constraints against, being a good student?

Figure 3 shows the relation for the boys between the social rewards for academic excellence (i.e., the frequency with which "good grades" was mentioned as a means for getting into the leading crowd) and the ability of the high performers, measured by the number of standard deviations their average I.Q.'s exceed that of the rest of the boys in the school. The relation is extremely strong. Only one school, a parochial boys' school in the city's slums, deviates. This is a school in which many boys had their most important associations outside the school rather than in it, so that its student body constituted far less of a social system, less able to dispense social rewards and punishments, than was true of the other schools.

Similarly, Figure 4 shows for the girls the I.Q.'s of the high performers.[6] Unfortunately most of the schools are closely bunched in the degree to which good grades are important among the girls, so that there is too little variation among them to examine this effect as fully as would be desirable. School 2 is the one school whose girls deviate from the general relationship.

The effect of these values systems on the freedom for academic ability to express itself in high achievement is evident among the girls as it is among the boys. This is not merely due to the school facilities, social composition of the school, or other variables: the two schools highest in the importance of scholastic achievement for both boys and girls are 1 and 8, the first a small-town school of 350 students and the second a city school of 2000 students. In both there are fewer students with white-collar backgrounds than in schools 9 or 3, which are somewhere in the middle as to value placed on academic achievement, but are more white-collar than in schools 7 or 4, which are also somewhere in the middle. The highest expenditure per student was 695 dollars per year in school 9, and the lowest was little more than half that, in school 4. These schools are close together on the graphs of Figures 3 and 4.

It should be mentioned in passing that an extensive unpublished study throughout Connecticut, using standard tests of achievement and ability, yielded consistent results. The study found no correlation between per pupil expenditure in a school and the achievement of its students relative

---

[6] For the girls, only girls with a straight-*A* average were included. Since girls get better grades than boys, this device is necessary in order to make the sizes of the "high-performer" group roughly comparable for boys and for girls. Schools differed somewhat in the proportion of *A*'s, constituting about 6 per cent of the students in the small schools, only about 3 per cent in schools 6 and 7, 1 per cent in *8*, and 2 per cent in *9*. In *8* and *9*, enough girls were added and assigned the average grade of the 7 (*A*—) group to bring the proportion to 3 per cent, comparable with the other large schools. The difference, however, between the large and small schools was left.

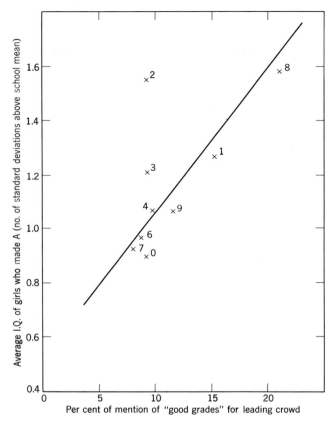

Figure 4. *I.Q.'s of high-achieving girls by importance of good grades among other girls.*

to their ability. The effects shown in Figures 3 and 4 suggest why: that students with ability are led to achieve only when there are social rewards, primarily from their peers, for doing so—and these social rewards seem little correlated with per pupil expenditure.

So much for the effects as shown by the variation among schools. As mentioned earlier, the variation among schools was not nearly so striking in this research as the fact that, in all of them, academic achievement did not count for as much as other activities. In every school the boy named as best athlete and the boy named as most popular with girls was far more often mentioned as a member of the leading crowd, and as someone to "be like," than was the boy named as the best student. And the girl named as best dressed, and the one named as most popular with boys, was in every school far more often mentioned as being in the leading crowd and as someone "to be like," than was the girl named as the best student.

The relative unimportance of academic achievement, together with the effect shown earlier, suggests that these adolescent subcultures are generally deterrents to academic achievement. In other words, in these societies of adolescents those who come to be seen as the "intellectuals" and who come to think so of themselves are not really those of highest intelligence but are only the ones who are willing to work hard at a relatively unrewarded activity.

The implications for American society as a whole are clear. Because high schools allow the adolescent subcultures to divert energies into athletics, social activities, and the like, they recruit into adult intellectual activities people with a rather mediocre level of ability. In fact, the high school seems to do more than allow these subcultures to discourage academic achievement; it aids them in doing so. To indicate how it does and to indicate how it might do differently is another story, to be examined below.

Figures 1 and 2, which show the way boys and girls would like to be remembered in their high school, demonstrate a curious difference between the boys and the girls. Despite great variation in social background, in size of school (from 180 to 2000), in size of town (from less than a thousand to over a million), and in style of life of their parents, the proportion of boys choosing each of the three images by which he wants to be remembered is very nearly the same in all schools. And in every school the leading crowd "pulls" in similar directions: at least partly toward the ideal of the star athlete. Yet the ideals of the girls in these schools are far more dispersed, and the leading crowds "pull" in varying directions, far less uniformly than among the boys. Why such a diversity in the same schools?

The question can best be answered by indirection. In two schools apart from those in the research, the questionnaire was administered primarily to answer a puzzling question: Why was academic achievement of so little importance among the adolescents in school 9? Their parents were professionals and business executives, about 80 per cent were going to college (over twice as high a proportion as in any of the other schools), and yet academic excellence counted for little among them. In the two additional schools parental background was largely held constant, for they were private, coeducational day schools whose students had upper-middle-class backgrounds quite similar to those of school 9. One (No. 10) was in the city; the other (No. 11) in a suburban setting almost identical to that of No. 9. Although the two schools were added to the study to answer the question about school 9, they will be used to help answer the puzzle set earlier: that of the clustering of schools for the boys and their greater spread for the girls. When we look at the responses of adolescents in these two schools to the question as to how they would like to be remembered, the picture becomes even more puzzling (Figures 5 and 6). For the boys, they are extremely far from the cluster of the other schools; for the girls, they are intermingled with the other schools. Thus, though it was for the boys that the other schools clustered so closely, these two deviate sharply from the cluster; and for the girls, where the schools already varied, these two are not distinguishable. Furthermore the leading crowds of boys in these schools do not pull the ideal toward the star-athlete ideal as do those in almost all the other schools. To be sure, they pull away from the ideal of the brilliant student, but the pull is primarily toward a social image, the most popular. Among the girls the leading crowds pull in different directions and are nearly indistinguishable from the other schools.

The answer to both puzzles, that is, first, the great cluster of the boys and now, in these two additional schools, the greater deviation, seems to lie in one fact: the boys' interscholastic athletics. The nine public schools are all engaged in interscholastic leagues which themselves are knit to-

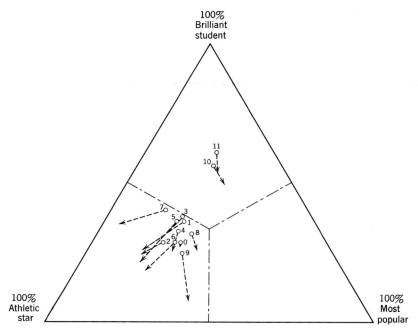

Figure 5. *Title as in Figure 1, but with added: (two private schools [10, 11] included).*

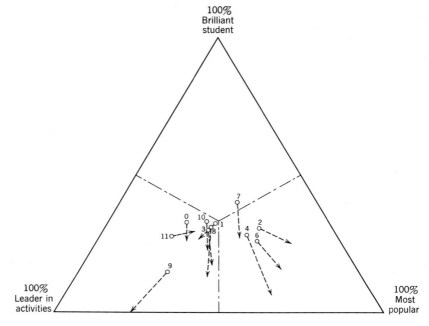

Figure 6. *Positions of schools and leading crowds in girls' relative choice of brilliant student, activities leader, and most popular (two private schools [10, 11] included).*

gether in state tournaments. The other school of the first ten, the Catholic school, is in a parochial league, where games are just as hotly contested as in the public leagues and is also knit together with them in tournaments.

Schools 10 and 11 are athletically in a world apart from this. Although boys in both schools may go in for sports, and both schools have interscholastic games, the opponents are scattered private schools, constituting a league in name only. They take no part in state or city tournaments and have almost no publicity.

There is nothing for the girls comparable to the boys' interscholastic athletics. There are school activities of one sort or another, in which most girls take part, but no interscholastic games involving them. Their absence and the lack of leagues which knit all schools together in systematic competition means that the status system can "wander" freely, depending on local conditions in the school. In athletics, however, a school, and the community surrounding it, cannot hold its head up if it continues to lose games. It *must* devote roughly the same attention to athletics as do the schools surrounding it, for athletic games are the only games in which it engages other schools and, by representation, other communities.

These games are almost the only means a school has of generating internal cohesion and identification, for they constitute the only activity in which the school participates *as* a school. (This is well indicated by the fact that a number of students in school 10, the private school which engages in no interscholastic games, have been concerned by a "lack of school spirit.") It is as a consequence of this that the athlete gains so much status: he is doing something for the school and the community, not only for himself, in leading his team to victory, for it is a school victory.

The outstanding student, in contrast, has little or no way to bring glory to his school. His victories are always purely personal, often at the expense of his classmates, who are forced to work harder to keep up with him. It is no wonder that his accomplishments gain little reward and are often met by ridiculing remarks, such as "curve-raiser" or "grind," terms of disapprobation which have no analogues in athletics.

These results are particularly intriguing, for they suggest ways in which rather straightforward social theory could be used in organizing the activities of high schools in such a way that their adolescent subcultures would encourage, rather than discourage, the channeling of energies into directions of learning. One might speculate on the possible effects of citywide or statewide "scholastic fairs" composed of academic games and tournaments between schools and school exhibits to be judged. It could be that the mere institution of such games would, just as do the state basketball tournaments in the midwestern United States, have a profound effect on the educational climate in the participating schools. In fact, by an extension of this analysis, one would predict that an international fair of this sort, a "Scholastic Olympics," would generate interscholastic games and tournaments within the participating countries.

10 Peer Influence on Personal and Academic Success

Roy J. Jones

The concept of "peer groups" continues to persist in spite of recent attempts to forge operational definitions. Definitions in the past have ranged from the very restricted traditional ones, that is, persons of the same rank, ability, age, and so on, to the more comprehensive one, such as that advanced by Newcomb (1962) and Merton (1956). Newcomb, in discussing student peer groups, contends that peer groups are likely to be found whenever local arrangements of living, dining, studying, and engaging in student activities result in frequent associations among a given group of students. To Newcomb, contiguity and common interest are central to the formation of peer-group relations. Merton has defined the concept in terms of reference groups. He states, "when operating as groups, members of the same social category can be thought of as *peer groups* or companies of equals."

There is considerable research on the influential effect of "peer groups" on personal and academic achievement (Coleman, 1961*b*). There is, however, a relative dearth of methodologically sound studies that deal directly with the specific factors and the resultant effects on mental health. Studies that have concerned themselves directly with this problem have utilized "peer groups" in the sense of their being therapeutic groups. Most of these studies have been in the clinical area and have been conducted in the out-patient clinic or hospital setting.

The precise measurement of peer-group influences on mental health prior to the appearance of aberrant behavior has been relatively sparse. Studies tangentially related to peer-group influences on mental health have been of the classical "Asch (1960) experimental" design. The evidence in this instance is that (1) individual judgment is influenced by peer-group pressure and (2) as peer-group pressure is increased, an increase in conformity results. Anxiety produced in the subject has been noted in this laboratory experience.

96

It has been pointed out by Withey (1962) that peer-group influences have differential effects depending on one's status in the group or groups to which one belongs. In a longitudinal study of blue-collar workers, French (1963) found that the lower the status of the worker, the greater the incidence of illness. When status was increased by promotion, an increase in health resulted. Conversely, when status was decreased by demotion, an increase in ill health resulted.

In a sample of 640 children in grades 2 and 5, Van Egmond (1961) found the level of utilization of intellectual ability in academic performance related to influence and acceptance by peers. The findings also indicate that disturbance in achievement is greatest for boys when they lack influence in the group, but greatest for girls when emotional acceptance is lacking. When academic achievement is viewed as a product of maturation and the interaction of this process with the psychosocial environment, there are many factors that take precedence over the use of peer-group influences per se as a unitary influence variable in personal and academic achievement.

There is little argument that the nuclear family, when it exists, occupies high priority as an influential variable. According to Peck and Havighurst (1960), it is only in those areas where the parents have defaulted that the peer-group influences become greater. They state specifically, "the peer group appears to be less an originator than a reinforcer of moral values and behavior patterns developed in the family." Bronfenbrenner (1962), however, cautions that relatively little attention has been focused on the impact of the influences beyond the nuclear family on behavior and character. The studies that have been conducted indicate that the influence is possibly greater than it is assumed to be. There is some evidence that outside influences have an impact equal to or greater than that of the family.

Factors such as socioeconomic status, race, cultural and subcultural values influence not only peer-group participation, but the standards that will be imposed for conformity by the peer group. Jones, Williams, and Riddick (1962), in attempting the development of an instrument to measure the influence of selected motivational factors and the relationship between these factors and medical-school success, administered a questionnaire to eighty Howard University medical students.

This study was premised on the fact that each year a number of medical students are referred to the Department of Neurology and Psychiatry with problems that apparently are retarding their progress in medical school. A cursory review of these referrals through the years indicated that a high percentage of these students were dropped from medical school prior to their graduation.

Examination of the area of problems presented by these students indicated a preponderance of conflicts with their teachers, economic factors, or family problems. In general, it seemed that the student was never motivated to cope with the problem until he had reached a danger point with respect to continuing his studies. It was reasoned that some technique should be attempted whereby the areas of possible difficulty could be predicted. If such a technique could be developed, it would not only serve as an additional predictor of medical-school success, but would aid the medical-school staff in giving the necessary assistance to the student in the particular area of difficulty prior to his reaching the danger point. The study was attempted as the first phase of a long-range study.

The original items for the questionnaire were developed by members of the Department of Neurology and Psychiatry. They were based on information contained in the clinic records of former medical students who had been seen by members of the staff. These items were grouped under subject-matter areas. The original instrument was an open-ended questionnaire in which the student was requested to write in his response. This instrument was administered to the freshman class of 1961–1962. The freshman class was used because it was anticipated that a wider range of responses would be obtained. The items and the responses of the original instrument were then edited for redundancy and ambiguity and re-phrased to meet the requirement of a summated-rating scale.

The scale contained fifty items. There were five subscales of ten items each which were intended to test (1) interest in subject matter and grades, (2) teachers and their effect, (3) economic factors, (4) competitive spirit, and (5) sociocultural factors. Included on the face sheet of this scale were background items including date of birth, previous school attended, sex, number of siblings and sibling position, and an estimate of the student's position in the class.

The majority of the students were male (90 per cent) with a mean age of 23 years. In general, the students had attended only one school prior to medical school and these schools were predominantly Negro schools located in the Southern part of the United States. The students were found to come from small families and in general had only one or two siblings.

The scale administered to these students was subjected to item analysis. Forty-one of the fifty items were found to discriminate between the high and low scorers at the .05 level of significance. The final forty scale items are listed below.

Scale A. Interest in Subject Matter and Grades (Seven Items)

1. Most of the subjects I have had are sufficiently stimulating so that I study them voluntarily.

2. Self-discipline and planning has been a factor in my success at medical school.
3. My knowledge of English makes a big difference in the courses I have had.
4. My grades have been a stimulating factor in my success.
5. Grades are stressed more in medical school than the subjects taught.
6. I am able to make associations quickly on most topics I read.
7. I prefer courses that require a great deal of reading rather than courses like math or physics.

Scale B.   *Teachers and Their Effects (Eight Items)*

8. Understanding my teachers has been a great factor in my success at medical school.
9. Most of the subjects I have disliked most have been taught by poor teachers.
10. Most scholars and good students have been inspired more by their professors than by any internal motivation.
11. Most teachers who have gained prestige in their specialties are, by comparison, poor teachers.
12. The reason most teachers push students on is because they can better see the need and value of an education.
13. Most students learn better from those teachers who are stern than they do from those who are warm and friendly.
14. The teacher is the greatest motivating factor in the learning experience.
15. If some counseling were not offered, most students would be unsuccessful.

Scale C.   *Economic Factors (Eight Items)*

16. One of the major contributing factors to my lack of success in medical school has been finance.
17. One of the greatest incentives for me to study and become somebody has been a constant fear of poverty.
18. I have an overwhelming need for security.
19. Most doctors do not pursue a specialty because they are tired of being broke and poor.
20. One of the most humiliating experiences for the bright young medical student is being broke and poor.
21. The economic status of my family has acted as an incentive for me to be a success.
22. The financial status of my family has acted more to impede my progress in medical school than any other single factor.
23. Most people need to experience being poor before they can learn to be humble.

Scale D.   *Competitive Spirit (Eight Items)*

24. The more I find that people dislike me, the more I am motivated to succeed.
25. My ability to adjust to almost any situation has been my greatest asset.
26. I tend to produce better when there is competition.

27. When I set up a goal for myself, I tend to let nothing interfere with achieving that goal.
28. I have always been popular with my classmates.
29. Those students who study together and pool their resources are usually successful.
30. Invariably those students who are chronic cheaters pay the penalty for cheating one way or another.
31. The students who are married usually set the pace for success in medical school.

Scale E.   Family and Other Sociocultural Factors (Nine Items)

32. The pressure that comes from my family seems to drive me on.
33. I must succeed because of my family tradition.
34. I pay tremendous personal price for failure.
35. Failure in my family almost always causes great alarm.
36. I seem to always be in competition with one or some of my family members.
37. The size of my family has impeded my progress.
38. If I fail, it will do damage to my family's standing in the community.
39. All that I am or that I will ever be, I owe to my close family ties.
40. Success in medical school is largely dependent on one's family background.

The responses to the items were distributed as indicated in Table 1. The categories "strongly agree" and "agree" were combined as were the categories "strongly disagree" and "disagree."

It can be seen in Table 1 that for Scale A (Interest in Subject Matter and Grades), the majority of students endorse Items 1, 3, 4, 5, and 6.

The majority of the students agree that (1) most of the subjects they have taken have been sufficiently stimulating that they study them voluntarily, (2) self-discipline and planning is important, (3) a good knowledge of English makes a difference, (4) grades are stressed more than the subject matter, (5) they can make associations on most topics that they read. The majority of the students do not prefer courses that require a great deal of reading—a general requirement for most of the crowded medical-school curriculum.

Data presented regarding Scale B (Teachers and Their Effects) indicate high disagreement on Items 10, 11, 13, and 14. In general, they do not feel that (1) professors provide more inspiration than one's own internal motive strength, (2) teachers who have gained prestige in their specialties are poor teachers, (3) students learn more from stern teachers than they do from warm and friendly teachers, (4) the teacher is the greatest motivating factor in the learning experience.

Analysis of Scale C (Economic Factors) data indicates rather strong disagreement on all eight items. The students feel that (1) lack of success

Table 1   *Distribution of Scores by Item*

	Response Category					
	Strongly Agree and Agree		Uncertain		Strongly Disagree and Disagree	
Item	N	%	N	%	N	%
1	54	68	7	8	19	24
2	56	70	12	15	12	15
3	57	71	15	19	8	10
4	26	32	15	19	39	49
5	43	54	15	19	22	27
6	48	60	17	21	15	19
7	27	34	11	14	42	52
8	34	42	19	24	27	34
9	36	45	10	13	34	42
10	16	20	20	25	44	55
11	11	14	24	30	45	56
12	39	49	19	24	22	27
13	10	13	14	17	56	70
14	25	32	13	16	42	52
15	26	33	22	27	32	40
16	9	11	9	11	62	78
17	14	17	7	9	59	74
18	14	17	10	12	56	70
19	16	20	21	26	43	54
20	12	15	13	16	55	69
21	23	29	8	10	49	61
22	6	7	6	7	68	85
23	20	25	12	15	48	60
24	19	24	14	17	47	59
25	58	72	12	15	10	12
26	50	63	17	21	13	16
27	51	64	14	17	15	19
28	53	66	20	25	7	9
29	45	56	30	37	5	6
30	55	69	12	15	13	16
31	26	33	29	36	25	31
32	19	24	8	10	53	66
33	11	14	8	10	61	76
34	44	55	7	9	29	36
35	24	30	8	10	48	60
36	6	7	5	6	69	86
37	1	1	5	6	74	93
38	15	19	6	7	59	74
39	36	45	10	12	34	43
40	23	29	11	14	46	57

is not attributable to financial status, (2) fear of poverty is not an incentive to success, (3) they do not have a strong need for security, (4) the pursuing of a specialty is unrelated to previous financial status, (5) family economic status is not an incentive to success in medical school, (6) family economic status has not been an outstanding impediment.

Of particular interest are the items related to peer-influence factors on personal and academic achievement found in Scale D (Competitive Spirit). These data show the majority of the students disagreeing on Item 24 and agreeing on Items 25, 26, 27, 28, 29, and 30. In general, the students feel that (1) their individual ability to adjust has been an asset, (2) competition influences their productivity, (3) nothing interferes with their goals once the goal is set, (4) they have been popular with their classmates, (5) studying together with other students is a positive factor, and (6) students who are chronic cheaters eventually pay the penalty for cheating.

The data presented on Scale E (Family and Other Sociocultural Factors) indicate a tendency toward agreement on Item 34 and disagreement on Items 32, 33, 35, 36, 37, 38, and 40. Analysis of the responses to these items show that the students feel that (1) family pressure is not a driving force, (2) family tradition is unimportant, (3) a tremendous personal price is paid for failure, (4) failure is not a cause for alarm in the family, (5) there is little or no continued family competition, (6) family size does not impede progress, (7) the family's standing in the community is unrelated to personal failure, and (8) they do not perceive family background as being related to medical-school success.

It should be noted that there were forty items in the full scale. The foregoing analysis indicates high agreement on thirteen items and high disagreement on twenty-one items. A total of seven items had less than 50 per cent of the respondents in any of the three categories.

The items included in these five scales were intended to provide response patterns that would serve as indication of subsquent success in medical school and to provide a basis for counseling the student experiencing difficulty.

The data on the "competitive spirit" scale is very relevant to the discussion here. It is therefore treated in more detail than the other four scales.

Presented in Table 2 is the relationship between age and score obtained on the "competitive spirit" scale.

The students in the age group 20–22, who score above the mean, tend to agree with the items in this scale preponderantly more than does the below-mean group in the same age category.

The implication here is that the younger the student, the greater the likelihood of his exhibiting the behavior being tapped by this scale.

Table 2   *The Relationship between Age and Above- and Below-Mean Scores on "Competitive Spirit" Scale*

| | Above Mean | | Below Mean | |
Age	N	$\%$	N	$\%$
20–22	13	31	7	19
23–25	16	38	14	39
26–28	6	14	7	19
29–31	4	10	4	11
32 and above	3	7	4	11
Totals	42	100	36	99

NI = 1 above mean, 1 below mean.

Note: A preliminary test of reliability was also conducted for each of the subscales. These data are presented below.

Scale	r_{tt}
A	.67
B	.62
C	.69
D	.69
E	.69

These coefficients were determined by use of the Hoyt's (Guilford, 1956) Method which is an analysis of variance technique. This method is of value in this instance because it does not require the usual retest of subjects for determining reliability. The obtained coefficients are relatively high and it seems safe to assume that the individual scales are essentially measuring what they were designed to measure. Further reliability studies will be conducted with data obtained by subsequent administrations of the scale.

The scale was administered to these students prior to their first-semester examination. The students, therefore, had no objective basis for rating themselves. They were requested to estimate their academic position in the class.

It was anticipated that these estimates would serve as a measure of level of aspiration for these students inasmuch as there was no objective criteria available for them to know their exact position in the class.

Table 3 shows how those students whose scores on the "competitive spirit" scale distributed themselves with regard to their estimated position in the class.

The majority (64 per cent) of the above-mean group tend to estimate their position as being in the upper half of the class. The distribution for the below-mean group is 48 per cent estimating their position as being in the upper half of the class and 51 per cent estimating their position as

Table 3   *The Relationship between Estimated Position in Class and Scale D Scores*

Estimation of Position in Class	Above Mean		Below Mean	
	N	%	N	%
1–10	2	5	–	–
11–20	2	5	2	6
21–30	8	19	5	14
31–40	3	7	3	8
41–50	12	28	7	20
51–60	4	10	8	23
61–70	4	10	2	6
71–79	3	7	5	14
80	4	10	3	8
Totals	42	101	35	99

being in the lower half of their class. Those students who feel that they have the ability to adjust to most situations, can produce better when there is competition, can achieve a goal once it is set, have been popular with classmates, can work well with others, and have a disdain for cheating, perceive themselves as performing in the top half of their class.

With regard to peer-group influences, the results of this pilot study tend to corroborate the position advanced by Bronfenbrenner (1962). The responses of these Howard University Medical School freshmen indicate less family influence on their behavior than specific economic factors and factors related to their own responsibility for their behavior.

The results of this pilot study are not definitive and there is an obvious need for further research with this derived scale. Further research would include correlating scale scores from subsequent administrations with other independent critieria such as letter grades, scores made on other objective tests, responses of successful practitioners, residents, and the higher grade levels in medical school.

One of the factors that may have contributed to the high-agreement score obtained on the scale designed to measure "competitive spirit" is that this test was administered to freshmen and, second, to freshmen prior to their first formal examination since their enrollment. In the first instance, the students were in the process of establishing new and different peer relationships. In the second instance, the students had no objective set of criteria on which to base their estimate of position in the class. Whether this factor alone may contribute to a subsequent shift in response will be determined on subsequent administrations of this scale and other similar techniques.

A panel study similar to the one conducted by Merton et al. (1957) would seem appropriate. In Merton's study the students were followed through their four years of training. This approach would allow for the more intensive study to determine the point at which factors related to personal and academic achievement undergo change.

It is of interest, for example, that the Merton study showed that students who depend on their parents for support, and the expense of school places a burden on their families, tended to let nothing interfere with their studies. The responses of the students in the present study indicate that economic status of the family is not a strong influence. One explanation for this difference could be that the items in this particular scale were too threatening to the beginning student or that their families in general had not yet begun to experience the financial burden involved in paying medical-school expenses.

Empirical observation indicates that medical-school students tend to form intensive peer-group relationships. These relationships tend to sustain themselves throughout the student's academic life, and they serve several purposes for the student. Examination of the records of those students experiencing difficulty indicates that there is a great deal of group pressure imposed on the youth to conform to the goal-oriented behavior of the group and that deviant behavior is severely handled. In many instances, these students become social isolates; and, because of the severity of peer-group reprimand, the deviant behavior is reinforced and goal-oriented behavior becomes increasingly difficult for the student.

A more precise examination of these and related variables is indicated.

11   *The Structure and Influence of Adolescent Peer Groups*

Percy Williams

In considering the influence of peer groups on the mental health of adolescents, one must understand clearly the nature of adolescents and the problems that they face. Important, also, is a recognition that adolescent peer groups, flexible and changing as they are in some respects, nevertheless manifest certain characteristics and values of the more fixed or permanent adult groups in the community. Many authorities believe that adolescent peer groups virtually echo the standards of the larger community, and there is growing evidence to support this position. Wattenberg, for example, states that "in each community there is likely to develop a set of attitudes on how life ought to be lived. Within this framework, there will be generally accepted ideas as to what teenagers are like and how they should be treated. Among the young folks themselves there will arise traditions as to relationships with grown-ups and a proper style of juvenile conduct" (1955).

The similarities that exist between the internal structure and values of the adult community and the adolescent peer group can be of real assistance, of course, in understanding more clearly the adolescent and his world. Yet by no means should adolescent peer groups be dismissed as mere imitations of adult society. The adolescent in mid-twentieth-century America functions, for the most part, in a world apart. He is preeminently concerned with problems and adjustments characteristic of his age group: physical and sexual development, social acceptability, morality, and so forth. In many of his activities he is free of adult supervision; his recreation is almost entirely separate from the recreation of adults and children. In many respects, he is much more self-reliant than the teenager of a few decades ago whose decisions often were made for him by the adult members of his family. Today's adolescent must make his own decisions. While he experiences personally the satisfaction that accompanies choices well made, he also feels responsibility for the distress and embarrassment that come with unwise choices. In the final analysis, the teenager of today must reconcile within himself the subtle pressures that evolve from his personal, family, community, and peer-group values.

FUNCTIONS OF PEER GROUPS

The peer group has always been important in the development of the adolescent; yet in recent years the functions and influences of the peer group seem to be expanding. The reasons for this development are fairly obvious. With the advent of more loosely knit family units and increasingly complex community structures, the teenager finds more and more a need for the security and acceptance that he can derive from satisfying peer-group relationships. Confused by the changing standards to which he is held by adults as he makes the often difficult transition from childhood to adolescence, the teenager seeks refuge from adult pressures and demands. He finds that his peers are puzzled by and seek answers to the same questions that perplex him: "Who am I?" "What am I expected to do?" "What can I do to make others accept me?" "What will I be like when I grow up?" Like most of his peers, the typical young teenager finds it difficult to make the transition from behaviors appropriate for children to those expected of adolescents. In this trying period of adjustment the company of other agemates provides a refuge from disappointments heaped upon him by the adult society.

Not only does the peer group provide the adolescent release from adult pressures; it is often his only source of real acceptance and approval. Frank and Frank (1956) maintain that the adolescent who finds that everything he says or thinks or does is criticized, opposed, or ridiculed at home may find in the peer group that others like him, accept what he says without dispute, encourage him to "*do* his stuff," and in general provide welcoming, reassuring company. Away from the scrutiny and demands of the adults' society, the peer group provides the needed opportunities for the adolescent to discover himself, to try out the new roles he must learn in company with other youth who are equally inexperienced. In general, the adolescent group works out its values largely in terms of the setting that the community provides. If the community setting is wholesome, the peer group usually will demand that each youth learn to act, live, and work with others in the community milieu and that aggressive feelings and desires be directed into acceptable channels.

STRUCTURE OF THE ADOLESCENT PEER GROUP

One of the first requirements for making a theoretical analysis of a group is to define its structure. What are adolescent peer groups like and how are they structured? The basic elements to be considered when analyzing any group structure are (1) members or personnel, (2) tests for admission of members, (3) distinctive roles or functions of members, and

(4) rules regulating the conduct of members (Hiller, 1941). Hence we shall try to determine the extent to which these elements impose restrictions or set up barriers to adolescent movement, adjustment, or if they in any way impinge on adolescent feelings of security and regard for themselves. In the next few pages we shall direct our attention specifically to the nature of each of these basic elements as it applies to and has significance in adolescent behavior.

Members or Personnel

The members or personnel in the adolescent peer group include a huge segment of our society. All youth who reach certain stages in their chronological, physical, or psychological development belong to this group for a period of time. The length of time during which any one youth may identify closely with the adolescent peer group varies with his developmental pattern. For some, the adolescent peer group may have significance for five or six years (ages 12–18); for others, the importance of the group may last a longer or shorter period, depending on the age at which physical and emotional maturation began and the rate with which it takes place.

Test of Admission

In a general sense, induction into adolescence is automatic and informal. It is achieved merely by having lived a given number of years and having achieved a given stage of physiological and psychological development. Youth need not seek or set out on a course of action to become adolescents. Each youth enters at his own rate according to the timetable of his physiological development. Just as there is little that can be done to accelerate the period from conception to birth, so too is there little that can be done by the individual to hasten the oncoming of his adolescent years.

Occasionally one finds parents who become anxious and try to accelerate the maturation process by surrounding their children with an environment filled with activities and social gadgets designed for older youth. However nobly motivated such parents might be, their attempts usually meet with failure because each youth enters adolescence at his own rate. Pressures to have him engage in activities that are beyond his psychological and emotional motivation merely result in confusion and frustration for the young person.

Tests of admission into a given group of adolescents in communities or neighborhoods follows the informal pattern indicated for entering into the adolescent years. That is, most youth simply tend to emerge and find themselves there, a natural part of the teenage group. The "badge of admission" into some groups of adolescents, however, may be very

different and specific and may have little to do with physiological maturation. Such "badges of admission" may influence and affect tremendously
the mental health of adolescents in these peer groups.

If the group is basically informal and friendly, members are gradually
inducted into codes of conduct acceptable to the group. On rare occasions adult counsel or guidance may be sought by these groups, but in
general adult interference or involvement is not welcome in the settlement of peer problems. Disapproval of a member's behavior is expressed
usually in teasing and taunting, and the adolescent soon comes to realize
that he must either act in accordance with the acceptable standards of his
agemates or withdraw from the group. Withdrawal, for most young
people, means a heightened sense of aloneness and rejection unless another, more acceptable peer group presents itself and is more personally
satisfying than the former.

Another type of adolescent peer group is the formal club, which is a
juvenile replica of adult lodges or college fraternities. Tests of admission
to these highly selective groups are closely related to the power structure
within the community and the degree to which the club tends to mirror
the adult community. In such groups there may be small or large dues,
specific types of costumes, and particular requirements with regard to
physical characteristics or family background. Tests of admission for
these groups pose tremendous problems for some adolescents who may
not be able to meet with ease the established standards or who, indeed,
may never be able to meet those standards. Adolescents for whom membership in these groups is desirable but unattainable tend to regard themselves as undesirables or to build deep-rooted feelings of resentment toward the favored "in" group.

Membership in some adolescent peer groups is occasional, whereas
in others it is of daily significance. The latter group includes the teenage
gangs that often emerge from informal street play groups. Test of admissions into such groups may be the most rigid and formal of all. Frequently members are taken in because they share problems common to the
group, such as defense from molestation by an outsider, or because they
support moves designed to gain greater freedom from parents or to
harass and vex unfriendly adults. Redl (1945) has given much information on the manner in which such peer groups—"gangs of a delinquent
nature"—are formed and the manner in which they approve or admit
members. From it one learns how innocent youth become involved and,
once involved, why they remain.

Roles or Functions of Members

Members in more formal adolescent groups usually take on specific
roles, including the recognized leader, the followers, and the "clowns" or

"stooges." The role that each member plays has tremendous influence on his personality and mental health.

The leader assumes responsibility for making decisions, for being bold in the face of conflict, and for being adept at organizing activities. When members of the group do not know what to do or are uncertain about what course of action to take, the leader's opinions or behaviors provide the answers. Redl (1945) cites examples of how the leader may indicate that a member is to be ridiculed for accepting the friendship of adults or how, on the other hand, the leader may cleverly indicate that the group may accept adult friendship under some circumstances and act as though he were wholly unaware of it in another situation. Being able to act at the leader's command is a role that many members must play. This does little to encourage or enhance self-esteem or the feeling of adequacy and security that most teenagers seek in the peer group. In a general sense, everyone who is not the leader is a follower, and, as with other groups, the role a given youth comes to occupy tends to be "buttressed by the phenomenon of role expectation" (Wattenberg, 1955). Once a youth has gained the reputation of playing a given role, the group seems to expect him to continue, and in order to maintain his ties with his peers he is likely to oblige. Because of this pressure of peer-group expectations and the tendency of youth to continue along lines they have followed, many youth tend to remain in the same positions within their peer groups. This tendency has been analyzed by several persons and was strongly supported by a sociographic analysis of peer groups by Clark (1952), in which he found that over a period of two years adolescent choices in position at the Guilford High School in Texas rarely changed.

If the roles of the members of the peer group seldom change, how do individual members who come to receive the unfortunate, minor, or drudgery roles keep their sense of balance—their feeling of belonging to the group, of being adequate and secure—without becoming frustrated and losing their mental balance?

Festinger (1957) in his theories of dissonance and consonance explains how an individual relates the things that he knows about himself— what he does, feels, wants, or desires—to the reality of the world in which he lives. He theorizes that when inconsistencies exist between what one knows about himself and the world in which he lives the individual will attempt to reduce those inconsistencies as best he can. When those attempts fail, he will manifest many symptoms of psychological discomfort. Why, then, do youth remain in groups that bring little pleasure and satisfaction to them? The answer may be partly that the rules and regulations governing teenage groups are so subtly felt that the adolescent himself is not concretely aware of the source of his dissatisfaction.

Rules Regulating the Conduct of Members

In most adolescent groups, there are no written rules and regulations that can be changed easily. Unwritten rules are passed on verbally or are noticed as one teenager observes what is done by his peers in given situations. Rules and regulations develop without formal meetings, seem to be agreed upon by the leaders of the group, and gradually gain general acceptance.

One regulation that seems almost universal among young people is the ban on tattling or discussing teenage activities with other than approved adults. Other regulations, not quite so universal but evident with some modification, pertain to ground rules for dating, to the type of clothes to wear, to the persons to be invited to parties, and to the kinds of things that must be kept secret. Sets of rules and regulations are appropriate to the age level of the group and are binding upon all within the group. As each youth grows older, he gives up his allegiance to old rules and regulations, only to find himself bound by new ones that seem more appropriate to his age.

In addition to the specific problems of his age group, the adolescent also bears with adults responsibility for his actions in general areas of human behavior. Like adults, young people struggle (1) for identity and support from authority within the family, (2) for identity and support from the authority of their peers, (3) for opportunities to work and share a portion of the world's goods, (4) for the satisfaction of loving and being loved, (5) for the self-control of sexual drives, and (6) for the security that God, the universe, and young people have meaning for each other. These problems are particularly acute for teenagers, who are subject to the multiple authority of parents, educators, law-enforcement officers, and peers and who often must divide their allegiance among groups with conflicting standards of behavior.

Like adults, teenagers tend to meet their problems in a variety of ways. Some try to compensate for disappointments and to secure a feeling of worth by turning their energies into new and untried areas. The teenage girl who is seeking to become identified with and accepted into a peer group, and whose image of self is not well established, frequently may try to solve her problem by unusual styles of clothing or by extremes in hair style and make-up. For many teenage girls one would say that such methods of compensation seem quite natural. If, however, her attempts to gain recognition and acceptance from her peers fail, then her image of self is clouded. Likewise any teenager who successfully learns to substitute one activity or interest that is acceptable to his peers for another that is unacceptable to the group has moved on the road to sound mental health. On the other hand, the youth who tries many times to substitute what he hopes are acceptable activities for one that he has found to be unacceptable is well on the road to frustration.

Some teenagers attempt to solve their problems through day-dreaming or living in a make-believe world. The extent to which adolescents indulge in fantasy because of problems with their peers may never be recognized outwardly. Frequently fantasy goes unnoticed or is confused with other adjustment techniques. There is some evidence that day-dreaming is more prevalent with girls than with boys. Kuhlen states that through day-dreaming "Reality is put aside while the individual gains vicarious thrills which relate directly to the desires he is unable to satisfy by direct participation; in these fantasies he may achieve ambitions irrespective of the mundane limitations of real life." Feelings of awkwardness because of a lack of bodily agility and the teasing and taunting by one's peers are thought to be among the most common cause for a youth's going off in a world apart from reality. Living in a dream world, whether brought on by teasing and taunts of one's peers or by the individual's hypersensitivity about his own limitations, is a state of mental health that may improve or grow worse as the individual matures.

Perhaps the most ordinary way in which adolescents make unpleasant situations more tolerable is to discover or create for themselves "good" reasons to replace the "real" ones. Rationalization is the verbal method of excusing failures and building up lesser goals so that they are accepted as more desirable actual goals that have not been obtained. In so doing, the individual can clear himself of any feelings of guilt or blame. Simultaneously, there is usually the tendency to blame others and thereby strengthen his own self-confidence. People use many techniques to "save face" or "explain away" deficiencies and thus protect the image they have of themselves. The peer group provides the adolescent many opportunities to try out rationalization techniques. Even though rationalizations are not deliberate acts performed with an awareness of what is happening, teenagers enact numerous sessions of "role playing." Youth gain practice in "building up" their cases in defense of lesser achievements and in explaining to others why they say they do not want some of the things they cannot achieve. These situations are repeated so frequently and so commonly that some have become accepted clichés that have connotations far beyond adult comprehenson. Typical among such clichés are, "Nobody wants to be a square," "Who wants to study that much?," and "You've got to have some fun some time."

None of the defense mechanisms just described is as wholesome for adolescent mental health as being able to acknowledge a problem frankly and to analyze the issues and make decisions on the basis of facts. Only the most secure and highly endowed youth, however, are able to meet their problems in this manner. Most adolescents need to try a variety of devices for adjustment until the time when they are psychologically and physically mature enough to cope with their problems directly. For many adolescents the peer group provides the ideal setting in which to try out possible solutions. On the other hand, the peer group may intensify a problem that needs solution.

Perhaps we can agree with Kuhlen (1952) that "adolescence is not to be thought of as an unduly stressful period." It is a period in American culture during which a particular group of adjustment problems are faced by teenagers. In general, these problems center upon breaking home ties, heterosexual adjustments, vocational choices, and moral codes. The peer group furnishes a buffer to absorb part of the shock by providing a sympathetic outlet for verbalizing and a try-out zone for acceptable behaviors. If parental support is good and community standards of trust and fair play are in evidence, most adolescents will profit by and enjoy their peer experiences. On the other hand, in adolescent peer groups in disadvantaged areas or any locale where there is inadequate parental support and where there are poor community models to emulate, peer-group activities can tend to impede, rather than facilitate, the individual's development of sound mental health. It is in these disadvantaged areas in which the peer group is disproportionately influential that both educators and many social agencies must continue to direct their concerted attention.

12 *Psychological Health and Cognitive Functioning in Adolescence*

Philip W. Jackson, Jacob W. Getzels, and George A. Xydis

Naïve conceptions regarding the relationship between psychological health and cognitive functioning pervade both the professional literature and the popular press. Most crudely stated, these conceptions imply that as psychological health goes, so goes cognition; that disorders and malfunctioning of the former will be accompanied invariably by disorders and malfunctioning of the latter. On the basis of such beliefs educators and other professional workers have been led to assume that any practice designed to promote a person's psychological well-being will produce direct and substantial gains in the cognitive acuity of that person.

When one seeks evidence to support this general conception, the results are disappointing. Both clinical and empirical investigations concerned with the interplay between psychological health and cognition attest to the complexity of this relationship. Rapaport (1945), for example, describes the dynamics by which intellectualization, or the libidinization of thought processes, comes to be used as a potent defense mechanism for the individual. More recently, Haggard (1957) and others have identified particular personality constellations in children, some involving pathology, that are associated with outstanding achievement in certain scholastic areas. In an earlier paper the present authors described the differences in scholastic achievement that accompany public-private conflicts within the individual (1958). From these and other investigations it is apparent that differences in the definitions both of psychological health and of cognitive functioning produce corresponding differences in the conclusions that may be drawn concerning the relationship between the two. The need to specify the conditions that affect this relationship is evident.

This research was supported by a grant from the United States Office of Education.

Reprinted by permission from *Child Development*, 31, 1960, 285–298.

PROBLEM

The research described here analyzes the effect of four major classes of variables upon the relationship between psychological-health criteria and cognitive performance. These variables include: (a) five measures of psychological health, (b) eight types of cognitive performance, (c) six school-grade levels, and (d) sex. It is the purpose of this research to study the contribution each of these variables makes to observed variability in the psychological health-cognition relationship. In addition, the interaction among these classes of variables is examined.

SUBJECTS, INSTRUMENTS, AND PROCEDURES

The subjects of this research were 292 boys and 241 girls enrolled in a Midwestern private school. These students were divided into six class groups ranging from the sixth grade to the senior year of high school. In this institution a single grade, the "prefreshman," is substituted for the usual seventh- and eighth-grade levels so that the high-school group is one year advanced when compared with most public-school adolescents. All subjects were given the following tests of cognitive ability:

1. *Individual intelligence tests.* In most cases, this was the WISC. A small number of children were given the Henmon-Nelson, the scores of which were converted by regression equation into equivalent WISC scores.

2. *Standardized numerical achievement test.* Differences in the curricula of various grade groups made it impossible to administer the same test of numerical achievement to all subjects. The following tests were given according to grade placement:
   Sixth Grade—Iowa Everypupil Arithmetic Test, Advanced Form O
   Prefreshmen—Snader General Mathematics Test
   Freshmen—Cooperative Elementary Algebra Test, Form T
   Sophomores—Cooperative Intermediate Algebra Test
   Juniors—Cooperative Geometry Test, Form 2
   Seniors—Cooperative Geometry Test, Form 2

3. *Standardized verbal achievement test.* The Cooperative Reading Test was given to all students from the sixth grade through the junior year of high school. Sixth graders and prefreshmen were given Test C1, Form Y; the remaining three groups received Test C2, Form T of the Cooperative Reading Instrument. The verbal achievement of seniors was assessed by means of the USAFI GED Test 1.

4. Five "creativity" measures adapted from the test batteries of Guilford (4) and Cattell (2), or designed especially for this study, as follows:
   a. *Word Association.* The subject was asked to give as many defini-

tions as possible to fairly common stimulus words, e.g., "bolt," "bark," "sack." His score depended on the absolute number of definitions and the number of different categories into which these definitions could be put.

b. *Uses for Things.* The subject was required to give as many uses as he could for objects that customarily have a stereotyped function attached to them, e.g., "brick," "paper clip." His score depended on both the number and originality of the uses that he mentioned.

c. *Hidden Shapes.* The subject was required to find a given geometric form that was hidden in more complex geometric forms or patterns.

d. *Fables.* The subject was presented with four fables in which the last lines were missing. He was required to compose three different endings for *each* fable: a moralistic, a humorous, and a sad ending. His score depended on the number, appropriateness, and originality of the endings.

e. *Make Up Problems.* The subject was presented with four complex paragraphs each of which contained a number of numerical statements, e.g., "the costs involved in building a house." He was required to make up as many mathematical problems as he could that might be solved with the information given. His score depended on the number, appropriateness, and originality of the problems.

The following psychological-health instruments were administered to all subjects:

1. *Group Rorschach.* Cards III, IV, IX, and X were projected on a screen. For each picture the subject was presented with 10 responses and was asked to choose the 3 which he thought to be most appropriate. Each list of 10 contained 4 "pathological" responses. The subject's score was the number of nonpathological responses among his 12 choices (Harrower, Erickson, and Steiner, 1945).

2. *Direct Sentence Completion.* The subject was asked to complete 27 sentences of the type: "When I saw I was going to fail I _____," or, "I think my father is _____." Each sentence was given a plus or minus score depending on the presence or absence of morbid fantasy, defeatism, overt aggression, and the like. The total score was the summation of the individual sentence scores.

3. *Indirect Sentence Completion.* This instrument was identical with the Direct Sentence Completion except that proper names were inserted for the pronoun "I," thus changing it from a "self-report" to a "projective" instrument. Boys' names were used in the male form of the instrument and girls' names in the female form. The instrument was presented as a "thinking speed" test. To reinforce this notion subjects were asked to raise their hands when they were finished and the

Table 1 *Correlations between Psychological-Health Variables and Cognitive Performance for Boys**

Grade	N	Fables	Uses	Hidden Shapes	Word Association	Make Up Problems	Verbal Achievement	Numerical Achievement	I.Q.
Group Rorschach									
6th Grade	46	016	168	206	303	249	224	260	573
Prefreshmen	55	046	−036	−157	−047	145	086	085	−108
Freshmen	77	−100	084	187	045	−014	−196	109	−100
Sophomores	46	−024	−285	044	−068	075	058	−010	042
Juniors	45	046	−241	170	114	101	−010	054	188
Seniors	21	126	−564	−247	−225	−023	−170	−030	−030
Direct Sentence Completion									
6th Grade	46	−009	106	−144	049	−029	170	105	138
Prefreshmen	55	−068	336	077	121	445	072	269	020
Freshmen	77	−100	044	−065	003	107	034	164	026
Sophomores	46	038	−143	−019	−003	018	−355	−049	−054
Juniors	45	076	−317	−055	−069	052	−461	069	−027
Seniors	21	−201	353	137	−086	116	−246	018	255
Indirect Sentence Completion									
6th Grade	46	145	−155	−120	141	−079	070	−095	012
Prefreshmen	55	−086	151	−036	146	016	111	135	−028
Freshmen	77	−283	−158	−008	033	−076	−087	076	−254
Sophomores	46	−048	−121	006	−046	000	−224	017	−122
Juniors	45	029	−200	−165	−060	−057	−389	−012	−016
Seniors	21	−320	121	211	−202	−024	−019	−141	204
California Personal Adjustment									
6th Grade	46	004	−017	114	304	166	414	291	−076
Prefreshmen	55	−016	201	077	121	094	023	187	183
Freshmen	77	093	078	205	086	112	041	078	120
Sophomores	46	035	−017	−217	018	−077	−062	−028	070
Juniors	45	201	−021	−007	−107	−095	−247	−178	−015
Seniors	21	080	237	265	−084	269	061	132	180
California Social Adjustment									
6th Grade	46	117	−025	069	237	320	435	223	−029
Prefreshmen	55	028	191	096	260	205	201	254	263
Freshmen	77	−075	−066	124	061	091	140	202	066
Sophomores	46	−060	−151	−215	−025	099	−159	−121	−050
Juniors	45	297	−047	087	043	014	−179	−015	−047
Seniors	21	−037	249	097	−293	254	−075	106	053

* For purposes of presentation, decimals have been omitted.

Table 2 *Correlations between Psychological-Health Variables and Cognitive Performance for Girls***

Grade	N	Fables	Uses	Hidden Shapes	Word Association	Make Up Problems	Verbal Achievement	Numerical Achievement	I.Q.
Group Rorschach									
6th Grade	32	205	143	407	461	215	396	118	105
Prefreshmen	41	−248	−125	497	−059	330	−021	166	264
Freshmen	65	048	253	203	357	193	204	230	171
Sophomores	43	−182	−159	−075	209	269	441	348	432
Juniors	43	173	235	168	309	192	391	347	551
Seniors	17	188	−043	104	166	449	330	322	373
Direct Sentence Completion									
6th Grade	32	−172	−019	040	−101	036	−291	287	−147
Prefreshmen	41	−232	−255	139	−148	−150	−176	−238	−153
Freshmen	65	−056	−032	−189	−194	−121	−028	182	076
Sophomores	43	−170	245	−368	−107	−287	−091	−295	−043
Juniors	43	064	067	029	063	−013	041	319	175
Seniors	17	163	−140	−062	267	071	059	−184	002
Indirect Sentence Completion									
6th Grade	32	−269	−029	−302	−461	−172	−492	270	−380
Prefreshmen	41	−145	087	190	154	003	−012	−086	123
Freshmen	65	−136	−013	−073	−207	−269	−256	−110	−176
Sophomores	43	−221	−250	−126	−029	−038	057	−067	073
Juniors	43	213	082	281	−131	177	070	296	144
Seniors	17	044	−354	−434	−062	−345	035	−065	−520
California Personal Adjustment									
6th Grade	32	−061	299	−022	−120	008	−221	332	−138
Prefreshmen	41	003	−171	070	−191	−182	128	−033	−018
Freshmen	65	−010	−114	−037	−104	−128	073	−146	−007
Sophomores	43	006	−174	−157	−171	−205	−162	−141	−134
Juniors	43	141	191	−345	138	−141	098	218	047
Seniors	17	511	203	−186	193	009	115	−124	107
California Social Adjustment									
6th Grade	32	−011	030	−080	022	064	−107	395	−059
Prefreshmen	41	032	−207	073	−114	−015	236	053	185
Freshmen	65	−001	−146	−088	−031	−022	109	−009	−011
Sophomores	43	043	−172	−091	−232	−081	−187	−074	037
Juniors	43	169	218	−325	171	−147	188	142	092
Seniors	17	151	−065	−361	−152	−432	−268	−513	−456

* For purposes of presentation, decimals have been omitted.

elapsed time was written on the front of their test booklet. This instrument was administered approximately two weeks *prior* to the administration of the Direct Sentence Completion.

4. *California Personality Test.* Two forms of this instrument were used. The intermediate form was given to sixth graders and prefreshmen; the secondary form was given to all of the older groups. Two subscores were obtained, one in "personal adjustment" and one in "social adjustment."

Correlation coefficients were computed for all cognitive-psychological health combinations.[1] The data were treated separately by sex and by school grade so that at each of the six grade levels 80 coefficients were produced, 40 for each sex. In order to test for the effects of sex, school-grade, and sex-grade interactions upon the variability of the correlations, the coefficients were transformed into Fisher z scores and standard chi-square statistics were computed. It was not possible to follow the same procedure in the analysis of main effects for the psychological-health and cognitive variables since the assumption of independence of observations (correlation coefficients) could not be met. In this latter section of the analysis tests of statistical significance were limited to selected combinations of variables.

RESULTS

Considering the total population of correlation coefficients, the relationship between psychological health and cognition appears to be rather weak although quite variable. These coefficients are shown in Tables 1 and 2. The mean of the correlations was .04, and the range was from —.56 to +.56. As the following analysis will show, however, it is incorrect to subscribe to the generalization that little or no relationship exists between psychological-health criteria and cognitive functioning. When the effects of the four major variables are examined, the relationship is seen to alter in a systematic fashion.

Chi-square statistics computed to test sex, grade, and sex-grade interaction effects among the correlation coefficients are given in Table 3. As this table indicates, the relationship between psychological health and cognition, as measured by specific criterion variables, reflects both sex and grade differences. Only two of the instruments used in the study fail to show significant variability with sex, grade, or sex-grade interaction. These Two variables are the California Personal Adjustment score and the Fables Test. It is also important to note that the effects of sex and grade are far from uniform throughout the table. Thus, depending on

---

[1] Coefficients describing the relationship *among* the two sets of tests were also computed, but are not treated in this paper.

Table 3 *Chi-Square Statistics Computed to Test Sex, Grade, and Sex-Grade Interaction Effects among Correlation Coefficients*

Cognitive Variable	Sex-Grade Variable	Psychological-Health Variable				
		Group Rorschach	Direct Sentence Completion	Indirect Sentence Completion	California Personal Adjustment	California Social Adjustment
Fables	Sex	—	—	—	—	—
	Grade	—	—	—	—	—
	Sex grade	—	—	—	—	—
Uses	Sex	4.52*	—	—	—	—
	Grade	12.96*	—	—	—	—
	Sex grade	—	16.75‡	—	—	—
Hidden Shapes	Sex	3.98*	—	—	—	3.84*
	Grade	11.30*	—	—	—	—
	Sex grade	—	—	—	—	—
Word Association	Sex	5.49†	—	—	—	—
	Grade	19.27‡	—	—	—	—
	Sex grade	—	—	—	—	—
Make Up Problems	Sex	—	5.19*	—	—	7.82‡
	Grade	—	—	—	—	—
	Sex grade	—	—	—	—	—
Verbal Achievement	Sex	9.31‡	—	—	—	—
	Grade	—	—	—	—	11.71*
	Sex grade	—	11.77*	13.94†	—	—
Numerical Achievement	Sex	—	—	—	—	—
	Grade	—	11.75*	—	—	11.93*
	Sex grade	—	—	—	—	—
I.Q.	Sex	5.34*	—	—	—	—
	Grade	—	—	—	—	—
	Sex grade	14.19†	—	—	—	—

Note: All correlations were transformed to Fisher z scores before chi squares were computed. Chi squares with a probability level less than .95 are not shown in this table.

* Significant at the .05 level.
† Significant at the .02 level.
‡ Significant at the .01 level.

the particular pair of variables chosen, one could find support for almost any hypothesis dealing with the effect of sex and grade variables.

The single psychological-health variable that seems most sensitive to sex and grade variability is the Group Rorschach. Nine of the 18 signifi-

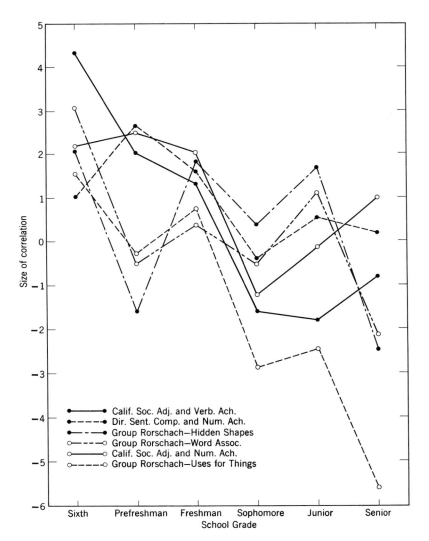

Figure 1. *Plots of correlation coefficients showing significant changes at various grade levels—boys.*

cant chi squares in Table 3 involve this variable. A more precise description of this variability will be given below.

The correlation coefficients that show significant variability with
grade are presented graphically in Figures 1 and 2. The sexes are pre-

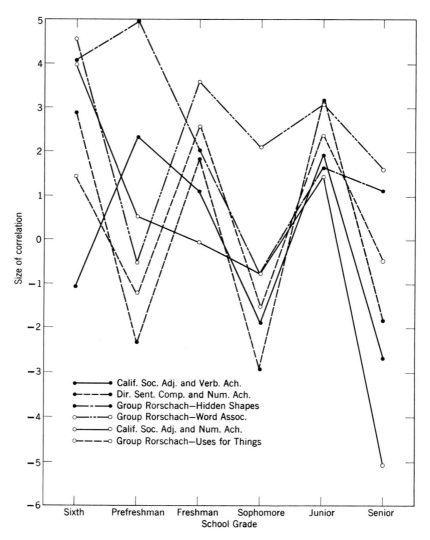

Figure 2. *Plots of correlation coefficients showing significant changes at various grade levels—girls.*

sented separately since some of the grade differences are also combined with difference between boys and girls.

The following observations concerning these two graphs seem appropriate:

1. For boys there is a general decline in the relationship with age. The sixth-grade period is the one during which the relationship between psychological health and the quality of cognitive performance appears to be highest. In addition, there is a tendency for the variability among these correlations to become greater as one moves from the lower to the higher grades.
2. Among senior boys there is a pronounced negative relationship between the Group Rorschach and three tests of creativity.
3. The correlation coefficients for girls are much more cyclic in their variability. They are highest, on the average, and much less variable in the junior year of high school.
4. Unlike senior boys, the senior girls show pronounced negative correlations between performance on academic tests and psychological-health measures involving self-report or personal appraisal.

When school-grade differences are removed by a procedure of averaging, the correlation coefficients yield the general patterns shown in Figures 3 and 4.

The major findings shown in Figures 3 and 4 may be summarized as follows:

1. The meaning of the sex differences associated with the Group Rorschach (shown in Table 3) becomes dramatically apparent in these two graphs. This instrument shows a striking relationship to cognitive functioning among girls, but not among boys. In fact, no other psychological-health variable in either figure approaches the degree of relationship between pathological fantasy, as measured by the Group Rorschach, and cognitive functioning. Further, the coefficients relating the Group Rorschach to cognitive variables increase noticeably as one moves from creativity tests to measures of scholastic achievements and I.Q.
2. For both groups the type of cognitive functioning which on the average shows the greatest sensitivity to psychological health is that which involves the manipulation of numerical symbols. This tendency is somewhat more pronounced in the boys' data.
3. For girls the great majority of the relationships are negative (with the obvious exception of the Group Rorschach); while for boys the majority of the coefficients are positive.

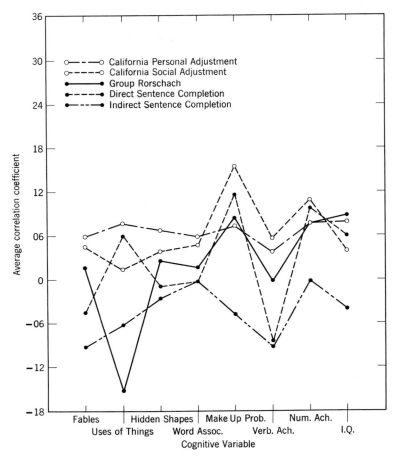

Figure 3. *Average correlations between psychological-health variables and cognitive variables—boys.*

DISCUSSION

The extreme range and average size of the correlation coefficients treated in this investigation point to the dangers inherent in making broad and sweeping statements concerning the relationship between psychological health and cognitive functioning in adolescence. These data make clear the necessity of qualifying such statements. More specifically, they demonstrate that sex, school grade, the type of psychological-health criterion, and the type of cognitive functioning are among the variables that must be considered when making these qualifications.

Among all of the findings described, those that concern sex differences and the role of pathological fantasy seem to us most worthy of special comment.

Succinctly stated, these data suggest that the cognitive functioning of girls is more sensitive to aberrations of fantasy than is the cognitive functioning of boys. Also it should be mentioned that no differences exist among boys and girls in the relative frequency of pathologic responses.[2]

[2] The mean Rorschach scores for the sexes at each grade level show no statistically significant differences. In five of the six grades girls choose slightly fewer pathological responses than do boys.

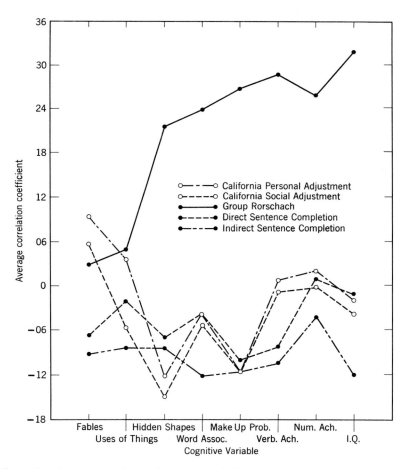

Figure 4. *Average correlations between psychological-health variables and cognitive variables—girls.*

Thus, although girls are as likely to choose pathological responses as are boys, this choice gives more information about the cognitive performance of the former than of the latter group.

A tentative explanation of this sex difference might focus on the nature of the responses to the Group Rorschach and the relationship of these responses to differences in cultural expectations for boys and girls.

Among the 16 choices that were considered to reflect pathology on the Rorschach, a great number appear to involve *morbidly aggressive* fantasy, e.g., "bloody stomach," "a burnt mass," "blood and dirt," "an explosion," "a dirty nasty mess," "bloody clouds," etc. Both common observation and recent studies support the notion that society tends to condone, if not encourage, the aggressive actions of boys, while discouraging, if not condemning, similar action on the part of girls. Given these social sanctions aimed at overt behavior, it is not far-fetched to hypothesize correlative self-imposed prohibitions referring to the inner world of the person. Although both sexes may think an equal number of "bad thoughts," the threat to the individual's concept of self-worth instigated by these thoughts may be far from equal for boys and girls. If morbid and aggressive fantasies tend to be less threatening to boys, their occurrence would be less likely to set off a chain of introspective events interfering with rational cognitive functioning. Girls, on the other hand, might be less capable of ignoring this "internal disorder," and accordingly there would be greater interference with rational cognitive functioning.

The relationship shown in this research between pathological fantasy and different types of cognitive performance is quite consistent with both traditional and recent formulations concerning the psychological functioning of creative people (Barron, 1958; Cattell, 1955). The suggestion that fantasy plays an important part in the creative act has been a matter of record for centuries. At times irrational fantasy itself has been the subject of artistic effort as in "Kubla Khan" or the surrealist's landscape. More recently the relationship between fantasy and creativity has become the focus of psychological investigation, and empirical evidence supporting the intuitive insight of artists and poets is steadily increasing. If it can be assumed that the presence of atypical fantasy is also a rough indicator of a general richness of fantasy life, then the relative decline in the relationship between the Rorschach and cognitive performance as one moves from scholastic performance to tests of creativity becomes more understandable. Since the tests of creativity call for original or unconventional responses, rather than "right" answers, it would follow that the individual who possesses a rich (and perhaps, at times, bizarre) fantasy life would be at an advantage. Conversely, the absence of an extremely rich fantasy life might be somewhat of a blessing when confronted with cognitive tasks which require intensive and prolonged absorption in a highly rational system.

The meaning of school-grade differences in the relationship between psychological health and cognition remains rather obscure. Grossly interpreted, the findings suggest that psychological difficulties intrude into the cognitive performance of boys during the pre- or early adolescent period while the same phenomenon among girls does not occur until the junior year of high school. Since the general level of scores on the psychological-health instruments shows no consistent age pattern, one can only assume that it is the quality rather than the quantity of the problems facing the students during these two periods that is important. Our general knowledge concerning the developmental problems facing adolescents during various periods suggests that the early adolescent period for boys is one in which physical maturity becomes crucial. It is during this period that general variability in size, strength, and the possession of secondary sex characteristics becomes most prominent. A tentative hypothesis would be that concern over delayed or extremely premature development during this period accounts for the general rise in the relationship between psychological health and cognition.

Girls, on the other hand, face an equally vexing set of problems in middle adolescence. These problems, rather than focusing on somatic changes, have as their general theme the resolution of social relationships. It is during this period that "chum" relations and involvement with "the crowd" gradually lose their appeal in favor of the more serious business of dating and "going steady." The demands which these more intimate heterosexual relations make upon the psychological well-being of girls may serve to explain the increased relationship between psychological health and cognition during this period.

SUMMARY

The relationship between psychological health and cognition in adolescence was examined using five psychological-health criteria and eight types of cognitive performance. The subjects were 292 boys and 241 girls enrolled in a Midwestern private school.

The major findings indicated that the relationship under question shows systematic variability with the school grade, sex, psychological-health criteria, and type of cognitive function. In particular, the interrelationship between sex differences and the role of pathological fantasy pose a series of promising research questions. A tentative theoretical framework was suggested for a number of the major findings.

Part Two The Changing School

The school has changed perhaps more than any other institution in our time. In response to the knowledge explosion, there have been innovations in curriculum, methodology, materials, organization, and teacher preparation. Currently serving students from prekindergarten through old age, many schools function day and evening throughout the entire year. Education is now expected to solve the dilemma of unemployment and welfare, to ensure economic efficiency for the young, and to provide mental health for all. But can these goals be reached? Is the school staff prepared for such tasks? Does efficient operation require an impersonal approach? The writers in Part 2 address themselves to the implications of change in the tangent of pupil-school relations, new expectations of the institution, and evolving staff functions.

There is danger that schools might become more impersonal as they grow in size and complexity. Perhaps, as Conner suggests, this process begins for the new pupil when, upon entrance to an institution, few if any efforts are made in his behalf to facilitate adjustment to classmates, school, and community. Nor is stability and self-concept enhanced by teachers who allow age-grade norms to govern their expectations of all class members. Those who do so imply that individuality is an extrinsic factor as to how pupils should act, think, or feel. Allport adds that predilection for objectivity has served to promote educator attachment to the rubrics of positivism and psychodynamics which perceive pupils as reactive stencils rather than active personal learners.

Then too, while few professional educators actually believe all human beings are alike, some grouping practices presuppose that large numbers of children are essentially similar. A continuing effort is being made to place those "alike" in the same group for the same experience at the same time in the same way. Also the lack of interpersonal relations is aggravated and the predicate for adult cooperation curtailed in classrooms where talking and collaboration are forbidden.

Administrators too promote an impersonal climate, write Rogers and Seymour, for as intricacies of school operation increase, it is possible for a principal or superintendent to become oblivious to the real objectives of his building or system. Mechanics of operation with many personnel can overwhelm a leader so that he comes to view his position only in relation to decisions regarding managerial efficiency. Finally, in many cases, the superintendent, principal, and teacher may reside in communities other than their place of work. As an itinerant commuter who is little involved in the larger community of the school, limited opportunity is available to see pupils in out-of-school situations. Consequently an expedient view is to envision pupils as products rather than persons, to be accepted only if academically acceptable. Is it any wonder, given all these instances of impersonality, that school dropouts report no one seemed interested in them, no one cared?

It would appear that schools must become more personal if holding power is to increase and pupil well-being is to proceed. Emphasis should commence at the time new pupils are admitted since then are they most in need of help to make new friends, meet new people, adjust to new circumstances. This is especially important in the central city of large metropolitan areas where a high rate of pupil turnover is common. In Los Angeles, where 100,000 student transfers are recorded each year, an exemplary program is underway to aid transient and in-migrant children. Reception rooms have been established in schools of high mobility where children seldom arrive with adequate records or background information. To facilitate placement and orientation, a testing counselor, teacher of remediation, and a child-welfare worker for family casework and referral are available. Milwaukee's program is similar except that each center includes a language specialist who helps provide educational programs for non-English-speaking children and serves as liaison between parents whose mother tongue is other than English, their children, and the schools. In both cities, project children have shown accelerated intellectual growth, lessened incidence of negative attitude and behavior problems, and appear more school oriented.

Classes will become more personal, writes Conner, when teachers are cognizant of learning styles, able to map strategies for individual success, and give consideration to interpersonal relations in grouping. Up to now educators have maintained a greater commitment to the priority of how teaching proceeds rather than how learning occurs. As a consequence, the paragon of individualized instruction has been perceived as simply a matter of smaller teacher-pupil ratio, more time per child, or better systems of grouping when in fact individualized instruction can occur only when teaching method is in conjunction with the preferred and most efficient learning style of the student. Ultimately educators may be able to see "sequence in education" as something that occurs within the individual child.

Allport reminds us that something more than understanding learning processes is required to promote mental health. The uncertain but inviting future makes it incumbent on educators to demonstrate empathy toward and interest in the personal problems unique to contemporary youth; to provide them with the attitudes of tentativeness and commitment. Seymour contends it is likely that more staff will promote pupil stability where a like concern for staff well-being is exhibited by the administration and where sufficient time is accorded teachers for interaction with pupils. That ample time can be made available and successfully used is shown by Hunt in his description of the new and exciting staff roles developed in Detroit's central-city experiment.

Can schools meet their commitment to extend quality education to every child? Or is mental health and achievement for children of poverty beyond the province of possibility? Such germane inquiries are presenting themselves in greater frequency than ever before. Certainly there can be little doubt that inequity exists, especially in the central districts of large cities. Project Talent of the National Education Association, in a 1964 analysis of scores of over 400,000 pupil aptitude and educational tests, reports that 90 per cent of youngsters from the culture of poverty rank in the bottom 10 per cent of the nation's 18-year-olds. The national committee assigned in 1964 to study Chicago's educational difficulties indicated that 40 per cent of the inner-city schools are overcrowded and that teachers in these buildings are less educated, less experienced, and less often certified than their counterparts in outlying areas. Similarly, State Education Commissioner Allen's 1964 report on New York City schools laments overcrowding and the incidence of less-trained teachers in central-city institutions.

High rates of staff turnover among slum schools in nearly every urban complex lend credence to the assertion that a more adequate type of training is needed by those assigned to such institutions. Certainly there is indigenous to the role of inner-city teachers a number of instructional and behavior problems that occur less frequently in schools of more favorable background. Consequently seventeen New York City colleges and universities in conjunction with the city board of education have begun teacher-training courses designed especially for those who intend to work in socially deprived areas. Student teachers have classes in connection with campus schools that are located in poor neighborhoods. Another promising practice is employed at Cardoza High School in Washington, D. C., where former Peace Corps volunteers are serving as teacher interns.

Discipline is perhaps the greatest difficulty confronting beginning teachers. It is unlikely this problem will be diminished, especially for those assigned to urban centers. A 1964 report by the National School Public Relations Association shows acceleration in the incidence of pupil misbehavior, staff-pupil conflict, and pupil attacks on teachers in New York City, Chicago, and Detroit. Yet, as Ausubel points out, a conspiracy of silence exists in teacher training about discipline with little or no attention given to its importance in relation to socialization, personality maturation, conscience development, and emotional security. Rogers, Armstrong, and Farnsworth each present views which imply effective classroom-discipline practices to be a requisite of mental health for students and teachers.

To prevent rather than assign pupil failure, schools need to augment their influence by creating new positions, by greater involvement with community agencies, and by upgrading staff efficiency. The services of a social worker trained to determine situational obstacles that deter academic progress is indispensable to a school system. As a liaison between home and school, the social worker described by Hayman is in a key role to bring about early intervention measures to prevent dropping out. That the school can and must utilize community agencies and voluntary groups to support and reinforce an education orientation is apparent in the rationale of programs described by Schreiber. Finally, appropriate pupil direction will not occur in the school, according to Hoyt, until counselors are better trained. Oriented to aid only the college bound, counselors usually manifest a deplorable lack of information about the world of work. Therefore they confine their service to counseling rather than guidance when confronted with vocationally minded students.

In conclusion, an analogy. Before the year 1500 Spanish coins were inscribed with the words "Ne Plus Ultra" (Nothing More Beyond). After the discoveries of Columbus and others, coinage inscriptions were changed to read "Plus Ultra" (More Beyond). Similarly, the future of our young people has more in its course than we who are now adults can imagine. Whether the years to come are, in fact, what they can be, however, depends in large measure on an adequate preparation to meet the times. Only education today can open tomorrow's door of opportunity. Every child must be provided a key!

R. D. S.

13 New School-Staff Roles in Poor Neighborhoods

Paul R. Hunt

The academic and social distance between the school-staff member and the child coming from a poor neighborhood has been of concern to the educator for some time. This concern has been reported repeatedly and perhaps needs further investigation. It will not be, however, the purpose of this chapter to enlarge on this particular phenomenon but rather to describe how this distance can be reduced through implementation of new school-staff roles.

The traditional treatment of subject matter through the curriculum, and implementation of teacher-student social relationships through extra-curricular programs, while narrowing the teacher-student gap in more advantaged neighborhoods, has widened or strained these relationships in some cases where such techniques prevail for children in less-advantaged social settings.

CHARACTERISTICS COMMON TO CHILDREN OF POOR NEIGHBORHOODS

When describing the children of poor neighborhoods, I find many characteristics peculiar to these particular children. Whether they are the products of either the urban or rural poor determines, to some extent, the nature of the characteristic. There are, however, three characteristics which I find common to the less-advantaged children living in a large city. Both indigenous and migrant children seem to share these characteristics. At the same time, I find these characteristics lend themselves to treatment through the school's role in the poorer neighborhoods and, if modified properly, will allow for new school-staff roles to emerge in these communities.

The three characteristics I find common to these youth, and around which I shall construct the new staff roles described in this chapter, have to do with (1) the child's lack of mobility within his broader community, (2) his lack of growth through juvenile employment and meaningful school experiences, and (3) lack of the adult guarantors who are needed to play an important part in any child's development. Although these factors seem common to elementary children as well as secondary-school youth in poorer neighborhoods, I shall confine my remarks to the latter.

There is little debate that mental health of teenage youths and their accompanying self-concepts are inextricably linked. This linking essentially provides the criteria through which we describe this age group's behavior. Moreover, when we describe the behavior of some children in poorer neighborhoods, particularly those with whom this chapter is concerned, too frequently we use such phrases as lack of social sophistication; not employment oriented; unable to get along with, or conform to, acceptable adult standards. The frequency of these comments, as relating to youth living in poorer neighborhoods, leads me to offer, for consideration, three objectives that may be considered for schools serving in such neighborhoods with suggestions as to how school-staff roles might be modified to support these objectives.

In the NEA's *Schools for the Sixties,* "Deciding What to Teach" (1963), the reader is led to consider first what children of specific ages do not know, and then to consider some very careful decisions concerning what they need to know at any given age in order to do the best they can in and for their homes and community. If these youth in poorer neighborhoods lack a certain mobility or have become disadvantaged because certain growth experiences and the adult support essential in the transition from childhood to adulthood were not available, it may be that these conditions can be considered as legitimate content in school programs. Thus new staff roles and curricula countering these deficiencies can be developed.

SOCIAL GROUP WORKER

It is not unusual for those of us who work daily with children from very poor neighborhoods to discover how little these children know about the city outside their immediate, daily contacts. For example, when we find youth who live within the glow of our downtown skyscrapers and have never walked between these buildings, or viewed the city from their heights, we learn something of their erroneous concepts about a big city. And, for example, when some children refuse to ride elevators or escalators because they have no familiarity with these machines, we begin to recognize their alienation to city life.

Not too long ago it was brought to my attention that a child in our school had never seen the Detroit River and had no idea about our Canadian neighbors on the other side. The sad part about this situation is that the child was seated in a school less than a brisk fifteen-minute walk from this famous river. And what about the cultural advantages great cities have to offer? Unfortunately, children in the poorer neighborhoods do not seem to feel a part of museums, libraries, and those institutions that help us blend the past with the future. Truly, then, there is a place for the "higher horizons" concept in the schools serving poorer neighborhoods. And how can this concept be realized through a new school-staff role? In our school we have added a *social group worker* to our staff and given him one-fifth of the instructional time available in our program to carry out his work.

The objectives behind this new school-staff role are to identify those areas of social and community awareness found to be lacking, and to bring into balance a program that in the two years we have the youth will tend to correct these deficiencies. A unique feature of this role is that, although it is the discrete responsibility of the social group worker to manage this portion of the instructional time, he shares his role with other staff members who in turn modify their roles in support of his program. For example, when trips to industry are made, the vocational teachers accompany groups of students giving them direct benefit of their special preparation and familiarity with industry during on-site visits. Such trips include visits to heavy industry, light-manufacturing facilities, and the commercial and distributive aspects of the community's economy. If, on the other hand, the objective of the social group worker's program for the week has a cultural bent, the academic teachers are invited to share in this experience. Usually academic teachers are found to delight in passing on their familiarity with the libraries and museums and even the more contemporary cultural aspects of the urban society. Teachers may even find a new communion with their students through such experiences. Essentially, then, this new staff role in the school introduces a whole new series of experiences to youth in addition to modifying, through sharing, the roles of other staff members.

It has been my experience that teachers for the most part do a good job in sharing and providing these mobility experiences where time permits. But it has also been my observation that, if some one person takes care of all the scheduling and "administrivia" in organizing such educational experiences, the teacher's contribution becomes even more significant during the experience. The social group worker in turn, in integrating his program with a variety of teachers, affords each teacher additional opportunities to involve youth within their own subject specialty.

One further point should be made concerning the role of the social group worker before going on to other new roles in our school. This has to do with his working with small groups of these poorer children. To think of the social group worker working by the "bunches," as it were, would be erroneous indeed and I would like to correct such an impression. Where youth have likes in common, and where these interests cannot be met through regular extracurricular programs, the social group worker can play a very important role. For example, small groups of a temporary nature may develop through common curiosities. Such curiosities center around sex education, smoking, dating, and other problems that occupy the minds of most youth. Such problems as these youth introduce in a small group setting may or may not warrant ongoing programs, but in either case the social group worker is available in the school to fill this usually unmet requirement of poorer youth.

WORK-SKILLS TEACHER

A second characteristic that seems to emerge as common to youth living in poorer neighborhoods, and around which new school-staff roles can be developed, has to do with the lack of work experiences these youth have. A curious circumstance about children in poorer neighborhoods is that they do not seem to have the opportunity to engage in the kinds of juvenile employment common to their peers in more economically advantaged areas. For example, as I drive the main arteries crisscrossing our mean-income neighborhoods, I find these streets lined with many small businesses offering temporary, part-time, or entry employment opportunities. And, adjacent to these streets, I find modest homes where lawns may be cut, windows washed, and garages cleaned for pay. Sometimes, just for the asking, juvenile employment is available to the youth who live in these areas.

Now, to continue, drive with me through the deprived neighborhood near the school where I work. Just west of us, a high-rise public-housing project, the residence for thousands of people. To the south, light manufacturing not open to young workers. To the east, the broad expanse of a public market where young people find a few jobs, but not without "cutting" school. And to the north, row upon row of substandard housing receiving little or none of the care that prevents a neighborhood from decaying.

In addition, we find virtually no small businesses lining the adjacent streets as once you could before the poor neighborhood became identified as such. A few stores remain. The "Mama and Papa stores," as they are called, offer little if any opportunity for youth to get their first experiences in the world of work. How, then, does a young person in a poorer neighborhood come by these experiences so essential to his development? What particular role can the schools play in this dilemma, and in turn what new school-staff roles emerge that will help to correct this deficiency?

Juvenile employment opportunities, in effect, offer a series of prevocational opportunities that allow youth to begin their evaluation of the world of work. Such opportunities, it is felt, give outlets for curiosity about jobs and offer realistic opportunities to test this curiosity. Such trial and error, or exploration into employment, helps youth make decisions concerning job choice, choices having much to do with aspiration development and vocational pursuits. Such trial and error is the pattern youth needs to follow in a society where the free selection of one's occupation ranks along with the other major concerns of our Bill of Rights. Paul Goodman (1960) has suggested that such opportunities to test the environment are extremely important in the whole process youth encounter in learning how to behave rationally and to manage themselves suitably in our society.

In the poorer neighborhood where our school is located, we are finding teenage youth who have not yet earned their first dollar. Earning experiences through juvenile employment, unfortunately, have not been available to them. Curiously enough, these youth report themselves as wanting to work and earn and see this as a responsibility, yet have had little if any opportunity to translate this desire into actuality.

To compensate for this deficiency, we have incorporated into our school program opportunities for youth to work and to earn. Their work consists of manufacturing training aids for the school system; assembling products coming to us through subcontract arrangements with local industry; and work responsibilities necessary to the operation of our school, that is, food service, custodial work, routine assistance to teachers and office staff. Students' earnings vary with their interest and ability. Each student receives a check every two weeks as testimony to his worth as a worker. Youth are also given an opportunity to test their interests in jobs outside the school. In such instances each student, when ready, is introduced to a small business or public agency by his prevocational teacher as a part-time employee. Several work experiences for varying periods of time may be offered. The teacher, working much in the same way we see teachers working in our commercial or distributive co-op programs, establishes a relationship with cooperating businesses and agencies where, together, these adults assist the youth in their initial attempts to behave as acceptable employees are expected to behave.

Although it is the discrete responsibility of the work-skills teacher to provide these production and work experiences within and outside the school, other learning experiences centering around the skill to work engage staff members whose roles allow them to share in his program. For example, since these youth earn money, a whole gamut of teaching opportunities is opened to school-staff members. The academic teachers can direct attention to such matters as budgeting, payroll deductions, computing earnings, and a variety of discussions around the whole area of money management. The group worker, on the other hand, has opportunity to discuss delaying one's immediate yen to gratify through impulse buying and other perils in misusing the money one earns. This misuse of money is particularly true of people in poorer neighborhoods.

Before describing yet another new school-staff role, that of the personal and academic-skills instructor, I would like to summarize these two new staff roles I have described and which are known to us as *work-skills instruction* and *prevocational coordination*. Together, these two new roles provide our students with opportunities generally absent in their adolescent experiences. After a few months with these teachers, youth know more about what may be expected of them on a job. For example, with these teachers they become familiar with what employees may expect from their employers and what employers may be able to expect in return. In addition, concepts such as quality of work expected, and quantities required, become more meaningful to them. Time, a factor not always appreciated by people in less-advantaged neighborhoods, becomes important to the youth through his recognition of its importance to the employer. Finally, young workers from poorer neighborhoods, where values associated with materials and equipment necessary for the worker and employer to do a job are often lacking, need to develop an appreciation for these essentials in work. *Work skills* and *prevocational coordination* assist immeasurably in the development of these and other appreciations of the world of work.

PERSONAL AND ACADEMIC-SKILLS TEACHERS

Personal and academic-skills instruction has, as its discrete function, the responsibility for assisting students in the whole process of learning to communicate with each other and with other groups. If deficiencies in communication skills are peculiar to any group of people, it would certainly be true of people living in poorer neighborhoods. Conant (1961), in his treatise on *Slums and Suburbs,* has borne this out. How communication skills may be developed are found to fill instructional-materials catalogues and research journals. Promising reading programs, such as the Progressive Choice Reading Method, work to correct the reading problems of youth in poorer neighborhoods. In addition to having limited reading skills, youth from such communities have many deficiencies that weaken their ability to achieve academically, particularly where traditional methods and school-staff roles reinforce rather than alleviate such resistance.

In our school we have adjusted the academic teacher's role to correct those deficiencies centered around a lack of skills and information needed for basic communication in our society. Such information includes a mastery of one's own personal data, and the skill to transfer these data to others. We recognize, too, ability to read correlates significantly with the youth's overall adjustment in his environment. Some have even said that low reading-grade levels relate significantly to youth who become tabulated delinquents or remain persistently unemployed and otherwise malfunctioning. Although, through our efforts, we do not find our students reading for pleasure, despite what they might benefit from such activity, we have been able to open the world to them a little more with reading materials as common as the daily newspaper. Several copies of the morning and afternoon editions are placed in the academic-skills classroom. And where youth do not have daily papers in their homes, they are encouraged to take them to their homes. In addition, we have found that some youth become more curious about reading as their interests develop in specific types of work. In such cases, teachers are diligent in helping youth find materials at a suitable reading level in order to capitalize on this new-found interest. Our academic teacher has also discovered that where youth with reduced reading skills tend to shy away from subject matter when presented in traditional format, such avoidance can be controlled through techniques associated with programmed-learning techniques. With each new staff role introduced in our school, complementing programmed materials are being developed.

If reading and writing are deficient as communicative skills, talking, as a means of expression, is not a strength either. Limited vocabulary, garbled speech, and poor eye contact while talking all lend to reducing their spoken words as effective communication. Moreover, if it can be said that some traditional school programs and teaching techniques are not reaching youth in poor neighborhoods, it may be assumed that in the area of verbal communication such programs and techniques are not as effective because of social and educational distance between child and teacher.

This assumption may be based on two conditions. It is a characteristic of youth living in poorer neighborhoods to relate with adults who may be even less articulate than they. For example, both adults and youth talk in an abbreviated fashion, not using words to give various dimensions to thought but, mainly, to communicate immediate wants and needs through limited speech, sometimes hardly more than an animal grunt. Just the other morning I heard a mother, as her child departed home for a neighboring school, dispatch this youngster with a tirade of inarticulate grunts of which I understood but little. It occurred to me that this same child, with ears tuned to such dialect, may not, during the day, understand much of what her more articulate teacher will say.

We do not encourage teachers to adopt the vernacular of the streets, however, so that communication will improve on this level. But we do encourage staff members to incorporate in their conversations with youth enough street language to reduce the gap that precise speech may create.

The new role for the staff member in an academic setting is not that of the precise academician who stands before the class as a dispenser of facts but, rather, that of a teacher who will interact with children in such a way that their ideas become a valuable contribution to the group. And in making this contribution new words are learned, pronounced with feeling and conveyed through the eyes, hands, and other personal techniques.

In addition, we are finding that verbal and performance scores increase significantly when these youth are provided with pupil-teacher ratios of ten to one. By helping youth to identify their interests in such an academic setting, a teacher can nurture these individual interests. Such a setting, in addition to being small, must encourage much free expression and ideas. Ideas, rather than facts, become the tools with which teacher and student now concern themselves. And what do we expect to observe as teachers play this role? Three expectations come to mind. First, we expect youth will learn something of managing themselves within and outside the classroom. Second, we expect the emotional involvement with those experiences the student finds meaningful in the classroom can be transferred to other areas of his life space. Third, the image of the teacher may change in the child's mind to that of an adult who is more approachable than some teachers and their teaching styles are found to be. It is, then, through this approach and with these expectations in mind that the academic teacher in our school emerges with this new role.

COUNSELOR

Thus far in my treatment of new staff roles in schools serving in poorer neighborhoods, I have attempted to describe roles as they relate to countering the child's limited mobility, limited social and academic growth, and limited adult guarantorship. We have added yet another new staff position to our school; not new as titles go, but certainly new as role is concerned. This staff member we call our *counselor*.

For years I have observed the role of counselors in the school system where I am employed. I have seen these individuals harried because each of them is required to care for the problems of 350 to 500 youths. Failure to alleviate this problem reduces the overall efficiency of the school. All kinds of problems are neglected, ranging from the critical aspects of college planning and vocational choice to the personal problems of indigent youth. As an extension of the principal's administrative arm, however, counselors often engage in activities that reduce greatly the time and energy they have for working directly with students.

Recognizing that, by changing the counselor's job to that of a new or more ideal role, certain administrative burdens would increase, we decided to allow counselors to spend all their time working with students.

The counselor's job, then, is to deal with problems revolving around immediate problems and life-plan preparation. The counselor does not deal with discipline problems as an authority figure, but many problems usually regarded as nuisances by administrators become a part of the counseling-session exchange and are ultimately resolved.

We do not always find youth immediately willing to accept the counselor in his new staff role. In many cases a lifetime of being suspicious of adults can make it difficult for youth to trust an adult who suddenly extends more than a courteous period of time listening to his problems. We are pleased, however, to see a developing respect for youth-adult confidences, confidences not unlike those we need to develop and share with our friends and professionals in urban life.

Although our school counselor is available to youth in the school setting, we recognize that yet another new role is needed to assist youth as they make the transition from school to work or engage in other alternatives our society permits its youth. This new school-staff role we call our *placement counselor*. Relating to youth in much the same way as the school counselor, this position, however, has a discrete function apart from the new staff roles described thus far.

Every school must terminate its service to its students at some point in time. Traditionally this termination occurs by age or semester. Furthermore, youth who become separated from school fall into two categories: the voluntary dropouts and the involuntary dropouts. In either instance, it has been my experience that most schools' contact with youth beyond this point has been nil. Recognizing that many youth are ill-prepared to greet the world they meet after leaving school, we have created the new staff positon of placement counselor. Essentially this new role maintains liaison with the "alumnus" particularly while the youth is making an adjustment to his new role. The availability of such a person, an adult remaining both available and congenial, tends to reduce the trauma some youth experience upon leaving school. This is not to say his former teachers do not remain congenial; it is to say, however, that because of the pressures of their responsibility in the ongoing school program, they may not always be available. In addition, for youths who cannot get back to the school because of hours of employment, our placement counselor is "on call" and frequently becomes acquainted with the student's employer or others who may be involved in the student's post-school life. For example, evening-school programs may be of interest to alumni who want further training. In such instances, the placement counselor can assist with school records and admission procedures. Moreover, youth who have other problems that might be shared by a community agency need to know about such agencies and how to approach them.

Our placement counselor, in addition to providing these services, works closely with the public employment services, supplementing their placement activities and employment counseling. Since some employers like to receive referrals directly from the school, particularly for short-term employment and where more refined screening as provided by the public employment service is not required, the placement agent offers such service to both youth and prospective employers. It is, then, the object of this new school-staff role to provide a continuum of care for youth beyond the traditional concern generally afforded youth by the school staff as they separate from school. Such concern provides for a much smoother transition from school than if such a school-staff role were not in existence.

NEW EMPHASES ON ADMINISTRATOR ROLES

Finally, in concluding my remarks on new school-staff roles in poor neighborhoods, it would be inappropriate not to mention the new emphases that must be given to the school administrator's role. The administrative style in large measure will determine the effectiveness of a school staff whether in a poor neighborhood or not. Moreover, the new school-staff roles I have presented could become meaningless if subjected to some types of traditional administrative styles. It was for this reason that the administrative structure in our school work took the following shape.

For many reasons the image of the traditional school is etched deeply in the minds of those who live in less-advantaged areas. Too often these people think in terms of the school's legal power, and perceive this power as a threat. They see this power being exercised through the principal, his assistants, and the counselors. In addition, other power figures involved are attendance officers and, unfortunately, those public agencies who use the schools as a lever in the interest of serving their own programs. Here I am referring to some agencies controlling public-assistance funds.

To reduce the "power image" of the principal and other administrative staff, new names were assigned along with the role. For example, the principal became the school's director. The title change occurred since principal means "main" and it was decided rather early that this school with its new roles did not have a "main" person. The director's job is to take charge of all administrative functions that directly serve those staff members traditionally known as the faculty. Such an arrangement places the director in casual contact with the student body, which in turn provides him with a figurehead type of rapport. For this reason the director takes charge of discipline problems where the pursuit of such problems by other staff members would damage their rapport with individual students or the student body. This does not mean that other staff members are totally relieved of this responsibility. Where such problems require a somewhat disinterested party, however, resolution of these problems appears to be expedited. Such an arrangement seems to appeal to both students and staff.

The director has yet another facet to this somewhat new school-staff role: evaluation. It is a rare school, indeed, where systematic evaluation of the school program is the primary concern of a single staff member. Furthermore, it is a frequent complaint of teachers that systematic evaluations of their work are not regularly made. For example, how many teachers, the question is asked, after student teaching practice, have the opportunity to be criticized by a master teacher? In our school the director is responsible for this phase of the program's evaluation. Frequently teachers and director review the objectives of the school's program, introduce or adjust content, and continuously improve the curriculum through in-service education based on research findings and new methods and materials found to be satisfactory in working with children from poorer neighborhoods.

In summary, then, the director serves the teachers first, by maintaining a comfortable physical plant, adequate supplies and equipment, equitable distribution of work load, and careful attention to his staff personnel-management problems. And, second, through his administrative style, he recognizes the value of and faith in providing his staff with ample opportunity to help jointly with the decisions that make the school a pleasant and meaningful place for both students and staff.

It is not enough to change the name of principal to director without making a similar change in the assistant principal's title and role. In our school the assistant principal is called a services coordinator. In some respects his contacts with the students are not unlike those of the director, but the services coordinator's role allows him to become much better informed than the director about individual students and their families.

A services coordinator coordinates services that exist within the school building and are the discrete responsibility of the school, and those services existing outside the school, services shared or provided by either public or private sources. Much of this chapter has dealt with services provided within the school. It is a peculiarity of poor neighborhoods, however, to find a number of public or private agencies interested in the children or families in these neighborhoods: public-assistance programs, public health, and law-enforcing agencies, to cite only a few.

Recognizing that shared services from the outside often mean the difference in whether or not a child is successful in school, our school assigns to the services coordinator the task of mobilizing these services in the interest of the child. In addition, the coordinator to some extent can regulate the intensity of the service required. Finally, through careful coordination, the child benefits more promptly, the sharing agency can approach its task more efficiently, and the overall confidence people have in the agency and the school becomes increased.

The new school-staff roles described herein work most effectively through a team approach. It is as team leader that the services coordinator makes his unique contribution through this new school-staff role. A teaching team, to be considered as such, by definition must have (1) a hierarchy; (2) members with discrete functions to perform; (3) opportunity to make specific recommendations concerning children and the means to carry out and evaluate these recommendations. The services coordinator is the team leader. As such, he uses his position to coordinate the services available to youth through new school-staff roles. In addition, he employs his contacts with services from outside the school in concert with his teaching team's recommendations, thus working in unison on behalf of the students.

Finally, recognizing that children in poor neighborhoods need to be processed more systematically through their school years, the services coordinator monitors the record keeping on each student. Since these youth tend to move from school to school, and since we have experienced delay in service to youth where adequate records were not available, our school has vowed to provide the school receiving our youth, should transfer occur, with complete, accurate, and current data on our students.

In concluding my remarks on the new administrative staff roles, one additional member should be mentioned. This member we call our administrative specialist. Actually this person is the school's office manager. The administrative specialist manages the clerical staff and is responsible for many of the duties traditionally handled by assistant principals. It does not require, we have found, a person with a master's degree in education to prepare requisitions, collect milk money, or check windshield stickers in the school parking lot. Professionally trained people, particularly those working in poor neighborhoods, have better things to do than these and the other "administrivia" I have cited. The administrative specialist, by taking over the business management of the school, not only frees the administrator for the real work of the school, but also allows for better distribution of administrative talent throughout the school system.

ADULT GUARANTORSHIP

To this point I have described the new school-staff roles as they are constructed around limited mobility and growth factors of children living in poor neighborhoods. The third factor, adult guarantorship, I shall treat in less detail, because implicit in the aforementioned school-staff roles is found the guarantorship these youth require. The new school-staff roles described herein assure closer adult and child relationships. In addition, these more intense relationships bring into play other adults who share the guarantorship role with the school staff. Together, a variety of adults remains available and congenial to these youth over a longer period of time.

Finally, I must add, the roles I have presented are not meant to replace the school-staff role found today in poorer neighborhoods. To do so would suggest that such schools are not performing their tasks in working with these children. This, of course, is not true. Excellent examples of school programs serving the poor are available in every city where poverty is a problem. In addition, it is not to say that every child living in a poorer neighborhood needs all the influence of these new school-staff roles. It is, however, my suggestion that where poverty exists and where schools are not satisfied with their progress in countering the influences of poverty, such new school-staff roles as I have described, if attached to the ongoing program, will assist as a countervailing influence.

CONCLUSION

The school staff working in a poorer neighborhood has a particularly challenging task. The rewards that dedicated teachers seek, moreover, are found in these neighborhoods. The reward of seeing a disadvantaged child take his place in the world as an advantaged adult is, indeed, a very satisfying experience. And tens of thousands of teachers working in poorer neighborhoods receive these rewards every day. But yet, not enough is being done to aid these children. Perhaps many more teachers will be attracted to work in these neighborhoods if given an opportunity to serve in new and vital school-staff roles.

14 Role of School in Coordinating Dropout Programs

Daniel Schreiber

I shall try first to outline broadly the present school-dropout problem. Such a survey will provide necessary perspective to any suggestion about what the school's role ought to be. This is difficult since "dropout" is rather a catch-all term, meaning just as many things as there are groups and institutions that might affect its solution.

In a sense dropout is an intrinsic problem in a democratic society where the function and interest of public education is to provide an informed and responsible citizenry. There is surely evidence that many schools, for this and other reasons, are increasingly assuming the goal of graduating every youngster. Still, compulsory school attendance extends only to a certain age—16 in most states. In the history of American public education, there are few accounts of dropout problems for the good reason, among others, that dropouts have until only recently always outnumbered graduates. It is ironic in view of the present dropout problem that this century has witnessed a steady and rather impressive improvement in school retention rates. For example, at the turn of the century only six or seven of every 100 ninth graders were graduated four years later. By 1930 the proportion of graduates had risen to one-half; at present it stands at about two-thirds.

Perhaps none would credit the schools for this program though the quality of education has been advanced. But the school, where presumably the future is forged, stands in a rather distinct relationship to society at large. It is by no means autonomous but largely expresses the contemporary spirit, purpose, and problems of the society whose continuity it is intended to ensure. Easily as much as to the schools themselves, for example, growth in retention rates owes to such contingencies as a rise in educational requirements for employment, extension of child-labor and compulsory school-attendance laws as well as the increased general affluence which enabled more parents to see their offspring through school.

148

NATURE AND DIMENSIONS OF THE DROPOUT PROBLEM

Just as forces extrinsic to the school have levered an increased school retention rate, so too contingencies from without have precipitated our current dropout problem. To begin with, the sheer number of young people expected to pass through school and into the labor market during the 1960–1970 decade is unprecedented. They are, of course, the crop of the post-World War II "baby boom" come of age. In 1960 some 2.8 million adolescents reached age 16—in 1963 the figure was 3.8 million. In 1965 college enrollments are expected to double those of 1960. Over the decade a place in the labor market will have to be found for some 26 million new entrants. At least 7.5 million of these will be school dropouts with few, if any, job skills; and 2.5 million of these dropouts will have had less than eight years of formal schooling.

Whether this figure of 7.5 million dropouts was equaled during previous periods when dropout rates were considerably higher is not known. The question is probably irrelevant. One major reason why the past was not confronted with a dropout problem is that there generally existed an at least adequate demand for low-skilled and unskilled workers, a demand that people of low educational background—dropouts—readily filled. In this light, dropouts traditionally served to reinforce the prevalent division of labor; and the process of school failure, whatever its basic rationale, ensured sufficient numbers of hod carriers and elevator operators.

The issue I am pointing to here is, in part, the social relevance of education in our society. By and large, the people who never completed high school constitute a fairly specific class in our society; and it is their offspring who constitute the current population of dropouts and potential dropouts we are anxious about. About two-thirds of all the country's workers who never completed high school are employed in low-skilled and unskilled jobs as laborers, household workers, and janitors. In an economy where the unemployment rate has not fallen below 5 per cent for over five years, two-thirds of the unemployed are men and women with less than a high-school education. Although the number of dropouts expected during this decade has no particular meaning in itself, it obtains great significance when juxtaposed to the diminution—or one might better say the demolition—of the low-skill job market of which the dropout was formerly assured. The U. S. Department of Labor estimates that by 1970 not more than 5 per cent of all available jobs will be of the unskilled variety.

The squeeze of this new unemployment is particularly hard on the young worker, especially where union seniority regulations are in effect. It virtually suffocates the youngster who has recently quit school. All other things being equal, employers will generally prefer an older worker, whether skilled or unskilled, who has validated work habits and who has acquired responsibilities that more or less guarantee his reliability. Similarly, whether or not the run of high-school curricula have much occupational relevance, the high-school diploma in recent years has achieved the status of a certificate of employability and a kind of admission ticket, in some instances, to occupations less susceptible to unemployment. Nor is the reasoning of employers altogether unacceptable. Many of them in the manufacturing and service industries are interested in developing managerial help and in retraining to the managerial level. Naturally they assume that the wider the employee's educational background the more available he will be to such advancement programs. Probably more important, the diploma certifies that the youngster has passed successfully through a social and socializing process that is apparently increasingly necessary.

In any case, the national unemployment rate among 16- to 21-year-old school dropouts is presently 24 per cent. As Conant showed in his *Slums and Suburbs* (1961), this rate is likely to rise to as high as 70 per cent in slum neighborhoods in the great cities. In New York City alone, a recent study revealed there are 77,000 out of school, jobless youth, of whom 33,000 are not even seeking employment. But again, it should be emphasized, these unemployed are not unemployed simply because they are high-school dropouts. They are unemployed because the kinds of jobs their training or lack of training fits them for are vanishing.

This disappearance of whole categories of jobs is, of course, a major consequence, a hard one, of the fairly fantastic pace of development of automation and technology. There is an argument, I am told, that automation creates as many jobs as it eliminates. Nonetheless it is estimated that during this decade an average of 50 to 60 thousand new jobs weekly need to be created to accommodate new entrants into the labor market and to replace the jobs taken over by machines. Needless to say, new jobs are not appearing at this rate; and the ones that do turn up are generally on a notably higher skill and technical level.

Let me cite a single graphic instance of the sort of silent devastation automation can wreak. Several years ago the National Tube Corporation in Lorain, Ohio, a division of the U. S. Steel Corporation, employed 10,000 men. Subsequently, among other innovations, a new technique of infusing oxygen was introduced which reduced the time required to process steel from ten to five and one-half hours. Today National Tube employs 5500 men to do the same amount of work as previously. This means that 4500 in a town of 60,000 were laid off, out of work. Moreover, since the company operated under a union contract, rights of seniority applied. The youngest workers were discharged first so that today in Lorain, Ohio, nobody under the age of 30 is employed in the manufacture of steel tubing.

What becomes of workers displaced under these conditions, and of youth for whom there is no opportunity in their hometown? In great part, they join an already incredibly large army of similarly displaced migrants. Within a month of today, more than 400,000 workers will have moved to a different labor-market area in a different geographical region. Not all of them, by any means, will have jobs.

It is seldom emphasized that perhaps rural areas (where, incidentally, dropout rates are as high as in the cities) and small towns and cities are most drastically ravaged by the pace of technological development. Eighty-five per cent of the country's population growth during the last decade took place in urban areas. Very few agricultural states grew in population commensurately with the country as a whole; in particular, several southern states lost in population. The U. S. Department of Agriculture calculates that by 1970 not more than 7 per cent of the labor force will be engaged in producing a more than adequate food supply for the entire nation; and, consequently, that 90 per cent of the youth presently growing up on farms will eventually have to migrate.

I can only suggest the plight of the majority of these people—the displaced farm laborer or small-city factory worker—as they cross the threshold of the industrialized cities. In great part, they are poor with little education and few marketable skills. Many are young with small children. Some groups such as the southern rural Negro, the Appalachian Mountain white, the Spanish American (Puerto Rican and Mexican), having been abruptly dislocated from centuries-old agrarian styles of life, are often dispossessed of all really operable sense of continuity and identity. Large numbers eventually become additions to welfare rolls; and their children in the core-city slum schools are immediately earmarked as what we call potential dropouts.

Nor let us be unduly illusionary or optimistic as to who the rest of the dropouts are, where they come from, where they are. Indeed, in a larger perspective, dropout seems nothing so much as another signal of the plight of that segment of our society which is, to borrow a phrase, "in" our society, but only marginally "of" it. For example, Professor S. M. Miller has pointed out that at least 70 per cent of the youngsters who quit school come from families whose annual income is less than 5000 dollars —a figure, be it noted, approaching the one (3000 dollars) generally used as a cut-off in definitions of the economic poverty which encompasses some 30 to 40 million of our fellow citizens. Similarly, one might mention only one among many highly interesting findings of Stetler's study of school dropouts in Connecticut; namely, that among sampled Negro students the rate of dropout was some 60 per cent higher than among their white counterparts.

The foregoing are some factors that determine the nature and dimensions of the present school-dropout problem. It is indeed of extremely wide and inclusive scope. Even from this cursory view, it should be clear that the dropout problem is not simply equivalent to the segregation problem, the unemployment problem, or the poverty and lower-class problem. It is not even simply a problem of chronic academic ineptitude. All the studies I have seen indicate that though the great majority of dropouts are school failures, at least two-thirds of them have registered I.Q. scores of 90—the minimum believed necessary to complete a high-school curriculum successfully. It is not simply a school problem. The school alone, despite all rhetoric about its levered relationship to the future, is not going to solve it. But it is a matter of people, and of young persons and children in particular; and the school, after all, remains the only social institution that has some contact with all children.

UNITED EFFORT: HOME, SCHOOL, AND COMMUNITY

Although the school must remain the focus of effort to ameliorate dropout, progress will be sooner forthcoming where community resources are utilized. In many parts of our country, programs are now underway in which schools in conjunction with business and industry are diminishing dropout rate. I should like to describe briefly some of these programs because, besides their intrinsic interest and relevance, they illuminate the scale along which the school's coordinating and focusing role can be defined.

In Green Bay, Wisconsin, there is a program that goes into operation in the seventh grade and extends through the senior high school. The purpose of the program is to alert students to the practicality of their present work in relation to their future, regardless of what it will be. Under this plan special programs are presented as interruptions in the schedule for an important message, rather than as an announced series. The programs seem casual but are actually carefully planned. In each instance the schools first draw up specifications for the approach and message that are needed, then go into the community to find the business leaders who can deliver them.

The senior-high phase of the plan is sponsored by the Downtown Kiwanis Club of Green Bay. It is conducted by the club's Vocational Guidance Committee and aimed solely at the potential dropout. For years the Vocational Guidance Committee had held luncheons for top-level students to give them a chance to meet Kiwanians and to discuss career possibilities with them. Last year, however, the Kiwanians realized that although the good student was presumably merely deciding on a profession, the potential dropout was debating a decision on which depended his future economic security. The club's members asked guidance counselors to bring selected potential dropouts to a luncheon at the city's leading hotel. A speaker from the Wisconsin State Employment Service was secured to give the boys and girls the "dollars-and-cents" reasons for staying in school. Students' questions were answered by a panel that included the personnel directors of the city's major utility and a large paper company, an Army officer, and the principal speaker. This past year the program was expanded and featured a special panel for girls.

In Indianapolis a few months ago the Western Electric Company instituted accredited high-school courses on its premises for its personnel. The program is projected over a six-year period; the courses in math, economics, history, government, and so on, are taught by both active and retired high-school teachers. Moreover, the courses are taught during three different periods to correspond to the schedules of personnel working the three plant shifts. The program is coordinated by the Adult Education Division of the Indianapolis schools, but in its uniqueness it ensures the participation of large numbers of people who probably would not otherwise have attended. A total of 400 workers, most of them former high-school dropouts, are enrolled in the program.

A Kansas City work-study program has just closed its second year of operation. This is a six-year controlled experiment involving a group of boys who when the program began were 13- and 14-year-old eighth graders and who had been identified as potential dropouts. During this past year each boy followed a special program in school for one-half of each day and worked the second half of the day on a special project. By the fifth year he will be working full time; and upon completion of that year, he will receive a special work certificate from the school system. Several Kansas City employers have agreed to keep one job permanently open as a training position for each boy in the program.

The school will by no means always be the source of initiative, but it must always be alert and ready to offer strategic assistance. For example, within the township of Kensington, Maryland, a suburb of Washington, D. C., is a small encapsulated community, predominantly Negro, called Ken-Gar. Ken-Gar has traditionally provided a steady source of maids and trash collectors to the surrounding communities. Over the years not more than a third of the children of Ken-Gar have completed high school, and none has ever gone to college. About four years ago a small group of private individuals from Kensington who wanted to help Ken-Gar help itself worked with the parents to establish a Home Study Program. Volunteer tutors were recruited, most of them residents of Kensington, all of them college graduates. One night a week each parent of Ken-Gar makes over some part of his home—kitchen, living room, or basement—

into a classroom where tutors meet with students who are grouped by grade for one-and-a-half-hour sessions. The program has realized enormous success so that there are about 75 volunteer tutors, with many more on the waiting list, teaching 100 Ken-Gar children. After operating for two years as an unofficial organization by contributions from the tutors and Ken-Gar parents, the program was taken under the wing of the Montgomery County Board of Education two years ago.

Increasingly, school systems are adding personnel skilled in techniques of mental health such as psychiatrists and social workers. In Philadelphia, as part of its "Grey Area" program, a mature adult with a high-school diploma who is a resident of the school neighborhood is assigned to the school staff. This person meets with parents on an individual basis in their homes, involves them in the school's activities, and enlists their participation in adult-education programs organized in conjunction with other community agencies. In Detroit this coordinator is a college graduate, a professional, usually a sociologist. The New York City schools with a large Puerto Rican population employ auxiliary teachers who are natives of Puerto Rico. Since they speak Spanish and have some proximate knowledge of the difficulties faced by the new migrants, they are able to help them register and to orient both child and parent to the new school environment and to urban living. Incidentally, in the original Higher Horizons school in New York City, the social worker who was attached to the school staff only as a result of additional funds found that the homes of 25 per cent of the students were so disorganized as to need outside help.

On the other hand, there are increasingly coming into appearance, mainly under the stimulus of the President's Committee on Youth Crime and Juvenile Delinquency, massive attack programs in which the school's role is interwoven with those of many other agencies. New York City's 13-million-dollar Mobilization for Youth Program, which is concerned with a 67-square-block area on the lower East Side, is a case in point. The program consists of an intricate variety of projects and approaches which certainly cannot be recapitulated here in any detail. Suffice it to mention that nearly 500 youths at present work as trainees in gas stations, luncheonettes, woodwork shops, and on similar projects, all sponsored by the program. Another 200 are holding down jobs in private industry. Mobilization for Youth is an independent nonprofit corporation, but the cooperation of the schools in the vicinity, although not particularly highlighted, is of crucial importance. Similar programs that coordinate efforts by such agencies as police, recreation, health, welfare, and the schools are underway in Boston and Oakland, California, and are in planning stages in a number of other cities.

REACHING THE POTENTIAL DROPOUT EARLY

Our dropout problem is a culminating signal—somewhat irrelevant in itself—of a tragic and unforgivable process that has its roots in the most fundamental social grounds. Whatever official records and studies report, most dropouts quit school because it has been meaningless to them —they have never got hold of it, they have let it pass them by, they do not believe (with good reason sometimes) what it says it will do for them. The real educational challenge is for the school to make itself relevant and meaningful and, in the process, to truly educate.

There are indications in a large majority of cases that dropout is not importantly determined even by the school process. That is, although dropout puts an emphatic end to a history of chronic academic failure, there is a sense in which many of these children never, in effect, started school. Because the roots of their failure lie in the deprivations of their preschool failure, they come to school with nothing like the tools, the experiences, the self-security that 5- and 6-year-old middle-class children possess. They do know and learn, as anyone who stops to watch them play recognizes; but their learning styles are not those that the school is generally geared to. For such children the first experience of school when they are forced to sit and listen attentively for ten minutes while a teacher speaks is one of failure, failure from which many never recover. I have seen reports that show whole classes to be seven months retarded at the end of the first grade. Is it any wonder that, by the time they reach the third grade, teachers often report these children to be unmanageable and without any idea why they are in school!

The potential dropout is often identifiable in the early elementary grades. Some promising programs are now underway that have as their purpose the early detection and prevention of dropout. For example, an interesting project was carried out in July 1962 by the Dunbar Pre-School Enrichment Group of Philadelphia. The program involved thirteen preschool disadvantaged children ranging in age from 4.5 to 4.11. I.Q. scores for these youngsters according to the Stanford-Binet ranged between 70 and 107 with a mean I.Q. of 88. Particular weakness was evident in test sections where language comprehension was a chief factor. These included giving reasons, following directions, giving simple word associations, and naming materials used to make common objects. Below-average verbal ability was observed by the failure of eight out of the thirteen children to identify pictures of objects at the four-year level such as tree, flag, arm, and leaf.

The program was conducted over a four-week period and consisted of group discussions, singing, working with materials, concept building, trips, and outdoor activities. Scheduling was flexible for at the outset none of the students maintained an attention span in excess of five minutes. In the beginning it was almost impossible to elicit any form of conversation or to get the group to sing or show an interest in stories. They had little or no group consciousness; they were shy and unattentive.

During the experiment the kindergarten supervisor conducted weekly workshops with the parents for several hours. Some of the immediate goals for the parents were to understand what 4- and 5-year-old children are like, what home and school can do to further their development; to give opportunities to discuss mutual problems concerning child rearing; to observe and understand the school environment and how it functions for the best development of children; to understand the importance of providing a rich cultural environment for youngsters; and to develop both in themselves and in their children a positive attitude toward school.

What happened to the children and their parents as a result of this enrichment program? You may recall that the mean I.Q. of the group was 88 with a range between 70 and 107. When retested again in August, an eight- to nine-week interval, the mean I.Q. had soared to 102, a gain of 14 points, with a range between 86 and 125. The group had changed from a "dull normal" to a "normal" group. Every child showed an increased score, one as much as 23 points, and not a single child showed a lower score. The psychologist reports that the difference in score is statistically significant at the 1 per cent level; that is, the problem of its recurrence by chance is less than 1 in 100: "Whereas no child had number concepts before his school experience, eight had established some concepts between two and ten."

The guidance given the parents, coupled with suggestions that they spend more time talking to the children, answering their questions, reading to them, and taking them to places of interest, was effective. Parents reported that their children "talk about school all the time." One parent offered the comment, "All I hear about all the time is the trips he takes. He knows about different animals now. He knows where milk comes from and what a farm is like." Another parent reported, "She's sick when she can't come to school on Saturday and Sunday."

Another exciting experiment designed to lessen the number of potential school dropouts is presently ongoing in Racine, Wisconsin. Although results of this project involving a new approach to kindergarten are not as yet available, teacher reports have been favorable.

The so-called "culturally deprived" children in this kindergarten follow the normal half-day kindergarten routine. During the afternoons, however, they are brought together as a group for additional activities designed to develop their background and horizons. They are taken on field trips at least twice a week, on nature hikes, to museums, parks, farms, and factories. They are being exposed to an abundance of reading materials; their classroom is outfitted with television and a tape recorder. All this additional activity and instruction is aimed at building a background of experience and understanding—at least somewhat comparable to what the middle-class child possesses—which can facilitate the learning of the art of reading.

I realize that in describing these programs what I have done is not so much to comment on and explore the question of the school's role in coordinating dropout programs as to indicate it. Briefly, as I mentioned earlier, I do not think it can be schematized, inasmuch as it should be one of ceaseless invention and initiative. It is to remain open to exploit every possibility that appears on the horizon.

In conclusion, school dropout is a serious national problem. Shortly before his assassination, John F. Kennedy said:

The end of the summer will be an especially critical time for 400,000 young Americans who, according to experience of earlier years, will not return to school. . . . Moreover, without a special effort to reverse this trend, another 700,000 students will return to school in September but will fail to complete the school year.

The greatest growth in labor demand today is for highly trained professional workers, with 16 or more years of education. The second fastest growing demand is for technical and semi-professional workers with one to three years of post-high school education. Jobs filled by high school graduates rose 30 per cent, while jobs for those with no secondary education decreased 25 per cent. We must therefore intensify our efforts to meet this problem. This is a serious national problem.[1]

It is serious because the prospect for employment for the dropout is dismal—almost 1,000,000 unemployed youth. It is serious because this large number of unemployed, out-of-school youth will result in an increase in rate of crime. It is serious because it will result in an increase in welfare rolls. And it is serious, most serious, because a sizable proportion of capable young Americans will be swept out of the mainstream of American experiences, hopes, ideals, and aspirations.

[1] President's News Conference Proceedings, NBC News, August 1, 1963.

15 *Improving the Mental Health of School Personnel*

Roderick A. Armstrong

The degree to which classroom instruction can be successful is in part contingent upon the mental status of the teacher. Should he be mentally healthy, there is greater likelihood his teaching will be more effective. But just what is a mentally healthy person? In 1962 researchers at Wayne State University determined to define this elusive goal basing their description on behavior patterns of persons considered by others to possess desirable life style. Five of the common characteristics chosen by experienced clinicians correlated well with trait descriptions given by 85 college freshmen.

The healthy person:

1. *Treats others as individuals.* He identifies himself with them and understands them. He is tolerant of others whether he likes them or not. He gives other people a sense of security and is not demanding. His recognition and acceptance of people is not limited by age or sex. He may be loving or stern, depending on his own limitations and the needs of other persons. He is esteemed for friendships that do not depend on rigid requirements or conditions.
2. *Is flexible under internal or external stress.* Such stresses may be imposed by the loss of relatives, possessions, or friends; by physical pain, illness and suffering, and by pressures exerted by those in authority. The healthy person reacts with control without becoming emotionally disturbed and is able to express his feelings. He finds a solution, such as a new job or a new direction for his love.
3. *Obtains pleasure from many sources.* The healthy person has a native curiosity about the world in general. He establishes friendships when possible but does not compulsively seek them and may even reject opportunity for friendships.
4. *Sees and accepts self-limitations.* The healthy person may often be

158

unsuccessful by cultural and social standards, but he is contented to attain limited goals.

5. *Employs his capabilities to fulfill personal needs in doing productive tasks.* He gets things done without feeling compelled to finish a task if it is impossible (Solley and Munden, 1962).

A DIVIDED INDIVIDUAL

It would be encouraging if all teacher behavior were in accord with those characteristics just cited. Unfortunately, frequency of neurotic incidents among educators does not favor such optimism. Like most other occupational groups, the teaching profession includes among its membership persons whose neuroses lead to disturbance sufficient to trouble either themselves or other people or both. Underlying the myriad causes of mental illness are like elements of stress inherent in our mode of space-age living to which teachers are as subject as their fellow adults.

A common source of stress arises from the nature of our complex societal structure wherein the individual is presumed divisible. Accordingly, the concept of "self" has been expanded so that each person is now considered to be many selves with his unique personality a composite of their integration. Every individual belongs to many "communities," each having its own customs, conventions, ideals, and aims which together constitute its status as a social entity. Each group has its influence in defining the motives and acts of the individual self.

There are primary groups such as the family to which nearly everyone belongs. Then follow the school and college with their very different membership and influence; the business or profession, the wife, and again the family. To these may be added social and voluntary organizations, sporting clubs, and literary societies. Further, each person is brought into close contact with the community, religious bodies, business and professional friends; and it must not be forgotten he is a member of a race, a nation, and usually a political party. Looked at from a subjective point of view, a man is a different self in every different social capacity, and the molding of these many selves into any working consistency of behavior is far more remarkable than that everyone should display inconsistencies of thoughts or actions.

The constriction of each man's environment is advanced as he becomes more isolated intellectually. With the tremendous increase in knowledge during the past century, no single person can know a lot about everything as formerly was possible; each now specializes and has a greater knowledge about less and less. Moreover, the rapid growth in population concurrent with the rapidity of change in knowledge imposes difficulties on self-expression, communication of reliable information, and learning and teaching.

Since it appears man is being confined socially with his small groups as well as intellectually, he pursues the ends of these various organizations more exclusively; he becomes a number, an automaton in a machine world whose only worthwhile goal appears to be materialism, because of the insidious infiltration of economic criteria into every phase of life. Materialism in turn generates dependence so that some persons no longer feel in control of their own destiny. Such a state of mind obliterates their sense of true values and self-worth resulting in a loss of individuality and freedom. This rudderless state, this environment of disintegration, is noxious and conducive to mental ill health.

STRESS REACTION: ADJUSTMENT OR BREAKDOWN?

How does one adjust to the multiple demands of allegiance made upon citizens in our culture? How can one function effectively amidst the daily pressures of stress? A knowledge of the general influence of stress is antecedent to answering such a query. Selye believes physical stress is something that tends to produce a change in an organism, a change to which the organism is bound to react. The object of this reaction would seem to be to restore as far as possible the inner equilibrium or homeostasis of the organism. In the first stage of alarm reaction the body reacts relatively violently to the stress for a comparatively short time, and bears all the signs of illness. If the organism survives, the next stage is one of adaptation; the stress has been successfully encountered at whatever cost, and relative equilibrium has been achieved; in this stage the organism is comparatively impervious to further stress of the same kind. When adaptation is incomplete because it is failing, or the stress continues too long, or when the nature of the response called forth is incompatible with normal health to a major degree, symptoms of illness become apparent. Continued stress results in a third stage, physical exhaustion and death.

While Selye's (1956) efforts primarily concerned physiological stress, they were helpful in fostering analogous studies in psychological adjustment. For example, the crisis theory of Gerald Caplan at Harvard University stems from the premise that throughout our lives each of us is exposed to a number of major trauma or stresses which can be the precursors of mental disturbance. Psychological stress of whatever etiology produces an appropriate alarm reaction in a specific part of the personality during which there are signs of mental disturbance. The second stage is one of adjustment to the stress which may either remedy the situation completely or else leave the personality with a lowered tolerance to stress of a different kind at a later date. Stress subsequently may produce a major mental illness.

According to Caplan, the most common human trials and tribulations constituting psychological crisis are adolescence, schooling, prematurity, loneliness, sickness or injury, bereavement, marriage, pregnancy, parenthood, religious differences, employment or its lack, leisure and its use or lack, retirement, and old age. For the most part people will cope with these difficult experiences satisfactorily but possibly 10 to 15 per cent will fail to do so or will do so inadequately. The latter of course are the ones whom mental health eludes.

STRESS IN THE SCHOOL SETTING

Aside from disruptive influences within the classroom, an individual's public personality as a teacher is exposed to stresses arising from the social system in his institution. These may be a consequence of long-standing defects of structure that lead to inefficiencies in specific areas or they may be traceable to recent and temporary difficulties which have led to the disordering of a previously effective organization. Areas of structure and functioning in which problems not uncommonly occur, and which lead to obstacles in catering for the mental-health needs of students, include the authority system, role conflict, broken communication, and personality difficulties.

Problems occur in the authority system when there is unclear or ineffectual leadership at various levels of the hierarchy both inside the school building and the central administration of the school complex. For example, the appointment of a new principal less experienced and capable than a senior teacher already at the school; or the issuing of contradictory instructions by two authority figures, such as a supervisor and a guidance officer, under circumstances where it is not clear who is the responsible authority.

Role conflicts are due to a variety of causes. For example, a new staff member may have a distorted perception of his role; or an old staff member in a new position may not yet have learned to play the role expected of him; there may be a discrepancy between personal ability and role demands. Incompatibility of goals may demand an impossible role of a teacher as when he is given responsibility without authority or school policy may conflict with differing community demands. So there are conflicting demands on teachers or between them and other institutions which may result in discordant performance and interfere with the smooth functioning of the system.

At times there is a disruption of communication networks either inside the school or within the school complex, between school and parents or between school and outside agencies. Channels of communication may not have existed previously or more often have become blocked for some reason; for example, new staff members may not be aware of the necessity to pass on certain information, or to pass it along a specific route; or perhaps staff members may be too preoccupied with duties that do not allow them time to communicate along certain channels.

Personality difficulties may upset the operation of the social system in any of the foregoing cases. They may express themselves in discordant performance of one individual, who because of acute or chronic difficulties is unable to carry out his allotted tasks in the school operations, and whose disturbing influence is felt in a wider or narrower circle depending on his role and status in the hierarchy. In the case of chronic personality difficulties a teacher may resemble a carrier of an infectious disease, a reservoir of emotional instability infecting many with whom he comes in contact.

CONCLUSION

There is no doubt that a teacher's life situation is a difficult one for he has to reconcile two personalities: a personal one for his own private life as spouse, parent, member of a community, and his public one of a teacher at school. He would be inhuman if he could dissociate himself completely at school from his personal problems, but whether he will allow features of student symptoms to stimulate his own unsolved concerns will depend on his mental state. If unable to deal effectively with his own difficulties, he will undoubtedly fail to see children with problems, rather he will see only problem children.

Much can be done to upgrade the mental health of teachers by increased clarity and efficiency within the social system of the school itself. For example, lines of authority should be spelled out; all personnel ought to be cognizant of the particular role expected of them; communication links between teachers and administration should be clear and contingent upon a minimum of red tape; and personality difficulties should be resolved whenever possible. Finally, although no universal prescription is applicable for coping with school pressures, educators can maintain a demeanor of flexibility. Indeed, in a time of rapid change, stability and adjustment can occur only within a frame of flexibility. To remain irresponsive to change is to become less than effective as a teacher and as a person; it is to become mentally ill.

16 *A New Look at Classroom Discipline*

David P. Ausubel

A few years ago, in one of our better New England high schools, two members of the school's counseling staff happened to be walking in the building when their attention was drawn to sounds of a disturbance in an adjoining corridor. Investigating further, they found that two boys, surrounded by a knot of curious onlookers, were engaged in an all-out switchblade fight. One counselor quickly whispered to the other, "We'd better break this up in a hurry before there's bloodshed." The latter replied heatedly, "For heaven's sake leave them alone or you'll ruin everything! Do you want the kids to think we are *disciplinarians?*" Fortunately, however, the native common sense of the first counselor prevailed over the doctrinaire permissiveness of his colleague, and a near-tragedy was averted.

This true story is admittedly a bit extreme and unrepresentative of disciplinary attitudes in American public schools. Nevertheless, somewhat less extreme versions occur frequently enough to suggest that American teachers are more confused and disturbed about matters of discipline today than at any previous time in the history of our public-school system.

It is true that superficial observation does not support this conclusion. On the surface, practically everything *appears* the same as it was ten years ago when, except in the so-called "Blackboard Jungles," these same teachers seemed supremely confident that the ideal of democratic discipline had been achieved in the American classroom. Substantially the same disciplinary philosophy is still preached in our teachers colleges; and teachers, by and large, still practice the same kind of discipline they practiced a decade ago.

To be sure, there is still an appreciable gap between the theory of

Reprinted by permission from *Phi Delta Kappan,* 43, 1961, 25–30.

discipline as taught in colleges of education and discipline as it is actually conceived and practiced in the schools. For example, in a recent survey conducted by the National Education Association, 72 per cent of the responding classroom teachers favored the judicious use of corporal punishment in the elementary school. But the gap is no greater now than it has ever been. In everyday disciplinary practice, American teachers have never gone along completely with the more extreme ideas of educational theorists. Elementary and high-school teachers, after all, have to be realistic in handling problems of discipline because they encounter them daily in doing their jobs. Unlike professors of education, who rarely if ever have to cope with disciplinary problems in the classroom, they can ill afford to be starry-eyed about these matters.

Why then should teachers be suddenly confused and disturbed about issues of discipline? Closer scrutiny reveals that everything is not *really* the same as it used to be. One important factor in the situation has undergone significant change: Although educational theory in the field of classroom discipline has remained virtually unchanged over the past two decades, the pendulum of public opinion in recent years has been swinging further and further away from the formerly fashionable cult of permissiveness. As a result, a growing estrangement has arisen between the general public, on the one hand, and educational and psychological theorists on the other—with the classroom teacher and the rank-and-file school administrator caught squarely in the middle. Teachers, of course, were also in the middle throughout the entire period of approximately 1935–1955, when American classroom discipline underwent a process of extensive democratization. But this middle position was decidedly more comfortable then than it is now, because all three groups—educational theorists, teachers, and the public at large—were moving toward the same culturally desirable goal of a less authoritarian classroom climate.

It is true that these three groups were moving toward this goal at quite different rates. Permissiveness, nondirective guidance, and the cults of extroversion, conformity, and social adjustment were much more extreme among child-centered educators, client-centered counselors, and psychoanalytically trained child-study experts than among American parents and teachers generally. By 1955, however, the entirely laudable objective of more democratic pupil-teacher relationships had been reached, and perhaps overreached. Public opinion began moving away from permissiveness, but educational and psychological theorists and professors of education, with few exceptions, stood their ground tenaciously. The same relatively extreme permissive doctrines of discipline are still dominant in teachers colleges, even though educational philosophy in the post-Sputnik era has generally become less permissive in most other areas, such as curriculum.

Now, it was one thing for teachers to swim in the middle of two streams moving in the same historically necessary direction, and to enjoy the approbation of both the general public and of their own professional leaders. It is quite another for them to be caught between two opposing streams, and to be faced with the problem of having to choose between the spirit of the times, on the one hand, and the historically obsolete ideological extremism of their former professors on the other.

HISTORICAL AND CULTURAL PERSPECTIVE

Before examining how particular concepts and practices of discipline have gone astray, it might be profitable first to view the problem in historical perspective within a broader cultural context. The revolution in classroom discipline that swept American schools between 1935 and 1955 was as necessary as it was inevitable. Teacher-pupil relationships had to be brought into closer alignment with the general spirit of adult egalitarianism in American society; and a more desirable balance had to be achieved between the actual dependence of children on adult direction and their realistic capacities for exercising self-direction and self-discipline. It was inevitable, of course, that we would go too far in redressing the balance—in overdoing the permissiveness and in cutting back adult control and guidance too drastically. Much more serious, however, were the deplorable consequences of deemphasizing certain other traditional American values in the enthusiasm of democratizing adult-child relationships.

Thus, in stressing the inherent right of children to receive the consideration to which they are entitled, we have neglected the equally valid claims of age and maturity. In debunking superficial and unilateral forms of etiquette, we have lost sight of the importance of genuine courtesy in human relationships. And in attacking despotic and abusive adult rule, we have failed to cultivate appropriate respect for just and rightful authority.

By respect for age I do not mean uncritical veneration or ancestor worship, but simply the consideration that is due all human beings at any stage in the life cycle. Yet our cultural attitude toward middle-aged and elderly persons tends to be patronizing and slightly contemptuous. Because they quite understandably lack the exuberance and venturesomeness of youth, they are often cavalierly dismissed as "has-beens" or as bumbling, ineffectual fuddy-duddies.

Courtesy is another of our most valuable cultural assets that was overlooked in the frenzy of extending democracy to home and school. It is fashionable in many quarters—not only among the younger set—to regard good manners and the more subtle amenities of interpersonal relationships as hollow formalities. But even the highly stylized bowing ceremony of the Japanese is far from being an empty gesture. It symbolizes deep and culturally ingrained respect for the dignity of the individual and genuine concern for his pride and feelings. Although bowing is obviously incongruous with our modern way of life, concern for the pride, feelings, and dignity of every human being is one of our most cherished American values. Hence, since courtesy is basically an institutionalized set of rules designed to safeguard and implement this legitimate cultural concern, those who sneer at courtesy, whether they realize it or not, sneer at nothing less than human dignity.

Finally, our culture has tended to put authority figures in an anomalous and untenable position, particularly in the school environment. We have assigned them the necessary and often distasteful task of authority figures the world over, that is, to enforce certain basic standards of conduct; but in too many instances we have failed to give them the respect, the authority, and the protection commensurate with this responsibility. When they conscientiously attempt to apply without fear or favor the community-approved sanctions for violating these standards, we accuse them of being punitive, vindictive, and authoritarian. School administrators, of course, are not above criticism and reproach when they use poor judgment or exceed their authority; but society has an obligation to protect them from disrespect and abuse for simply doing their duty and exercising their just and necessary disciplinary prerogatives. In our present cultural climate, therefore, it is small wonder that many principals and superintendents of schools are more concerned with courting general popularity than with enforcing desirable norms of pupil behavior.

THE BRIGHTER SIDE OF THE COIN

In pointing out some of the failings of our recent approach to discipline, I do not mean to detract in any way from our genuine accomplishments. The latter are extremely impressive when compared with disciplinary practices in many other countries. I recently had an opportunity to study secondary schools in New Zealand, an English-speaking welfare state of British origin with a pioneering tradition not unlike our own. School discipline in New Zealand high schools connotes explicit subjection to authority and implicit habits of obedience that are enforced by a very heavy-handed set of controls and punishments. It implies a very identifiable atmosphere of classroom control which the teacher maintains with much deliberate effort—in much the same sense that he strives to have his pupils understand and assimilate the subject matter he teaches. For example, it is not uncommon for a New Zealand high-school teacher to begin the school year by exhibiting a cane to his class and announcing that he fully intends to use it on the first pupil who steps out of line.

By contrast, the American approach to discipline seems laudably incidental. Our teachers tend to feel that the cause of discipline is adequately served if pupils exercise sufficient self-control and observe a minimum set of rules with sufficient decorum to enable classroom work to proceed in an orderly, efficient manner. They do not, in other words, strive deliberately for discipline as an explicit goal in its own right. They assume instead that good discipline is *ordinarily* a natural by-product of interesting lessons and of a wholesome teacher-pupil relationship; that the vast majority of pupils respond positively to fair and kindly treatment; that respect for the teacher is a usual accompaniment of the latter's superior knowledge, experience, and status as a leader, and does not have to be reinforced by such artificial props and status symbols as differences in clothing, mode of address, and fear of the strap. Hence they treat adolescents as maturing young adults rather than as unruly children, and implicitly expect them to respond in kind—which they usually do. And it was a very gratifying experience to discover that despite the absence of strict authoritarian controls, American high-school students, on the whole, behave more decorously than their New Zealand counterparts—particularly when not under direct supervision.

SCIENCE OR OPINION?

Discipline today is much less a science than a matter of opinion. It not only shifts in response to various social, economic, and ideological factors, but also manifests all of the cyclical properties of fads and fashions. Objective scientific evidence about the relative merits of different types of discipline is extremely sparse. Indeed it is highly questionable to what extent valid objective data are obtainable and even relevant in matters of discipline. Whether or not particular disciplinary practices are appropriate depends, in the first place, on the particular values, institutions, and kinds of personal relationships prevailing in a given culture; and, second, any definitive empirical test of appropriateness would have to be conducted over such an extended period of time that its conclusions would tend to be rendered obsolete by intervening changes in significant social conditions. For all practical purposes, therefore, the choice of disciplinary policy involves taking a rationally defensible and self-consistent position based on value preferences, on relevant considerations of child development, and on individual experience and judgment.

The fact that discipline cannot be placed on a largely scientific basis, however, does not mean that one position is as good as another or that no public policy whatsoever is warranted. Society is continually obliged to resolve issues of much greater moment with even less objective evidence on which to base a decision. Under the circumstances, all we can reasonably expect is greater humility and less dogmatism on the part of those engaged in formulating disciplinary policy. Thus the most disturbing aspect of the entire problem is not the fact that there is precious little scientific evidence to support the disciplinary doctrines expounded in our colleges of education and educational journals and textbooks, but rather the ubiquitous tendency to represent purely personal opinions and biases as if they were the incontrovertibly established findings of scientific research.

THE DEFINITION AND FUNCTIONS OF DISCIPLINE

By discipline I mean the imposition of *external* standards and controls on individual conduct. Permissiveness, on the other hand, refers to the absence of such standards and controls. To be permissive is to "let alone," to adopt a *laissez-faire* policy. Authoritarianism is an excessive, arbitrary, and autocratic type of control which is diametrically opposite to permissiveness. Between the extremes of *laissez-faire* permissiveness and authoritarianism are many varieties and degrees of control. One of these, to be described in greater detail below, is democratic discipline.

Discipline is a universal cultural phenomenon that generally serves four important functions in the training of the young. First, it is necessary for socialization—for learning the standards of conduct that are approved and tolerated in any culture. Second, it is necessary for normal personality maturation—for acquiring such adult personality traits as dependability, self-reliance, self-control, persistence, and ability to tolerate frustration. These aspects of maturation do not occur spontaneously, but only in response to sustained social demands and expectations. Third, it is necessary for the internalization of moral standards and obligations or, in other words, for the development of conscience. Standards obviously cannot be internalized unless they also exist in external form; and even after they are effectively internalized, universal cultural experience suggests that external sanctions are still required to ensure the stability of the social order. Finally, discipline is necessary for children's emotional security. Without the guidance provided by unambiguous external controls, the young tend to feel bewildered and apprehensive. Too great a burden is placed on their own limited capacity for self-control.

DEMOCRATIC DISCIPLINE

The proponents of democratic classroom discipline believe in imposing the minimal degree of external control necessary for socialization, personality maturation, conscience development, and the emotional security of the child. Discipline and obedience are not regarded as ends in themselves but only as means to these latter ends. They are not striven for deliberately, but are expected to follow naturally in the wake of friendly and realistic teacher-pupil relationships. Explicit limits are not set routinely or as ways of showing "who is boss," but only as the need arises, that is, when they are not implicitly understood or accepted by pupils.

Democratic discipline is as rational, nonarbitrary, and bilateral as possible. It provides explanations, permits discussion, and invites the participation of children in the setting of standards whenever they are qualified to do so. Above all, it implies respect for the dignity of the individual and avoids exaggerated emphasis on status differences and barriers between free communication. Hence it repudiates harsh, abusive, and vindictive forms of punishment, and the use of sarcasm, ridicule, and intimidation.

The aforementioned attributes of democratic classroom discipline are obviously appropriate in cultures such as ours where social relationships tend to be egalitarian. This type of discipline also becomes increasingly more feasible as children become older, more responsible, and more capable of understanding and formulating rules of conduct based on concepts of equity and reciprocal obligation. But contrary to what the extreme permissivists would have us believe, democratic school discipline does not imply freedom from all external constraints, standards, and direction, or freedom from discipline as an end in itself. And under no circumstances does it presuppose the eradication of all distinctions between pupil and teacher roles, or require that teachers abdicate responsibility for making the final decisions in the classroom.

DISTORTIONS OF DEMOCRATIC DISCIPLINE

Many educational theorists have misinterpreted and distorted the ideal of democratic discipline by equating it with an extreme form of permissiveness. These distortions have been dogmatically expressed in various psychologically unsound and unrealistic propositions that are considered sacrosanct in many teachers colleges. Fortunately, however, most classroom teachers have only accepted them for examination purposes—while still in training—and have discarded them in actual practice as thoroughly unworkable.

According to one widely held doctrine, only "positive" forms of discipline are constructive and democratic. It is asserted that children must only be guided by reward and approval; that reproof and punishment are authoritarian, repressive, and reactionary expressions of adult hostility which leave permanent emotional scars on children's personalities. What these theorists conveniently choose to ignore, however, is the fact that is impossible for children to learn what is *not* approved and tolerated simply by generalizing in reverse from the approval they receive for behavior that *is* acceptable. Merely by rewarding honesty and good manners one cannot, for example, teach children that dishonesty and rudeness are socially unacceptable traits. Even adults are manifestly incapable of learning and respecting the limits of acceptable conduct unless the distinction between what is proscribed and approved is reinforced by punishment as well as by reward. Furthermore, there is good reason to believe that acknowledgment of wrong-doing and acceptance of punishment are part and parcel of learning moral accountability and developing a sound conscience. Few if any children are quite so fragile that they cannot take deserved reproof and punishment in stride.

A second widespread distortion of democratic discipline is reflected in the popular notion that there are no culpably misbehaving children in the classroom, but only culpably aggressive, unsympathetic, and punitive teachers. If children misbehave, according to this point of view, one can implicitly assume that they must have been provoked beyond endurance by repressive and authoritarian classroom discipline. Similarly, if they are disrespectful, then the teacher, by definition, must not have been deserving of respect. It is true, of course, that some pupil misconduct *is* instigated by harsh and abusive school discipline; but there are also innumerable reasons for out-of-bounds behavior that are completely independent of the teacher's attitudes and disciplinary practices. Pupils are also influenced by factors originating in the home, the neighborhood, the peer group, and the mass media. Some children are emotionally disturbed, others are brain-damaged, and still others are aggressive by temperament; and there are times when even the best-behaved children from the nicest homes develop an irresistible impulse—without any provocation whatsoever—to test the limits of a teacher's forbearance.

Both of the aforementioned distortions of classroom democracy are used to justify the commonly held belief among educators that pupils should not be reproved or punished for disorderly or discourteous conduct. I have, for example, observed classrooms where everybody talks at once; where pupils turn their backs on the teacher and engage in private conversation while the latter is endeavoring to instruct them; and where pupils verbally abuse teachers for exercising their rightful disciplinary prerogatives. Some educators contend that all of this is compatible with wholesome, democratic teacher-pupil relationships. Other educators deplore this type of pupil behavior but insist, nevertheless, that punishment is unwarranted under these circumstances. In the first place, they assert, reproof or punishment constitutes a "negative" and hence axiomatically undesirable approach to classroom management; and, second, the misbehavior would assuredly have never occurred to begin with if the teacher's attitudes had been less autocratic or antagonistic. I have already answered the second group of educators, and to the first group I can only say that I am still sufficiently old-fashioned to believe that rudeness and unruliness are not normally desirable classroom behavior in any culture.

When such misconduct occurs, I believe pupils have to be unambiguously informed that it will not be tolerated and that any repetition of the same behavior will be punished. This action does not preclude in any way either an earnest attempt to discover why the misbehavior occurred or suitable preventive measures aimed at correcting the underlying causes. But, by the same token, the mere fact that a pupil has a valid psychological reason for misbehaving does not mean that he is thereby absolved from moral accountability or rendered no longer subject to punishment.

Still another related distortion of democratic discipline is reflected in the proposition that it is repressive and authoritarian to request pupils to apologize for discourteous behavior or offensive language. However, if we take seriously the idea that the dignity of the human being is important, we must be willing to protect it from affront; and apology is the most civilized and effective means mankind has yet evolved for accomplishing this goal. In a democratic society nobody is so important that he is above apologizing to those persons whom he wrongfully offends. Everybody's dignity is important—the teacher's as well as the pupil's. It is no less wrong for a pupil to abuse a teacher than for a teacher to abuse a pupil.

If apologies are to have any real significance in moral training, however, it is obvious that, even though they are explicitly requested, they must be made voluntarily; and they must be reflective of genuine appreciation of wrong-doing and of sincere regret and remorse. Purely formal and mechanical statements of apology made under coercion are less than worthless. Apologies are also without real ethical import unless their basis is reciprocal, that is, unless it is fully understood that under comparable circumstances the teacher would be willing to apologize to his pupils.

A final distortion of democratic classroom discipline associated with the extreme child-centered approach to education is the notion that children are equipped in some mysterious fashion for knowing precisely what is best for them. "Scientific proof" of this proposition is adduced from the fact that nutrition is adequately maintained and existing deficiency conditions are spontaneously corrected when infants are permitted to select their own diet. If the child can successfully choose his diet, runs the argument, he must certainly know what is best for him in *all* areas, including curriculum and classroom management.

This doctrine, however, has even less face validity than the three other distorted concepts of school discipline. Because the human being is sensitive in early childhood to internal cues of physiological needs, we cannot conclude that he is similarly sensitive to complex intellectual and moral needs, or that he has sufficient experience, perspective, and judgment to make intelligent decisions in these latter areas. Even in the field of nutrition, self-selection is a reliable criterion of need only during early infancy. The current interests and opinions of immature pupils can hardly be considered reliable guideposts and adequate substitutes for seasoned judgment in designing a curriculum or in formulating rules of classroom behavior. Hence, while it is reasonable to consider the views of pupils in these matters, teachers and school administrators cannot abdicate their responsibility for making the final decisions.

WHAT NEEDS TO BE DONE

In seeking to correct these undesirable permissive distortions of classroom democracy, it would be foolhardy to return to the equally undesirable opposite extreme of authoritarianism that flourished in this country up to a quarter of a century ago, and still prevails in many Western nations. Democratic school discipline is still an appropriate and realistic goal for American education; hence there is no need to throw away the baby with the bath water. It is only necessary to discard the aforementioned permissivist doctrines masquerading under the banners of democracy and behavioral science, and to restore certain other traditional American values that have been neglected in the enthusiasm of extending democracy to home and school.

More specifically, we first have to clear up the semantic confusion. We should stop equating permissiveness with democratic discipline, and realistic adult control and guidance with authoritarianism. Permissiveness, by definition, is the absence of discipline, democratic or otherwise. We should cease instructing teachers that it is repressive and reactionary to reprove or punish pupils for misconduct, or to request them to apologize for offensive and discourteous behavior.

Second, we should stop misinterpreting what little reputable evidence we have about discipline, and refrain from misrepresenting our personal biases on the subject as the indisputably established findings of scientific research. The available evidence merely suggests that, in our type of cultural setting, authoritarian discipline has certain undesirable effects—*not* that the consequences of *laissez-faire* permissiveness are desirable. As a matter of fact, research studies show that the effects of extreme permissiveness are just as unwholesome as are those of authoritarianism. In the school situation a *laissez-faire* policy leads to confusion, insecurity, and competition for power among pupils. Assertive pupils tend to become aggressive and ruthless, whereas retiring pupils tend to withdraw further from classroom participation. The child who is handled too permissively at home tends to regard himself as a specially privileged person. He fails to learn the normative standards and expectations of society, to set realistic goals for himself, or to make reasonable demands on others. In his dealings with adults and other children he is domineering, aggressive, petulant, and capricious.

Third, we should stop making teachers feel guilty and personally responsible for all instances of misconduct and disrespect in the classroom. We do this whenever we take for granted, without any actual supporting evidence, that these behavior problems would never have arisen in the first place if the teachers involved were truly deserving of respect and had been administering genuinely wholesome and democratic discipline.

Finally, teachers colleges should terminate the prevailing conspiracy of silence they maintain about the existence of disciplinary problems in the public schools. Although discipline is the one aspect of teaching that the beginning teacher is most worried about, he receives little or no practical instruction in handling this problem. Colleges of education, as already pointed out, rationalize their inadequacies in this regard by pretending that disciplinary problems are relatively rare occurrences involving the disturbed child, or more typically the disturbed teacher. Due respect for the facts of life, however, suggests that prospective teachers today not only need to be taught more realistic propositions about the nature and purposes of democratic discipline, but also require adequately supervised, down-to-earth experience in coping with classroom discipline.

17 *The Teacher in a World of Increasing Impersonal Relations*

James Conner

One day I went into a kindergarten room and there I watched a blooming Rembrandt go about the arduous task of painting her masterpiece, which in this case resembled many pictures one can see in museums today. Being a curious person, but informed of the way in which one should approach these matters, I asked not what the picture was but gave the artist an opportunity to tell me about this ambiguous red blob which was tacked to the easel. Scarcely missing a stroke, the young lady said, with some impatience, "It's a turkey, and tomorrow I'm going to put the skin on it."

I hope the understructure I shall try to fashion will not be as formless and ambiguous as the red blob in the painting. Also, it is not my purpose to put the "skin" on the subject of impersonality. It should be noted at the outset, however, that the world of impersonality is not off in some obscure place—in some Wagnerian twilight world—but impersonality is something that has to do with all of us in very personal ways.

EDUCATION IN RAPID TRANSITION

Since Sputnik I, education has been in a state of rapid change. The single most important outcropping of this hysterical period, however, was in the form of an admission that education is important to our national survival. This admission was spelled out not just in high-flown phrases but in legislative action. Never before had education been given such a high priority.

For the third time in our history, the federal government equated education with national survival but this time there was a difference; whereas with the advent of World Wars I and II there was concern for mass literacy, the concern during the post-Sputnik period was for scientific and mathematical literacy. Consequently the federal government under the National Defense Education Act poured millions and still is pour-

174

ing millions into the public schools to promote the improvement of science teaching and facilities. Teachers, conscientious as they were, were indeed illiterate scientifically. They were inundated with a good amount of apparatus that they could not use. Consequently much of it sat on shelves and gathered dust.

But out of the mad running of the mazes, reason emerged. The "crash program" philosophy was abandoned to some extent and intelligent people sat down to work. At Yale, Illinois, and the University of Maryland, groups began to construct a mathematics program that emphasized mathematical understanding and concepts and deemphasized social arithmetic; names such as Skinner and Pressey were again heard as people ardently expounded the virtues of the teaching machine; foreign languages were being taught in the early elementary grades; first-grade children were being exposed to geometry; and people were beginning to admit that perhaps a child can learn to read before the golden age of six mental years; a man at Yale with the first and middle name of Omar Khayyam, respectively, was teaching preschool children to read through the use of a special typewriter; largely through the encouragement of the Ford Foundation's Fund for the Advancement of Education, all kinds of experiments in groupings were undertaken.

Team teaching, which is more than forty years old, was given new respectability; platooning of children as low as the first grade was undertaken; large-class instruction was said to be more efficient in many instances than that of small classes; individualized reading, the Joplin Plan, the Newcastle Plan, the economy method, and the Gillingham Method of reading were all tried; the school board in a small Wisconsin community urged to return to the McGuffey Reader; all over the country, harried fathers were working on projects for science fairs; high over the farmlands of Ohio an airplane circled transmitting signals to television sets in hundreds of classrooms in five states; an admiral with a penchant for atomic submarines stated that Swiss education was far superior to that offered by the American public school; typewriting was taught in first grade; in a few scattered places teachers began to teach English as though it had a relationship to oral language; everybody began to talk about creativity; Massachusetts Institute of Technology and later Educational Services, Inc., began to work on programs concerned with the science education of young children; and a man at Harvard by the name of Bruner wrote a book that will be quoted at educational meetings for many years to come.

The preceding is but a sample of changes that have gone on within a few short years. There seems little chance that this intellectual agitation will abate. Change will be an accepted condition of life. Not only can you not stick your foot in the same river twice, but, as some sage pointed out, you can't stick the same foot in the same river twice. It would appear that there is no chance that we shall in the foreseeable future return to the relatively slow pace of several years ago—the good ol' days. Yet it seems urgent that amid the frantic activity we find solace.

IMPERSONAL FACTORS IN THE SCHOOL

The problems of impersonality have been treated by many writers. Fromm (1956) refers to man's aloneness, his separateness, his alienation from the human enterprise. He speaks of his exploitation and treatment as a product rather than a person (1947, 1955). More recently Whyte in *Organization Man* (1956) wrote of man in our industrial democratic society as seeking the warm, comforting womb of conformity.

The world of impersonality is a world of machines. In our democratic, technological, industrial society, unskilled and semiskilled man is being phased out. He is slowly and inexorably being replaced by more efficient and impersonal machines. A high official of the AFL-CIO told me of a plant that had employed scores of semiskilled men. This plant, which makes engine blocks, was now manned by one person sitting at a console. His job mainly consisted of keeping his eyes on dials and indicators. As soon as the machine had served a certain number of hours, a button pushed, the machine moved out of the production room automatically on tracks and a new machine moved in to take its place. All this was accomplished in a period of a very few minutes.

Certainly I do not pretend to grasp the full import of the writings of the social scientists—nor is it my task to do so. It is my objective to touch on some of the factors and conditions that operate in the impersonal lesser world of the school. What are some of the things that the school does and has done which create impersonal relations?

The first point I would like to discuss is the normalizing of children. We not only normalize them according to age and sex but by grades as well. We normalize children by regions and sometimes by race. This normalization of children leads to the expectancy of how children should think, speak, feel, and act according to the standards of their grade, or age, and so on. The norms more often than not (taken as a quantitative index of absolute accuracy) dictate to the teacher just how much Johnny can absorb. It is true that all teachers are not guided by the determinism of norms, but it is equally true that there are teachers who, acting on the basis of test scores, classify children as potential successes or failures before there is any involvement with them. I know of one case in which a fifth-grade teacher arranged her seating by I.Q.'s.

Sometimes the business of I.Q.'s takes on a comic aspect. I shall never forget a teacher I supervised who taught retarded children. The class I.Q. range was from 35 to 65. During the course of discussing her pupils she waxed enthusiastic about Johnny. "Oh," she said, "Johnny is bright; he has an I.Q. of 60."

One of the causal factors of increasing impersonal relations is the uprooting of children from their homes. The amount of mobility in this country is astronomical. Most teachers do not need to be told the extent of this problem. Results of this national game of musical chairs are incalculable. It is a fact that every twenty-four hours approximately 76,000 people in New York City move. Many children are "lost" as far as school officials are concerned. We can appreciate the mobility of population if we realize that 24 per cent of college graduates move each year—some several times.

All these migrations place considerable strain on children; they must adjust to a new world of age peers and to new and different people; they may move out of a society of understanding relatives to a world of impersonal adults. All of the moves and shifts may result after a while in a hardening of their psychic arteries. Impersonality under these conditions may serve as a kind of protection against affective amputation. The mobility may result in what Fromm calls "emotional bleeding." There is, however, another possible consequence of this mobility. The child may learn the surface ritual for induction into a group but such a child may need "radar" to pick up the proper signals. In his repeated attempts at adjustment to various groups, it should not be surprising that he develops conformist behavior.

But of all the migrants it is the young child who may need the tenderest care. The warm, sympathetic adult who is the teacher or the principal becomes a pivotal person in the intricate ritual of inducting the newly arrived child into the school society. I must say that my heart has been warmed more than once by the sensitive handling of new arrivals by both teachers and children. On the other hand, I have been shocked by situations in which a tactless teacher complained because she had to put an additional desk in her classroom.

What of the child who is entering the new world of the school? Although the child entering school at 5 or 6 must relinquish the close affectional relationship with his mother, he can do this without damage if he can replace it with a warm friendly relationship to a respected adult who will respect him, treat him with the dignity to which he aspires, and enable him to accept a less personalized relation of pupil to teacher and nonsibling peers. Because the school may be the child's first experience with impersonality, it is possible that a school not attuned to his needs may develop in him patterned ways of dealing with the nonpersonal world he senses by adopting a repressive impersonality that may easily become a life-long mode of behaving toward others.

We add to the atmosphere of impersonality in the schools by limiting the transaction between pupils. Instead of encouraging interpersonal relations, we construct situations which isolate children into separate units within the classroom, forbidding talking or collaboration. Because our system is founded on the competition of grades, the child is expected to refrain from talking or seeking information from others because this is construed as cheating. It is a sad fact that thousands of children are incarcerated in classroom cells and encapsulated within the unseen barriers that surround their desks. Children, instead of learning from interaction with their peers or (even in this day of automated learning) from their teachers, are asked to serve in the capacity of digital computers giving back bits of inert material. For knowledge has been seen too often as not something that may give satisfaction to the learner but may contribute to his worth as a commodity.

Make no mistake about it—many children upon entering school have entered the market place. I do not want to give the impression that the school is anything but an agent of the larger society that surrounds it. But man or children as a commodity—children who are norm-confined— are being alienated from themselves and from mediating human influences. Those living in a market economy where they are commodities rather than persons may find, as Fromm notes, that:

... his self-esteem depends on conditions beyond his control. If he is "successful," he is valuable; if he is not, he is worthless. The degree of insecurity which results from this orientation can hardly be overestimated. If one feels that one's value is not constituted primarily by the human qualities one possesses, but one's success on a competitive market with ever-changing conditions, one's self esteem is bound to be shaky and in constant need of confirmation by others (1947).

The human condition that Fromm describes is noted by Riesman (1953) in *The Lonely Crowd* and by Whyte (1956) in *Organization Man*. More recently Friedenberg (1960) commented on the effect on the high school of the adolescent.

... In this respect, the high school has been getting worse for years, for society has. It has always devoted itself to the interests of uniformity more than to individuality; but the uniformities used to be more external than they are now. ... The school today is less a stewpot than a blender. What comes out, when it is functioning effectively, is not merely uniform but bland and creamy; by its very nature inimical to clarity, yet retaining in a form difficult to detect all the hostile or toxic ingredients present in the original mixture (Friedenberg, 1960).

Certainly not a pretty picture!

Now we have the teaching machine. Although this is admittedly an impersonal instructional device, it is perhaps no more so than the textbook or seatwork. In fact, the teaching machine if properly used might well free the teacher for more "interactional" teaching. It is not the teaching machine that is impersonal, unless we contrive situations in which we demand more and more digital learning from the student and less *holistic* learning and interactional learning.

If we adopt the fallacy that facts are more important than process then our instruction cannot help but become more and more impersonal. Paul Torrance tells the story of the dean of education at the University of Minnesota who taunts his staff by telling them that half of what they teach is not true. "Now if we but knew which half." At this point I would like to relate the story of a second-grade teacher whom I shall identify as Mrs. X. This story goes back to the time when I was a principal of an elementary school. One day at about two minutes of nine, Mrs. X approached me and stated in a dead-pan voice, "I can't teach today." Now it should be pointed out that Mrs. X had a dead-pan face to go with the voice. I was quite upset that she had waited to the last minute to tell me of her misfortune, whatever it was. "Are you sick?" I asked. "No," she said, "the ditto machine broke down."

The next point of consideration is that of grouping. There are some indications that considerations of grouping may be based more on concern for mastery of subject matter than for interpersonal relations. Such grouping as platooning where mass movements of students take place with the ringing of bells is an example. To my knowledge this practice has extended down as low as first grade. It is likely that the teacher who is faced with shifts of children will not know their names but will remember them only in a topological sense. H. Gerthon Morgan, Director of the Institute for Child Study at the University of Maryland, tells of visiting a class where the teacher was carrying on a recitation. Calling on one student, the teacher said, "The student in the third row, second from left." It may be that certain kinds of large-class grouping will not be nonpersonal, but it is worth noting that it is impossible for a teacher to relate to more than a certain number of students in a significant way.

I do not want to appear negative to all the current attempts at grouping students. The increasing number of nongraded schools is a favorable omen. I have seen very good team-teaching situations that provided excellent individualization of students. I visited one junior high school in Michigan which must be one of the most orderly places in the country. The students were not subdued; in fact, there was considerable social exchange among them. When the classes changed I did not find it necessary to find a bomb shelter. Youngsters walked down the halls in two's and three's, conversing as they went. There were no monitors providing supervision and control. In the classrooms I visited I observed youngsters sitting in desks that formed a rectangle around the room. Here too they seemed to be comfortable and assured.

After my visit around the school I sat down with the principal who was a warm, accepting person. I expressed my astonishment and asked how he had done it. I was not prepared for his answer. He stated, "We group by sizes." I could not help but feel I was the victim of a practical joke and expressed my doubt as to the causal factor of his extraordinarily tranquil school. He invited me to go back for a second look, which I did. There was no doubt—they were indeed grouped by sizes. I do not quite know what the point of this is, but I suspect it is that the principal and teachers in this school, although appearing to use a highly impersonal index for grouping, were motivated by their personal concern for these children.

Many years ago most teachers lived in the community in which they taught; today a teacher living in his or her school neighborhood is the exception. The teacher may have no involvement in the community in which the school is located. Like the itinerant preacher, the teacher comes into the community and leaves. He is probably uninvolved in its civic and political affairs. Because in many cases he must commute long distances he may leave as soon as the bell rings. The children are dispensed with and drift off home where more than likely no parents are waiting.

The teacher labors under an additional handicap because he knows little about Johnny's life space, his affectional relationships, the family constellation. He rarely visits the home to talk to the parents and see the place where Johnny spends most of his hours. If a home visit is made, you may be sure that Johnny is in trouble and that the home visit is made by the pupil personnel worker—a specialist in such problems.

The world of the teacher and the student have become highly depersonalized; the student has been considered a product rather than a person and has been accepted only if he is successful; very often the routinizing of school experiences and the rigidity of school programs has created conditions of impersonality; the anonymous authority of the board of education and that of the curriculum makers bears down on teachers and students alike; the use of tests for improper purposes has had a deleterious effect on students; and last, the frequent migrations of families has added to the problem of impersonality.

PROSPECTS FOR PROGRESS

Perhaps the previous remarks might lend credence to despair but this has not been my intent. Indeed there appear to be many important things that may be done to render the classroom effective and stimulate the positive mental health of students. I humbly submit the following:

1. The teacher has a real opportunity to become the most significant adult outside the child's family. He should be for the child a model of maturity. Equally important the teacher should realize just how important he is to the healthy growth of the child.
2. We need to give careful attention to the migratory child—how we will induct him into the new school society.
3. We need to reappraise our ideas on teaching and learning and make provision for more interaction among students in the classroom. We should consider the cooperation a desired goal, and should provide the opportunity for students to assist and collaborate but also to disagree if such seems inevitable.
4. The schools should do all they can to involve parents and people in the community in its programs.
5. Instead of relying so heavily on standardized tests, the school should begin to look at the unique learning styles of children. Admittedly this is a virgin field but as soon as we accept the highly idiosyncratic learning styles of children we shall be well on the way to accepting them as individuals. It would be helpful if the school in general, and the teacher in particular, could make provision for the formulation of a *strategy for success*. This would necessitate an understanding of each child's unique way of learning. Perhaps what we need in education is the concept of quality control. Such a concept would force us to go back and review the educational processes that contributed to the child's growth or lack of growth.
6. This was not mentioned in the body of this chapter, but large school systems should decentralize. Teachers who have to go through bureaucratic mazes to get things done cannot but feel isolated in their rooms. Breaking down large administrative structures into smaller units should provide better communication within the education hierarchy.
7. The classroom teacher must be given more sanctions that will allow him to use more judgment than he is now allowed.

In conclusion, let me note that impersonal is not what other people are. It is what we are, what the world has become!

18 Mental-Health Implications for Teachers

Dana L. Farnsworth

Mental health has been talked about so much in recent years that in some quarters it has almost become a topic of derision. Movements for its promotion have such diverse aims that they have become overloaded with persons who mean well and with programs of desirable but vague generalities. Rigorous scientific thinking in the development of such programs has not always been evident, but no one seems to regret having mental health even if he does not know how to define it or how he got that way.

SOME FACTS

A major effort in gathering much-needed facts concerning the extent and results of emotional distress has been under way since 1956, under the direction of the Joint Commission on Mental Illness and Health. This study, sponsored by numerous private organizations and financed largely by the Congress of the United States, has resulted in several volumes of reports (eleven in all, when completed) that are of immense value to everyone and particularly to teachers. In the volume on *Community Resources in Mental Health* (Robinson, de Marche, and Wagle, 1960), some idea of the challenge posed for education is disclosed in these facts: In nearly half the 3103 counties in the United States, no public funds are available for persons in dire distress. Very few communities make even minimal provision for needy nonresidents and transients. Some communities, notably in New England, still publish paupers' lists. Treatment in many sections is "primitive and calculated to damage instead of help" these people. Two million children in America not only are financially destitute but also have experienced family disruption, conflict, and emotional deprivation. Attention is too often focused not on the needs of the

Reprinted from *Teachers College Record*, 62, No. 4, January 1961.

children, but on the moral behavior of their mother. In 1958, 6,400,000 children were living with only one parent, another 1,100,000 with other relatives, and about 400,000 in institutions, foster homes, or with other unrelated persons. Thirty-seven per cent of the nation's counties have no child-welfare services of any sort, and 49 per cent have no public child-welfare services. About 60 per cent of the children in foster homes are emotionally disturbed. Thirty per cent of all mothers with children under 18 were working outside the home in 1958. Many welfare agencies force the mother to work, giving little thought to the effect on the personality and emotional development of the children when the mother is out of the home (Robinson, de Marche, and Wagle, 1960).

From other sources we learn that, among the young men and women attending our colleges and universities, emotional disorders are widely prevalent. The commonly accepted estimate that 10 per cent of all college students can be expected to have emotional conflicts of serious proportions each year has not been seriously challenged, some observers even believing the estimate to be too low (Farnsworth, 1959; Group for the Advancement of Psychiatry, 1959).

CULTURAL CONSIDERATIONS

The idea that emotional disturbances, tension, anxiety, and restlessness are products of Western industrial civilization is widely entertained. Those who hold this view are prone to think of primitive people as being happy and serene, living a plain, simple, happy, and healthy life with few of the complications that are so prevalent in more advanced societies. Many studies of the habits and customs of other cultures reveal that mental illness is a problem everywhere, though not all countries and regions treat the problems with similar basic preconceptions. If the authorities who compile statistics in a particular country are not familiar with the causes of emotional illness or the determinants of mental health, or do not think in those terms, the incidence of emotional problems may appear very low. But such anthologies as those of Opler (1959), Mead (1955), and Soddy (1956), furnish abundant evidence that emotional problems are universal, even though expressed in an infinite variety of ways, depending on social customs and cultural patterns.

Fereidoun Esfandiary, an Iranian social scientist, has described (1957) with skill and convincing logic the basic threats to the mental health of men and women who live in what we now call "underdeveloped" countries.

Terror fills the hearts of all those who live in the lingering shadows of past centuries. The native of most backward countries goes through life in the constant grip of fear, afraid of the elements, afraid of the knife that might strike back in the darkness, afraid of the darkness itself, afraid of neighbors, afraid of foreigners whom he cannot understand and, therefore, cannot trust—afraid of the real threats and afraid of imaginary threats.

Esfandiary sees a close connection between the unchecked emotional illnesses and harmful social pressures of Asia and Africa and the amount of violence there, an observation amply justified by events since he made this statement.

Similarly, observers in India and in Japan have recently described how profoundly students in those countries are affected by the dislocations caused by excessively rapid social changes with the resulting destruction of the usual stabilizing influences. The past is discredited and the future filled with uncertainties. Poverty is crushing. Much tolerance and understanding will be needed in the nations of the Western world if students in these countries are not to be led into some form of an authoritarian social system, even Communism (Grimes, 1960; Rockefeller, 1960), in the hope of easing intense emotional pressures consequent on cultural change.

A recent international conference on the mental health of college students (Funkenstein, 1959) reported that students everywhere have severe emotional problems. For example, in the Philippines far more students go to college and become theoretically qualified for various professions than there are positions available for them. Thus large numbers of people are trained to be teachers or lawyers but must earn a living by manual or unskilled labor. These unfulfilled people constitute a large reservoir of unrest and dissatisfaction.

SOME DEFINING IDEAS

If we are to think lucidly about the relationship of the educational process to mental health, it is necessary that we be clear as to what is meant by the term. I think of it as the state of mind in which one is able to carry on his private life and his work without crippling anxiety or other disabling manifestations of emotional conflict. But that is not enough. A robber or murderer may have mental health by this criterion. The element of value must also enter the definition. Mental health entails freedom with responsibility, flexibility, self-reliance, and a genuine concern for the common welfare. It is *not* freedom from anxiety and tension, *not* freedom from dissatisfaction, *not* conformity or constant happiness or a lessening of accomplishment and creativity or the absence of personal idiosyncrasies. Furthermore, it does *not* imply the undermining of authority, nor is it in any way opposed to religious values.

Some persons become uneasy about mental-health promotion when they find evidences of concern for morals and other value judgments in many of the programs put forward. In view of the confused state of most people about the meaning and purpose of their lives, this objection might well be a recommendation unless one group tried to force its ideas on another. Mental health and democracy are peculiarly compatible.

Any teacher who reflects on the behavior and background of students in his class who are apparently handicapped by emotional problems will almost invariably find them behaving overtly in very diverse ways. They may work too hard, or they may be unable to work at all. They may be exceedingly tense and irritable, or they may be disinterested and apathetic. They may be very aggressive and make a nuisance of themselves to others, or they may be exceedingly shy and sensitive. They may act out their feelings by being argumentative, destructive, and completely lacking in concern for the rights of other people, or they may be so precise and careful as to appear to be model children. In fact, psychiatrists and clinical psychologists are often more concerned about the excessively proper youngster than about one who expresses his feelings in more direct ways. For some young people, the indices of discontent may be various forms of dishonesty, difficulty in speech, reading, or spelling, or undue concern for their own physical condition. A teacher may be rightly concerned whenever the behavior of one of his students does not "make sense" to him, to the student himself, or to the student's parents. The focus of concern is not the form of the symptom but the *meaning* of the behavior exhibited by the student.

It should not be the function of the school to take over the responsibility of the family or of the church. But when personality factors interfere with the educational process, it is reasonable to expect that the school should become professionally concerned. This would not be practical unless teachers themselves had some knowledge of and were serious students of personality development and of the elements that are most desirable in the maintenance of good interpersonal relations.

If teachers are to advance their own knowledge of the personality characteristics of their pupils, some reliable frame of reference is certainly desirable. The study of personality is beset with enormous difficulties. Definitions are seemingly without limit; Allport's (1937) famous work on the subject gives us fifty to start with. A common approach that is both profound and simple is urgently needed. It should be one that merits the respect of scholars in the field and at the same time can be understood by those who are not specialists. The most fruitful work toward this end that has been done so far is that of Erikson (1950, 1959, 1960).

In briefest outline, Erikson views the developing person as going through a sequence of stages in which certain key problems have to be resolved successfully for subsequent development to proceed in an optimum fashion. These stages, eight in all, include the development from birth onward of a proper balance between trust and mistrust, autonomy and doubt and shame, initiative and guilt, industry and inferiority, identity and identity diffusion, intimacy and isolation, generativity and self-absorption, and finally, integrity and disgust. Of all these stages, the attainment of an appropriate sense of trust is probably of greatest importance in developing the proper balance in all the succeeding crises in the life cycle. To teachers and others interested in high-school and college students, the attainment of identity is of particular interest and relevance.

ROLE OF THE TEACHER

When teachers are reasonably aware of the factors that promote or impede mental health in their students, then each student is considered individually as far as is practicable, and his background is thought of as relevant to his present behavior. When things do not go well for him, the reasons underlying his difficulties are sought. This is not done to find excuses for his shortcomings but to plan effective ways of furthering his growth. The teacher who is aware that one of his students is encountering unusual problems seeks such information by opening his mind to all the possibilities that may be present, but particularly he listens to what the student wishes to tell him. The teacher is the first line of defense, the person who is in a position to note attitudinal changes, discouragement, depression, "acting out," or any other behavior that signifies a possible request for help.

But the teacher should not attempt to be a therapist. His primary purpose is to teach, to encourage the student to use his mind in the most effective way possible, hopefully with enjoyment. He deals with his students in educational terms, thinking of their total growth and development. He should scrupulously avoid interpretations of possible unconscious motives. Although good teaching and an understanding of the personality of students may well aid in resolving emotional conflicts, the teacher is not primarily concerned with psychopathology. Competent professionals, psychologists and psychiatrists, should be brought in when psychotherapy seems desirable.

A crucial question concerns how a teacher may become an ego ideal or appropriate role model for his students. A number of issues are involved here. It is not proper to expect the teacher to be perfect. He is a human being like anyone else. Neither is it desirable for his private life to be extinguished in order that his public life may appear blameless. What is desirable is that students see in their teachers adults who are alive and zestful, enjoying their work, enthusiastic, and exhibiting sincere signs of commitment to the intellectual life in which they are engaged. Young people may then feel that there is meaning in what they are doing and may be stimulated to strike out in similar directions. The potential worth of the teacher as a model, as an admirable human being with whom his students can profitably identify, is hard to overestimate.

With presently available resources, there seems to be no chance whatever that an appreciable percentage of those who are emotionally disturbed can be helped by individual attention from psychotherapists. The number of psychiatrists, psychologists, social workers, and specialized counselors available is inconsequential in relation to the need in both the underdeveloped countries and those with high material standards of living. However valuable psychotherapy may be in instances of acute individual need, it is certainly uneconomical and may not be the best method of approach on intrinsic grounds. Some institutional line of attack is needed.

If the basic problems of promoting and maintaining mental health are considered relevant to the educational process, some methods should be devised whereby all teachers may become aware of their nature. Opportunities should be opened up for continual development of skill in dealing with them. An in-service training program, well organized but of modest proportions, is essential in every school system.

One reasonable approach for a single institution or school system is to select some teacher in the organization who has been notably successful and vitally interested in the behavior and attitudes of students, who would be both willing and eager to make himself informed in the broad area of the emotions and their influences on education. At present, it would not be easy to get special training in this field but it is possible. Such a teacher might go to a school of education which has strong courses in counseling: he might spend some time in a counseling center, or he might divide his time between independent study of the literature and visits to departments of education, counseling, or student health in various institutions to observe the nature of their problems and how they are handling them.

As such a teacher becomes more and more interested and skilled in the utilization of mental-health resources, he should be quite careful not to lose his identity as a teacher. Some persons believe we should develop specialists in mental-health education, a wholly new and separate profession. I believe we would be wiser to insist that every person who indulges in extensive mental-health education should first have a basic orientation in one or more of the traditional subject-matter areas. Whether that be English, mathematics, modern languages, psychology, or fine arts does not particularly matter. What is important is that mental-health promotion should be considered a means to an end, not an end in itself. The desired result, so far as our schools are concerned, is the development of boys and girls, young men and women, who can use their minds well and responsibly and who take pleasure and realize significance in what they are doing.

INFORMATION SOURCE

What should be the focus of interest of a teacher endeavoring to become the disseminator of constructive mental-health principles in his institution or school system? Of necessity, tentative answers to this question must be quite general and partly philosophical in nature. At the same time, it is apparent that much valid information of great potential value to teachers and administrators is not used or even appreciated. We need to devise methods of using effectively what is already known about intellectual development as urgently as we need research to advance our knowledge.

Many of our ideas of human behavior come from well-designed experiments and observations by psychologists, more recently by anthropologists and sociologists. Another rich source is the study of abnormal behavior or psychopathology. At first glance this type of knowledge may seem to be of small relevance to educators, but recent experiences of psychiatrists and other clinicians in our schools and colleges suggest that it may be of immense importance. For example, those who try to help the students handicapped by emotional conflict are impressed with the frequency of disturbances in the relations of such youngsters with their parents or with those whose love and esteem they value most. These disturbances do not appear to be inevitable; they result in part from a lack of parental awareness of the essential conditions for the development of strong, independent, and responsible personalities in their children. A moot question is whether or not the quality of child-rearing practices and family life can be improved by educational procedures. Brim's recent study (1959) indicates that there is as yet no proof that it can be done. Studies by Sheldon and Eleanor Glueck (1959) strongly suggest, however, that obviously faulty attitudes and practices of parents are of crucial importance in steeling children toward delinquent behavior.

There is urgent need for a combination of experimental and clinical types of information about personality and character formation, followed by elaboration of new methods in the presentation of subject matter that will help more of our young people to confront their problems constructively and positively. It seems likely that many emotional conflicts of this sort can be resolved by the timely efforts of sensitive, intuitive teachers, using appropriate pedagogical techniques, at times with the background aid of psychiatrists and psychologists. We are handicapped in the achievement of such goals not so much by our lack of knowledge and what is necessary for the attainment of these ideals, but rather by our inability to disseminate and apply what we already know.

A third source of information is studies of the development of personality. A child who is brought up under circumstances in which his basic needs are met is in a much better position to learn effectively than is one torn by anxiety, conflict, and experienced inconsistency. Every child needs love and affection, the feeling of belonging and being wanted, respect as a separate person, and proper standards of behavior to emulate. He also needs room to move about and to experiment with his emerging abilities. He needs firm discipline from a respected source, but he should be free from excessive domination. Throughout his early developmental years, there should be a thread of consistency, enabling him to predict what kinds of consequences his behavior will evoke in others and to learn standards of appropriateness.

PROFESSIONAL CONSULTATION

Psychiatrists who work with college students are constantly concerned with the question of how to make their services most helpful in furthering the educational aims of their institutions (Blaine and MacArthur, 1961; Group for the Advancement of Psychiatry, 1955, 1957). They are sure they have learned much from their student patients about the influences that encourage or inhibit learning, but as yet this knowledge has not been well organized or expressed in general principles.

From my own experience, it seems obvious that any student can learn rapidly and with satisfaction if (1) he has a good mind, (2) if he sees those about him whom he admires as clearly gaining satisfaction and pleasure from their intellectual activity, (3) if a high quality of school work brings him rewards in the form of esteem and prestige, and (4) if he has the stimulus of association with other persons with good minds with whom he can exchange ideas. But these positive factors may not be enough. All these influences may be neutralized by anti-intellectual influences in the community, often mediated by the mass media of communication, or the student may be paralyzed by severe emotional conflict.

There is a general consensus among educational psychiatrists that the brief treatment of dissatisfied, unhappy, and ineffective students is desirable in a school or college setting. Most of them agree that extensive or definitive psychotherapy should not be the responsibility of any educational institution. Unfortunately, in most institutions even minimum treatment is neither practicable nor possible. It is not realistic to expect all schools and colleges to have psychiatrists on their staffs. There are simply not enough to go around. We should look, therefore, for the most effective way of making use of the professional knowledge of those we do have. Instead of spending all their time consulting with unhappy and ineffective students, psychiatrists and clinical psychologists can greatly enlarge their sphere of usefulness by working with teachers and counselors, aiding them to understand the factors preventing their students from working effectively.

There are many aspects of teaching and learning in which the mutual collaboration of educators and psychiatrists or psychologists can be helpful. For example, if the quality of the early years in the family are of crucial importance in determining a child's ability to cope successfully with problems of growth and development, it follows that one of the marks of the educated person is his understanding of these human-growth dynamics. Such an awareness of those factors promoting strong and stable personality development is a prerequisite to sound parenthood and, hence, to our national future. With a decline in the centrality of the family, the facilitation of these responsibilities could well become the joint responsibility of the school and its professional consultants.

Again, mental-health proponents are vitally concerned with the way in which authority is exercised in schools or colleges, as well as in the community generally. Students sense the basic attitudes of principals and deans toward them very quickly and almost automatically mold their reactions accordingly. If the person in authority believes in the basic good judgment of his students or assumes that they will use good judgment if and when they are fully informed of the issues in any given situation, he is much more likely to influence them quietly and favorably than if he is abrupt, authoritarian in attitude, or sensitive about his own prerogatives. If the latter conditions prevail, students can usually find weak spots in the principal's or dean's armor, and the clever ones can readily bring about a cleavage in which the administration (and possibly the faculty) are pitted against the student body instead of the ideal situation in which administration, faculty, and responsible students are aligned against whatever forces and tendencies threaten and demean the educational community.

STANDARDS AND COMPETITION

Pressures for high standards from persons in authority will have little effect if they are constantly neutralized by pressures for mediocrity exerted by customs within student groups and by community agencies. The peer-group pressures within an educational institution may be especially powerful when tacitly supported by parental attitudes and weakened when these attitudes are aligned with faculty and administration objectives. Peer-group attitudes and pressures deserving study include those favoring or discouraging high scholastic standards, methods of showing school spirit, the prestige and influence exerted by fraternities and sororities, toleration or disapproval of commercialized athletics, and dozens of similarly sensitive issues. Likewise, techniques of maintaining order, cheating in examinations, and excessive competition for grades are fruitful subjects for collaborative study by educators, clinical workers, and behavioral scientists.

The role of competition is especially important now that admission to the college of his choice is becoming increasingly uncertain for every secondary-school student. There is a danger that the necessity of high grades may change the major emphasis from mastery of subject matter to sheer marks, with a resultant lowering of ethical standards. In many areas of public life, we see evidences that remaining within the technically legal limits of behavior is of more concern than observing moral principles and standards. From overcompetitive attitudes and a lowering of ethical standards, it is only a natural step to assume that education is chiefly a means of increasing one's earning capacity rather than an experience liberating one from the bonds of ignorance, chauvinism, bigotry and prejudice, and dull routine.

The wisest and strongest efforts of teachers, parents, and student leaders toward developing high standards of intellectual and moral excellence are continually checkmated by large segments of the productions of our mass media of communication. Incorrect English is deliberately used by advertising agencies to attract attention. Programs on radio and television often capitalize on cheap and immediate sensationalism. The dramatic headline in a newspaper gets the attention, whether correct or not. Censorship of such agencies creates more problems than it solves. A proper—even an urgent—subject for consideration in our schools is the level of taste in the surrounding community. Our schools could do much to strengthen the efforts of the encouragingly large number of editors and producers who are eager to keep their standards high. They cannot survive giving us good programs if we do not want and articulately appreciate them.

Psychiatrists and psychologists are greatly concerned with the methods by which scholastic standards are established and maintained. I believe in a system in which standards of intellectual performance and proper behavior are kept at a high level, but with a considerable degree of permissiveness as to how those standards will be attained. It is quite possible that our present procedures for enforcing them may not be ideal. Let us suppose for a moment that teachers, businessmen, and all who hold responsible jobs were checked regularly as to whether they performed their duties, given regular periodic tests to determine their progress (with careful proctoring to avoid cheating), and assigned a monthly grade to show where they stood with respect to others in similar work. I wonder whether such procedures would bring out our good qualities or if they might rather excite some of our sporting tendencies or desires to outwit the system. Just as our traffic rules, with their haphazard enforcement, may be instruments for teaching disrespect for law and order, so may some of our customs in schools be stimulants to antisocial behavior.

DISCIPLINE AND RELATIONSHIPS

Administration of discipline is another factor affecting students' attitudes in a variety of ways. Most students prefer a community in which standards of behavior are high and rules against improper behavior are rigorously enforced. The more they have to do with formulating the standards and the rules for their enforcement, the more likely they are to support them. The maintenance of the web of morality in a community calls for the assent of the great majority of the people in it. With such assent, those who indulge in behavior harmful to others or to themselves can be dealt with effectively. Without it, enforcement of order is almost impossible. Furthermore, if the guilty person senses that the institution or community is more interested in rehabilitating him than in punishing him or casting him out, discipline is likely to have added effectiveness.

There are many other aspects of life in schools and colleges in which behavioral scientists are professionally interested and on which they can be constructively consulted. The style of dormitory architecture may be quite influential in creating favorable or unfavorable conditions for work. Parietal rules in colleges or preparatory schools may be so strict as to invite violations or so liberal as literally to force young people into behavior for which they are not ready and of which they do not really approve. Fraternities and sororities may be vital forces in training for citizenship and responsibility, or they may be foci of anti-intellectual attitudes. Institutional religious practices and attitudes may be conducive to reverence and worship, or they may create attitudes of protest and disgust. The quality of faculty-student relations may depend on basic concepts of human worth and dignity held by faculty members, these being somewhat dependent on what teachers know about the developing personalities of their students. Erik Erikson says, "We ought to regard the breaking of a child's spirit—by cruel punishment, by senseless spoiling, by persistent hypocrisy—as a sin against humanity" (1960). He was referring to parents when he made this statement, but the basic point is relevant to teachers and public officials.

Psychiatrists and psychologists are interested in sharing concern with their academic colleagues about how to recognize early signs of emotional distress in children and adolescents. Stammering, reading and spelling deficiencies, behavioral symptoms of excessive rebellion, marked shyness, constant preoccupation with physical conditions, stealing, and accomplishments grossly inconsistent with known ability are among the possible indicators that all is not well in emotional development. Recognition of a covert cry for help, followed by discreet investigation into the background of the child, may enable the school to institute corrective measures quietly and unobtrusively.

To identify these possible areas for joint study by psychiatrists, psychologists, teachers, and administrators does not imply that psychiatrists or any other specialists have readily available solutions for these problems. They emphatically do not. But collaborative investigation may help to clarify situations that had not previously been understood and to suggest courses of action that can contribute to student growth.

Knowledge derived from the study of emotional conflict in students does not suggest that all that goes wrong is the fault of parents or of schools or of society generally. Neither does it indicate that students are not responsible for what they do. In our discussion of basic causes of unsatisfying and unacceptable behavior, we often appear to cast aspersions on some one group such as parents or "the school," causing feelings of guilt and self-condemnation when they are not justified. Our intent should be how to discern causes of emotional distress and to bring about its resolution, not to point a finger of scorn and disapproval toward some scapegoat. Our present knowledge indicates that we all share a portion of the responsibility for improper practices, just as we share in the credit for desirable accomplishments. Our purpose is to determine what is right or wrong rather than who has made errors.

CONSTRUCTIVE PREVENTION

It is now high time for leaders in education and the other helping professions to find ways and means of using to better effect the vast array of knowledge derived from research in the behavioral sciences to promote strong personality and character development. Much more is known than is being used. The development of preventive and constructive mental-health programs is the portion of this task that falls into the combined fields of effort of education and psychiatry. The goals of these programs include the following:

1. Helping all teachers to accomplish what a few excellent ones have always been able to do—urging students to perform at their highest level of ability and to enjoy their work.
2. Resolution of an increasing number of the problems of growth and development in children and adolescents by improved educational methods before they become so exaggerated that they require professional help from psychologists and psychiatrists.
3. Helping both teachers and students to understand themselves in such a way that their conscious control of themselves is steadily increased and their domination by primitive and unregulated emotional drives derived from unconscious sources is subsequently lessened.

A teacher who has taken a specialized interest in the mental-health aspects of education could work helpfully with his colleagues toward such objectives, using discussion groups, conferences about worrisome student cases, and outside consultations. Widespread involvement of school personnel is desirable. Free communication between all responsible persons is essential to a good in-service training program.

In our schools and colleges, mental-health education is inseparable from good education. In practice there is nothing to be gained by making an artificial separation. Knowledge of mental-health principles should be considered fundamental in the training of all teachers. Attention to them should serve not to burden still further an already overloaded curriculum, but to enable students and teachers alike to work for higher standards of academic and personal excellence.

19   The Social Worker's Role: Detection and Prevention of Dropouts

Charlotte Hayman

Today we are experiencing nationwide concern for increasing numbers of intellectually well-endowed children who encounter difficulties in academic learning and in adjustment to the school setting. By and large these students express their frustration and unhappiness through symptoms of nonattendance and eventual dropout. Until recently only slight attention was given to understanding causative factors precipitating early school termination. It is encouraging that educators presently consider dropout symptoms as breakdowns in a child's total life (Altmeyer, 1951). As a consequence the problem is one of early detection and prevention rather than crime and punishment.

Contemporary interest in the early school dropout has also produced valuable research relevant to the nonattendance syndrome. We have come to recognize that a combination of various pressures—social, parental, and familial—are usually involved both in learning blocks and behavior difficulties of youth identified as potential dropouts. Accordingly, our limited concept of nonattendance has been expanded to include those children attending school but whose performance indicates their psychological absence (Talbot, 1954). For this group, it is lack of interest and motivation that constitutes distance from the learning province. Efforts are now being made to develop techniques that might arrest, reverse, or modify some of those factors predisposing adolescents to withdraw from formal education.

As a social worker, I claim no competence to suggest methods for improving present educative processes. Experience with dropouts and their families over the years, however, has led to a conviction that increased understanding of home background will substantially enhance the school's potential for aiding such children. At this juncture it may be helpful to survey some of the information we have regarding (1) the types of homes from which dropouts come; (2) the emotional pressures and types of deprivational themes to which they are subject; and (3) some personality characteristics of dropout children.

FAMILY OF THE DROPOUT

Experience in the New York Bureau of Child Guidance reveals that similar factors prevailed in the homes of students who were either early school leavers or underachievers. The dozen most common family problems of these youngsters have been found to be:

1. psychological neglect by family;
2. psychological abuse by family;
3. family relationships unstable;
4. sibling rivalry;
5. rejection;
6. ambivalence in parental attitudes;
7. ambivalence of child toward parents;
8. broken home;
9. illness of parents;
10. parents emotionally unstable;
11. both parents working; and
12. poor housing.

In relation to family background and underachievement, significant differences have been found between practices of child rearing and parental attitudes in families of achievers and nonachievers:

1. Underachievers tend to come from homes in which parents have less education than do parents of achievers.
2. Parents of underachievers tend to be either neutral or negative in attitude with respect to education whereas parents of achievers tend to value education positively.
3. The relationships that exist between the underachiever and his parents tend to be more distant psychologically than those that exist between the achiever and his parents.
4. Broken homes, working mothers, and other family disruptions are found in much higher proportion among parents of underachievers.
5. Family size and constellation appear to be factors since underachievers tend to come from larger families (Jansen, Huggard, and Krugman, 1956).

DEPRIVATIONAL THEMES

Family backgrounds also suggest similarities in the types of anxieties to which dropouts are subject. Those quitting school who come from more economically privileged areas have generally experienced early psychological neglect and rejection by their parents, particularly the mother. In addition, these youngsters have sustained a distance in parental relationships resulting in dilution of affection. On the other hand, less-privileged youngsters have endured pangs of reality-oriented existence, witnessed basic struggles for survival as well as suffering psychological rejection. In situations affecting the culturally and economically deprived, lack of food, shelter, and prolonged periods of separation from mothers add to emotional cost (Gruenbaum, 1960). The resulting anxiety, fear, frustration, and anger for all these groups of children is equally traumatic and damaging to ego development and normal growth.

There is frequently a close correlation between earlier deprivation of parents and transmission of its various aspects to their children. An example is the limitation and repression of subtle communications of parent to parent and parent to child. This was observed in a study of learning problems which began ten years ago at the Judge Baker Guidance Center in Boston. Although the majority of families in the study could be grouped in the lower-middle to middle-middle class, a review of clinical material revealed deprivational themes containing anxiety measures of the order usually observed in patients where there is a real struggle for existence. The observation was made that, both within these families and as they related to the outer world, communication of feelings and often even facts were greatly distorted (Gruenbaum, 1960).

It is understandable that parents who in their early years handled suffering by denying feelings of loss and subsequent anger are as adults unable to express emotions on this level. In treatment these parents must first be accepted at the level of their dependency needs; they must be given to before they can give to their children. Often they forbid themselves expression of feeling even in the most mildly provocative situation lest it arouse such expression from their children. Anger is not the only emotion given this taboo—it is extended to voicing love, needs, longings, and the like. Little wonder that a child reared in such an environment is less than popular among his peers and teachers.

PERSONALITY CHARACTERISTICS OF DROPOUTS

Perhaps because the types of emotional deprivation outlined have been instrumental in shaping his personality structure, the dropout is found to be a person lacking in ego strength and subject to feelings of low self-esteem. More negative in his attitude toward self than his achieving peers, he also manifests stronger feelings of inferiority. Lack of self-discipline usually is demonstrated by his inability to complete unpleasant tasks. A need for immediate results on all activities indicates a difficulty in working toward distant goals.

When in school he encounters a situation in which lack of recognition or worth is sustained, where there is a lack of activities and atmosphere to accentuate his feelings of importance, he has little motivation to attend. In spite of normal intelligence, failure often ensues. Unfortunately this neurotic symptom, indicating emotional conflict, is too often perceived by teachers as laziness, passive refusal or failure to learn. Although wishing to learn because his peers do and it is expected of him, learning may be resisted because avoidance of success quiets anxiety, brings momentary peace. Symptoms of failure bring the dropout some advantage no matter how self-defeating it may appear to others (Kunst, 1959).

Frequently potential dropouts react to excessive parental demands for achievement by avoiding reading or learning in other subjects. In addition to feelings of despair, they may transfer hostility felt for a rejecting mother to the teacher, using a learning situation to punish the parent. Teachers should be aware in these instances that a child's disruptive, sometimes hostile, behavior is not directed personally to her. In fact, reticence or disinterest in learning may stem from the fact that there is no one for whom to work. Although such a child needs the security and love of his family, he may respond to an interested and accepting teacher.

A dropout's feelings of little self-worth related to weak ego structure are likely to become exacerbated by real defeat, failure, and frustration in high school, which feeds into feelings of despair in home and community. Leaving school may well represent for him a turning away from dissatisfaction but in so doing he may invite the very rejection he is trying to escape. Unless the school is cognizant regarding the deep-seated causation of withdrawal, appropriate help will not be forthcoming. To determine cause and treatment lies within the province of clinical knowledge and is best ascertained by a school social worker.

THE SOCIAL WORKER AND DROPOUT FAMILIES

The overall aim of a school social worker involves examination of the child's total situation to determine what factors are contributing to social maladjustment or impinging on school performance. Training has equipped the clinician to investigate psychological, economic, and cultural elements affecting the social functioning of children and their families. Those caseworkers who have been most successful in working with dropout families suggest the following guidelines as being of prime importance.

A foremost principle for those engaged in the art of helping people is a concept of individual differences. Recognizing the invalidity of using broad generalizations with respect to behavior and needs of social-class groups, the clinician can effectively approach her task without categorizing families in terms of prevailing labels. To assume that middle classes are eager for professional help or that lower classes are hard to reach is an error that will be compounded in practice when one takes for granted that a family living in a certain neighborhood has the same values, same concept of roles, "same everything" as the neighborhood.

An important adjunct attending concern for individual differences is the social worker's concept of expectation and role. Should all groups be expected to meet middle-class norms or be found wanting? This consideration is especially pertinent for those who labor among disadvantaged or minority groups where frequently ignorance regarding cultural mores leads one to practice as though in a foreign land. A caseworker's task under these conditions is not only to help the reach of families exceed their grasp but to aid in making such a reach realistic.

Patience and understanding are requisite virtues for successful casework. These attributes will need be manifest frequently in underprivileged areas where a tendency to be late for appointments is observed. Punctuality, a norm of middle class, is seldom practiced in depressed districts and as one practitioner pointed out, "How often have you seen one of our clients with a watch?" Then too, appointments requested by mail might not transpire as many persons in low station are inclined to disregard mail except when expecting checks. Or they evidence reticence to accept any correspondence on official stationery lest it contain additional liabilities.

Wise scheduling, paramount in school social work, involves maintenance of a flexible work program for the clinician. Office hours should be adjusted so that parents are not inconvenienced to attend lest they fail to continue cooperative efforts. For example, high unemployment among unskilled workers understandably deters one from leaving a job at midday for an appointment with the social worker. In such cases, evening or weekend appointments should be arranged so as to coincide with the worker's free time. Relations will be more amicable not to mention those diagnostic values that derive from visits when one can observe family interaction, role expectancies and performance (Hayman, 1962).

Willingness to be inconvenienced is often the difference between success and failure in this work. To view people who do not reach out for help as lacking motivation keeps one from understanding a host of mitigating circumstances that prevent clients from meeting appointments. In the poorer areas of New York City it was found that broken appointments most often occur because parents lacked clothing to go out of the neighborhood, lacked carfare, sustained inflexible working hours, or experienced illness in the family. To find out why appointments were not met and then, if necessary, to reschedule them at the client's home will be helpful.

Finally, techniques employed in casework should always be ego supportive to the client. Should one encounter an atmosphere of school hostility, consideration might be given to a group approach such as that used in New York City where eight to ten parents meet with a school social worker who outlines school plans in behalf of their youngsters. The fact that they are in a larger group enables the parents to be less defensive and less reticent to participate in a question-answer period. Much of the distrust and resistance to school help is dissipated when clients realize the clinician's purpose is not to point out family failure. If we can convey to parents our feeling of their importance they will usually reciprocate with a willing cooperation to help those children whose importance we mutually admit.

RESPONSIBILITY OF THE SCHOOL

Failure of the school to provide success for dropouts usually comes into bold relief at the end of the sophomore year in high school consistent with pupils' reaching age 16 when legal absence is sanctioned. At this point an adolescent demands our attention when he asserts his intention to withdraw from formal education. Sincere but overdue is the intense concern that educators usually evidence in this circumstance. Efforts are toward, shall we say, a patching-up process of a problem that earlier detection and treatment might have prevented.

Since evidence exists that modifiability of the whole syndrome of habits and attitudes which foster optimal development is greater in earlier than in later years and since the abilities of young children must be known if appropriate instructional programs are to be planned, it appears obvious that initial efforts toward diminishing school dropout rate be made in elementary schools. An example worthy of note is the action program for kindergarten through third grade established in September 1959 by the New York City Board of Education. The primary objective of this program, operative in 37 schools, is the identification of problems, abilities, and talents early in academic life. A team of psychologist, social worker, guidance counselor, teacher, administrator, and consulting psychiatrist has been helpful in meeting needs, aiding in adjustment problems, and providing enrichment for talents and abilities (Rinaldi, 1961–1962).

Continued efforts are needed, of course, at the secondary level in providing adequate programming for potential dropouts. Significant experiments at George Washington and Morris High Schools in New York City (Hillson and Meyers, 1961) are providing for (1) special instructional programs; (2) remedial courses; (3) job-placement facilities; and (4) pupil personnel services. Efforts of clinical workers in cooperation with administrative and instructional staff in these two institutions have been instrumental in enabling many students to remain in school, to improve scholastically, and to complete graduation requirements.

As vital as any program is the objective analysis by each school of its learning environment to ascertain whether the institution itself engenders situations encouraging dropout. Most children enter school with eagerness. What happens to dampen their enthusiasm as they advance through the grades into high school? Could it be that some children do not have the experiences to cope with what is expected of them by group standards? If the school is not important to the potential dropout, why not? How can we help all children build on their original eagerness to learn? These questions are incumbent upon any school staff that is serious about diminishing dropout rate.

Another crucial concern should be the emotional climate of the school. Attitudes of teachers and attending staff are ingredients that may enhance or destroy efficacy of the educative process. For example, the child who early in his school experience is exposed to a severe and overly demanding teacher might become so conditioned to the unpleasant aspects of education that he can never find pleasant experiences that are available (Altmeyer, 1951). The average child will usually possess sufficient security, stability, and ego strength stemming from parental and family relationships to allow his toleration of some adverse experiences without suffering distorted views of school. It is the child with weak ego structure, however, who lacks parental and familial understanding and support, who has already experienced negative parental attitudes in child rearing, who will be adversely affected. His suspicion concerning adults who do not care for him and his feelings of constant threats to his security are thus reinforced. The teacher who is prone to ridicule may contribute to symptoms of nonattendance and to the need of pupils to escape from negative school environment. Especially is this true for preadolescent children who are beginning to experience conflicts in their relationships with adults.

CONCLUSION

In conclusion, essential ingredients to be included in programs for preventing dropout are: skilled study of the sociocultural impact on child and family; thorough psychological, social, and physical study of the dropout; and increased investigation of school instruction for its relevance to pupil needs. This venture is a joint one because positive emotional climate in the youngster's total milieu is essential to school achievement and to preparation for a satisfying, productive, and useful life.

20 *Counselor Self-Understanding and Responsibility for Those Not College Bound*

Kenneth Hoyt

The attainment of increased self-understanding for many years has been one of the major goals school counselors have held for their clients. Recently there has been a considerable amount of attention devoted to the problem of helping counselors in training increase *their* level of self-understanding as an integral part of the total counselor education program. I would like to extend this concept by speaking of self-understanding of school counselors as it pertains to operational functioning of counselors on the job. That is, my goal will be to encourage each of you to think about your own role and function in the school setting from the standpoint of your personal motivations.

So far as I know, this has not yet been attempted in any paper. As I approach the topic now, several reasons why it has not been done previously become obvious. In the first place, to raise questions concerning personal motivations may, to some, sound like accusations. Let me assure you this is not my intention. Second, to talk about personal motivations is sure to create certain feelings of uncomfortableness. I do this intentionally here because of my conviction that counselors have now reached a level of maturity that will enable them to cope with such feelings productively and resolve them satisfactorily in a way that will result in personal growth. Third, to raise questions regarding personal motivations is not going to make you view what I have to say as pleasant and pleasing to hear. You will not like some of the things I will say. I must take the risk that you will not automatically transfer your dislike of what I say to a personal disliking for me. Finally, to speak of personal motivations must carry some implication that I believe I know what these motivations are. Let me assure you that I make no such pretense here. My intent is to raise questions. Answers to these questions must come from each of you as individuals.

The approach I shall use will be to urge you to consider two counselor needs, each of which could be viewed as a reason for certain kinds of counselor behavior. These two counselor needs can each be represented by the initials "SS." In one sense, these initials can be thought to represent counselor need for "Satisfaction of Status." In another sense, they could be thought to represent counselor need to be of "Service to Students." Both of these "SS" needs of counselors are legitimate and proper. My question is, which is really in first place?

I use the word "really" for obvious reasons. That is, the first reaction of any of us would be to contend that service to students comes first and counselor status is only a by-product in terms of counselor motivation. But is it? To what extent is our rationale for certain kinds of counselor behavior more nearly a rationalization? To what extent are counselors content with earning status, and to what extent are they busy proclaiming their right to it? To what extent are we repressing some unconscious motivations while emphasizing a set of conscious ones? Questions such as these have been worrying me lately. I would hope to pass some of this worry on to you.

In an attempt to do so, I shall discuss briefly four examples of counselor behavior. These are: (1) our tendency to spend a disproportionate amount of time with the college-bound student; (2) our tendency to favor the academic over the vocational-educational curricula in our schools; (3) our tendency to place relatively little emphasis on the information service in guidance; and (4) our tendency to place a major emphasis on the counseling function.

THE EMPHASIS ON THE COLLEGE BOUND

I know of no guidance book that fails to proclaim service to all students as a basic goal of guidance. I know very few counselors who appear to recognize this goal operationally in the school setting. In most schools I visit, the college-bound student receives much attention and significant assistance from the school counselor. Many of you already know your schedule this year for such activities as administration of the PSAT, NMSQT, and ACT. You have already scheduled visits from college recruiters (sometimes referred to by the strange term "college admissions counselors"), assisted students in filling out college application blanks, collected college catalogues, and organized your "College Night."

The clamor for college has approached a magnitude approximating that of the rush toward religion in this country. Both are commonly viewed as representing a "good thing" for those who make such decisions and a prediction of less than maximum success, if not a sentence of failure, for those who do not. Youngsters making these decisions and those who assist in the decision-making process are applauded by society for their efforts. School counselors in this decade will receive much credit and a considerable amount of status for their efforts in helping 6.5 million students enter college—including the 2.6 million who will drop out prior to entering the junior year. There is little doubt but that school counselors can claim they have served well at least 3.9 million college-bound students in this decade. I do not mean to detract from the credit due counselors for these efforts. The needs of these students are obvious and must be met. Counselors must continue to serve these needs and these students. As you do so, I would ask you to reflect occasionally on your motivations —to what extent are you helping these students because you recognize their needs and to what extent is your help a reflection of status that will accrue to you as a result?

The reason for this question, obviously, lies in other questions such as: (1) What are counselors doing about the fact that there will be at least one million more students dropping out of high school in this decade than going on to college? (2) What are counselors doing about meeting the changing educational-vocational guidance needs of the twelve million students who will graduate from high school in this decade, but will never enter college? If both of these questions could be answered satisfactorily from the standpoint of service to students, it would then be both easy and appropriate to ascribe a pure service orientation to current efforts being made toward helping the college bound. But can they? Can you, as counselors, be satisfied with results of the "crash" program carried out in selected cities during August 1963 aimed at encouraging dropouts to return to school? Can you be satisfied with the fact that, at one point in July 1963, there were over a million and a half new high-school graduates unsuccessfully seeking employment in a labor market calling for skills they do not possess? I am concerned that you should not. I hope that you will not.

We have not adequately met the guidance needs of these students. During this period when we have been ignoring these students in favor of the college bound, their needs for guidance have both changed and increased. These guidance needs are such today that they can no longer be ignored. If we are to profess a "service-to-students" rather than a "search-for-status" orientation, it is time for those of us identified with the school-counseling movement to reorient our thinking and our patterns of behavior.

GUIDANCE AND VOCATIONAL EDUCATION

This brings me to a second area of counselor behavior—namely, that concerned with relationships between guidance and vocational education. It should be obvious that part of the reorientation in thinking to which I have referred has to do with this topic.

I am aware of the dangers of presenting a brief historical sketch—including the danger of overgeneralization and the danger of boring an audience. Yet this is where I feel we must begin. Guidance and vocational education began as separate movements in education. They became closely bound together with passage of the George-Dean Act in 1938, and this relationship was strengthened through passage of the George-Barden Act in 1946. This professed close relationship existed in most parts of the country between approximately 1938 and 1950. Since 1950 these relationships have been less than optimal. In some schools relationships have gone from good to poor to a point where one today would have trouble discovering *any* significant relationship between these two movements.

As with the emphasis on the college bound, counselors have often voiced a fine rationale for this chain of events. Among the reasons we have given are: (1) Guidance has broadened to include more than vocational guidance. (2) Vocational education requiring specific occupational choices at an early age is inconsistent with what we are learning about the psychology of vocational choice and vocational development. (3) The vocational-education programs in public-school settings have not been sufficiently broadened in scope, flexible in nature, or specifically appropriate for meeting the guidance needs of students they are intended to serve. (4) Post-secondary-school public vocational-education programs have not been available for youth in many school districts. (5) Private schools are profit-making businesses that often fail to provide students with the kinds of training they promise. This list could be expanded, of course, to include rationale for lack of counselor activity in helping youth plan for training in the military services and under the OJT, BAT, or MDTA programs. Overriding all these elements in the rationale has been the claim that our responsibilities are to students and not to programs.

But to what extent have these been the real reasons behind our increasing lack of enthusiasm for vocational education? Is it possible that a fear of loss in status among our colleagues in college prep teaching has had anything to do with our actions? Could the fact that we would have to admit our ignorance regarding the nature and extensiveness of opportunities to people we consider not as able as ourselves have anything to do with it? It is possible that we have fallen into the trap of equating differences in level of training with differences in quality of instruction? Could it be that sophisticated school counselors have fallen into the even more serious trap of defining as "sinful" those things that are unavailable to us—for example, could our criticism of the profit motive of the private school be related in any way to the fact that most of us do not have much money of our own? Does the fact that most parents of the students involved lack prestigeful community positions have anything to do with our attitudes here? Have we *really* been thinking about students as we formulate policy and operational procedures for dealing with vocational educators in public and private-school settings?

These are cold and, in a sense, cruel questions. I raise them not as accusations but simply as a means of helping each of you think through your own motivations in this area. If they cause you to stop and reflect a bit, they will have served their purpose. I do not raise them here to make you angry. If, as a matter of fact, you find yourself resentful that I have asked them, you must be either *very* good or *very* guilty. Maybe this is worthy of reflection.

My biases here are clear. I believe school counselors should be working much more closely with vocational educators in both public and private-school settings. These settings represent opportunities for students to acquire the kinds of marketable job skills that will enable them to enter today's labor market. Public-school post-high-school vocational-education opportunities for youth are bound to increase dramatically if the Vocational Education Act of 1963 now before the Congress becomes law. For many youth the private vocational school will continue to represent his only real opportunity for attaining entry into the labor market. If we want to serve students more than we want to acquire status, it is essential that school counselors recognize the potentialities that both public and private vocational education at the post-high-school level hold for meeting the needs of youth.

THE INFORMATION FUNCTION IN GUIDANCE

I would like now to turn to a third area of counselor behavior—namely, the tendency to place relatively little emphasis on the information function in guidance. It is significant, I think, to recall that guidance was first organized in 1938 in the United States Office of Education in what was known as the "Occupational Information and Guidance" Section of the Division of Vocational Education. The words "occupational information" were as significant at that time as the word "counseling" is today in the present Counseling and Guidance Institute Section of the U. S. Office of Education.

There is no doubt that our emphasis on the information function in guidance has declined since 1938. As with relationships between guidance and vocational education, school counselors have built a strong rationale for this deemphasis. This rationale includes the following observations: (1) Occupations are changing so rapidly that it is almost impossible to keep current on actual occupational opportunities. (2) The only thing certain about our occupational structure appears to be certainty of change. (3) There is good evidence that dissemination of information to clients is not sufficient for them to resolve their counseling problems. (4) There are many counseling problems where the need for information is relatively small and, in some cases, entirely nonexistent. All these factors have operated as rational reasons for a decline in our emphasis on the information function in guidance since 1938. They make an effective rationale.

But again we can ask, to what extent is this rationale operating because of a concern for service to students and to what extent is it operating because of counselor needs for status? For example, does the fact that counselors do not know very much about occupational information have anything to do with their deemphasis on this function? Does the fact that to answer a student's request for information constitutes a less dramatic challenge than his request for assistance in solving a personal problem have anything to do with this deemphasis? Could it be that counselors perceive requests for the kind of help that might be considered more "therapeutic" in nature? Is it possible that counselors view an emphasis on supplying information to students as a threat to their claims for a unique function in the total school setting? Does the routine nature of collecting and disseminating information threaten the high status level that school counselors seek? Again, I am making no accusations. I am simply raising questions for each of you to consider as you think about your operations in school settings this year.

It seems to me that the time is here for a rededication to the information function in guidance. Because information has been shown as not *sufficient* for meeting the counseling and guidance needs of students does not mean that it is not *necessary*. Because students in high school today are likely to change occupations more than once in their adult life does not mean that there is no need for them to make some specific occupational plans now. Because it takes a great deal of counselor time to keep up to date on occupational and educational information does not mean this function should be abandoned or greatly neglected. Because some have said each student has within himself the capacity to solve his own problems does not make this a proven fact. Because providing information to students is not exciting does not mean it is not a worthy counselor function. If service to students is to take precedence over satisfaction of status as a counselor need, then this reemphasis must take place.

THE COUNSELING FUNCTION

As a final example of counselor behavior, I would like to consider the counseling function in secondary-school guidance programs today. In contrast with the other functions I have discussed, this one has grown rapidly in importance and prestige in recent years. One of the ways some counselor educators have tried to acquire status is to compete with each other in terms of how much of the counselor's time they feel should be spent in counseling. If one says "50 per cent," his competitor in a neighboring institution is likely to say "60 per cent," whereupon yet another counselor in an education institution will say "70 per cent." The glorification of the counseling function is evident in the Wrenn (1962) Report, in the APGA Policy Statements, the APA Policy Statement, and the proposed ASCA Policy Statement. It is equally evident in the nature of NDEA Counseling and Guidance Training Institutes conducted since 1959.

The usual rationale given for this emphasis on the counseling function is very simple. In essence it says that counseling represents the best way we know of helping students solve their problems which clearly protects the right of the individual to make his own decisions. The right of the individual to privacy in the decision-making process is an essential ingredient of the rationale as is the decision-making process itself. It is a rationale that, in every basic element, is strictly "service-to-students" oriented. As with the other rationales presented, it is one that no professional school counselor would want to oppose.

Most of you are already scheduling counseling interviews this year. You are busily engaged in emphasizing counseling as a unique function of the school counselor and in protecting the counselor's counseling time. You are fighting hard for counseling facilities that will provide the privacy demanded by counseling. You are fighting equally hard to protect the confidentiality that is such an essential part of the counseling process. As with attention being given the college bound, all these activities are laudable and must be continued.

On the other hand, in some schools I have visited counselors who have carried these practices far beyond that dictated by a "service-to-students" emphasis. I have seen schools where the counselor's cubicle for which so many of us fought so long has become, in effect, a counselor's cocoon—a place where the counselor can isolate himself and his clients from the real world—including the real school. I have seen the appraisal service, the information function, and the role of the classroom teacher in guidance suffer because of the almost blind worship given to counseling. I have seen the emphasis on counseling carried too far.

Could it be that counselor behavior with respect to counseling is also being unduly influenced by counselor needs for satisfaction of status? Does the fact that "counseling" sounds to many as more prestigeful than "guidance" have anything to do with counselor behavior here? Is there a possibility that counselors see counseling as resulting in more "credit" being given counselors than they do guidance? Is the confidentiality of the counseling interview being used by some counselors more for the protection of the counselor than the client? Why do some continue to insist teachers cannot perform any counseling function? Do the claims for counseling continue to be heard more because of status needs of counselors than because of inherent values of counseling?

To me there is no doubt that, if service to students is our goal, guidance should be emphasized more than counseling. I say this not only because of the clear lack of evidence concerning the efficacy of counseling by itself but also because of the promising evidence with respect to the efficacy of schoolwide guidance procedures. We cannot hope to meet the counseling needs of students in our secondary schools today in the absence of a great deal of both appraisal and environmental information available for use in counseling. We must, it seems to me, begin worrying less in counseling about how students feel and more about how they think—less about what they believe and more about what they know. We must be more concerned with the amount of help that can be provided students and less about whether or not we receive credit for the help provided.

SUMMARY

At this point it would seem reasonable to expect you to be wondering what it is I am asking you to do. I have discussed four areas of counselor behavior and indicated my basic agreement with the rationale behind each. I have pictured these behaviors as having a sound base in a "service-to-students" orientation. This has been followed by a series of questions concerning the extent to which a "search-for-status" emphasis may be causing us to overemphasize the importance of these four counselor behaviors. In each case I closed with a plea for some change in perspective and action. All I am asking you to do now is to think about what I have said, to examine your own behavior in terms of the "service-to-students" and "satisfaction-of-status" dimensions, and arrive at a clear self-understanding with respect to your own values and motivations. If these remarks will accomplish this much, I shall be satisfied.

21 *Psychological Models for Guidance*

Gordon W. Allport

However excellent his natural eyesight may be, a counselor always looks at his client through professional spectacles. It could not be otherwise. After all, he has invested time and money in his psychological training. Of what use is it unless it adds special prisms to his own unaided eyesight?

The lenses we wear are ground to the prescription of our textbooks and teachers. Even while we are undergraduates a certain image of the nature of man is fitted to our eyes. We grow accustomed to the image and when we become practitioners or teachers we may still take it for granted.

But every so often comes a time for optical reexamination. Perhaps the image we have is still the best fit we can get; perhaps it is not. We can tell only by examining alternative lenses. In particular I believe that three are worthy of special scrutiny.

1. *Man seen as a reactive being.* Under this rubric I would include outlooks known as naturalism, positivism, behaviorism, operationism, physicalism; these are also sometimes called—mistakenly, I think— "scientific psychology."
2. *Man seen as a reactive being in depth.* Here I include what is variously called psychoanalysis, psychodynamics, depth psychology.
3. *Man seen as a being-in-process-of-becoming.* This label covers recent trends known as holism, orthopsychology, personalistics, existential psychology.

These three images provide a focus not only for guidance practices, but for all other professional psychological activity whether it be teaching, research, counseling, or therapy.

From *Harvard Educational Review*, 32, 1963, 373–381.

MAN: A REACTIVE BEING

One hundred years ago in his *Beiträge* Wilhelm Wundt mapped a program for the newly conceived science of psychology. His own view of the proper development of this science was broad and permissive, especially in the field of social psychology. But what has taken hold in the Anglo-American tradition is the experimental outlook of his *Physiologische Psychologie*. Fusing with Darwinism, Machian positivism, the quantitative outlook of Galton and his successors, as well as with techniques invented by Binet, Pavlov, Hull, and others—this experimental outlook prevailed and has ground the lens that is fitted to the eyes of almost all undergraduate students of psychology. Many of us who continue in the profession feel no need for further correction in this image of man.

Seen through this lens man is no different in kind from any other living reactor; and therefore, like the paramecium or pigeon, may be studied biologically, behaviorally, mathematically. To be sure a few special concepts need to be devised to take care of the vast complexity of human behavior, but all these concepts—among them habit hierarchy, secondary reinforcement, input and output of information, and the like—are consistent with the postulates of physicalism and naturalism.

If we ask, "What does it mean to be a human being?" this school of thought replies, "Man is one more creature of nature; his behavior though complex is predictable in principle. His present state is determined by his past state. A man's consciousness is unreliable and must be distrusted, preferably disregarded altogether. We seek the general laws of nature, not personal uniqueness. We study man, not men; objective reality, not subjective."

In principle this broad positive tradition, which we all know so well, puts a desirable end to psychological naïveté. It cautions us not to believe every verbal report that comes to our ears; it warns us to be skeptical of our own naked eyesight; and from it we learn to check ourselves for observer reliability. It teaches us to use precise and repeatable methods. Because of its stress on reliable methods this favored tradition in psychology has become known as "scientific psychology." Its methods are indeed scientific; but its primary postulate—that man is simply a reactive organism—is no more scientific than any other postulate.

It is here that the counselor encounters his first difficulty. Trained in tests, statistics, and experimental design, he may think, quite mistakenly, that to employ these useful aids he must also view his client as a reactive being—an exclusive product of stimulus impact, homeostasis, drive reduction, and reinforcement learning. The term "scientific" has spread like a grease spot from method to theory. Just because most of our methods evolved through the positivistic tradition does not mean that the postulates of this tradition concerning the nature of man are the only acceptable postulates for scientific psychology.

A counselor whose theoretical spectacles disclose a merely reactive being is likely to think of his client in terms of past conditioning and potential reconditioning; in terms of reinforcements, in terms of environmental determinism. He will assume that his client's basic motives are drive reduction or second-order conditionings which in some shadowy way are supposed to account for all his adult interests and vocational ambitions.

The vocabulary emanating from this type of postulate is replete with terms like *reaction, response, reinforcement, reflex, respondent, reintegration*—all sorts of *re*-compounds. The reference is backward. What *has* been is more important than what *will* be. Terms such as *proaction, progress, program, production, problem solving,* or *propriate* are characteristically lacking. One would think that the client seated opposite would *pro*test, for the language of response negates the subject's immediate certainty that his life lies in the future.

The positivistic view of man as a reactor has performed a good service, shaking us out of commonsense naïveté, endowing us with useful methods, and correctly informing us that man is, in *some* aspects of his being, a simple respondent to simple pressures. Its postulates are, however, questionable. It sees reality as ordered but not as personal; it sees consciousness as a nuisance; it looks at man as reactive, not proactive.

It is probably true that no counselor fully follows this creed in his daily practice. Indeed he could not do so. It is too impoverished a view of real life. When a convinced positivist attempts to fit his image of man to concrete human situations, as B. F. Skinner has done in *Walden Two,* the result strikes many of us as threadbare, even pitiable.

Probably for this reason many behaviorists (starting even as far back as E. B. Holt in *The Freudian Wish and Its Place in Ethics*) attempt to combine stimulus response with psychoanalysis. John Dollard and Neal Miller in their *Personality and Psychotherapy* (1950) offer a good example. Man as a reactive being is combined with man as a reactive being in depth.

MAN: A REACTIVE BEING IN DEPTH

So influential is this image of man that we find it everywhere: dominant in literature, in social work, in guidance, in therapeutic practice, and in the market place. There is no need today to describe this image to any educated, or even semieducated, American adult. Freudianism, like positivism, is our daily dish.

What I should like to do is to make clear that Freudianism (in spite of its less reliable methods) is a close kin of traditional positivism. The only change in the image of man lies in adding the depth dimension. To the long psychological vocabulary of *re*-compounds, depth psychology adds *repression, regression, resistance, abreaction, reaction formation,* and many others.

Like other simple naturalistic views of man, psychoanalysis puts its chief weight upon the press of pleasure and pain. This pressure produces in the organism a tendency to seek an equilibrium between the force of his drives and the circumstances of reality. The fact that Freud maximizes the role of sex and locates the whole constellation of reactive forces chiefly in the unconscious does not alter the essential similarity.

For Freud causation lies in the past history of the individual just as it does for the conditioned-response theorist. Both have a dismaying disregard for the person's phenomenology of the future, for his sense of personhood and sense of freedom. The ego is a reactive agent, having no energy of its own, but borrowing from the unsocialized id.

Central to depth psychology, and important for guidance, is the doctrine of *recall* and *recovery* (two more *re*-compounds). Therapy, and presumably guidance, proceeds by disclosing to the client some buried motive, or a troublesome and repressed psychic trauma. The client's salvation, if indeed he has any, lies in this vital recall. A troublesome memory is brought to cognizable form. Presumably the result is helpful to the individual in solving his conflicts. The theory, however, does not allow for any interaction between the person and the recovered memory. Simple reinstatement is itself, as Freud says, the "pure gold" of psychoanalysis. What values a client should live by when once the reinstatement has taken place is not the "pure gold" of psychoanalysis. That all adult values are simply sublimated aim-inhibited wishes is the central doctrine. Freud never allows for the individual's capacity to disregard his past or to reshape it freely. Indeed, since the structure of the id never changes, the future can at best be a redirection, never a transformation, of one's purposes. What one becomes is essentially what one is, and what one was.

Among the valid portions of psychoanalysis of special use to all counselors is the brilliant account given us by Freud and by his daughter Anna of the defensive mechanisms of the ego. In dealing with our client we do well to follow the advice of psychoanalysis and watch for rationalizations, denials of reality through repression, and displacements of aggression. All these and other ego defenses belong to the nature of man and therefore must find a place in any theory of human personality.

But what perplexes me is why so many of the ego processes described by psychoanalysis should be merely protective strategies. Are there no ego processes that lead to a transformation of what is recovered? To a creative cognition? To a revised sense of personhood and a new phenomenology of the future? To Freud the person seems never to be truly proactive, seldom even active. Almost always he is seen as reactive to early fixations—perhaps to some castration threat that occurred years ago, or to some other unsocialized infant complex, especially to Oedipal fantasies. My difficulty with this image of man is summed up most tersely by the late satirist, Max Beerbohm, who said, "They were a tense and peculiar family—those Oedipuses."

There is, I am well aware, a large group of theories that derive from the psychodynamic tradition but at the same time deviate considerably from the orthodox view of reactivity-in-depth. All these theories, in my judgment, move in a desirable direction. Here I shall mention only some of the relevant authors: Adler, Jung, Hartmann, Horney, Erikson, Fromm. Still more deviant from Freud are Goldstein, Maslow, Rogers, and Robert White. These and other writers offer a type of theory that views man as a being in the process of becoming. Many of them ask the pivotal question differently from the reactivist schools of thought. And it makes a good deal of difference just how a question is asked.

A story is told about two priests. They were arguing whether it was proper to smoke and to pray at the same time. One said "Yes," the other "No." To settle the matter they decided that both should write to the Holy Father for his opinion. Sometime later they met and compared notes. Each claimed that the Holy Father had supported his view. They were perplexed. Finally one asked, "How did you phrase your question?" The other replied: "I asked whether it was proper to smoke while one is praying; and the Pope answered, 'Certainly not, praying is serious business and permits no distractions.' And how did you phrase your question?" "Well," said the other, "I asked if it were proper to pray while smoking, and the Pope answered, 'Certainly, prayer is always in order.'"

Instead of asking Aristotle's question, "What is the place of man in Nature?" many authors today are asking St. Augustine's question, "Who am I?" This question, rephrased in the twentieth century, has opened the floodgates to a new theorizing of the broad type often labeled *existentialist.*

MAN: BEING IN THE PROCESS OF BECOMING

Seelye Bixler, former president of Colby College, tells of a student who recently remarked, "I can't tell you how much satisfaction I take in my existential despair." In some student circles despair has always been popular. To label it "existentialist" makes it doubly attractive, in fact irresistible.

But overlooking the fashionable flavor of existentialism it is surely necessary for the modern counselor to take seriously the present-day anxieties of the younger generation. No longer can youth contemplate its future under the protection of the great social stabilizers of the past.

No longer can one counsel within the framework of Victorian decorum, theological certainties, or the Pax Britannica. It is obvious to us all that some sort of shattering transformation is underway. The comfortable stabilities of culture, caste, the gold standard, and military supremacy are no longer ours.

Nor are the comfortable stabilities of traditional psychology adequate. Of what use is it to invoke an impersonal theory of learning, a biological theory of motivation, and a late-Victorian formula for the unconscious, when youth's problems today are acutely conscious, intensely personal, and propelling him like an unguided astronaut into an unknown future? A counselor is not equipped for his job unless he can share in some degree the apprehensions of modern youth, and sense the swampy underpinning on which youth treads. Over his desk the counselor might well tack the wisdom of the Spanish writer Unamuno, "Suffering is the life blood that runs through us all and binds us together." While not every youth who comes to the counselor is at that moment a sufferer, it is a safe assumption that he comes for guidance that will fortify him for the inevitable suffering that he will encounter in his course of life.

TENTATIVENESS AND COMMITMENT

From the existential point of view the ideal counselor will strive to develop two attitudes in his client. Taken separately they seem antithetical; but fused into a world view they provide strength for the future. One attitude is *tentativeness* of outlook. Since certainties are no longer certain, let all dogmas be fearlessly examined, especially those cultural idols that engender a false sense of security: dogmas of race supremacy, of naïve scientism, of unilinear evolutionary progress. Let one face the worst in oneself and in the world around one, so that one may correctly estimate the hazards.

Taken by itself such tentativeness, such insightfulness, might well lead to ontological despair. Yet acceptance of the worst does not prevent us from making the best of the worst. Up to now psychologists have not dealt with the remarkable ability of human beings to blend a tentative outlook with firm commitment to chosen values. The poet Tennyson perceived the point.

There lives more faith in honest doubt,
Believe me, than in half the creeds.

A commitment is, as Pascal has said, a wager. One may lose it, but one may also win. Cardinal Newman warned us that our religion can never be a matter of certainty. It is at best a subjective condition of certitude which he defined as "probability supported by faith and love." Yet a mature religion, thus defined, can be infinitely sustaining and heroically motivating. Existentialism, whether theistic or atheistic, makes the same point. We have the freedom to commit ourselves to great causes with courage, even though we lack certainty. We can be at one and the same time half-sure and wholehearted.

William James, probably America's greatest thinker, tried to teach us this lesson, but fifty years ago we were not ready for it. It is surely noteworthy that, writing as he did in a period of social stability, James saw clearly how ultimately uncertain are our foundations of value. Wealth, he saw, was a false god, leading us into a national disease that has recently been called "galloping consumption." The more we build up our material resources, the more we fear poverty. In religion, James knew, there was no certainty; yet, like Cardinal Newman, he recognized the constructive power of a mature religious commitment. Whatever ideal leads to long-range constructive consequences is psychologically sound. It is also pragmatically true. And who is to say that we have a test for truth more absolute than our own commitment insofar as it is validated by fruitful consequences?

Neither positivistic nor psychodynamic schools of thought allow for the fact that our psychological constitution permits both total tentativeness and total commitment. Such a paradox reminds us of the electron that is able to go in two opposite directions at the same time. Taken by itself tentativeness is disintegrative; commitment is integrative. Yet the blend seems to occur in personalities that we admire for their soundness and perspective. Presumably through teaching and guidance we may develop both attitudes in our youth.

Whenever the two attitudes coexist in a life we find important desirable by-products from the fusion. One is a deep sense of compassion for the lot of the human race in general and in each separate social encounter that marks our daily life. The other by-product is likewise graceful; it is the sense of humor. Humor requires the perspective of tentativeness, but also an underlying system of values that prevents laughter from souring into cynicism. As Meredith said, humor is a capacity to laugh at the things you love and still to love them.

RATIONALISM VS IRRATIONALISM

The chief criticism made of existentialism is that it leads away from reason and exalts irrationalism. While this charge may apply to certain literary and theological trends in the existential movement, I doubt that it jeopardizes the future of scientific psychology. The attitudes of tentativeness and commitment of which I speak are perfectly sound concepts—call them "intervening variables" if you wish. Indeed insofar as they reflect important states in human personality, and thus lead to improvement in understanding, prediction, and direction of human behavior, they are sounder scientific concepts than many of those we have been using.

And just what is rationalism? We venerate the ancient Greeks for their exaltation of human reason; and as psychologists we venerate Aristotle for asking the question, "What is man's place in nature." But Greek rationalism was broader than the limited, method-centered, scientism into which it has degenerated. The Greeks themselves saw a place for tentativeness and commitment within the scope of reason. The case is beautifully stated in an ancient inscription found somewhere on the coast of Greece:

A shipwrecked sailor buried on this coast
Bids you set sail.
Full many a bark, when we were lost,
Weathered the gale.

The dead sailor urges us to make the wager, take the risk, although we cannot be sure of coming through to our destination.

IMPLICATIONS FOR THEORY

What does all this mean in terms of psychological theory, and in terms of guidance? First of all it means that in order to achieve a more realistic image of man and his potentialities, we need to revise our current theories of learning and growth, of motivation and personality structure. Elsewhere (in *Pattern and Growth in Personality,* 1961) I have discussed some of the needed changes in detail, and so shall say only a few words about each.

The trouble with our current theories of learning is not so much that they are wrong, but that they are partial. They fit best the learning of animals and young children. The concepts of conditioning, reinforcement, identification, seem a bit hollow when the counselor tries to apply them to his work. They are not very helpful, for example, in explaining how a youth may learn both tentativeness of outlook and firmness of commitment. Supplementary theories in terms of organizational, biographical, and propriate learning are needed.

Except in the sense of physical maturation the concept of *growth* scarcely exists in psychology at all. Nor will it have its proper place until we have agreed upon normative standards for the maturity of personality. Up to now normative problems, except in the sense of statistical norms, are much neglected.

As for motivation and personality structure psychologists are in a state of turmoil and disagreement. That the past stages of a life do not fully explain the motivational "go" of the present, I for one am firmly convinced. Therefore we need a concept (*functional autonomy,* I think will do) to represent that portion of a life that is oriented toward the future and not toward the past. Also we need a theory of personal structure (of *personal dispositions*) to represent the important cleavages and foci of a given, concrete personality. Such a theory will, I am convinced, carry us much further than a conception of uniform variables to which every client is forcibly ordered, whether we call these variables factors, needs, dimensions, or common traits.

Most of all we need to surrender the models that would compress human personality into the routine homeostatic situation that we find in quasiclosed systems. Human personality is a wide-open system, responsive to tangible and intangible culture, on the lookout for new ideas, and capable of asking an altogether new type of question—asked by no other creature in nature—namely, "Who am I?"

There are, I am glad to say, many psychologists who feel as strongly as I that these various types of improvement need to be made before the counselor will have a fully fashioned science of psychology to undergird his practice.

IMPLICATIONS FOR GUIDANCE

Guidance is not a matter of gimmicks, nor of rules of thumb. A guide, like a philosopher and friend, is a person who loves wisdom and loves his fellow men. True, he has skills to mark him off from the professional philosopher or the untrained friend. To some extent the counselor's present-day skills are useful. Standard tests and measurements are helpful; so too achievement records and focused interviews. Most of our devices come from researches conducted under the positivistic outlook, or (in the case of projective techniques) under the psychodynamic. While many of them are serviceable I look forward to the invention of new instruments still better suited to the study of the central or propriate aspects of single personalities.

Most important, of course, are the spectacles the counselor wears. The image should no longer be borrowed from the tradition of simple naïve reactivism. Just as centimeters, grams, seconds are outmoded in modern physics, so too are simple stimulus-response connections in modern psychology. In psychology, even more than in physics, we need theory capable of dealing with fluid becoming.

The plain fact is that man is more than a reactive being, more even than a reactive being in depth. If he were comfortably fixed at these levels we could with confidence apply a uniform stencil in studying his nature. But the life process is no less paradoxical than the processes of modern physics. How can one deal with space that is both finite and unbounded, with light that is both wave and particle, with electrons that pass from orbit to orbit without traversing the space between? Similarly, a human person is both structure and process, a being both biological and noetic, a being who changes his identity even while he retains it. Small wonder that at the end of his life, the famous physicist, P. W. Bridgman, said, "The structure of nature may eventually be such that our processes of thought do not correspond to it sufficiently to permit us to think about it at all."

We need not, I think, be quite so pessimistic. Our first duty is to affirm a new and wider rationalism; that is, to redouble our efforts to find a more adequate image of man to guide us in fashioning a more suitable science of personality.

And what about our personal attitudes as guidance specialists or teachers? Should we not cultivate the same twin virtues that we recommend to client and student: tentativeness and commitment? We can hold our own present image of man on trial, reviewing our own past psychological training in critical perspective. At the same time we can embrace courageously our task of interpreting the wisdom of the past in such a way as to make it most available to the youthful personality who is facing an uncertain, but not uninviting future. Tentativeness and commitment are twin ideals for both counselor and client. To my mind they lie at the heart and center of guidance, of teaching, and of living.

22 Role of the Principal in Fostering Mental Health

A. Raymond Rogers

With a topic as broad as education itself, it may be appropriate to consider the directions of public schooling that tend to encourage development of youth and in so doing enhance the mental well-being of individual pupils. This will include the unique role of schools in our society, the responsibilities of professional staff, and the educational process itself. As a working administrator who has served institutions varying in population from 29 to 3500 students, it has been my responsibility and intent to meet a multitude of daily problems in plant management and operation. Yet I have found the most challenging task for a principal to be that of helping youngsters realize their potential, pursue their interests, maintain their mental health.

THE PRINCIPAL: CARETAKER OR COORDINATOR?

The influence of the principal should be both pervasive and harmonious as he assumes a designated leadership position in building, maintaining, and continuously developing an educational climate that is conducive to the mental health of all school people, staff and pupils. An administrator ought not to confine his function to seeing that schedules are kept, records are in order, necessary materials are available, personnel needs are handled, and physical aspects of the plant are operative. To be sure, each of the foregoing are important tasks, but the prime duty of a principal is one of coordination, or bringing together the individual strengths of teacher, counselor, social worker, and librarian in order that this group might make its efforts more effective through concerted action.

In a sense the role of an administrator might be analogous to the function of a gardener in that while he should encourage pupil and staff growth and foster the development of ideas, he should also weed and prune so that positive direction is established and maximum growth assured. In effect, a principal must be primarily concerned with indi-

220

vidual pupils, their instruction, their development, their well-being. It is not uncommon as complexities of a school increase for an administrator to become oblivious to the real aims of his institution. The mechanics of operating a large plant with a large staff is sometimes overwhelming so that he comes to view his position in relation only to decisions regarding managerial efficiency or community relations, with little or no attention to the educational process, to learning, or to the beneficiaries of school, the learners.

ADULT EXPECTATION AND PUPIL BEHAVIOR

An important responsibility incumbent on those involved in school management is the constant encouragement of classroom teachers to organize and present learning experiences that are significant for youngsters, to assign only those tasks that are reasonable, to determine expectations of individual pupils within a realm of possibility. The key here is reasonable expectation; it occurs when the student is cognizant of what the school staff expects of him in terms of performance and behavior; it occurs when there are no doubts in his mind as to what is required of him; it occurs when goals assigned him are emotionally comfortable. Realization of these objectives demands that the principal not spend his major energies developing grandiose organizational schemes but rather that he work to make possible a vital involvement of teacher and pupils. To make the extent of this interaction sufficient, to assure the result of interaction productive, to observe and assess the progress of interaction; these are the tasks and satisfactions of a principal.

Since emotional maturity of students is a goal that schools should foster, it is apparent that administrators must have a keen sense of what experiences are appropriate for pupils, what expectations are reasonable. The field of experiences to which a student is exposed might be likened to a pasture or corral that has known bounds. Included within these bounds are experiences that we presume an individual able to handle with a degree of success. This is giving freedom within known bounds. If many experiences that cannot be handled successfully are included, we can shrink the boundaries. Conversely, as students master experiences and competencies build, boundary lines can be expanded. It is important that limits be set because when they are excluded it has been found that students are often overcome with indecision and self-doubt. Yet, with limits, as learners add one experience to another, they have a chance to develop confidence in their own judgment and thereby both to feel and become mature.

Discipline, derived from the word disciple, is a vital element in the learning process. To be a disciple one must be able to go along with a system of control set up by someone else. As an individual develops and matures, he gains self-discipline which includes those elements from various systems of control that have been meaningful for him. In order that teenagers can develop self-discipline and evolve their own value structure, it is necessary for the society, church, community, parents, and schools to be specific about what is expected of them. We sometimes fail to define the limits for behavior of youth, not realizing that limits afford a certain degree of security.

The Hechingers (1963) said it well in *Teen-Age Tyranny:*

Rebellion and protest have, of course, always been important ingredients of adolescence. But like any other vital, youthful force they can be controlled, directed and civilized by a purposeful and cohesive adult society. Today's danger is that, instead of giving young people some tough and specific rules on which to cut their teeth, society is reorganizing around the demands and preferences of youth (to the accompaniment of the sideline cheers from commercial exploiters). Ironically, it is possible to provide young people with so much "understanding" of all their actions that they are robbed of the chance to rebel and test their strength, and in testing learn, grow up and mature. Turning merely to the proper chapter in an approved advice book to determine the next step is no substitute for testing and searching.

Part of growing up is the increasing ability to handle failure in a mature fashion. There is a significant difference between one who has failed and has learned from the experience and one who has failed and who feels he is a failure.

Other pressures regarding behavior in our mobile society tend to undermine the discipline, the authority, the effectiveness of our homes. The authors (Gordon and Gordon, 1961) of the *Split-Level Trap* eloquently probe life in suburbia, labeling it "disturbia," with its "gimme" kids who really don't know who's the boss. As more adults become less sure of themselves and seek to avoid stress, they tend to shield their children from anxiety and become extremely permissive, intensely concerned. American parents have been described as letting their children do anything they want and then worrying about everything they do. From time to time we must remind ourselves that each of us will encounter stress and that mental health is not based on its avoidance.

EDUCATION: KEY TO ADAPTABILITY

To be effective schooling must equip students to meet challenge and change. Education is not a collection of facts but a process that enables one to organize known materials, to develop new ideas, to use knowledge in new ways. It is desirable that learning processes employed in one subject area transfer as workable approaches to problems in other areas of life. It is this adaptability of what one knows to new and unique situations that makes education requisite to mental health. One simply must be able to adapt to changing conditions today. At a conference on mental health, Dr. Francis Braceland (1963), Director of the Hartford Institute of Living, recalled to his audience Edna St. Vincent Millay's "Conversation at Midnight":

All creatures to survive
Adapt themselves to the changing conditions
    under which they live;
If they can grow new faculties to meet the new
    necessity, they thrive;
Otherwise not; the inflexible organism, however
    much alive
Today, is tomorrow extinct.

Recent innovation in methodology requires that teachers aid students in making the transition from old learning to new. With adaptability as a key, most educators no longer insist on strict reproduction or recall as the criterion of growth. Some teachers and pupils, however, still equate knowing with knowledge, perceive education as a collection of facts rather than a process, and when unable to depend on recall become frustrated. The questing approach is new for them, the search for meaning is alien. These persons need to know that the educated man is he who can ask pertinent questions about what he wishes to know; he is not the person who assumes what he needs to know resides in his memory. If a spirit of inquiry is to prevail among students, it becomes necessary for teachers to create a learning climate that makes this approach both academically legitimate and emotionally comfortable.

GUIDANCE: A SHARED RESPONSIBILITY

Guidance is perhaps the most direct and vital function a school performs in relation to student mental health. The improved training of counselors is evident not only by their demonstration of competence to help pupils with vocational planning, learning problems, and personality conflicts, but is manifest also by an increasing confidence in and demand for their services by pupils and parents. Certainly counselor sensitivity to the unique needs of individual learners can do much in helping an institution maintain curricular offerings of positive consequence. But we do an injustice to young people when responsibility for guidance is consigned exclusively to counseling personnel. Indeed guidance, in its context of providing direction for growth, should permeate the role of every professional staff member.

At this juncture it is pertinent to interject a note of caution, namely, counseling and behavioral analysis are not synonymous in the educational sphere. It is when a teacher, a guidance officer, or an administrator forgets this that his capacity to help is diminished. The search for hidden motivation, the psychological categorization of students into types, and the inappropriate probe into a youngster's private life space can have dire ramifications. Such approaches may serve to raise anxiety levels, lessen positive rapport between student and school, and generally contribute to disorientation by acting as a deterrent to understanding and resolution.

Rather, the educator's initial approach should be directed toward the attainment of an acceptable solution to the specific problem a student may pose. For example, the issue of academic failure can best be handled by determining the specific study areas contributing to incompetence. These questions might be a tenable beginning: Does the pupil understand what type of commitment is necessary to get good grades? Does he do an adequate amount of studying? Does he take advantage of extra help extended by the institution? Does he understand what is expected of him in his classes? Has he consulted with instructors in those disciplines where his grades indicate failure? These kinds of query, in deference to psychological fishing trips, are requisite to school guidance in its most comprehensive sense.

Those who work closely with teenagers are aware that students sometimes go on pseudo-psychological kicks and may during interviews rationalize as to causation of their problems by citing teacher conflict, parent conflict, or emotional trauma of one sort or another. It is not suggested here that such probable difficulties be ignored but instead that first concentration be given to resolving school manifestations of an issue, realizing that student interviews may be as concealing as they are revealing. For all who counsel adolescents, it is well to remember that as awareness of self increases, some pupils tend to feel they are different, strange, "kookie." In their attempt to escape meeting a particular problem, students may make requests for specific concessions; if we concede, we may reinforce a negative self-concept, thereby encouraging the pattern of escape.

It has been said that one adolescent in ten has some emotional disorder. Schools can never give the amount and nature of psychological help commensurate with the need this number suggests. Moreover, because of difficulty in communicating with teenagers and the often transitory nature of their problems, it is becoming increasingly obvious that we must look to a more comprehensive approach utilizing to a greater extent various mental-health agencies and private professional sources.

The clergyman, psychologist, social worker, guidance officer, psychiatrist, and teacher each have particular strengths that best qualify them to handle certain types of difficulty. Each, in effect, must screen out those individuals whose problems are of sufficient complexity to warrant specialized help from another source. Since this is true, schools cannot be all things to all people, but administrators can encourage and reinforce roles that other sources play in making all people what they can become: mentally healthy.

23 The Superintendent and Mental Health

Howard C. Seymour

INTRODUCTION

Every individual makes an effort to achieve balance—the magical equilibrium that exists when the forces within him are at peace with the forces that make up his environment. The drives for security, recognition, success, affection, creativity, and acceptance by the group are a part of each individual's personality. Oversimplified as this statement may be, it is the existence and identification of satisfactory outlets for these drives that enable the human personality to operate in balance.

Obviously there is no state of perfect equilibrium. Nor would much ever be accomplished if every person were so blissfully balanced. It is the striving for goals and the interweaving of desire and partial success that spurs the individual toward unachieved goals. The mentally healthy person must be at least partially successful. To prevent serious maladjustment, the school, home, and community must offer each person continued opportunities to realize some success.

But before proceeding further with this discussion, it is important to establish what constitutes good mental health. The mentally healthy person is one who:

1. Knows his own abilities, interests, assets, and limitations.
2. Stretches himself sufficiently to know realizable and realistic limits.
3. Respects others and makes a real effort to understand their assets and to bear with their limitations.

The writer wishes to express his appreciation to the following associates who contributed ideas and criticism to this chapter: Dr. Harold C. Miles, Director of the Monroe County Board of Mental Health, Rochester, N. Y.; Dr. Earl Telschow, Director of Mental Health Clinical Services, Rochester, N. Y.; Miss Eda Gorrie, formerly Coordinator of Mental Health Clinical Services, Rochester, N. Y.; Miss Helen Weston, formerly Director of School Social Work, Rochester, N. Y.; and Dr. Walter O. Smith, Psychologist, Board of Education, Phoenix Union High School District, Phoenix, Ariz.

226

4. Attempts to replace emotional responses with analysis and scientific thinking.
5. Recognizes that achievement is acceptable compensation for previous failure or inadequacy.
6. Faces the reality of daily routine with initiative and purposefulness, never losing sight of long-term goals.
7. Demonstrates an ability to accept balance between his own drives and those of the individuals with whom he is associated.
8. Coordinates these qualities in such a way that he is able to deal positively with the ebb and flow of life around him and to do so with courage, purpose, and satisfaction.

Perhaps the following quotation (author unknown) summarizes the kind of person the schools should be seeking to produce.

No human being can be invulnerable and immune to life. It follows that mental health does not express itself in an invariable serenity of circumstances, events and other people; that it may be impaired by clinging to an established security and further that it may be imperceptibly forfeited by an adjustment to unfavorable conditions. Actually, we know that mental health is contingent upon the individual's capacity to experience pain as well as pleasure, each fully enough not to be caught in its toils.

It is the purpose of this chapter to note in what ways the superintendent can contribute to this objective.

THE SUPERINTENDENT AS A LEADER

Ralph Waldo Emerson, in his essay on self-reliance, wrote, "The institution is the lengthened shadow of one man." Many factors contribute to the success of an institution, not the least of which is its leader. Certainly the superintendent of schools is not the only person responsible for the success of public schools in America, but it cannot be denied that he casts a long shadow.

What he is, what he believes, what he considers important to no small extent determines the success of the school system he heads. It is not only what he knows, but what he feels, how he acts, how he treats others that determines whether it can truthfully be said that his school or system possesses high morale.

No position in the educational profession is as demanding as that of the superintendent. He is expected to be a master of the curriculum, well versed in teaching methods, adept at working with the school board and the community, and proficient in overseeing all the complex operations of the modern school. His most important role, however, is working with people, inspiring them and guiding them into their appropriate school tasks.

There is no more powerful influence than good example. Its effect on others is cumulative and pervasive. If the superintendent gives evidence of sound mental health, notwithstanding multiple pressures upon him, the atmosphere of the school system that he serves will be more conducive to mental health. What the superintendent does is important. How he does it is equally so. The superintendent, assumed to be in good mental health, gives evidence of the following:

1. Draws around him staff members who question his actions and who are free to disagree with him.
2. Welcomes constructive criticism.
3. Rewards when rewards are merited.
4. Censures, when necessary, privately and in such a way that the person is stimulated to improve.
5. Encourages freedom of expression and is not made insecure by the questions of others.
6. Makes a conscious effort to draw around him those who have competencies that he lacks.
7. Can live with partial success.
8. Reserves decisions until the facts have been collected. He does not, as the old saying goes, "Act in haste, repent at leisure."
9. Is sensitive to the need for communication, conferring with his staff often in order that its members may know themselves to be important elements of the team.
10. Creates a spirit of mutual trust and confidence. He backs his staff members when they are right.
11. Makes a conscious effort to evaluate frequently how well he, as a superintendent, is performing.
12. Uses his mistakes as springboards to better solutions.
13. Appreciates the use of humor as a release valve.
14. Approaches unpleasant tasks promptly and disposes of them with dispatch.
15. Deliberately plans for variety in his life by taking on hobbies and community interests as unrelated as possible to his daily activities.

Anxiety is infectious. If the leader feels in control of his job, his confidence is communicated to his staff. The reverse is equally true. If the administrator has had a bad day or has been under considerable tension and as a result is nervous and tense, teachers and school personnel are almost immediately aware of it. Inevitably classrooms and students are affected. How, then, can the administrator keep his own anxieties under control?

Otto (1961), in an article on the subject of the administrator's mental health, asked administrators what practices they believed had a positive effect. The response can be summarized as in Table 1.

Table 1 *Practices That School Administrators Believe Improve Their Mental Health*

	Number of Responses	Per Cent of Responses
1. Talking it out or talking it over.	86	26.7
2. Developing good administrative working relationships.	81	25.3
3. Handling work pressures, routines, and office atmosphere smoothly.	57	17.8
4. Following a balanced life outside of the office.	48	14.9
5. Improving communication and listening.	23	7.2
6. Others	26	8.1
	321	100

The superintendent must know something about mental health and the mental-health movement. He can acquire this through study and from consultation with someone either on his staff or in the community—a consulting psychiatrist, a staff psychologist, or a school social worker. Any one of these can be a source of strength to the school leader who needs to know the full implications of his decisions as they affect people.

THE SUPERINTENDENT AND THE TEACHER

The superintendent can subscribe to all the tenets and manifest the benefits of good mental health, but if around him and with him he does not have a staff with similar attitudes, any program of promoting system-wide mental health will be handicapped. Probably the most important delegation of responsibility is that for teacher selection and employment to a discerning, well-qualified personnel department.

It is not enough for the personnel department to test applicants on what they know. An attempt must be made to examine feelings and attitudes. What does the record reveal regarding the candidate's versatility and "bounce"? What is his childhood and school background? Does he demonstrate that he knows the relationship between permissiveness and authority? What are his feelings toward the less able or the differently colored? Does he feel himself threatened by students with brains? Does he radiate warmth? Does he generate confidence in others? Much can be determined from an examination of the record, through a series of interviews, and from reference material in which a deliberate attempt is made to appraise these qualities.

No teacher should be employed by any school system sight unseen. The interview is one of the most important devices for revealing the nature of feelings, attitudes, responsiveness, and flexibility. During the interview the shrewd superintendent or personnel director will be asking the candidate such questions as these: What are the characteristics of the best teacher you ever knew? What is most important for young people to learn? What is your view of your role in education? Why do you want to be a successful teacher? Where do you feel you have the greatest chance for success as a teacher? Where do you feel most limited? The answers to these questions and others like them help the school system determine something of the applicant's sense of values, his feelings, his likes and dislikes. It is the flexible, versatile—the desirable—teacher who really understands individual student differences and makes provision for them.

Once employed, teachers should be frequently observed and conferred with, particularly during the important pretenure period. It is during this testing time that the school system can discover whether what the teacher has learned is put together in such a way that his students are motivated to learn, do learn, and find pleasure in so doing. This is the time to assess feelings, attitudes, and flexibility. It is important for the superintendent to visit, observe, listen, commend, or suggest improvements. This administrator-teacher relationship needs to be a rich, rewarding one in which the teacher gains confidence, whittles away at his inconsistencies and drawbacks, finds his niche and discovers where he can make his best contribution to helping young people learn.

Once he has been accepted for permanent employment, the teacher is not forgotten by the superintendent. There is really no more lonely situation than the classroom unvisited by principal and administrator, and in which daily contacts are largely with pupils only. The superintendent drops in on the new teacher's classes, lets him know when he has done an outstanding job. The top administrator knows something of the background of each teacher, what shape his life takes, what his outside interests are. While visiting classes the superintendent accents the positive. He reassures each teacher of his tremendous importance in the classroom. He demonstrates, when he can, that the administration exists only to support the activity of the teacher in the classroom. When it is appropriate, he says a kind word and, in fact, looks for the opportunity.

For example, when the teacher retires, the superintendent writes a note of regret, listing the outstanding services the individual has rendered the young people of the system.

The superintendent deploys skillfully those whose interests, abilities, and attitudes are particularly effective with certain kinds of young people. He does not become overfamiliar with any one member of his staff. The tenor of his relationship is one of respect for the qualities that each brings to the learning process. He is never too quick to condemn. He recognizes that there is a reason, cause, and circumstance for everything that occurs. He attempts to examine this causation process before he questions, ridicules, or reprimands.

The degree to which the superintendent can achieve and maintain this kind of relationship depends, of course, on the size of the system. Fortunate is the superintendent who has a small enough system to permit this close, intimate, and rewarding supervision.

THE SUPERINTENDENT AND THE CURRICULUM

The superintendent will need to give more than lip service to the concept of meeting individual student differences. Youngsters in school differ markedly. One of the purposes of the school should be to encourage differences. This means a constant search for curricular experiences and situations that probe for and reveal nonconformity. On the other hand, differences can exceed desirable limits.

One group of young people labeled as different are the emotionally disturbed. All too frequently the school uses excuses to release the pupil with emotional difficulties. What it should do is determine ways of adjusting his problems. This means special classes at various grade levels for emotional underachievers. Such classes permit specialized support for youngsters who are not doing well in regular classrooms. They require specially prepared teachers selected on the basis of their native ability, flexibility, and knowledge of mental health. Such classes need to be smaller in numbers in order to provide special individual attention.

The superintendent should recognize that the seriously emotionally maladjusted youngster should not walk the streets or be relegated totally to a home that may be the cause of his disturbance. This type of child needs to learn, to read, to compute, and to walk with normal youngsters and be as much like them as possible. The superintendent should see the curriculum not as a static band of knowledge to be absorbed but as a flexible instrument to meet the needs of these young people. Inherent in every resource unit and course of study should be ways in which these youngsters can achieve or approach a sense of personal balance or equilibrium.

The superintendent sees curriculum not as set but as adjustable, leaving to the expert and intuitive teacher the opportunity to modify the program within classes in order to meet the needs of his emotionally starved pupils.

THE SUPERINTENDENT AND THE COMMUNITY

The superintendent should ally himself with the forces in the community dedicated to mental health. He cannot afford to do otherwise. Continually he must bring to the attention of the community the mental-health needs of school children, what the school can contribute to the improvement of the situation, and suggest ways in which the community can help.

The superintendent will stimulate programs that help to produce a satisfactory relationship between the home and parents on the one hand and the school on the other. He will admonish those who work with him that school people must never give the impression that the school is all-knowing or always right. He insists that all school personnel respect the sovereignty of the home. He emphasizes the fact that the child is the parents' choicest possession. "They pass this way only once."

He requires that the school know something about the parents and the home environment of each child. The superintendent and his staff can take steps to help the home understand why a child is as he is, why he is different from the parents, and why he has not reached the level of accomplishment the parents had established for him. He can do this through personal interviews, through bulletins to parents, through his influence on teachers, through his support of the parent-teachers organization, and other means of communication between the school and the home.

The superintendent becomes a member of the community mental-health team because of the services he can get from it. If it does not exist, he helps to create one. If a mental-health committee exists, he makes himself available for service on it.

Through contact with psychiatrists, psychologists, and social workers he learns of the valuable services these other disciplines can add to the school effort. He discovers how little he really knows. His humility becomes a source of strength to himself and to his associates. Clarity of vision and understanding can be achieved only through actual contact, alertness, and a receptivity to continued learning. This must be his attitude toward a practical mental-health program.

THE SUPERINTENDENT AND PREVENTIVE MENTAL HEALTH

The superintendent must be alert to the need for providing a positive mental climate in each classroom in each school and in all contributing services.

It is possible that good mental health in a school is caught, not taught. If this is so, it is important that the conditions for good mental health exist for administrator, the teacher, and other staff members. If their mental health is on a high level, it is highly probable that the conditions will eventually include students.

As was indicated, the school administrator's influence on the emotional climate of the school is of considerable importance. If his relationship with the members of his board of education is good, this atmosphere will embrace teachers and students as well. If school-board policies are well spelled out, outlining conditions under which teachers are freed from worry, undue restraint or uncertainty, the teachers are then freed for total absorption in the all-important teacher-pupil-learning relationship.

Salaries and working conditions are the responsibility of the superintendent and the board. If these are cooperatively worked out, they are more likely to be satisfactory to the teachers. This contributes to a high state of morale. If each teacher has adequate supplies and equipment to support him in the task of teaching, this contributes to good morale. If guidelines concerning the relationships of teachers and administrators, teachers and board, teachers and parent are cooperatively arrived at, the atmosphere of the school is more likely to be favorable to sound mental health.

If the school system has developed a meaningful, practical, and cooperatively determined philosophy that is understood by all staff members, the atmosphere of the school is likely to be healthy. If the proper balance of authority and permissiveness has been established between administrative and teaching staff, the climate of the school is usually favorable. If the physical plant is well planned, well constructed, and well maintained, this contributes to total morale.

Possibly most important of all is the superintendent's influence in helping teachers and staff members develop a program sufficiently broad in structure and content to meet the needs of all kinds of pupils.

The superintendent recognizes that many teachers and administrators do not have as much training in mental-health practices as present-day conditions demand. It is unfortunate that teacher-training institutions have been forced into a position of emphasizing acquisition of traditional subject matter to such an extent that programs and subject matter having to do with human relations, individual differences, and the teacher-pupil learning relations have been underemphasized. It is therefore essential that training in mental-health practices for teachers be continued while on the job. The superintendent will try to have every teacher participate in such experiences as a case conference, a clinical discussion of behavior, and an explanation of the teachers' role in diagnosis and treatment.

The superintendent recognizes that if a positive approach to good mental health in the classroom is to be maintained, some pupils must have special programs and corrective services. It is recognized that approximately 3 per cent of all pupils in all classrooms are seriously out of balance either with the school, the home, other institutions in the community, or with themselves. The superintendent must make every effort to demonstrate to his board of education and to the community the need for employing a properly trained staff to work with such persons.

THE SUPERINTENDENT AND CORRECTIVE MENTAL HEALTH

The school system should have available within its own resources the three disciplines commonly called for in an adequate mental-health program—psychiatry, psychology, and school social work. Limitations of budget and distance from source of supply may make it necessary for the superintendent to modify this rather absolute requirement. However, some combination of those disciplines should be available to some degree in every school system. The superintendent should make provision for them in his budget. Perhaps he can afford or obtain only the part-time services of a social worker, a psychologist, or a consulting psychiatrist. Whatever the combination, some form of mental-health service should be available to help diagnose and treat the 3 per cent for whom some assistance is necessary.

There are three main aspects of mental-health service provided by these three disciplines: (1) diagnosis, (2) treatment, and (3) consultative service.

It is important to know why an individual acts as he does. Inherent in diagnostic techniques are the suggestions of what remedial or positive measures can be taken to enable the individual to reach a satisfactory equilibrium for himself and for those who live with him.

But diagnosis is not enough. The school should be thought of and should function as a very definite part of the treatment process. Counseling, regular interviews, and consultation with psychiatrist, psychologist, and social caseworker are all important ingredients. It is difficult to treat the young person of elementary-school age or the adolescent outside the normal framework of the school system.

When the pupil is being served by community mental-health services, the school should be made aware of what is being attempted so that it may synchronize its efforts, in behalf of the child, with those of the community agency. The superintendent must take the initiative to draw agency representatives together for the purpose of agreeing on acceptable policies and procedures. The school, of course, must respect the confidential aspects of each case. All it needs to know is its role as a member of a mental-health team.

One of the finest services that a mental-health team in the school can provide is consultative service for teachers and principals. When teachers and principals are involved by school psychologist, social caseworker, or psychiatrist—in whatever combination—much of what constitutes good mental health rubs off on them.

Perhaps the mental health of the teacher improves best when he is in almost daily contact with these special disciplines. The classroom becomes a practicum, each child a learning device. The teacher at firsthand recognizes the real significance of individuality, the importance of ferreting out causes of activity and how he can best contribute to the everlasting search for mental equilibrium for each child.

The preventive mental-health experiment of the Rochester, New York, school system is an excellent example of the interaction of teacher, principal, parent, and mental-health services and how these services help teachers grow in insight and perceptiveness.

CONCLUSION

No one formula for good mental health of the school system exists. It is the total of a number of practices and procedures. One development triggers another. Each in its little orbit stretches out to affect others. The superintendent's acceptance of staff and teachers suggests that others do likewise. The superintendent who works cooperatively with staff helps leaders to work cooperatively with pupils and parents and peers.

A school or school system is mentally healthy when the superintendent gives every evidence of good mental health himself, when he communicates thoroughly and appropriately with staff, when the teachers feel confident that they have the security of his support and when he reacts positively to their suggestions.

Mental health begins with the superintendent's "Good Morning" and ends when the teacher departs for the day with the feeling that education is still a noble profession and that he has contributed something to the learning and mental well-being of the children. The superintendent frees the teachers for these all-important tasks. The atmosphere will embrace pupils, parents, and the community. It will be said of such a superintendent that "He runs a healthy school system."

24 *Educating for Mental Health*

James Conner

We are in a hurry. We are in a hurry to build a new world, to create a new educational order. We are in a hurry to get to the moon. We are in a hurry for children to read, to write, to compute, to perceive, and to comprehend the varied and complicated phenomena of this world. We are being rocketed at fantastic speeds from an ambling past to a sprinting present and a challenging future. One characteristic looms above all others, impatience. It is as though we have suddenly awakened from the proverbial twenty years' slumber and, rubbing the sleep from our eyes, find ourselves in a new world. We are in a pedagogical twilight zone.

Yesterday we could afford the leisurely pedagogical stroll that led some to conclude that the lag time between an educational invention and its implementation into the schools was fifty years. The prevailing tempo of the times reminds one of the following lines from *Alice in Wonderland*:

"Why, I do believe we've been under this tree all the time. Everything is just as it was."

"Of course it is," said the Queen, "what would you have it?"

"Well, in our country," said Alice, still panting a little, "you'd generally get to somewhere else—if you ran very fast for a long time as we've been doing."

"A slow sort of country," said the Queen. "Now here, you see, it takes all the running you can do to keep in the same place. If you want to get somewhere else, you must run twice as fast as that" (Chorpenning, 1946).

For though the revolution is upon us, I strongly suspect many of us do not know why we are running.

DIMENSIONS OF EDUCATIONAL REVOLUTION

On the one hand, there is reason to be pleased about the new ferment in education. After all, if we can't have exploration and discovery in this

236

field, where can we have it? It is well that some of the stale, educational dogmas have been laid to rest; some of the pedagogical theologians have been put to rout, and that there is less method or formula in our intellectual diets.

In spite of the joy in being active in these wondrous changing times, however, we must act in the cause of sanity. I would agree with Bruner who said:

> We are indeed on the edge of a great period of revolution. But it would be a great pity if our zeal were too easily assuaged by partial victories. We do well to recall that most revolutions have been lost precisely because they did not go far enough (Bruner, 1963).

Yet one cannot help remembering that history is also replete with examples of excesses of revolutions, of abuses to human rights. We must be equally careful that while keeping the torch of revolution alive we do not indulge ourselves by holding "purge trials" for those of the "old order."

What is needed along with the state of unrest is a continuing dialogue, a critique. We need outstanding people in educational philosophy and learning theory to give order to what appears to be a highly differentiated and often unrelated series of discrete educational events. In short, we are sorely in need of people who can orchestrate the various tones and pitches that characterize our times. It is very encouraging that a body such as the Association for Supervision and Curriculum Development may be pointing the way. In a series of brilliant essays in its recent yearbook (Frazier, 1963), this NEA department gave a refreshing perspective to the myriad happenings of our time.

Another group that has sounded the alarm over current developments in education is the Association for Childhood Education International. In an extraordinary colloquy held in Washington and chaired by one of the outstanding orchestrators of our day, Lawrence K. Frank, the group tried to identify some value constants in this age of great change. The problem was summed up in the first paragraph of their resulting booklet.

> "Things are so complicated" is a common plaint of adults. Too rapid, too many, too different, too interrelated are the many changes which crowd in our busy day-to-day world. But in a very real sense each of these complications, each of the pressures leaves its impress on children too. Problems seem to have a way of seeping down until they reach and affect the all unsuspecting children; problems in the community which cause tensions between people; problems in the neighborhood, of families going and coming, of new standards and customs; and problems of parents, in meeting these new demands and keeping to some of the old values too. Among all of these changes, there ought to be some guidelines, some values which hold steady (Goodykoontz, 1963).

Terry Ferrer, education editor of the *New York Herald Tribune*, dramatically outlined the Homeric sweep of current educational events.

The "bold changes" are already taking place in hundreds of schools throughout the country. The gifted, the average and the slow pupil have already begun to benefit, from new readers for the disadvantaged child geared to his real and often ugly world to advanced mathematics for the able high school student to foreign language in elementary school for the average.

If the tough subjects are pushing further and further down in a child's school life, the pressure is pushing up, too, on the colleges. It is almost inevitable that as the school revolution goes on, the patterns of college will have to change too, as well as the subjects taught there.

Thus the whole educational process, from kindergarten to graduate school, is beginning to seethe with fresh ferment. A longer school day and school year—which could be necessary in the coming years—may well blend with year-round college. Graduate education may begin much sooner, as better school-prepared students absorb college courses quicker.

The prospects are dizzying. Each ten and a half seconds, the United States makes a net gain of one person (the deaths against the births). That is 3 million children a year who must be educated with an eye to the future rather than the past (Ferrer, 1963).

In the preceding statements we have expressed what we all know—that the pressures on children and adults are increasing and that these pressures for good or ill will become worse because the simple truth is that we cannot stop the world and get off.

The booklet resulting from the "Colloquy on Basic Human Values" sponsored by the ACEI listed the pressures and stresses to which children are being subjected. We cannot consider the problem of mental health in a school context without taking recognition of these pressures. The following is a list of eleven pressures that were enumerated by the select group which met in Washington, D. C.

1. Pressures for early academic achievement. What is disturbing is that the organizational patterns of the high school are pushing down even lower into the grades. Also, we may be demanding that children learn things which could cause physical damage.
2. Pressures for conformity to standards.
3. The stress of nuclear war.
4. Pressures of an unknown future.
5. Emphasis on excelling in sports.
6. Pressures to be clean, neat and well groomed.
7. The nation's search for talent.
8. Difficulties in identifying parents' roles.
9. Difficulties in identifying one's own sex role.

10. Pressures on handicapped children to live and conform in a world geared to normal children.
11. Frustrations of nothing to do, no one to play with (Goodykoontz, 1963).

MENTAL HEALTH IN THE CLASSROOM

Reflecting on the foregoing pressures and change to which children are subject one might ask what of the teacher and mental health? What can the teacher do to help the child become a more adequate, productive, secure person? No attempt will be made to offer prescriptions for the teacher and administrator, to offer what Gordon Allport calls the "simple and sovereign solution."

First of all, it seems to me that we must give attention to the role of the teacher in promoting better mental health. It is my opinion that the teacher should first and foremost serve as a model of maturity for the child. We must realize that the teacher and the school may represent the only base of stability for the child in his otherwise disordered life. The teacher may well determine whether the child will have a trusting attitude toward other adults, or whether he will view them with suspicion and fear. The teacher needs to be aware of just how important he is and of the profound effect what he may do and say has on the child. Biber expresses this well:

> . . . What can she give and be to a child that can constitute the enabling ingredients for positive growth?
>
> She can lead him to become skillful, knowing, perceptive, and effective in this world; to master confusion; to communicate in the modes of his culture and sustain the idiom of himself; to extend his interest in the world to far places and times; to act, or organize, to accomplish, to reason, to reflect (Biber, 1958).

Next, in my opinion, the teacher should be a good observer and interpreter of child behavior. In a sense he should be a classroom meteorologist who is aware of the climatic highs and lows in the ecological setting that is the school. Early prevention and detection is an absolute requisite. As a "meteorologist" he will keep records and charts of human activity. The least we might expect is that the teacher would recognize the difference between problems of maturing and problems that may indicate a thwarting and distorting of the self. The teacher should come to recognize the kinds of signals children send out when they are distressed—to perceive the various adjustive mechanisms children adopt.

Admittedly, to become an observer and interpreter of behavior is no simple matter; it takes training—but I would point out that with the heavy emphasis on subject matter and academic achievement, we may be in danger of having some of the human growth and development courses taken out of teacher-training programs and removed as a teacher-certification requirement. The result may be that the teacher may know more mathematics but less about children. Obviously, such choices should not have to be made.

The next thing that would help matters would be for teachers and administrators to ask for help and to know where to get it. True, some of the climate of suspicion regarding outsiders should be removed. This could be accomplished by having resource people such as pupil-personnel workers, psychologists, and psychiatrists participate in the program planning of the school.

One of the blocks to securing outside help for youngsters is the feeling that referrals indicate a lack of control within the school or classroom. I was in one school where the principal stated with pride that she had not referred one child to the pupil-personnel worker or to a psychologist. This was a tragedy compounded of stupidity. Let me hasten to add that in my experience most elementary principals make use of all the help they can get. The problem is that they must wait for long periods of time before help is forthcoming.

My next point is that if we are to foster mental health in the schools, we will need to plan success. Perhaps we would do well to adopt the staffing procedures of child-development clinics and hospitals, but with one difference—to devote the energies of the group to planned success. Planned success means that we must consider each child individually and not as a person who is related to a measure of central tendency.

TOWARD INDIVIDUALIZED INSTRUCTION

In order to have planned success, we will have to undertake to explore and understand the highly idiosyncratic learning styles of children. Determining the cognitive styles of children should be the first order of business for the school. There is no better time to begin than in kindergarten or first grade. Ascertaining individual styles of learning will mean that we will have to provide opportunities for manipulating and experimenting.

If we are to interest ourselves in the cognitive styles of children, it will mean that we will need to understand the differences in digital and analogical thinking. It is important that we learn the nature of the two modes of thinking because the schools have tended to reward digital thinking while often discouraging analogical thinking. It might be useful if we could review the definitions of these two kinds of thinking.

Digital operations are those that involve the handling of discrete units by adding, subtracting, multiplying, and dividing. They are essentially linear operations achieved by the accumulation of digits or "bits" of information. Our language is digital in that we have the stringing together of words in a linear fashion. Such operations may be thought of as constituting a part-to-whole procedure.

L. K. Frank describes well analogical modes of thinking:

> Analogical operations take place, not step by step, bit by bit, by manipulations of single, discrete bits or digits, but as a holistic, integrative process that produces a product that can be immediately perceived and grasped. Thus a photograph, especially a moving picture of some event, communicates what happened where, when, how, and in what context, at one time, while a verbal or written description of that same event may require a long drawn out series of verbal statements, of nouns, verbs, adjectives, and adverbs presented serially in sentences, which may omit much that is relevant, may be erroneously heard, decoded or misunderstood by the hearer, and must be "added up" and combined if the words are to be meaningful (Frank, 1959).

It has been pointed out that the learning of children when they come to school is largely analogical (Ruesch and Kees, 1956). They need many direct sensory experiences before they can move into the world of symbols with adequate understanding. We must be willing to examine our school programs to determine if we are not overrewarding verbal behavior while discouraging behavior of a nonverbal nature. Of course, it should be realized that a textbook has little in it that would promote nonverbal learning. It is encouraging that people of the stature of Dr. E. Paul Torrance in their work in creativity are pointing out that our perception of intelligence has been quite narrow.

We need to look carefully at the things in the schools which are disturbing children. If schools can view their own operations carefully with a view to primary prevention, then giant strides can be made in mental health. For example, a prime area of concern should be what I would term abuse of mental functions; there are a minimum of three classifications of "thinking." I put thinking in quotes because I am not sure that is what I am talking about. The classifications are rational, freewheeling, or noncritical, and automatic or habituated learning.

The rational is the thinking that goes on at the conscious level. It is evaluative and critical. Freewheeling is largely intuitive and noncritical. It is "preconscious." This may be classified as "vagrant" thinking. It comes and goes and is not subject to our wills. Automatic or habituated thinking is the thinking that is stored in the muscles—it is reflexive. This type of learning allows us to type and walk without thinking about it. This "thinking" is characterized by "unconscious feel."

I submit we are often out of tune with ourselves because these three kinds of thinking are not working in harmony. We have had children thinking when responses should be automatic because somewhere in the learning sequence we failed to provide sufficient experiences in order that certain things could become habitual. On the other hand, we may have killed creativity by too frequent and immature evaluation. I think we need to look at the process of evaluation most carefully.

The whole point that I am trying to make is that mental health in the school may be greatly secured if we provide opportunities for successful experiences. Mental health is not some rarified, extrinsic goal. It is not achieved by formulas, but by careful attention to the child's operational world.

In sum, if we are to have planned success for children, we need to learn more about the individual cognitive styles of children, and, in order to recognize individual learning styles, we must look at learning that is analogical and nonverbal as well as digital and verbal.

INCREASING HUMAN STABILITY

It was stated in the beginning that no prescriptions would be given, but I cannot resist relating two separate experiments which I feel have great significance for learning and mental health. The first experiment was related to me by Ron Lippitt at the University of Michigan Group Dynamics Laboratory. He had undertaken a program whereby children who were discipline problems in the upper grades would act as big brothers or sisters for children in kindergarten. The upshot of the experiment was that real changes took place in the upper-grade children over a period of time and the upper-grade children were able to handle problems that the teacher was not.

The second experiment was carried on by a friend of mine who teaches young brain-damaged children. She was sitting in the teacher's room where she overheard an upper-grade teacher complain of a child in her room. The teacher went on to say that she wished she could get the child out of her room for a part of the day. My teacher friend stated that she would like to have the child come down to her room and help her. She undertook a program of training a number of school misfits in how to work with the children. Although all the results have not been analyzed, there is the positive subjective appraisal on the part of the upper-grade teacher. One of the youngsters made an occupational choice—he wants to be a teacher.

I point out these two similar experiments as examples of how we might be able to salvage some children by giving them a sense of competency. I very much like the statement of Earl Kelley: "When we see ourselves as inadequate, we lose our 'can-ness.'"

The next thing I think we can do to promote better mental health is to end what Lawrence Kubie calls "the conspiracy of silence." The simple truth is that many children carry perplexing problems within them with little opportunity to express their concerns and anxieties. Many of these feelings, though strong, may not be stated verbally because the child does not have the symbol system for doing so. Others may not be expressed verbally because to do so would involve a great amount of guilt.

We are in danger of increasing the "conspiracy of silence" because we are becoming increasingly academically oriented so that we have less and less time for nonacademic matters. The things in the school program that help the child give expression to his feelings are in danger of being curbed or lost, particularly at the presymbolic and early symbolic stages, nursery, and kindergarten. Art, music, creative dramatics, rhythms, and the like are much-needed modes of expression but they are not considered nearly so useful as science and mathematics. There is considerable pressure to eliminate these things because they take away from the "hard core" subjects of reading, arithmetic, and science.

Perhaps the more sensible among us in our society will recognize the value of the arts in the wholesome development of human beings. It is harder to make a case for the arts because they are not quite so utilitarian. Perhaps the difficulty in making a case for the arts was expressed by Francis Keppel, United States Commissioner of Education. "Nobody ever died of a split infinitive." Although Commissioner Keppel was urging more research in education when he made his cogent remark, it nonetheless is appropriate. So in an age when there are fewer and fewer opportunities being given for expression, we must as professional people protect the arts from the incursions of the pragmatists of this technological age.

In addition to what we have identified as the arts, we cannot fail to help children develop the symbolic language to express themselves adequately. We must be willing to roll back the barriers on what can and cannot be talked about. I am not too sure how prepared our society is for freedom of speech and inquiry, but we certainly need to begin to think about it.

What kind of classroom fosters wholesome mental and emotional growth? We might have some disagreement as to all the factors that should be included but I rather like the words of Lorrene Love Ort:

... There must be "enough for all"—enough teacher and enough care and enough encouragement and enough space and all the other "enoughs" to accommodate everyone. So often these are dimensions of the mind and heart rather than mere spatial measures.

Flexibility and availability are in evidence in the classroom . . . when a teacher remarks, "Let's look at this problem together."

Not, "Didn't I tell you to do it this way?"

... when a teacher nudges a person or a group but does not make a fool of anyone.

. . . when a teacher has enough of himself to share with everyone and when his attitude implies that there is a sufficiency of time even unto the least.

. . . when a teacher cares enough to help children expect and give a consistent best part of themselves.

. . . when a teacher's sound waves are consistent and not erratic.

. . . when there is room for whimsy and fun and the creative warmth of understanding laughter.

. . . when a teacher respects a student's choices, suggestions and ideas and does something constructive with the class about these.

. . . when a teacher can frankly and candidly admit that he does not know all the answers and that knowledge for him and them is a continuing and re-shaping process that goes on apace at all ages.

. . . when a teacher can accommodate with grace to the unexpected and is able to modify and modulate interestingly and well.

. . . when a teacher helps children recognize and accept those important aspects of social life and living in a classroom (Ort, 1963).

Part Three Curriculum, Learning, and Evaluation

Recent research and theory concerning the curriculum, learning, and evaluation have some important things to say about the problems of mental health and achievement, especially if we are interested in increasing potential and reducing school dropouts. If the curriculum is too difficult, too easy, or inappropriate, a child's school life becomes so stressful that he loses his motivation to learn and either fails to achieve his potential or drops out. If he is given too much, too little, inconsistent, or confusing guidance in learning or is forced to learn in ways inappropriate to his mental abilities and learning preferences, he will fail to learn and perhaps become ill. If evaluation is too severe, too easy, inconsistent, or inappropriate, the child lacks the guides to behavior that he requires and is likely to become mentally disturbed and unable or unwilling to learn. The papers included in this final section attempt to capture the essence of recent research and theory concerning these problems and bring it to bear in practical ways upon the problems of mental health and achievement.

In the opening chapter I attempt to show recent research demonstrates that there is a relationship between different kinds of mental ability and different ways of learning. Methods of instruction appear to make a considerable difference in who learns and fails to learn. In general, traditional measures of intelligence and scholastic aptitude predict achievement under authoritarian methods more accurately than under methods of discovery, experimentation, and other creative ways of learning. Measures of originality, however, predict more accurately achievement under creative ways of teaching than under the more authoritarian ways of teaching. Even clearer is the fact that the method of evaluation (multiple-choice test; short-answer questions requiring recall; problem solving, judgment, and decision making; creative application; and so on) makes a significant difference in who achieves high grades and who fails. Obviously these are facts that must be dealt with in any honest attempt to help increase potential and reduce school dropout.

Although it is true that some children will always learn "in defense of themselves," we cannot depend on this in the case of children who are subject to the stresses of poverty, the isolation and discrimination of a minority-group member, or other social and cultural disadvantages. The advantaged child with high creative-thinking abilities and preferences for learning in creative ways may somehow learn on his own, even if he is taught in authoritarian ways. If a child must cope with the additional stresses of poverty and other disadvantages, he may not have the adaptive energy to continue trying to learn under ways unsuited to his best abilities and preferred ways of learning. He becomes overwhelmed by the stressfulness of his life, loses his motivation to learn, and stops striving to achieve.

In recent years in England some interesting questions are being asked about the matter of different ways of learning for different kinds of children. Some of the children who were failures on the "Eleven Plus" Examination under the traditional system have achieved exceptionally well in the curricula that have been provided them. The explanation seems to involve something more than "late maturers" or "late bloomers," and the most common and reasonable explanation is that the new curriculum is more appropriate to their abilities and preferred ways of learning and is taught more interestingly than prior to the Eleven Plus Examination. Quite properly, many are asking why these children are not taught more appropriately and interestingly to begin with before they fail.

In spite of the great promise this line of development offers, we must face the fact that we have slow-learning students or less-able learners and that we have a responsibility to educate such youngsters. Several of the papers in this section deal with these special problems. Wesner's paper offers many practical suggestions regarding curricular considerations for less-able students. He argues that offering the same curricular opportunities does not give everyone an equal opportunity to become educated. He describes and evaluates such alternatives as homogeneous grouping, work-school programs, and special efforts to identify and capitalize upon whatever potentialities a child has. He points out that children of poverty and other disadvantaged groups come to school with basic needs not ful-filled—not just the physiological needs such as food, clothing, sleep, and the like, but also the psychological and social needs such as security, love, and status. In his chapter Wesner offers a wealth of specific, practical sug-gestions for dealing with these problems among less-able students. He believes that these curricular considerations should begin in the early school years and be continued at least through the high-school years. He thinks new types of tests, adapted textbooks, and programmed instruc-tion may revolutionize education but that the main link will continue to be the teacher.

Many of the papers in this volume in one way or another refer cas-ually to the discontinuity between the culture of the school with its pre-dominant middle-class values and the culture of the disadvantaged fam-ily. Most of these papers, however, emphasize the discontinuities as they exist for the adolescent. In Chapter 27 I have focused attention on the dis-continuity that occurs for all children the first time they come to school, but which is most severe, of course, for children from disadvantaged groups. I argue along with Alfred Binet for the point of view that it is natural for mental development to be continuous rather than discontinu-ous and that periods of decrement in achievement and mental function-ing are unnecessary. Specific, positive suggestions are given for reducing the common discontinuities in education by grafting education onto the learning skills that the child brings with him when he comes to school for the first time. The application of this idea to the education of disad-vantaged children would require that we learn more about the learning skills of preschool children. As Schreiber points out in an earlier chapter, children from disadvantaged families do have learning skills but they are quite different from those to which the school is geared. Schreiber may be correct in his assertion that the trauma experienced by some of these children when they are made to sit down and listen is one from which many of them never recover. The handling of the common dis-continuities in education (first entry into school, the fourth grade, and the seventh grade) appears to be of tremendous importance in achieve-ment and mental health.

These discontinuities doubtless play important roles in the increasing rejection of school by some children. Mary Saterlie defines the potential dropout as one who is rejecting school. She describes his most common mental, emotional, and social characteristics and offers a wealth of ideas for motivating and helping the potential dropout continue trying to learn. She offers separate sets of suggestions for emergency and long-range programs. She sees emergency programs as temporary solutions only and much less realistic than long-range programs that are initiated in the early school years and continued at least through the high-school years. She argues for a curriculum that is "different" rather than a watered-down version of what is offered to college-bound students. She treats separately the problems of the "slow learner" and the "underachiever." A realistic program for the underachiever would involve a highly motivating atmosphere and deal with causes of learning difficulties and lack of motivation.

Charles Savitsky, in his chapter on reaching the disadvantaged, reinforces the case Saterlie makes for curricula that are different rather than watered-down versions of existing curricula. He believes these weakened or watered-down courses do not bring about much genuine growth. He argues for curricula and instruction with a broader meaning, greater flexibility, and special consideration for motivation, meeting basic needs, and search for potential.

Frank Riessman offers a very refreshing approach for reaching the culturally deprived child. He has little to say about overcoming the handicaps or defects in the backgrounds of such a child. He builds his proposals around the common strengths of the culturally deprived child. For example, he maintains that such a child may be slow but not dull and suffers when speed is rewarded. There are virtues, however, in slowness and programs can be built on them. He also offers positive proposals for action on the culturally deprived child's hidden verbal ability and his positive attitude toward education. Riessman sees the lack of "know-how" as the culturally deprived child's basic weakness—how to fill out forms, to take tests, to answer questions, to listen, and to appear for interviews. He also feels that the culturally deprived child's anti-intellectual attitude is a handicap and should be modified.

Deutsch presents another interesting viewpoint concerning the achievement and mental health of disadvantaged children. He sees deprivations resulting from cruelty, neglect, and parental separation as more damaging than the deprivations commonly associated with economic and cultural disadvantages. These deprivations, he maintains, leave children unprepared to cope with the formal intellectual demands of the school. Deutsch is also concerned about the discontinuity between the disadvantaged child's background and school programs and contends that the school further estranges the disadvantaged child by its low expectations of him. He points out that the reduction of this discontinuity will require that teachers learn a great deal more than they now know about specific intellectual sequelae associated with economic impoverishment. He suggests further that serious consideration be given auto-instructional and programmed devices, since their use by the child will not involve the emotional rejection that he usually experiences in his interaction with a teacher.

In her chapter Merle Karnes has done a painstaking job of identifying the common characteristics of slow learners and discussing their implications for mental health and school achievement. She includes: physical inferiorities, mental immaturity for age, short attention span, poor memory, below-average incidental learning, poor abstract reasoning, poor response to long-range goals and delayed evaluation of work, poor ability to follow instructions, inadequate self-evaluation, deficiency in creativity, difficulty in transferring learning, retardation in academic areas, poor work habits, poor adjustment, and poor attendance. Karnes uses this background to propose positive suggestions concerning administrative plans for slow learners, the selection of teachers for them, and the modification of grading systems.

In my own chapter following Karnes' I present data and arguments which indicate that potentially gifted but unmotivated students may appear to have all of the characteristics that Karnes enumerates for slow learners. It has always been difficult to differentiate between slow learners and unmotivated gifted learners. In fact, many of the most eminent men and women in history have manifested at times during their school careers the characteristics Karnes lists for slow learners. Few of them come from economically and culturally disadvantaged backgrounds, however. There have come to my attention enough cases of unmotivated gifted youngsters from disadvantaged backgrounds to indicate the existence of a tremendous waste of potential. Such was the case of Kathy Daniel, an 18-year-old Negro girl (*Minneapolis Morning Tribune*, April 13, 1964, p. 15). Kathy is now recognized as a promising fashion designer with a real flair for originality. She grew up in a racially mixed neighborhood in Minneapolis. Her most lasting impression of her early teens was that she hated school. In her early teens she became in her own words, "a real juvenile delinquent."

In junior high school she skipped more than she attended. She spent most of her time plotting ingenious misdemeanors but most of them never got beyond the planning stage. Finally she was expelled from high school for wearing "crazy, funny clothes" and for "smarting off to the principal," according to her report. She picked up dressmaking on her own and her designs began reflecting her originality or, as some put it, her rebel instinct. Prominent designers believe that Kathy has the imagination and drive for a successful career in the field of creative dress design and she has already staged, primarily on her own initiative, a large fashion show of her own creations. It remains to be seen, of course, whether the potential that is now recognized will be realized.

In Chapter 33 I suggest that the mental health and achievement of unmotivated students can be improved by (1) providing more opportunities for doing something with what is learned, (2) increasing concern about what is learned rather than about grading, (3) adapting the difficulty level of curriculum tasks, (4) teaching in ways that give opportunities for using a variety of different mental abilities and learning preferences, (5) rewarding a variety of kinds of achievement, and (6) giving purposefulness to learning activities.

Allport's chapter on crises in normal development provides us with some potentially useful baseline data from which to interpret the meaning of the ongoing experiences of young people who are not achieving their potentialities. Using data from young people he identifies and discusses problems of apathy and anxiety, intellectual crises, specific inferiorities, religious crises, ideological crises, and sex and family conflicts. He does not regard as very useful such sloganized concepts as Oedipal complex, character disorders, identity difficulties, schizoid reactions, and the like. He prefers to examine the problems of young people in the more constructive terms of "becoming," maintaining that even in crises young people try to consolidate their gains and continue on the path of "becoming."

As a further means of providing and using baseline data concerning adolescent development, Strom describes in Chapter 35 an instrument for evaluating whether outcomes of learning in human relations and conduct are being realized. Strom believes that helping adolescents achieve their potentialities involves more than identifying an individual as an isolate. He would compare the deviate's norms and behavior with those of his peer group in such a way as to reveal the conditions under which exclusion occurs.

Lois French's chapter on how it feels to fail makes this book distinctive among books in the mental-health field. Rarely is the matter of failure even discussed in mental-health textbooks. For example, I examined the indexes of fifteen of the most commonly used textbooks in the field (Bernard, 1961; Bonney, 1960; Carroll, 1956; Henry, 1955; Jourard, 1963; Kaplan, 1959; Klein, 1956; Lazarus, 1961; Leeper and Madison, 1959; Redl and Wattenberg, 1959; Sawrey and Telford, 1963; Seidman, 1963; Shaffer and Shoben, 1956; Smith, 1961; Thorpe, 1960). Only three of them even include "failure" as a category. The Carroll and Seidman books each have five citations and Redl and Wattenberg's book has fifteen references to the category of "failure." I have long believed that education to cope with failure should receive far more attention than it does. An understanding of the effects of failure and the development of constructive strategies for coping with failure are especially important in any kind of educational program that seeks to develop potential and reduce school dropouts. Those who achieve their potentialities must fail and cope with failure or else they will never test the limits of their abilities and cannot know what their potentialities are. French offers some useful ideas about the neglected concept of overpunishment and the limitations of punishment, especially in dealing with slow learners, disadvantaged minority groups, delinquents, and the like. Perhaps more importantly, she offers positive suggestions for helping youngsters cope with failure.

In the final chapter Strom discusses another neglected topic in the field of mental health—that of school evaluation and grading. He identifies and discusses some of the dangers of current emphases on correcting and grading everything that a pupil does, the confusion of grades with conformity and losing sight of genuine achievement, and the confusion of completion with achievement. Strom cautions that there is a danger that those who choose grades as goals will cease to learn upon graduation from school or college and pleads for emphasis on the evaluation of what is learned and skills in using what is learned.

E. P. T.

25 *Different Ways of Learning for Different Kinds of Children*

E. Paul Torrance

To me, by far the most exciting insight which has come from recent research is derived from the finding that different kinds of children learn best when given opportunities to learn in ways best suited to their motivations and abilities. The evidence seems rather clear that whenever we change our ways of teaching in significant ways, a different group of children become the star learners or high achievers. I should like to review some of this evidence and consider with you what this means for educating a larger number of children to a higher level and for achieving a higher level of human dignity and a higher level of mental health in our society.

I suppose alert teachers have always been intuitively aware of the fact that when they change their method of teaching that certain children who had appeared to be slow learners or even nonlearners became outstanding achievers and some of their former star learners became slow learners. They have also learned that when they change the nature of the test used for assessing achievement, such as from a multiple-choice test to one requiring creative applications of knowledge and decision making, the star learners may change positions in class rankings markedly.

With some of the recent developments relative to mental abilities, some of the formerly puzzling phenomena are becoming clarified. There are now many convergent lines of research that make it clear that when a teacher changes methods of instruction or the nature of instructional materials that children with different kinds of mental abilities become the star learners and nonlearners. Differences in methods of evaluation bring out still further differences.

I shall review briefly several rather diverse studies that lead to the

Keynote address, Ontario Association for Childhood Education, Toronto, Canada, October 31, 1964.

253

conclusion that children with differentially developed mental abilities profit differentially from different methods of instruction. To reduce bias I shall not rely at all on my own studies or those conducted by students under my direction. I shall begin with one reported by T. R. McConnell in 1934.

AUTHORITY VERSUS DISCOVERY

McConnell's study is somewhat typical of earlier studies that emphasized the relationship between individual differences and methods of instruction or learning. It was a rigorous, carefully conducted study of learning by discovery versus learning through authoritative identification in second-grade arithmetic. The study encompassed a period of seven months, involved fifteen different schools, and 653 pupils. It made use of a comprehensive program of pre- and posttesting, as well as testing during the process.

In Method A, number combinations were identified authoritatively by a teacher who had established his reliability as an authority. The pupil supposedly took the word of the teacher that his work was correct or incorrect and depended on the teacher to supply him with the correct answer. In Method B, the number combinations were identified by the child through the process of discovery or verification. The child was taught the skills of discovering his errors for himself and found the correct answers on his own initiative. Learning was a relational process.

On five of the seven posttests, children taught by the discovery method tended to perform better than those taught by authoritative identification. The greatest superiority for Method A was on a test of speed of computation. The greatest superiority for Method B was on a test that required pupils to write as many different (but correct) answers to problems as possible during a 20-minute period. What puzzled McConnell most about his results was that mental age as measured by the Pintner-Cunningham Test was a better predictor of achievement under Method A than under Method B. In other words, the coefficients of correlations between mental age on the test of intelligence and scores on the final tests were higher among pupils taught by authority than among those taught by discovery methods. The difference was greatest for the test on which pupils under the discovery method were most superior to those under authoritative identification (r's of .401 and .177, with a critical ratio of 3.61).

McConnell was puzzled because he believed that insightful learning involved in the discovery method should have increased the relationship between the measure of intelligence and the measures of achievement. What McConnell did not recognize at that time was that the abilities involved in the measure of intelligence are more useful in learning by authority than in learning by discovery, whereas the reverse is true of the abilities represented by measures of divergent thinking, creative thinking, or productive thinking—whichever term you prefer. These results need no longer be puzzling, I believe, in the light of a variety of recent studies by investigators such as Hutchinson (1963), Stolurow (1962), Gotkin and Massa (1963), and various others.

HUTCHINSON'S STUDY

Hutchinson's study involved high-school students and more closely parallels McConnell's than any of the others. In the experimental condition, the methods of instruction were more nearly geared to the full range of mental abilities (divergent, evaluative, and so forth) found in the normal classroom and not just to the high I.Q. students. Meticulous classroom observations showed that there was a significantly higher proportion of productive thinking in the experimental classrooms than in the control classrooms. From the description of the teaching methods and the classroom interactions, I would describe the experimental method as creative teaching and the control method as authoritarian teaching—teaching for facts, logical reasoning, and the like.

Among the control subjects there was a significant correlation between mental age and the difference achieved on the subject-matter test from the pretest to the posttest. In contrast, there was no correlation between mental age and differences achieved on subject-matter tests for the experimental groups. The normal classroom instruction thus seems to have been geared to bring into play the abilities measured by the intelligence tests to a greater degree than in the experimental groups.

In the experimental groups where the methods were more nearly geared to the full range of mental abilities and not just to those abilities measured by intelligence tests, new productive and creative stars emerged and the correlations between measures of achievement and measures of creative thinking rose. In one of the experimental groups, for example, three of the students in the lowest quartile on mental age were the creative and productive stars.

If Hutchinson had been concerned about transfer of training, it is quite possible that his results would have been even more dramatic. In the experimental groups it appears that students were acquiring information with a larger number of possible ramifications and in an organized manner. Research over the years seems to indicate that if information is to be functional later, it should be acquired with as many ramifications as possible, in an organized manner, so that cues may evoke the information at some later time.

PROGRAMMED-LEARNING STUDIES

Two programmed-learning studies, one in language arts with fifth-grade gifted pupils and another with high-school students in mathematics, support Hutchinson's findings and add new insights in their own right.

The language-arts study reported by Gotkin and Massa (1963) involved 42 highly intelligent (I.Q.'s of 136 and higher) fourth- and fifth-grade pupils. They were provided about 30 minutes per day of programmed instruction in language arts for a period of about two months. The program used was the first four books of Susan Markle's *Words*. The subject matter was labeled vocabulary building and word-attack skills. Emphasis was placed on the development of ability to infer meaning. Prior to the initiation of the study, pupils were administered the Minnesota Tests of Creative Thinking (Forms VA and NVA).

Gotkin and Massa (1963) report that their subjects made significant gains as determined by the pre- and posttests of achievement but that among the fifth-grade pupils it was the *less*-creative students who made significantly greater achievement on *both* posttests and in gain scores. There were no significant differences in the achievement made by pupils of the two teachers nor were there any significant interactions. The correlations between the measure of creative thinking and pretest scores were not significant. The relationship between the creativity score and posttest achievement was —.34 and —.29.

Although Gotkin and Massa do not mention the fact in their final report (1963), they reported to me that in interviews conducted with the children, they found that many of the highly creative children expressed a strong dislike for this way of learning while almost all of those in the lower half of the distribution on the creative-thinking measure liked this way of learning. My guess is that the highly creative children disliked this way of learning and failed to learn very much from it because it was contrary to their preferred or best way of learning. They disliked being forced to make only tiny leaps because they are accustomed to making longer mental leaps and checking, testing, and correcting their errors. The less-creative children, however, prefer the safety of the tiny mental leaps and the authoritative feedback of their errors.

In discussing their results Gotkin and Massa (1963) express uncertainty as to whether the negative correlation between the creative-thinking measure and achievement under this program is a function of programmed materials in general, a function of the characteristics of this particular program, a function of the maturity of the subjects, or what.

Stolurow's studies involving measures of mental age and measures of originality in relation to achievement following a programmed-training experience throws some additional light on the problem raised by Gotkin and Massa concerning programmed material in general and specific strategies of programming material. In some of his early experimentation with different strategies of programming arithmetic material, he had discovered that as he and his associates improved the effectiveness of their programming the relationships between intelligence-test scores and posttraining achievement faded out. After further experimentation Stolurow (1962) predicted that as programming develops those students who do well on programmed instruction will tend to be those who are more original than those who do less well. In fact, some of Stolurow's own experiments support this prediction.

With 20 high-school students ranging in age from 13 to 15 and in I.Q. from 112 to 157, Stolurow and his associates conducted a summer institute in problem solving. He used self-instructional materials in logic, mathematics, and statistics. These students were given three Guilford-type tests (Consequences, Unusual Uses, and Plot Titles) and two Thematic Apperception cards with instructions to make up a story. All of these productions were scored for originality. The originality scores obtained from the Consequences, Unusual Uses, and Plot Titles tests correlated significantly with achievement on the statistics unit and with the final examination covering the entire statistical program. The originality scores obtained from the imaginative stories correlated significantly with the mathematics final examination. Mental age or scores on intelligence tests did *not* correlate significantly with any of these scores based on programmed learning. Correlations between mental age and originality and I.Q. and originality were essentially zero.

Stolurow believes on the basis of this and earlier research by him on troubleshooting or diagnostic decision making that effective autoinstructional materials should build specific, but multiple, associations to a stimulus. Since originality is operationally defined as the ability to make specific, but multiple, associations to a stimulus, it is expected that posttraining performance should be related to measures of originality. Thus Stolurow sees in this type of programmed instruction a realistic possibility of implementing the concept of individualized instruction.

MACDONALD-RATHS STUDY OF DIFFERENT CURRICULUM TASKS

MacDonald and Raths (1964) wondered if children should be grouped according to their creative-thinking abilities so that curriculum tasks could be adapted to their learning preferences and styles. Using the Minnesota Tests of Creative Thinking (Torrance, 1962a), they divided 81 children in the intermediate grades into three groups (high, middle, and low creativity). In a rather carefully controlled experiment the three groups of children were given a series of twelve fifteen-minute curriculum tasks. Three of the assignments were frustrating tasks, one each in the areas of ideas, numbers, and words. Three of the tasks were "open" in nature and were designed to encourage differences or divergencies of behavior. Three were "closed" in nature and were constructed so that everyone would have to respond alike to be successful. The other three tasks were called "passive" and required the children to listen as materials were read. In each instance there were tasks in the areas of ideas, numbers, and words.

The children high in creative-thinking ability were rated by observers as significantly more productive on the frustrating tasks than were the children in the other two groups. The children low in creative-thinking ability rated the frustrating tasks significantly lower than did the children in the other two groups.

On the "open" tasks the group low in creative-thinking ability was rated by observers as significantly less productive than the other two groups. The children in the middle creative-thinking group reacted less favorably to the "open" tasks than the other two groups.

The observers noted no statistically significant differences among the three groups on the "closed" and "passive" tasks. On the "closed" tasks the high creative-thinking group reacted less favorably than the other two groups, but there were no statistically significant differences in reactions to the "passive" tasks.

Thus it appears that children who are low in creative-thinking ability tend to dislike frustrating curriculum tasks and to respond in an unproductive way to open and frustrating tasks. Those high in creative-thinking ability tend to dislike closed assignments. The results suggest that pupils of varying levels of creative-thinking ability react differently to different kinds of curriculum tasks and are possibly best taught by varying procedures.

RELATED OBSERVATIONS

Many of the observations coming from users of the new curricular materials such as the PSSC physics, SMSG mathematics, and some of the chemistry materials are pertinent to the problem of differences in learner characteristics. Many of the users of these materials have reported that many students who had formerly been high achievers are no longer high achievers and that some who had been only average or below-average achievers became outstanding achievers. When statistical studies were made to evaluate some of the outcomes of the introduction of the PSSC physics, it began to become clear that old predictors of achievement could no longer be used with much success. Ornstein (1961) has reported some of the results obtained by the Educational Testing Service in their 1958–1959 study of the new physics materials. It was found that a substantial number of students who had scored only slightly better than average on the School and College Aptitude Test made gradually higher scores on the special physics tests given throughout the year. Many of these students scored higher than a large number who were at the top on the predictor tests and presumably were specially gifted. One possible explanation is that the students whose high aptitude scores did not correlate with their achievement-test scores were much better at remembering facts and formulas than at the creative thinking and intuition required by the new approach.

If we look at the nature of these new learning materials, it is easy to understand the phenomena which have been served by Ornstein and others. Learning by discovery and direct observation is a key to the teaching approach developed around most of these materials. As we have seen from McConnell's early study, measures of intelligence do not yield the best predictions for learning under such methods. Learners are taught to become sensitive to problems and to the gaps in their knowledge and inquire in ways that will yield solutions. They learn to keep records of their observations and to use information in solving other problems that require logical reasoning. They work with raw data and generate and test ideas from these data. It seems to me that these new curricular materials are resulting in an increase in the extent to which knowledge, skills, and attitudes are being learned in ways that bring into play imagination, intuition, divergent thinking, judgment, and decision making. Learners are required to do more inquiring, questioning, hypothesizing, experimenting, testing hypotheses, and communicating what they discover. These kinds of learning experiences draw more heavily upon what I have been calling the creative-thinking abilities and what others have termed divergent thinking or productive thinking.

Educators at work on problems of school dropout and on the education of culturally disadvantaged children, economically impoverished children, and the like have made some interesting observations about the styles of learning of these children. These observations indicate that such children have in the past shown up rather badly perhaps because the schools did not give them opportunities to learn in ways that are compatible with their best abilities and preferred styles of learning. Schreiber in his chapter in this book maintains that children from culturally deprived or disadvantaged families can and do learn but that their learning styles are not those the school is generally geared to. Schreiber believes that for such children the first experience of school when they are forced to sit and listen attentively while a teacher speaks is a traumatic one from which many never recover.

One of the most interesting things I have noted from the reports of teachers using the experimental materials developed by my associates,

Myers and Cunnington, is that children who are not ordinarily motivated to learn become excited about learning for the first time. For example, teachers using our audio-tapes and the related guided, planned experiences in creative thinking report that some of their most enthusiastic learners are children who ordinarily do very little studying, tend to be isolated and nonconforming, and the like. Boys, more than girls, appear to show a greater interest in learning. It is my contention that many children and young people not now motivated to learn in school will become excited about learning and will achieve in line with their potentialities, if given a chance to use what is learned, if given a chance to communicate what is learned, if we show an interest in what is learned rather than in grades, if learning tasks are not too easy or too difficult, if there is a chance to use their best abilities and preferred ways of learning, if we reward a variety of kinds of excellence, and if learning experiences are given purposefulness.

A SUGGESTED ANALOGY

It may be an overwhelming task to tailor-make the educational experiences for every child, but the task becomes more manageable if we can identify important variables about which instruction can be individualized. Although I am sure that we shall eventually, perhaps quite soon, be able to identify a number of these variables or types of individuals, I would like to propose an analogy that I believe is useful in helping to understand the learning problems of at least two types of learners.

This analogy comes from my personal experiences with pets and their learning problems. As a child I had dogs for pets. Somehow I managed to train them so that they became reasonably well-behaved, apparently happy, affectionate, and loyal pets, as well as productive killers of rats, mice, and moles. My teaching skills did not match those of instructors in dog obedience schools, but I think my methods were basically similar to those of the obedience school. Essentially, I punished undesirable behavior and rewarded desirable behavior. Dogs, anxious by nature apparently to please, respond to this kind of treatment.

In recent years my pets have been cats. I undertook to train Hazel, my first cat, in very much the same way that I had, as a child, trained dogs. I still bear some of the physical marks of this error and I suppose Hazel still bears some of the psychological scars of my inhumane treatment. The more I punished undesirable behavior the worse she behaved; the more I rewarded desirable behavior the worse she behaved. In time I began to gain insight into the ways by which cats learn and I changed my treatment of Hazel accordingly. She is now a well-behaved, apparently happy, loyal, and affectionate cat. She is infinitely curious, independent, proud (sometimes appearing haughty and self-satisfied), possessed of great dignity, manipulative, experimental, playful, quiet, adventurous, highly sensitive to ridicule or criticism, energetic, persistent, yet affectionate and considerate.

Hilda, the second cat, was trained according to my new understanding of the cat's way of learning. When she and the other kittens in the litter first chose to use a different corner of the basement for their toilet than the one I had intended, I provided facilities in the corner that they had chosen. Formerly I would have punished them to try to force them to use the location I had chosen. Later they started using the facilities that had been established for Hazel. Hilda has never scratched me, yet she puts to flight hostile cats far larger than she. She has never been difficult. Her greatest delinquency is that she pulls books from the shelves when she is frustrated or angry with my wife or me. We can assess the degree of her provocation by the number of books she pulls down. If we grant her the right to become provoked when she is frustrated and simply place the books back on the shelves, all goes well. Creative children experience frustration too and respond to limits in ways similar to Hilda's book pulling.

It is my belief that the reason why creative children frequently become difficult children is because we have been unwilling to recognize fundamental differences in the ways by which cats and dogs learn. In the main, dogs tend to learn by authority. They are anxious to please and respond favorably to the stimuli provided. Cats, on the other hand, tend to learn creatively—by exploring, testing the limits, searching, manipulating, and playing. They have been noted throughout history for their curiosity and venturesomeness. This is (I believe) the basis for the tremendous differences in the ways by which cats and dogs learn. This does not mean that dogs are totally lacking in curiosity and that they learn exclusively by authority. Dogs also learn in creative ways. Similarly, cats do not learn exclusively through spontaneous ways. They respond to firm limits and deliberate methods to some extent. There are big differences, however, in preferred ways of learning. Similarly, I believe that one of the most fundamental ways in which children differ in learning springs from their creativity.

The cat and the creative child both need a responsive environment more than a stimulating one. Many teachers and parents ask, "What can we do to stimulate creativity?" It is not necessary to stimulate the creative child to think creatively, although it may be necessary to provide a stimulating environment for the child who prefers to learn by authority and the child whose creativity has been suppressed for a long time. With the creative child, adults need largely to avoid throwing off course the child's thinking processes, guiding him by providing a responsive environment.

It is my belief that this approach will lead to the controlled kind of freedom that seems to be necessary for productive, creative behavior. In defending the possible consequences of this approach, I point to the fact that the dogs in our neighborhood are kept on leashes so that they will remain under control. No one would think of placing a leash on any of the cats in this same neighborhood.

A responsive environment is something quite different from what is commonly termed a "permissive atmosphere" or a "laissez-faire" environment. A responsive environment requires the most alert and sensitive kind of guidance and direction. It involves absorbed listening, fighting off criticism and ridicule, stirring the unresponsive and deepening the superficial. It requires that each honest effort to learn meet with enough reward to ensure continued effort. The focus is on potential rather than on norms.

26 *Curricular Considerations for Less-Able Students*

Gordon E. Wesner

Our progress as a nation can be no swifter than our progress in education. Our requirements for world leadership, our hopes for economic growth, and the demands of citizenship itself in an era such as this all require the maximum development of *every* young American's capacity.—John F. Kennedy

The class period, as usual, seemed wholly inadequate to the earnest young teacher who stood facing a roomful of expectant faces. Test papers, painstakingly graded and recorded, lay in a neat stack on her desk, ready for distribution; and yet, a glance at her watch confirmed that there could be no time for discussion or explanation.

Already she could anticipate the whoops of joy from the eager few, excited with the adventure of learning, who would dash off, waving success overhead like a victorious banner. Others would respond with the indifferent shrug to which she had become accustomed, and, easily shedding their problem, hurry off to more entertaining pursuits. It was those remaining who, reluctant to leave, would crowd around her desk, the puzzlement and defeat in their faces seeking answers that could not readily be found. There would be no easy words or reasons to explain to these anxious youngsters their inability to keep pace with the leaders of the class. Still, no single one was without a certain measure of ability. Where and how could it be developed? Who would find the time? Reluctantly she began to hand out the papers, calling the names one by one.

For teachers all over America there is, perhaps, no problem of greater concern than that of the slow learner. From the time teachers arise in the morning until they switch off the light at night, the problem of the slow learner confronts them. This awareness of the slow learner is necessary and desirable—but concern is not enough!

LET'S FACE THE ISSUES

American public schools are faced with a real challenge, the task of providing appropriate education for more than ten million less-able students whose presence is felt in almost every community in the United States—in large-city slum areas, in wealthy suburbia, in small towns, and in rural communities.

The unsatisfactory term "slow learner" has come into general use to designate the individual who is equipped with less-than-average native capacity to learn. Before we as educators can be of much help to the less-able learners, as we reluctantly label them, we not only must recognize them as *being* different, but we must, alerting ourselves to certain identifying characteristics, understand *how* they are different. The problem becomes oversimplified in merely noting:

1. Severe retardation in reading skills and comprehension.
2. Lack of interest in academic subject areas.
3. Limited attention span in learning activities.
4. Poor study habits.
5. Feelings of anxiety and neglect.
6. Tendency to anticipate failure and eventual dropout of school.

G. Orville Johnson (1963) clearly defined the slow learning or less-able pupils

as a group which differs from children identified as mentally retarded, disturbed, delinquent, or remedial problems. But the close interrelation of these children, so defined, with culturally disadvantaged and delinquent groups compounds the educator's approach to careful identification as well as the development of appropriate curriculum. . . . Slow learners are usually accepted in adult society as normal members of the community, requiring no special consideration, but are restricted in finding a job and a social group where they can fit in comfortably.

According to Arthur A. Hitchcock, Executive Director of the American Personnel and Guidance Association,

many of these less able pupils fail—withdrawing from the scene of failure to follow a narrowing path to a sign, "Not a Thruway"—become detriments to themselves and losses to society. Disaffiliation and the sense of having been handicapped by the very school that should have helped individual development may lead from failure to open hostility.

Communities have a stake in every child's education, for schools are the channel through which our American way of living is handed on and the responsibility of citizenship is fostered. As a nation we cannot send into the labor market an ever-increasing number of unskilled workers while jobs for the unskilled are decreasing sharply every year.

Educators are slowly awakening to the fact that offering the same curricular opportunity for all does not give everyone an equal opportunity to become educated. Johnson (1963) feels that the less-able learners should be grouped homogeneously for instruction as soon as they enter school, especially at the junior and senior high-school level. Stressing the importance of continuing the education of these pupils until age 18, he recommends that the last three years become a work-school program leading to the gradual transition from school to normal community life.

The majority of large-city schools have attempted to solve the problem of educating the less-able pupil by attempting more or less homogeneous grouping. Mere grouping for purposes of isolation, however, is not only wrong but it is ineffectual. Education for these students must be accompanied by more careful thinking and planning on the part of teachers, and greater differentiation of teaching materials and teaching methods. The fact must be accepted that slow learners *are* learners, nonetheless, and that curricular approaches can and must be developed to reach more appropriately the classes for these pupils.

Featherstone (1951) recommends that

in thinking about planning for slow learners, the term, "slow learner," should be interpreted consistently to mean slow in learning intellectual things. They are not equally slow in all kinds of activities or abnormal in all their characteristics. Even though they do not do well in mathematics or reading, they may get along quite well with respect to social adaptability, mechanical ability, or artistic sense.

Where the student's slowness is due to lack of native capacity, however, it is erroneous to assume that he will "catch up" in time with the more capable students. He must be recognized for his potential, "where he is," and provision should be made to develop this potential to the maximum.

IDENTIFYING THE LESS-ABLE STUDENTS

The *Dictionary of Education* defines the slow-learning boy or girl as one "who, though capable of achieving a moderate degree of academic success, will do so at a slower rate with less than average efficiency." The general practice is to place students in this classification when they score between 80 and 95 after the administration of several valid intelligence tests. The problem faced by the schools comes into sharp focus when we recognize that one out of every five pupils falls into this classification.

No pupil, however, should be labeled a slow learner without the benefit of many tests, both medical and psychological. Failure in academic achievement may not always be due to a low mental ability, but to some physical disability, such as loss of hearing or vision, or to some emotional problem that temporarily may prevent the pupil from functioning at his true level.

Ideally a school-system routine would include examination by a psychologist of all pupils before starting school, but, in the absence of this procedure, the teacher's report must furnish first indication of slow learning rate and poor retentive ability. Further screening for identification then must follow, based on actual intelligence tests. The California, Kuhlmann-Finch, Lorge-Thorndike, and SRA Primary Mental Abilities Tests are among those considered most useful in the elementary schools, with the Differential Aptitude Tests and the School and College Ability Tests being most widely used by the secondary schools.

After group-screening processes have been thoroughly evaluated, final identification should be attempted through an individual comprehensive examination administered by a school psychologist, who will have at his disposal an extensive battery of testing instruments that includes achievement tests, personality tests, interest inventories, and so on. All these aids will serve to distinguish the true slow learner—his limitations and his abilities—from deviates due to emotional maladjustment, mental retardation, or extreme cultural deprivation.

The foregoing analysis, combined with cumulative data gleaned from school records, home visits, and the careful anecdotal reports of teachers, can well serve in helping to understand and reach these less-able students. For a school to do less is like trying to reach an unfamiliar and distant point without adequate direction or a highway map.

GENERAL CHARACTERISTICS OF SLOW-LEARNING STUDENTS

In working with the slow learner, the first thing that the teacher must recognize is the fact that these students have the same basic needs as those of the normal or gifted student. They have (Bernard, 1952) the

organic needs of food, air, clothing, shelter, et cetera, the fundamental psychological needs to feel secure, to manipulate and to satisfy their curiosity, to achieve, and to be independent; and the social needs to be loved, to be accepted, to be recognized as being of worth, and to have companionship.

According to Robert F. DeHaan (1956), and others, in *Identifying Students with Special Needs,* the following are the characteristics of the slow learner:

(He) is unable to think abstractly or to handle symbolic material
is unable to understand and carry through directions for assignments
is below the so-called "common sense" and reasoning level of the class
is unable to understand complex assignments or game rules
is slow in all areas: academic, social, emotional, and physical; breaks
    rules of conduct or of games and is often unaware of doing so
is unable to work independently
is easily confused
has a short interest and attention span
seems unable to concentrate voluntarily
finds it extremely difficult, if not impossible, to keep up with the class
    in academic work
is behind normal grade achievement in school.

Because it has been found that many slow learners come from "less-favored" backgrounds or from homes in which their fundamental needs—especially the psychological and social ones—are not adequately met, the teacher often needs to provide experiences in which the slow learners can feel "success" more often than do the other pupils, and can feel that they are accepted and loved. While working with slow learners, teachers have observed that desire for acceptance and need for reassurance appear much stronger in slow learners than with the other students. Such attitudes would seem to indicate that this feeling of insecurity, and the desperate need on the part of the slow learner to be accepted, might be due to his past experiences of failure and of rejection within the classroom, the community, or even in his own home.

Psychologists assert that the slow learner goes through substantially the same mental processes as the average or rapid learner, except that he seems to have a different rate of perception and moves at a very much slower pace. Consequently, teachers must allow these slow pupils a much longer time to "catch" and understand what is to be learned, even if it means repeating each step several times. Experienced teachers have found that many of these students are helped by the use of visual and manipulative devices. In arithmetic, particularly, where learning is cumulative, the slow learner may soon fall hopelessly behind if pressure exists to keep pace with the average and above-average members of his class. Here, especially, more reinforcing practice exercises must be provided in order to establish more permanent learning.

One investigator believes that another major characteristic of the slow learner is his lack of creative ability, which is manifested in a weak "associative memory." Placed in a heterogeneous classroom, in which pupils with a wide range of ability are taught and in which setting he is socially immature, the slow learner is generally made aware of his "stupidity." Such awareness frequently leads to social withdrawal and subsequent antisocial behavior, further blocking the learning process.

SUGGESTIONS AND TECHNIQUES FOR TEACHING LESS-ABLE STUDENTS

Teachers should realize that the broad objectives for education of the slow learners are the same as those for the normal and for the gifted students. These objectives, according to the Educational Policies Commission (1946), are "self-realization, human relationship, economic efficiency, and civic responsibility." The difference between slow learners' education and that of the other students is found in the types of experiences provided by the teacher, the kinds of materials and equipment he or she uses, and in the curriculum adjustments that he or she makes in order that the slow learner may attain these objectives. Specific objectives (Kirk and Johnson, 1951) for the less able naturally will be much simpler and more practical, and will stress the areas of "occupational adequacy, social adequacy, and personal adequacy." Teachers are reminded that all of the educational and vocational planning made with the slow learner must take into consideration the fact that many of them will not go beyond the secondary school, if they go that far, and that most of them will find their future employment in the "unskilled or in the semiskilled field" (Ingram, 1953).

Some teachers encourage success and enjoyment in reading through use of high-interest, low-reading-level materials, recommending such vehicles as *Teen-Age Tales,* the Ginn reading books, condensed publications, various reviews, and "adapted" materials. When books in the school library seem "too hard," teachers often form a book-review committee, with students assisting in reviewing books and offering oral and written recommendations based on class-developed criteria.

Many teachers promote reading interests through extensive use of the daily newspapers. The front page is studied for new words and their meanings; the index becomes a tool to locate information; the student learns to "skim" for essentials; advertisements are analyzed to develop importance of reading words with care; the editorial page becomes an instrument to encourage discussion, debate, and to promote critical thinking in an interpretation of the news. The "social-studies" aspect of this activity is further developed through the use of *Read* magazine and its timely news articles and geographical materials.

Preparing material for broadcast over the school public-address system provides committees of slow learners with incentive for doing reference work, furnishes opportunity for the necessary written and oral composition, and focuses attention on their own speech patterns, looking toward improvement. Teachers are taking advantage, also, of suggestions contained in Bell Telephone's new "Telephone Activities" as a means of improving telephone techniques.

History writing can offer a unique and challenging vehicle for the improving of English-usage skills. Class members team up to write for personal interviews with local resource people of the community. The interview itself furnishes practice in introductions, questioning procedures, and note taking. Finally, the information thus gathered may be shared and compiled by the class into a collected local—community, town, city—history, a practical example of English at work.

TEACHERS AND TEACHER SUCCESS WITH THE LESS-ABLE STUDENTS

The teacher working in this area should recognize that every slow learner is a unique individual and not merely a typical member of a group. The teacher should become thoroughly acquainted with her slow learners, how they differ from each other, and how she must provide for these differences. The teacher should understand the child and help him to feel a part of the group by working through his strengths and showing a personal interest in his accomplishments.

Certainly teachers should be alert to problems too severe to be solved in the classroom, and work effectively as a part of the professional team by promptly making referrals for special services available in the school.

Basically, however, a teacher's qualifications for success with the slow learner should include an emphasis on patience, firmness, a good sense of humor, teaching skills and techniques that will stimulate pupils to reach their potential, and, above all, an abiding faith in the personal worth of *each* of these less-able children.

In a research study carried on in New Jersey, secondary-school teachers reported the following practices found to be most effective in teaching the slow learners (Langworthy, 1961):

1. Using substantially more praise than reproof.
2. Extensive use of audio-visual aids.
3. Using students' experiences to stimulate interest.
4. Giving students many chances to apply what they learn.
5. Small-group instruction within the class.
6. Using projects in which students evidence interest.
7. Encouraging cooperation within the class.
8. Keeping students carefully apprised of their progress.
9. Emphasizing vocational values in materials studied.
10. Emphasizing the social value of the materials studied.
11. Use of school and/or community resource people.
12. Individual work-study contracts.
13. Doing much planning of the classwork with students.
14. Encouraging competition with the class.

These practices imply that teachers find their students learning more effectively when they feel successful; when they feel good use is being made of their experiences; when the work relates to their interests; and when they feel they can apply what they are learning.

Viewing this same study from the opposite angle, the question, "What are the major contributors to the difficulties teachers have in working with slow learning youth?" presented the following problems (Langworthy, 1961):

1. Lack of knowledge of the students as individuals.
2. Lack of knowledge of suitable materials for slow learners.
3. Lack of knowledge of the learning process of slow learners.
4. Too much emphasis on textbook-dominated teaching.
5. Inflexible courses of study not permitting adjustment.
6. Too many students to permit individualized instruction.
7. Lack of interest in youth who are slow learners.

8. Inflexible standards, unreasonable for slow learners.
9. Lack of ability to help slow learners with reading.
10. Instructional materials suited only for more-able students.
11. Inability to teach small groups within classes.
12. Too little use of audio-visual aids.
13. Lack of knowledge of the patterns of human development.
14. Lack of knowledge of vocations or occupations.
15. Periods too short to individualize instruction.

These opposing sets of problems pose interesting questions to teachers, school administrators, and to people charged with teacher education. Unfortunately, teachers will find disappointingly little help from literature on teaching slow learners. If their work is to become more effective, they must confer with other teachers, be given time and encouragement to conduct studies of their own slow learners, and get expert help from specialists in this area.

CURRICULAR CONSIDERATIONS FOR CLASSES OF LESS-ABLE STUDENTS

Numerous educators point out that curricular programs for the less-able learners should begin as soon as they enter school and should continue until they are ready to take their places in the community. This means the planning of a total program K–12 or K–12–Adult education. Slow learners tend to become serious problems in the upper grades of the elementary school and in the junior high school, as lack of achievement begins to cause serious disruption in regular classes, and truancy and harassing delinquent behavior comes to be a common denominator. The aim of the school systems should be to prevent from the beginning development of this unhappy problem, rather than devoting years of haphazard attempts at correction or in remedial programs. This new approach calls for continuous surveys of kindergarten or first-grade populations, with group placement, followed by carefully planned programs that begin in the primary, advance to intermediate, and continue through the junior and senior high-school years. Teachers selected to work with children in such a program should be interested in working with children who have learning problems typical to this population group.

Locating teachers with appropriate ability and attitudes for this task is not easy. Probably one of the most neglected areas of preservice education of teachers is the in-depth preparation for teaching classes for the less-able student learners. Every effort should be made, however, to employ teachers who have come through teacher-training institutions that are seriously trying to produce trainees who understand slow-learner characteristics and learning problems, and who can perform well with these deviate children. Here, teacher-education institutions need to carry on more extensive research and field work, encouraging future teachers to accept the challenge to teach this one-fifth of our growing school population.

The curricular program should be developed based on understanding of the characteristics of these slow learners and embodying plans for the fulfillment of their emotional, social, physical, and achievement needs and interests. Such a curriculum should focus on background environment of these children rather than those curriculum programs that traditionally have carried heavy investments of "middle-class" biases inappropriate for children coming from less-favored environments.

If a curriculum continuum (K–12–A) is to differentiate properly from the general curricula of the past, curriculum planners and teachers must be responsible for carrying on learning activities, geared to these specific local environments, which will help boys and girls develop purposes and values looking toward improvement of their home environment.

New tests, adapted textbooks, and programmed learning may revolutionize methods, but the main link in the learning process still resides in the relationship of the individual teacher to each slow-learning student. Teacher enthusiasm for the course he is teaching is contagious. The classroom teacher can be the strongest force from the primary grades on, for upgrading the quality of work that the less-able students will do, and for keeping them in school.

Many school systems are now establishing specific programs for the less-able or slow-learning students, whatever the cause of their difficulty may be. None of these programs, however, particularly those of New York City, is designed for rigid permanent groupings. The less-able students can and do move into high-level course materials as substantial skill and individual competency is demonstrated.

In the Kansas City, Missouri, Public Schools a three-year Work-Study Block-of-Time Curriculum, beginning in the eighth grade, is attempting to reach more effectively the less-able students among the boys, and is an experimental program under the direction of the Work-Study Project of the Practical Arts Division and the Secondary Curriculum Department of the Instructional Division. The aims of the research project are to:

1. Build better pupil self-concepts and self-understandings by establishing more realistic goals.
2. Improve basic skills in reading, speaking, listening, writing, and computation.
3. Develop success habits and attitudes toward work and job activities.
4. Provide a functional curriculum that will meet pupil needs.
5. Establish a school climate that will help improve pupil social and emotional adjustment to our democratic culture.
6. Encourage the pupil to explore wholesome recreational and vocational opportunities.

7. Develop a functional knowledge of our government and the American heritage.
8. Recognize the importance of science in daily living.
9. Develop an understanding of the pupil's role as a consumer and as a worker in industry.
10. Encourage worthy home and family relationships.

Each teacher carries on a guidance-centered approach to the class group and a counseling-centered approach with the individual students, using anecdotal records and accounts focused on growth, progress, and encouragement. Such growth records serve the pupil well as a basis for personal conferences and in helping interpret his progress to his parents. Periodic consultation and planning sessions between the teachers and the work supervisors assure best results for both the in-class learning activities and in the pupil work experience.

Structured in flexible patterns that are geared to the needs of each individual pupil, the curriculum base, however, relates—within the limits of the pupil's ability—to the general grade curriculum, to the end that he is not set apart from his peer group in the junior or senior high-school setting. The work part of the project, designed with the hope of equipping each boy to better meet the challenge of today's social and vocational world, strives to stimulate in the individual boy the following qualities:

1. neat personal appearance
2. punctuality
3. dependability
4. ability to work with others
5. personal application on the job
6. cooperativeness and initiative
7. enthusiasm for work and its rewards

Beginning in the ninth grade, adapted courses for classes of less-able students—both boys and girls—have been developed in English, mathematics, science, and social studies, thereby providing appropriate learning experiences as well as selected instructional materials on a reading level more suited to the slow learner.

GUIDELINES FOR ACTION

Forward-looking school administrators and curriculum workers are backing strong convictions with a determination to establish a developmental curriculum that meets the needs of their less-able pupils. In seeking sound general principles on which to base such programs of instruction, they may well need to look no further than G. Orville Johnson's (1963) *Education for the Slow Learner*. His excellent, well-defined "guidelines," offered for professional consideration, leave little to be desired as a blueprint for just such a timely, functional curriculum. There exists a mountainous task, however, in providing effective curriculum—a task too extensive to be left to individual teacher production of instructional materials. Textual materials for teaching the slow learner need to be produced in substantial quantity by publishers. These should include the complete "kit" approach, plus an abundant supply of instructional media directly related to the appropriate level, thereby making basic textual materials easily available for classroom use. This provision of basic learning need not abrogate creativity or initiative on the part of the classroom teacher. On the contrary, if teachers of less-able classes could receive such instructional materials, increasing amounts of teacher time could be freed to devote to individual student learning problems.

In planning further for the less-able student, teacher and staff utilization should be organized to provide for year-to-year continuity of the program, taking care to see that the slow learners enjoy the same access to all school facilities and receive the same attention from school specialists as do their more-able peers. It is essential that the professional relationships in the program, as well as the relationships of the slow learners themselves, be accepted as an integral part of the total school.

More encouragement and respect for education at home, improved teaching, more effective guidance, and differentiated curricula in schools, these factors, along with expanded employment opportunities, all have a place in keeping the less able in school. Every student, regardless of ability, craves the recognition and self-respect afforded by a friendly adult. Warmth, interest, and sound guidance, such as the school counselor can give, will go far toward preventing human waste and suffering, and often becomes the crux in avoiding dropout of the slow learner before high-school graduation.

If the administrative officers, counselors, and teachers initiate and encourage such procedures and attitudes in the school environment, inevitably community feeling toward these students will begin to replace the outmoded notions of disrespect, suspicion, or often downright rejection with attitudes of tolerance and acceptance of the less able in our population.

More curriculum development for the less-able student is long overdue. There is no magic formula. But teaching effort directed to these learners, for the establishment of their personal self-confidence, dignity, sense of accomplishment, and personal worth, can be very rewarding. After all, they too have a right to their fair share of the educational dollar; they too must develop an abiding faith in the real meaning of democracy.

27 Continuity in the Creative Development of Young Children

E. Paul Torrance

One of the most persistent and recurrent findings in creativity research with children is that there are discontinuities in creative development in most societies, apparently accompanied by loss of interest in learning, increase in behavioral problems, and increase in emotional disturbance. These discontinuities have been noted by a variety of investigators for many years (Andrews, 1930; Colvin and Meyer, 1906; Kirkpatrick, 1900; Mearns, 1941, 1958; Simpson, 1922; Whipple, 1915; Wilt, 1959; Torrance, 1962a, 1963). At least in Anglo-American cultures these discontinuities seem to appear at about the kindergarten, fourth-grade, and seventh-grade levels. Children at these stages of development perform less well than children at the next lower educational level on tests of imagination, originality, creativity, and divergent thinking, regardless of the level. They also participate in fewer creative activities on their own, appear to lose some of their curiosity, manipulativeness, and excitement about learning. There are also some indications that these are peak periods in psychiatric referral, remedial instruction, and behavior problems. They are certainly peak periods of concern for parents who write me letters concerning the struggles of their creative children.

In the past, little significance has been attached to these discontinuities in development. Observers have generally concluded that these are natural, genetically determined phenomena about which nothing could be or need be done. MacKinnon, who has studied the personalities of many highly creative people, maintains that there must be periods of socialization and increased conformity and that there are probably no better periods for increased pressures to conformity than in kindergarten, fourth grade, and seventh grade.

Presented to Institute for the Exploration of Early Childhood Education, Wheelock College, Boston, Massachusetts, November 6, 1964.

274

Other workers have discounted the significance of these findings by pointing out that there are plateaus in almost all kinds of development. It has seemed to me, however, that these drops in creative functioning are more serious than learning plateaus and are man-made or culture-made. As we have begun to concentrate on the discontinuity that occurs at about the beginning of the fourth grade, we find that the pupils in one fourth-grade class in a particular school may continue to show creative growth while those in another class show a decrement. Or, all the fourth-grade classes in one school may show growth while those in another school may all show decrements. No discontinuities occur in such continuous cultures as Western Samoa, the Sikhs in India, and the like (Johnson, 1963; Torrance, 1963). Thus it appears that teachers, school cultures, and larger cultures play roles of varying importance in determining continuity of creative development.

What most people have failed to recognize is the evidence that many types of intellectual development can be quite different when children experience guided, planned experiences than when they experience only what the environment just happens to provide (Ojemann, 1948; Ojemann and Pritchett, 1963). My associates and I have demonstrated (Torrance and Gupta, 1964) that the concept of guided, planned experiences in creative thinking can be translated into instructional materials in the form of audio tapes, teachers' manuals, and exercises that eliminate for most children the fourth-grade slump in creativity and result in fewer children hating school and greater participation in self-initiated activities of a creative nature. As in other concepts of guided, planned experiences, the development of materials and activities is guided by an analysis of the structure of the learning task, the nature and status of the learner, and the motivation of the learner to participate in the sequence of activities designed to facilitate a particular kind of development.

In my opinion we find many of the essential clues for developing methods and materials to eliminate discontinuities in creative development in the theory behind the Mental Orthopedics designed by Alfred Binet and discussed in his 1909 publication (*Les Idées Modernes sur les Enfants*). Binet maintained that all, or almost all, children begin school with highly developed skills in learning by experimenting, manipulating objects, rearranging them and combining them in different ways, singing, drawing, dancing, story telling, and the like. It was his contention that we should graft education on these already highly developed learning skills rather than suddenly requiring the child to abandon learning in these ways for learning in ways strange to him.

In designing educational experiences to reduce discontinuities in creative development, efforts should be made to make positive, constructive use of the early mastered and practiced ways of learning. If educators could accept the advisability of grafting education on the skills the child initially brings to school, we would have less concern about regressive behavior. We would then look upon the child's learning skills in a more positive, pushing-forward light rather than as regressive behavior. In adulthood it would not be necessary for Synectics groups (Gordon, 1961) to work so hard to create the psychological state of play, nor for the brainstorming groups (Osborn, 1963) to refrain deliberately from negative evaluation and to encourage "free-wheeling."

NATURAL WAYS OF LEARNING

Let us examine now the nature of the learning skills young children bring with them when they first enter school and see how we can build onto them as Binet suggested.

Skills in Creative Ways of Learning

When children enter school, they are experts in creative ways of learning because they have already had quite a lot of experience in learning in these ways. They have not yet abandoned creative ways of learning by questioning, searching, manipulating, experimenting, and playing, always trying to find out in their own way the truth. If they sense that something is wrong or missing, that there is something that they do not understand, they are uncomfortable until they do something about it. So they start asking questions, making guesses, testing, revising, and retesting. When they discover something, come upon some new (to them) truth, they want to tell somebody about it. It is such a natural process. At other times we must wait patiently—and then it may come lightning quick. Ann taught me how it could be lightning quick and Ollie taught me that there are times when it is best to wait.

Ann and her kindergarten classmates were busy with the Circles Test. She had been given a page of 35 circles and asked to sketch as many objects as possible from these circles in ten minutes. She had been instructed to sketch as many *different* objects as possible, to make each one tell as complete a story as possible, and to try to think of objects that others would not think of. After about eight minutes I said, "We now have about two more minutes before our time is up." Ann lacked about two lines of circles. Immediately she drew a girl blowing bubbles and the unused circles were bubbles already blown by the girl.

Ollie taught me a lesson about interrupting children's thinking while taking the Picture Construction Test. In administering this test, I had shown how to use a triangular piece of colored paper as the roof of a birdhouse with all of the trimmings. I then said, "Now, don't draw a birdhouse. This is just an example." All of these 33 kindergarteners except two could hardly wait to start. One began in about a minute, so he did not bother me much. Ollie bothered me greatly as he just sat there. I wanted to go to him and find out why he was not working. Perhaps he did not understand what was wanted. I waited, however, and in about four minutes Ollie began drawing with great intensity. I discovered that he had been sitting and thinking how a birdhouse would look on the inside and he was trying to draw this. Have you ever tried to imagine how a birdhouse would look on the inside? Ollie would not have been able to do this if I had interrupted him.

It is interesting to note (Singer, 1961) that highly creative children have greater ability to sit still than their less-creative peers. Under the guise of administering a test to identify future space men, it was found that highly imaginative children would sit still for longer periods of time than their less-imaginative classmates.

Interest Span

When I began including preprimary children in studies of creative thinking, advisers cautioned me that I could not conduct an experiment that would last longer than ten or fifteen minutes at the very most. I respected expert opinion, but I was not altogether willing to accept this advice, because earlier work with four- and five-year-olds in religious education had convinced me that young children can become deeply absorbed in a task for 30 minutes or longer. Thus I dared go ahead with an experiment that extended from kindergarten through sixth grade and lasted for about 60 minutes. Of course, there was considerable variety in the activities included. There was pasting, drawing, discussing, looking at one another's work, and even a brief "candy break" after 30 minutes. Usually the kindergarten children were so absorbed in their tasks that they kept working through the candy break. Some even put the candy aside until later or ate it as they worked.

Several problems may actually arise from a kindergarten or first-grade teacher's insistence that children move promptly from one activity to another. Chess and Thomas (1964) cite an interesting case of this type. Billy had shown no symptoms of disturbance at home or in nursery school. His first tantrum in school apparently occurred when the teacher shifted activities while Billy wished to stick with what he was doing at the time. Billy's temperamental pattern from birth had been characterized by persistence. He would become absorbed with his toys in his playpen, playing in his bath, or whatever he was doing. He would want to go on and on with an activity. The family learned not to let Billy get involved in any activity if he would have to be pulled away in less than an hour. His real trouble began when the curriculum called for many shifts in activity during the day. In a new school Billy was permitted to spend a good part of one morning reading and a good part of another morning doing arithmetic. He was not interrupted as long as he completed his required work and did not interfere with the other children's schedule. His classmates respected his scholastic performance and accepted the fact that he did not always do the same things they did.

I find it difficult to believe that it is natural for young children to skip from one activity to another. I am willing to admit that it may not be natural for an entire group of young children to sustain interest in the *same* activity, but in almost any exciting activity there are likely to be some who want to continue. Our mistaken idea that the curriculum must be the same for all of the children in a class makes it difficult to respect and make constructive use of this absorption in an activity. This point is illustrated in the following incident described by one of my students when I asked the class to describe an incident in which they had encouraged or permitted a child to learn in creative ways and it had made a difference in subsequent behavior and achievement.

A three-year-old on a walk with the class was shown a snail. Completely fascinated, he spent the remaining school time (one and one-half hours) observing and touching the snail, rather to my annoyance, but I let him alone while the rest of us went on with crafts. The child consequently became so interested in nature's small creatures that at age five he is quite an authority on small creatures. He approaches them stealthily and while looking for lizards practically looked a rattlesnake in the eyes. He immediately recognized it and retreated just as quietly and was unharmed.

Ability to Organize

Young children are grossly underrated regarding ability to organize their behavior. This is one of the surprising discoveries of Maria Montessori (Standing, 1962). She recognized that children wanted things to be organized but at first thought that adults must organize them. She soon discovered that children of kindergarten age had a real interest and talent for organizing things themselves. The following report of a kindergarten teacher illustrates how opportunities present themselves for permitting children to organize their behavior.

This teacher's class of 28 kindergarteners was presented with the problem of planting bulbs in containers and cleaning up within a 30-minute period. Some of the children rushed to get their containers and several quickly said, "We won't get it done that way." Spontaneously some of the children recognized that they must act in a more organized manner in order to accomplish the task. One child suggested that they do the planting by rows, each taking a turn without rushing or pushing. After the class organized the groups to come to the back of the room, the planting was accomplished in an orderly fashion without accidents, spilled soil, or spoiled bulbs. Each one planted a bulb, learned which side of the bulb had to be up, watered the planted bulb, and set it in the dark. All were finished before the allotted time. One child remarked, "It sure pays to think."

Looking at Things a Different Way

A number of the deliberate ways for increasing creative output makes use of the technique of looking at something in a different way. Synectics (Gordon, 1961), for example, stresses the principle of making the unfamiliar, familiar, or the familiar, unfamiliar. One idea was sparked when one member of the team tried to imagine himself as a drop of paint struggling to get some kind of hold on a wall that had been painted and had not been scraped or cleaned before repainting. Children use the techniques of synectics and brainstorming naturally. This lesson is symbolized dramatically in little Catherine Babcock's (1962) recorded song, "Did You Ever Read a Clock Upside Down?" with (sound effects):

Did you ever read a clock upside down?
  Upside down!
Did you ever read a clock upside
  down?
It is very hard but I think you
  should
Learn how to read a clock upside
  down.

Children's skills in looking at things in a different way will be sharpened if they have a chance to investigate and explore the detailed nature of objects and situations and to perceive them from many different angles and points of reference. Studies of perception show that the meaning and grasp of an object changes as we shift the point of observation. Details missed altogether may become important. By changing purposes, obtaining different information, or the like, the meaning of objects and experiences also changes.

Four- and five-year-old children can make excellent use of opportunities for investigating things afresh and anew, and more thoroughly. I learned this in reading books to this age group. Frequently when I would read a book to the group, they would ask immediately that I read it again. At first I thought that I would have to go through the book rapidly each time, lest they become inattentive and bored. I soon discovered that they wanted just the opposite. Now that they had seen and heard the book through, the urgent tension to get through had been satisfied, and they were prepared to examine it more thoroughly. They were not bored and did not want to be hurried. They could now savor the experience to the fullest, elaborate upon it, and think more deeply about it.

Postponement of Learning by Authority

There are times when the teacher of young children might as well accept the fact that children prefer to learn creatively and postpone for a while learning by authority. An example of such a time is the day young children are first given rhythm-band instruments. Most teachers are almost driven to distraction on this day. They want to tell the children about their instruments, but they usually fail to gain attention for more than a moment. The alert and experienced teacher will realize that on this day the children must be permitted to encounter their instruments creatively and find out what the instruments will do to them. They want to feel the instruments, smell them, look at them, tap them, and sense them in every way possible. After this, the children are ready to learn by authority. They will listen and watch.

Here, as in many other situations, the learning process is thrown off course when the teacher tries to hurry and push the children to do what the teacher wants to tell them to do—namely, how to use the instruments properly. It happens almost any time when we try to prepare children through verbal or authoritarian orientations.

Periods of Silence and Hesitation

Work with young children has taught me to be tolerant of moments of silence and hestitation. In administering tests of creative thinking, it is apparent that it does not pay to hurry, urge, or push children to give responses when they are hesitant. Many of the hesitant children become quite responsive when told that "it is just for fun." When they discover that the examiner is really listening and taking down whatever they tell him, they tend to become quite productive. It is better to make no evaluative remarks and only write down what children dictate than to give disruptive remarks of approval and encouragement.

In discussing what he calls the "slow gifted child" who is culturally deprived, Riessman (1962) cautions against misinterpreting periods of hesitation and points out that many of these children are better at doing and seeing than at talking and hearing. They often appear to achieve better on performance tests than on verbal ones. They like to draw, role play, and the like. They appear to think in spatial terms rather than temporal ones and often have poor time perspective. Riessman also recommends the games format for use with the "slow gifted child." He points out that Davis and Eels capitalized on this idea in the development of an intelligence test in the form of a game for use with underprivileged children.

Children may seem hesitant and slow because adults do not give them time to respond. This difficulty is illustrated dramatically in the story of one mother (Miller, 1961) who was shocked when her five-year-old daughter asked to be permitted to eat in her room when Mrs. Green came for lunch. When asked to explain, the child said, "Oh, you know. She talks to me in a baby voice—and keeps asking me things and never lets me answer."

Then the mother recalled that every remark Mrs. Green made to the child was some little question she obviously did not expect answered. "Where did you get that pretty dress? What have you been doing today? What makes Julie grow so fast?"

As a result the child clammed up tight. Then Mrs. Green made matters worse by adding, "My, Julie is a shy one, isn't she? Are you bashful, honey? She doesn't talk much, does she?"

Taking a Closer Look

With young children nothing can take the place of personal observation. They enjoy using a magnifying glass to get a closer look. The young child will be satisfied to watch from a distance at first. This look from a distance, however, does not satisfy his curiosity. Creative thinking and learning is driven off course when children have no opportunities for a closer look, when they are forbidden to touch, when there is no real chance for the creative encounter.

We place many restrictions on the child's manipulativeness and curiosity. We discourage him by saying that curiosity killed the cat. If we were honest we would admit that curiosity makes a good cat and that cats are extremely skilled in testing the limits and determining what is safe and what is dangerous. Apparently, children as well as cats have an irresistible tendency to manipulate and explore objects and this very tendency seems to be the basis for the curiosity and inventiveness of adults. Even in testing situations, children who do the most manipulating of objects produce the most ideas and the largest number of original ideas.

Learning through Fantasy

Fantasy is one of the young child's most valuable tools for learning and should be kept alive, developed, and guided. Many teachers and parents try hard to eliminate fantasy by the time children enter school. They do this because they believe that fantasy is unhealthy and fail to recognize that fantasy can be useful even to adults. Imaginative role playing, telling fantastic stories, making unusual drawings, and the like are normal aspects of a child's thinking and a part of his way of experimenting and problem solving.

Both children and adults need time for absorbed thinking and dreaming. When we are absorbed in thinking about the problem, we may be "good for little else" at the time. It might be helpful to leave a part of the young child's day unscheduled with activities in which he has to appear busy. We are interested, of course, in developing a sound type of creative problem solving and decision making. Fantasy must be kept alive until children achieve the intellectual development that makes this type of thinking possible. For some time it is through fantasy that children must do much of their experimenting and exploring, and there should perhaps never be any complete discontinuity of fantasy as a way of exploring possibilities.

Ruth Griffiths (1945), a British student of imagination in early childhood, maintains that fantasy or imagination provides the normal means for the solution of problems of development in early childhood. Through fantasy the child attacks problems indirectly, often disguised by symbolism. The child is only vaguely aware of the goal toward which he is struggling. The problem develops through a series of successively imagined solutions that constitute a gradual resolution of the problem. As a result the child acquires information, makes changes in attitude, and becomes more socialized and objective.

Chukovsky (1963), the Russian child psychologist, also defends fantasy among both young children and adults. He believes that fantasy is "the most valuable attribute of the human mind and should be diligently nurtured from earliest childhood." He insists that we not interfere with its natural development. He sees the reading of fairy tales as very important for young children and supports his contention by referring to the use of fantasy by such eminent men as Darwin and a number of eminent Russian physicists and mathematicians. He asserts, "Without imaginative fantasy there would be complete stagnation in both physics and chemistry, because the formulation of new hypotheses, the invention of new implements, the discovery of new methods of experimental research, the conjecturing of new chemical fusions—all these are products of imagination and fantasy" (Chukovsky, 1963). Thus does Chukovsky posit the need for continuity between childhood fantasy and adult creative achievement.

Story Telling and Song Making

Children are natural story tellers and can compose charmingly and excitingly if encouraged to do so. Furthermore, this tendency can be used as a bridge to the acquisition of information and important educational skills. Seldom are children's compositions appreciated and given adequate treatment in publications. I would like to call attention to a few notable exceptions. One of these is on an exciting little book by Susan Nichols Pulsifer entitled *Children Are Poets* (1963). In this book Mrs. Pulsifer joins me in contending that the drop in creative behavior that occurs at about age 5 is not a natural developmental change. Instead, she contends that it is due to the influence of other children, group activities, the imposition of correct techniques and facts, rules, and regulations. She believes, as I do, that with wisdom the home and the school can do much to reduce this discontinuity in development and lessen this serious loss of creativity.

Another exception is the work of Kathleen Wrenn with her son Robert (1949). When her son was about 2 years old, Mrs. Wrenn discovered that he was responding much more readily to suggestions that were sung to him than he did when the same requests were spoken. Soon she discovered that he was responding by singing and rapidly developed a sense of rhythm and a singing scale. When Bobby was about 4 years old, the idea of making a book of songs began taking shape. These were simple songs about everyday happenings—songs about the fireman, the milkman, the zoo, balloons, traffic signals, and the church bell.

With new experiences Bobby would think of ideas for songs and work them out. On one occasion his mother asked him to put some leaves over the tulips planted in the yard so that they would not freeze. He came back with the following idea for a song:

Here come the flowers out of the ground.
Spreading happiness all around,
Daffodils, hyacinths, tulips gay,
Oh, how I wish you were here to stay.

His mother suggested that "hyacinth" was a very difficult word for little children to sing and why not say "daisies" instead. His reply was, "I'm a little child, aren't I, and it's my word." (Yes, children dislike for others to tamper with their compositions and their reasons may be well founded.)

Some people have commented that it was only because Mrs. Wrenn was musically talented that this procedure was successful. Another mother (Hargrove, 1964), avowedly untalented musically, made similar discoveries quite independently of Mrs. Wrenn. This mother maintains that "all children have heard the angels sing." Her advice to parents and teachers is simple: "How do you begin? Follow the leader—your child. Children often make music as they play. Sometimes they hum wordless tunes. At other times, they break into words and music. You can listen and join in. Don't make the mistake, however, that I once did. Sing *with* them, not *to* them. Otherwise, you may hear something like this: 'Go away, and sing your song. This is *my* song.'" This mother also found that singing her instructions as she assigns various duties gives work a flavor of creativity and enjoyment.

Difficulties in Maintaining Continuity

Some of the difficulties of permitting continuity in creative development are evident when we examine the concepts of the ideal child of a
sample of 100 nursery and kindergarten workers. These workers were
asked to describe the kind of person they would like to see the children
they work with become. They were given a checklist of 66 characteristics
that have been found significant in studies of eminent creative people.
They were asked to check all the characteristics they considered desirable
and that should be encouraged, to double check those that should be especially encouraged, and to strike through those that should be discouraged
and punished. By assigning weights of 2 to double checks, 1 to single
checks, and — 1 to strike throughs, it is then possible to obtain an index
and rank order for each characteristic for a given group. Since we had a set
of rankings by an expert panel that judged the ideal, productive, creative
person, it was also possible to correlate the rankings obtained for the
sample of nursery and kindergarten workers with the rankings of the
expert panel (students of the creative personality).

A coefficient of correlation of .37 was obtained for them compared
with one of .51 for a sample of 264 teachers in Buffalo, New York; one
of .47 for a sample of about 100 teachers in Berlin, Germany; one of .35
for a large sample of teachers in India; one of .32 for a sample of about
100 teachers in Greece; and one of .30 for a sample of teachers in the
Philippines (Torrance, 1965).

An examination of the grosser differences between the rankings of
nursery and kindergarten workers and those of the expert panel identifies
some of the areas of possible discontinuity for the child when he first
comes to school. Compared with the expert panel, the kindergarten and
nursery workers are *more discouraging* of asking questions, preoccupation
with tasks, disturbing the procedures and organization of the group,
dominance, emotional sensitivity, fault-finding, guessing, haughtiness,
independence of judgment, intuitiveness, liking to work alone, preference
for complex tasks, occasional regression, unwillingness to accept things
on mere say-so, vision, and willingness to take risks. The early-childhood
educators placed higher value than the experts on conformity, courtesy,
consideration of others, promptness, neatness and orderliness, obedience,
receptiveness to the ideas of others, sense of humor, social adjustment,
striving for distant goals, truthfulness, versatility or well-roundedness, and
willingness to accept the judgment of authorities.

I do not want anyone to infer that I deny the necessity for the latter
group of characteristics. My guess is that early-childhood educators tend
to produce discontinuities in creative development by their heavy emphasis on the latter set of characteristics such as courtesy, obedience, and

promptness and fail to build on the child's natural curiosity, intuitiveness, liking to work alone at times, and the other characteristics in the first group.

It is my belief that indeed children can and will learn more whenever we learn to maintain a higher degree of continuity in creative development and overcome these difficulties. It is my belief on the basis of the incomplete evidence available that continuity of creative development is healthy and normal and that it can be achieved by grafting on to the learning skills that the child brings with him when he first comes to school.

28 *Realistic Studies for Potential Dropouts*

Mary Ellen Saterlie

WHY PUPILS REJECT SCHOOL

A potential dropout is an individual who is rejecting school. His reasons are highly complex and many of them even unknown to him. He may have begun rejecting school before he was old enough to attend one because his parents also rejected school and passed this feeling on to him. However deep seated or elusive some of the reasons may be, this child is aware that certain elements of school are unsatisfactory to him.

First, the school does not allow him to succeed very often. It has not taught him to read and to do arithmetic as well as he should. School has held him back by failing him so that he is older than others in his grade. It has forced him to compete when he knew he could not win. It has insisted that he learn in ways that are unnatural to him.

Second, the school does not interest him. The teachers are engrossed in some academic world that exists in their minds and which they can discover and explore vicariously. He lives in a world that he can touch and see and smell. Reality is the thrill and concreteness of meeting basic needs for food, clothing, shelter, and acceptance in his world.

Third, the school does not provide really satisfactory social relationships. His teachers and other school personnel are concerned about pupils who like school, but they are frustrated by him. He does not have the same interests as most other pupils, and he feels rejected by them. The standards for social acceptance in the middle-class school environment are different from those in his home and neighborhood.

Finally, the school costs too much money. Activity tickets, uniforms, dues, and special equipment require money which is either not available or which he does not want to spend for those purposes. So he cannot take part in many extracurricular activities even if he wants to. School also stands in the way of his having a job which would make him inde-

286

pendent of the adult jurisdiction that seems to be making his school years so unbearable.

Although these four considerations may not tell the whole story, they are frequently the pupil's reasons and should be carefully considered by educators who are organizing realistic programs of curricular offerings for potential dropouts.

School is not unsatisfactory for all children, so the next step educators must take is the identification of the unique characteristics of the child who is rejecting school.

WHAT PUPIL REJECTS SCHOOL?

The pupil's characteristics give important insights not only into what the child desires to know about but also into what things are basic to his functional survival. In many cases only the school can provide the latter.

His academic characteristics are usually the first to be identified by the school. He has difficulties with abstract reasoning, generalizing, analyzing, and inferring relationships. His spatial relationships, sensory-motor relations, and form-perception abilities are below normal. He shows limitations in his ability to communicate effectively, at least according to the accepted classroom pattern. His attention span is short, and he has difficulty in planning and carrying out school work without supervision, at least in the activities that the school gives him to do. His interests seem limited.

The pupil who rejects school often evidences some unique emotional characteristics. His self-image is unrealistic, usually in a negative sense. Frustration frequently leads him to quick discouragement and early abandonment of a task. His moods may be unpredictable, often reflecting antisocial behavior that is either aggressive or withdrawn. He has difficulty in adjusting to change. He is often preoccupied with himself and seems to daydream.

This pupil exhibits social characteristics that may set him apart from others. Frequently he is a loner, rejecting or being rejected by his peers. When he associates himself with others, he often chooses leaders with the greatest emotional appeal. He is often prejudiced or resentful toward those who are different from himself. Social experiences in middle-class situations are often limited and are neither natural nor meaningful to him.

Home and neighborhood environment may also make the potential dropout different from the child who adjusts to school. A disorganized home life may deprive the child of security, health care, and the development of positive value patterns. His home may be culturally barren because of poverty or lack of interest on the part of his family. He may be discouraged in educational progress by limited understanding, intellectual ability, and family interest. His neighborhood and home may reflect cultural patterns not compatible with those reflected by the school.

In attempting to analyze the potential dropout's academic, emotional, and social characteristics, one finds it difficult to differentiate those that are products of the pupil's own basic intellectual, physical, and emotional structure from those that result from unfavorable home and school environments. Whatever the sources, the characteristics of school rejectors must be used as a second factor in developing realistic curricula.

THE WORLD OUTSIDE THE SCHOOL

The third basic consideration for planning curriculum offerings for potential dropouts is the world these pupils will face at the termination of their schooling.

The rapidity of changing job opportunities is staggering. The 1963 *Occupational Outlook Handbook* attempts to project employment possibilities over a fifteen-year period between 1960 and 1975. During that period it is anticipated that employment opportunities for professionals and technicians will increase by 65 per cent. Over the same period, however, need for machine operators and other semiskilled workers will increase only 17 per cent. The report further indicates that jobs for laborers and unskilled workers will remain at their present number and that the need for farmers and farm workers will decline. At the same time, career types are changing as new knowledge accrues so that many of the jobs that will be held ten years from now do not presently exist. The *Handbook* states, "To enter the job market without at least a high school diploma is now 'economic suicide.'"

Guidelines for curricular offerings then can be established on the basis of what educators know about why some pupils reject school, the unique characteristics of these pupils, and the outlook for the future. This knowledge in turn leads to the recognition that the curriculum must be intensely interesting and rewarding for this child. It must provide an atmosphere in which a desirable self-image can be developed. It should enable the pupil to learn and use basic reading, writing, and arithmetic skills. It should provide basic knowledge and develop attitudes required of a contributing adult citizen. At the same time, the curriculum must enable the pupil to recognize needs for adjustment and to understand ways to go about it. For some pupils the curriculum must lead directly to employment.

Two approaches can be taken to the preparation of curricular offerings for the potential dropout. Schools can provide an emergency program for the pupil who is nearing the legal age for school leaving and who is already evidencing all the signs that have brought about school rejection. In other words, the child is already retarded in reading and arithmetic; he has failed several other subjects and at least one grade; he is frequently late and absent; he does not participate in extracurricular activities; and his behavior is considered unsatisfactory. Other factors may be present also, but the pattern is well established in the child. The other approach is one in which schools develop a K through 12 curriculum that recognizes the problems faced by a significant segment of pupils who do not adjust to the organization of the school as it now exists.

THE EMERGENCY CURRICULUM

The first approach to curriculum is at best only a stop-gap procedure. But it is inescapable in areas of high mobility and in areas where the tide of dropouts must be stemmed or a quick terminal program provided until long-range provisions can be put into effect.

In developing this kind of curriculum, the educator is caught in the dilemma of providing a program that hopefully will keep the pupil in school through the twelfth grade, but at the same time realistically recognizes that this probably cannot be done. The curriculum must reflect special interest in the child as an individual and must provide him more freedom of expression and experience to encourage him to remain in school. But it must also cram into the child all the advice and skills that will immediately equip him to enter the world outside of school.

The junior high school is generally the area where this program is organized. The traditionally departmentalized nature of the junior high school as compared to the elementary school requires organizational modification in order to provide individualized guidance and instruction. The philosophy of the junior high school for this child cannot be the same as for the rest of the student body. The opportunity to explore is drastically changed to a necessity to specialize. The specialization must be in the areas of basic skill remediation and development, and of preparation for rudimentary function as an independent adult.

The curriculum cannot easily take into account differences in intellectual abilities because superficial factors may have partially concealed them and because time is short. But an attempt at recognition of ability levels and special abilities should be an important responsibility of the teacher and of supportive personnel. The curriculum must reflect the startling needs of these pupils in terms of their present inadequacies and of their almost inevitable future.

The Language Arts

The language-arts offerings must equip this child to communicate with understanding in increasingly interdependent conditions. Basically, he must read. Corrective and remedial help as well as developmental skills should be employed to upgrade reading ability to the highest level possible. Reading necessities such as forms, written and symbolic directions, newspapers, and menus must be introduced. New York City in its Career Guidance Program calls this "survival reading" (Board of Education of the City of New York, 1963). Some insights into reading as a pleasurable experience also need to be provided.

Speaking and listening skills should enable this child to give and receive basic directions, to carry on acceptable conversation, and to use the telephone as a tool in the giving and getting of information, and to employ polite speech forms. Writing experiences should prepare the child to fill out essential forms, to write letters of application, to construct simple expository paragraphs, and to spell basic words with some degree of accuracy.

Concepts in grammar should be kept at a minimum. The pupil frequently sees no use in and probably will have little use for grammatical understandings more complicated than noun-verb agreement, fundamentals of complete sentences, and mechanics of basic capitalization and punctuation. Whatever grammar is taught should be presented in a functional writing or speaking setting.

The Social Studies

The social-studies curriculum should be geared to the setting in which the pupil finds himself. A large city school must organize a curriculum which is much different from that developed by a small town, suburban, or rural school. The pupil should gain certain understandings about his immediate environment through: (1) an orientation to the community through maps and field trips, (2) an investigation of transportation facilities, (3) a study of specific responsibilities of a community citizen, (4) an overview of job opportunities and of ways to investigate them, (5) an understanding of agencies at work and their direct relationships to the citizen, (6) an observation of cultural opportunities in and near the community, and (7) an investigation of ways to spend leisure time wisely in the community.

It would be a mistake to allow this child to sever his relations with the school without some general understanding of the scope of national affairs and the influence of other nations on him as an individual. Time should be provided for developing fundamental understandings about the federal government. These should include basic rights guaranteed by the Constitution, the heritage of this somewhat unique form of government, the responsibilities required to maintain it, and the benefits that accrue to people living under this government. The curriculum should also contain a look at world political geography including the location of continents and important countries through the use of map skills, a general understanding of ranges of characteristics of climatic regions and their effects, a review of the basic areas of disagreement among conflicting ideologies of world powers and the involvement of other nations, and some idea of the influence of history on world affairs. Trends in the modern world should be developed in the curriculum with special emphases on automation, the population explosion, and nuclear and space advancements. Current affairs should be used extensively in weaving together portions of the social-studies program, and the use of adult news media in the classroom should perpetuate this means of keeping informed in the years to come.

These social-studies areas should be built into the curriculum in what may be the terminal years of education not only to provide some perspective for the long years ahead but also to establish deterrents to early school leaving. The concepts for the most part, however, cannot be treated academically. The pupil must visit automated industries, see overcrowded conditions, listen to political leaders, and talk to unemployed persons and those who handle employment problems. At this stage stark realism with some hope of less depressing experiences in school are the only means of overcoming the pupil's desire to leave school.

Mathematics and Science

The mathematics and science program must enable the pupil to measure and compute accurately and to understand basic scientific principles which he must cope with in his daily living.

The basic skills of fundamental arithmetic operations must be developed to the fullest with the same degree of persistence as those in the reading-skills program. Wise consumership is a requisite to this adolescent's independent survival. The use of simple measuring devices, the computation of costs such as maintenance of an automobile, the development of a family budget, and the ability to compare qualities, quantities, and prices are a few of the essential elements of consumership which the school can help to develop.

The handling of money, although a part of consumership, has many ramifications which must be understood to some extent by this child. Tax deductions and tax payments, banking procedures, credit, wages, and insurance involve mathematical concepts that are also required for any degree of financial independence. Teachers should not overlook the possibilities of using real situations, materials, and experiences in developing these understandings.

Science is intricately woven into many areas of the curriculum including social studies, physical education, industrial arts, and home economics. Some special emphasis should be given, however, to two important areas that may be correlated with other subjects. This pupil needs a basic understanding of life processes and of the physical structure of the human body.

This understanding should be directed toward enabling him to maintain good health, to detect physical problems, and recognize the need for legal and moral obligations regarding his physical being and that of others. An understanding of the fundamentals of physical science should enable him to comprehend the function of simple machines, to operate and repair simple household appliances and fixtures, and to recognize and eliminate causes of accidents.

Science is rich in possibilities for extending special interests into leisure-time pursuits. Teachers should capitalize on every opportunity to help a pupil learn ways of pursuing such interests independently.

Industrial Arts and Home Economics

The curricular offerings in industrial arts and home economics should be the closest to reality of all the other school offerings. Since actual specialization in a single occupational area is nearly impossible, these subjects must basically orient the pupil to the scope of the field, develop some positive attitudes, and develop as many manipulative skills as practical.

Industrial arts in this setting can provide fundamental training in the use of basic tools, assembly-line production, wood and metal work, home maintenance and repairs, automotive mechanics and service operations, and the interpretation of labor laws. It also can establish the essential concept of the need for accepting and pursuing retraining opportunities. Close contact with the community and its needs by the industrial-arts department will increase effectiveness of offerings.

The girl who is a potential dropout is especially important since it is she who will be largely responsible for perpetuating her own kind or for providing a home atmosphere that is more conducive to the development of sound values. The home-economics department should provide this pupil with training in home management considering the kind of home the child will probably occupy, in child care, in the preparation of a budget for household finances, in providing balanced diets, in maintaining safety and sanitation in the home, in buying wisely, and in avoidance of wasteful practices.

Correlated work-study experiences for both boys and girls can prove useful in situations that can be carefully controlled and where the pupil is 16 years of age or older.

Other Curricular Offerings

Art and music should be provided as frequently as possible. This child responds to properly motivated esthetic experiences as enthusiastically as do other pupils. The utilization of the cultural and ethnic backgrounds of the pupil may give more meaning to these subjects. Folk music and jazz may be more realistic than Bach or Beethoven and may bring the same depth of feeling to this pupil that the latter bring his teacher. Colorful, active realism may be more appropriate than abstract or impressionistic art. As important as listening to and observing music and art is the creation of both which can unleash self-expression and emotion as no other media can.

Physical education should be included in the curriculum not only to build skills but also to provide opportunities for the pupil to excel. A part of the physical-education curriculum should enable pupils to know about recreational facilities in the community and how they may be used for leisure-time activities.

Although the curricular offerings for emergency programs have been developed by subject areas, a high degree of correlation and articulation is desirable. Wherever feasible, one competent teacher should handle several areas, classes should be small, and guidance should be an important aspect of the program. Studies such as the foregoing will not eliminate dropouts; but, developed in a carefully designed and administered school setting, they can provide some of the basic tools for productive citizenship whether the child continues his schooling or terminates it.

THE LONG-RANGE CURRICULUM

Although the emergency curriculum may solve some immediate problems, the long-range approach is more realistic. This approach to education is the organization of curricular offerings, not on the negative basis of studies for potential dropouts, but rather on the more positive premise that a segment of pupils requires a curriculum that is different in many respects from the kinds currently in effect. The urgent need for a different program is clearly evidenced through the negative factors influencing this type of pupil to reject school in its present form. A close look at the characteristics of the child indicates that he may fit into one of two categories, terminology for identifying both of which is once again negatively based on our limited concept of curricular offerings and achievement expectations in education today. However, since the terms "slow learner" and "underachiever" are widely understood by educators, they will be used throughout this description of curricular offerings. Many of the characteristics are also applicable to mentally retarded pupils, but since most school systems have developed realistic programs of special education for them, they will not be considered in this paper. Long-range organization of curricular offerings provides an opportunity for richer, more satisfying learning experiences for the pupil who is now rejecting school.

Educators must recognize that fine distinctions in this modified curriculum need to be made in order to provide for the differences between the slow learner whom we identify as one whose measured mental ability is below average but who is not mentally retarded and the underachiever as one whose achievement level is well below his apparent intellectual capacity. Since the dividing line between these two groups is often exceedingly difficult to define, much care must be exercised to identify learning problems and to guide pupils realistically toward scholastic experiences consistent with their potential ability.

The goals for long-range curricular development for the slow learner, as well as for the underachiever, should not be greatly different from those for other pupils. Basically, "the major goal is the development of individuals who can fulfill their responsibilities to society and find personal satisfaction in creative and constructive activity—people who think clearly, feel deeply, and act wisely" (NEA, 1963a). More specifically, a goal for both the slow learner and the underachiever should be the development of improved self-concept and self-realization.

Scholastic provisions for both kinds of children must begin at least by the first grade. Kindergarten and prekindergarten are highly desirable as experiential bases. When preschool tests indicate a child has below-average intelligence or will experience delay in reading and arithmetic, the pupil should be placed in a small group with an experienced and specially trained teacher in a nongraded primary program. Fundamental skills in reading and arithmetic along with many of the conventional primary experiences should be taught in an orderly sequence but at the pupil's rate. Four years should be set aside for the primary program. During this time several important goals can be achieved: (1) An adequate readiness period can be established. (2) A positive attitude toward self, school, and peers can be established through a series of success experiences. (3) Basic skills can be developed systematically. (4) The potentially average or above-average pupil can be identified and some of his delays in learning overcome. (5) Slow learners can advance at a realistic rate without the needless repetition of the same curriculum. The four-year period also provides an opportunity for the development of social maturity frequently needed by these kinds of children.

The negative aspects of retention have been clearly defined in personal interviews with 16- to 18-year-old potential dropouts. They have described a feeling of inadequacy, not belonging, and contempt for the school because of failure in two or more grades which has made them older than their classmates. Goodlad and Anderson in *The Nongraded Elementary School* (1963) support these pupils' remarks by summarizing research conducted primarily with the slow learner. "Promoted slow-learning children achieve at higher levels, are involved less often in aggressive acts toward school and schooling, get along better with their peers, and appear to have more wholesome feelings of personal worth."

Following the primary years, the curriculum should become more differentiated for the slow learner as compared to the pupil who continues to underachieve in spite of intensive efforts to identify and alleviate his learning problems in the primary program. The bases for determining the curriculum for the slow learner must necessarily be the somewhat limited scope of his occupational opportunities and his needs for concrete, specific guidance for undertaking his lifetime pursuits. On the other hand, the intellectually average or better underachiever has potentially unlimited possibilities for his endeavors; and his need is largely the awakening of interest and purpose to pursue them with success.

Curriculum for the Slow Learner

The structure of the curriculum for the slow learner must be based on the characteristics and special requirements of this kind of pupil. The intermediate years should reflect a nongraded organization similar to the primary so that realistic pacing of skill development can continue. The usual three-year period, however, should be maximum so that age differences do not segregate him from other pupils. The junior high school should begin in earnest the development of the concepts of occupational responsibility and of competent home management for the slow learner. Social studies, mathematics, science, language arts, home economics, and industrial arts should be correlated, but the pupil should not be denied the opportunity to work with many of the same aspects of history, geography, civics, and science which his chronological peers are learning. Other subjects should be available to him as well. Art, music, literature, and physical education are as essential to the slow learner as to any other learner. In fact, these subjects may prove to be the key to unlocking the potential of some of these youngsters.

The senior high school should begin to channel the slow learner into occupational fields that are realistic in terms of intellectual demands as well as in terms of breadth for future adaptations as technological, economic, and social changes take place during the individual's working lifetime. Even as more time in the curriculum is devoted to occupational responsibility and competency in the senior high, the slow learner should not be denied other curricular experiences that will enable him to become a more adequate person. A great deal of flexibility should be built into the curriculum to allow for additional experiences for the pupil who learns slowly to some extent but not in totality. The school should bear most of the responsibility for the slow learner's next steps whether they be enrollment in a more specialized training school following high-school graduation or placement on a job.

An underlying factor in the development of the slow learner's total program is the realization that, if correctly identified, he will rarely ever reach the level of achievement of an average child, and that the provisions of educational experiences should be guided not by grade-level expectations but by the readiness and ability of the pupil to work with them.

The language-arts program for the slow learner should provide experiences that equip the pupil with tools for communicating effectively in society with the guiding criteria being utility, concreteness, and pleasure.

The primary period should include if necessary a protracted readiness period for language. Special suggestions should be developed for teachers which describe activities and experiences that will facilitate the individual's receptivity to reading, speaking, listening, and writing. Throughout the elementary years, emphasis should be placed on functional development of skills rather than on grammatical technicalities. Steps in language maturation should guide the placement of increasingly difficult concepts. The pupil should be given as much exposure to good literature as possible with any accompanying experiences that may be necessary for full appreciation of the selections. Story telling and reading to the class by the teacher enriches the curriculum for the slow learner.

Basic skills should be continued into the junior high school. Reading materials consistent with the social maturation of the pupil should be provided on his sight recognition and interpretive level. Most slow learners should be able to write legibly, construct simple sentences, use correct capitalization and basic punctuation, and develop simple expository paragraphs from outlines in the junior high school. The basic uses of the library, the dictionary, and sources of public information such as the telephone directory, newspapers, and signs are within the capabilities of this pupil. The values and pleasures of forms of mass media such as the newspaper, selected magazines, radio, television, and motion pictures can become an important part of the language arts since these forms will play a fundamental role in perpetuating the individual's education.

In the senior high school, language activities can be more closely integrated with the program in social studies and industrial arts. Continued development of basic skills may be necessary but these skills now need to be directed toward the realism of adult use. Reading and writing directions, informative letters, and explanations; speaking with poise and clarity to individuals and groups; and listening courteously and with understanding are goals to be achieved. The more realistic the application of these concepts the more lasting their effect will be.

Literature should be included throughout the slow learner's school experience. It is most appreciated when it has a clear plot that is suspenseful, humorous, or adventurous and is within the realm of the pupil's real or vicarious experiences. Some means of identification for the child with a character or an idea and a vocabulary which can be understood are requisites for meaning. The pleasure of literature is lost when the reader must wade through it. The pupil should be encouraged to read on his own, but, by the same token, teachers throughout the grades should read to the pupil or use recordings to bring these experiences to him and to instill in him the appreciation of the vistas that can be opened through the printed page.

The social-studies program provides rich opportunities for developing understandings and attitudes that are essential for the success of the slow learner in society. These include a better understanding of himself, of his place in the community and beyond it, and an enthusiasm for the learning process.

The social-studies curriculum more than any other can be based on the social characteristics and needs of the pupil himself. The slow learner often accepts uncritically the leadership with the greatest emotional appeal, and he may be either belligerent or obsequious in dealing with persons in status positions; therefore the social-studies curriculum should emphasize important qualities of good leadership, the intelligent selection of leaders, and the choice of courses of action based on probable effects rather than on emotional appeal. The slow learner tends to be prejudiced toward people who are different or who may hold different points of view, so the social studies should stress the common characteristics of mankind and help the pupil to understand racial, cultural, and political differences. The pupil's feeling of inadequacy and peer rejection can be combatted with the development of a classroom atmosphere that recognizes the value and develops the understanding of human dignity and respects the ability of all groups to contribute to society.

Since "not until adolescence do most children develop the sense of time which is required for historical perspective" (Watson, 1961), it is safe to assume that this sense comes even later for the slow learner. The social studies, however, should give some concept of the vast sweep of history and prehistory as well as the sense of space and variation that characterizes the planet and its people. The direct effect of time and space on the pupil as an individual often needs to be established. An example of this on the secondary level is the development of units that first identify the pupil with the issue and establish its significance to him, then place the issue in its historical and geographical setting, and conclude with a return to the here and now where the issue is associated with current affairs of national and international significance.

The slow learner will be a voting, reacting, working citizen. He will need to know about his own drives and physical needs, his relationship to his home, community, and nation as an elementary-school child, as an adolescent, and as an adult. He needs to know basically how the governments that affect him operate and the part he plays in their effectiveness. He needs to know how and why other people in other places and times affect him. He needs to know in what ways his environment is different from that of others. Above all he needs to know why his role in society is essential to others.

In the last years of secondary school, social studies can be closely related to occupational preparation with opportunities to put into practice many of the social attitudes and understandings gained in prior years. This phase of the social studies must be taught by a skillful and perceptive teacher who can not only recognize realistic opportunities to develop concepts but also who can enable the pupil to identify principles and practices that will increase the effectiveness and satisfaction of his existence.

The mathematics program for the slow learner should establish as its major purposes the understanding of fundamental mathematics processes and the recognition of the social applications of these processes for the effective solution of quantitative problems in daily life.

The primary years should include an extended readiness period for the introduction of quantitative concepts along with the basic vocabulary for numbers. The normal sequence of arithmetic skills can be pursued by the slow learner, but these must be adjusted to the learning and readiness rate of each pupil with no grade standards as criteria.

The junior-high-school slow learner is, for the most part, neither ready nor interested in learning about such topics as taxation, banking, and interest, and these learnings should be reserved for the senior-high-school years when there is more likelihood of their immediate use. This does not preclude the use of practical mathematics in the junior high school. However, the practicality should reflect adolescent experiences such as aspects of part-time employment, wages and hours, travel distances, measurement of athletic fields, recipe ingredients, and computation of lapses of time. The discovery method of learning mathematics is appropriate for the slow learner, and the modern mathematics programs seem to have considerable promise for these pupils. Rosenbloom has found that students low on traditional methods of scholastic aptitude by comparison profit more from the School Mathematics Study Group program than students in the upper brackets. This may be due largely to the fact that the program brings into play kinds of abilities not especially useful in mastering traditional materials (Torrance, 1962*b*).

Mathematics in the secondary school must also have many direct relationships to the industrial-arts and home-economics experiences. As the pupil is guided toward occupational fields, his mathematics instruction should be directed toward proficiency in specific areas including consumership and taxation. At the same time, the program should maintain basic understandings that allow for adjustment to varying situations requiring computational application.

The science curriculum for the slow learner should enable him to investigate intelligently but it should also provide concrete information about the pupil himself and about the physical and biological world around him.

Science is inherently interesting to most pupils. Units can be developed on all levels of the slow learner's maturity which provide stimulation and learning based on observation and experimentation rather than on reading and writing. From studies of force and motion through such investigations as "What makes our toys move?" to an understanding of the behavior of lower animals through observation of mealworms to a senior-high course in physical science which deals with electrical appliances, home maintenance, and safety is an illustration of increasingly complex, yet realistic ways of learning about science.

Much of the curriculum in science now used by average pupils can be made applicable to the slow learner. The criteria for maintaining or eliminating such units should be: can the slow-learning pupil experience stimulation or satisfaction from the study; will the unit provide applicable skills and information; and does the unit represent a step related sequentially in concept or in skill-development level to prior learnings.

Science, like other subjects, can be closely articulated with the occupational orientation toward the end of the secondary school. Opportunities for developing scientific concepts directly related to jobs and homemaking are numerous and can be made stimulating. But educators should not lose sight of the fact that science can be intrinsically rewarding as an aspect of leisure time. This point of view should be woven into curriculum planning for the slow learner throughout his schooling.

Although *industrial arts* traditionally has been associated with the secondary schools, there is a growing concern for its increased utilization in the elementary years. There seems to be considerable justification for early opportunities for slow learners to engage in industrial-arts activities. Wonacott, Giovannoni, and Hedrick (1964) indicate that

Elementary industrial arts is concerned with educating boys and girls to live in a technological world, to understand and to be able to use many of the technical devices around them. As the children engage in activities that help them to understand the world in which they live, they also acquire certain worthwhile work attitudes, such as cooperation, precision, and appreciation for a job well done.

Beyond this, the use and manipulation of tools and materials can provide concrete experiences and objects to enhance language arts, mathematics, science, and social studies.

Following introductory and exploratory experiences with industrial arts in a self-contained classroom in elementary school, the slow learner beginning in the seventh grade should develop more refined skills and attitudes and begin to gain appreciations in shop procedures and environment. The junior high school should allow slow-learning boys to continue to explore interests and to discover special abilities in wood and metal shops. Industrial-arts departments should be alert to such accusations as that made by Hechinger in the *New York Times,* "Vocational education exists in a kind of fairyland that has not much relation to the real world of work" (Boodish, 1962). Opportunities to visit local industries to correlate skill and attitude development in the shop classroom will enhance the reality of industrial-arts experiences.

The focus of the slow-learning boy's education becomes his preparation for occupational competency by the conclusion of his schooling. The development of occupational centers in comprehensive high schools can provide realistic training opportunities in attainable production and service vocations. The centers should reflect community and nearby employment opportunities and should be comprehensive enough in nature to enable pupils to develop a number of occupational competencies in fields that have promise for foreseeable future employment. Work-study programs have important values for slow learners when work experiences are well selected, carefully supervised, and correlated with the remainder of the curriculum. According to Burchill (1962),

Curriculum based on academic preparation and supervised work experiences can satisfy some adolescents' needs for recognition. In these programs, youngsters may develop feelings of individuality by occupying roles meaningful to themselves, to their peers, and to adults. Identification with work may provide many youngsters with an avenue for recognizing their approaching maturity with its concomitant responsibilities.

The increased focus on occupational competency as schooling nears termination tends to give direction to the pupils and to close the gap between school and work with its accompanying social and economic responsibilities.

The elementary school can also introduce important information and appreciations concerning home economics for girls. Such concepts as helping at home and responsibilities to the family are appropriate in the primary and intermediate years. However, home economics should begin to be focused in the junior high school in a way similar to the industrial-arts program. A major contribution that schools can make to future generations is to enable slow-learning girls to provide homes that are conducive to the development of healthy minds and bodies in a responsible family setting. A sequentially organized program beginning in the early grades and continuing through the senior high school can do this if it is geared to an understanding of value patterns in the community and is closely correlated with other phases of the curriculum.

Schools also have the responsibility of developing salable skills among girls as well as with boys. The occupational centers and work-study situations are equally valuable for and adaptable to girls.

Art and music are essential parts of the total curriculum for slow learners. They afford unique opportunities for deriving esthetic values from life and also allow pupils to realize greater self-expression through creative experiences. Educators need to develop teaching guides that develop appreciation largely through participation. Observation and listening appreciations can be developed to a degree by appropriate realistic experiences in anticipation of the more subtle activity. Once again, capitalizing on cultural background and natural talents can provide avenues for approaching esthetic experiences. The slow learner often has an opportunity to compete successfully with his peers in art, crafts, instrumental and vocal music.

Physical education is a fundamental curricular offering for these pupils. Although slow learners as a whole may evidence slightly inferior physical development to that of average pupils, it is not sufficient to differentiate them markedly. Physical education then allows these pupils to develop their physical abilities, to participate on an equal basis with other pupils, and in many cases to excel in their chronological peer group in a school setting.

Electives such as home maintenance and repairs, typing, record keeping, and driver education should be available to slow learners and adapted to their rate of learning as well as to their prospective use of the subject.

Long-range curriculum offerings for the slow learner should enable him to develop to his full potential, to be as well rounded and well informed as his intellect will allow, and to obtain a job which he is emotionally and physically trained to hold.

Curriculum for the Underachiever

The structure of the curriculum for the underachiever must be somewhat different from that of the slow learner. Following the nongraded primary years this pupil should continue to receive systematic skill development in a highly motivating atmosphere that utilizes many kinds of intellectual endeavors beyond the reading and writing of the word and number symbols. Curriculum content on the intermediate and junior-high-school levels should not be drastically different from that of the normal achiever. Its organization and presentation, however, should be quite different from traditional methods. Creativity utilizing questioning, searching, manipulating, experimenting, guessing, testing the limits, risking, and occasionally even playing around should be fundamental to every phase of the curriculum. Units may be shorter and more pointed than abstract but not necessarily less difficult. Opportunities should be provided through flexible scheduling and specialized help from teachers or supportive personnel for individuals to pursue particular interests during school hours and after school. Special services in counseling, health, and social work with the home should be a part of the underachiever's curriculum.

The senior high school provides even greater challenges for those who work with the underachiever. Continuation of principles outlined for the intermediate and the junior high school should be maintained with increased emphasis on individuals. Hopefully, throughout the twelve years of special emphasis on the underachiever, he will have been enabled to utilize more nearly his full potential and will have become able to adjust to the regular curriculum. Some, however, will continue to function as slow learners. If, by the latter years of schooling, these pupils indicate no appreciable sign that the school can enable them to overcome their reasons for learning and operating on a level indicating low ability, there seems to be only one recourse for the school—that is to make the pupil as useful a citizen as possible by providing him with the somewhat specialized and directive social and occupational preparations designed for the slow learner.

Paul H. Bowman in *New Insights and the Curriculum* (Frazier, 1963) suggests that education may be defined

in terms of process rather than content of knowledge; thus, the central problem of education would be to help each child experience success in the mastering of new ideas. This goal is based on the theoretical assumption that the personal experience of success by the pupil in using his own resources to solve new problems is exciting, satisfying, and habit-forming. The thrill of discovery whets the appetite for more problems and solutions.

This attitude toward education has special significance for the underachiever. The pupil with average or better potential is not rejecting school necessarily because of the curriculum content, but because of his attitude toward learning. Realistic studies for this child are those that are made stimulating to him, not ones that force him to conform. Furthermore, since probably no two children have identical reasons for underachieving, classes must be small and teachers and supportive personnel highly trained to diagnose and treat causes for low performance.

Although most underachievement probably is produced by a multiplicity of factors, there may be a basic cause that triggers other factors making the situation more complicated the longer it goes undetected and untreated. The curriculum needs to cope with physical, environmental, social, and emotional factors that frequently are characteristic of these people. Physically, the child may have undetected hearing, vision, or speech defects along with defective teeth, adenoids, and tonsils as a result of poor health standards and general neglect in the home. Malnutrition, lack of sleep, and irregular growth patterns also may inhibit achievement. Not only should the school initiate the provision of health services where necessary, but teachers should weigh demands on productivity in light of these conditions. Environmentally, the child may be restricted by poverty so that cultural and social horizons are limited, home facilities are inadequate, and preoccupation with meeting basic physical needs becomes dominant. In such cases, teachers should capitalize on the real concerns and interests of the child, should broaden cultural and social experiences, and should provide for him a time and place to work independently in school. Emotionally, the pupil may lack maturity and seriousness of purpose, awareness and concern for others, a sense of responsibility, self-confidence, and motivation to achieve. The school needs to provide opportunities for development of desirable self-images through tangible success experiences and recognition of achievement, but at the same time it needs to challenge the pupil. Variation in activities should be made which gives each pupil opportunity to contribute to group effort. Socially, the pupil may feel inadequately prepared to handle middle-class social situations, and he may feel rejected by his peers. In such cases, the total school staff should develop a climate which respects the potential contribution of every pupil and which engenders that feeling throughout the student body. The school also should build an understanding of acceptable personal qualities required of individuals who expect to function positively in society.

Individual and group counseling should be considered an essential part of the underachiever's curriculum. As soon as an underachiever is identified, he should be assigned to a guidance counselor for regular and consistent follow-up.

There is little the school can do to prevent negative influences of the home which apparently have vast effects on children. Disorganized family life and its resulting insecurity; inadequate parental discipline resulting in substandard physical, moral, and mental behavior; indifferences and contempt toward school resulting in similar pupil responses; and parental establishment of unattainable goals resulting in frustrations are all problems whose sources are nearly impossible to treat. An active program of parent education is one approach, and the development of positive attitudes toward school and society in this generation as a hope for the next is the other.

Basically, school must provide a highly individualized and stimulating curriculum for the pupil who under present conditions does not achieve to the level of his capacity.

Essentially then, realistic studies for potential dropouts are those that are developed to educate children with special types of learning processes. Educators can no longer afford to merely hope that this group of pupils will adjust to the regular curriculum. A curriculum, with new and adjusted content and with creative and sparkling approaches, must be provided for them.

29 *Reaching the Disadvantaged*

Charles Savitsky

THE CHALLENGE TO OUR EDUCATIONAL STRUCTURE

In broadening the base of educational opportunities and extending, by law and policy, the age for leaving school, we are beginning to face the realities of hard facts by reexamining our educational structure. We are no longer committed solely or primarily to preparing students for college, but we are not too sure how and what to offer those not college bound; we are challenged to submit fast and easy solutions on the dropout and related problems in answer to growing social and political pressures, and groping is inevitable; we observe with dismay the revolutionary technological advances daily closing avenues of job opportunities for the nonskilled and semiskilled and recognize that the disadvantaged may not, in fact, be confined to the culturally deprived, to specific low socioeconomic groups or geographic areas. Failure to recognize the latter fact is an injustice to an increasingly large number of students being nudged ahead to shuffle through the popular educational "catch-all basket," the general course; the refuge, in most cases, for those responding to stay-in-school campaigns.

A number of school systems are employing specific programs to aid the more disadvantaged high-school students, the slower learners and the non-college bound, as well as providing for upgrading and uncovering latent abilities and potential—modifications of Higher Horizons, to a degree. Thus the District of Columbia has a general-track program in clerical subjects and a basic track adapted to slow and retarded students; in Portland, Oregon, there are special achievement classes that lead to special diplomas; in San Diego, students who are unable to profit from the regular high-school program are enrolled in a special school where they progress at their own rate and follow individualized programs; New York City has in operation a general course (about one-third of the total graduates are in this category) for students who have serious difficulties achieving in academic or high-level commercial subjects, providing more than fifteen modified courses within an educational cluster that emphasizes training in marketable skills, basic language and arithmetic skills, and citizenship. New York City also provides a work-experience program (School to Employment Program) to meet the needs of potential dropouts and encourage them to remain in school and graduate. None of the programs is designed rigidly for permanent groupings; students can and do move into higher-level tracks; and parents, too, are beneficiaries of supportive action from the school.

CHANGING PROGRAMS AND INADEQUATE CURRICULA

Unfortunately, curriculum planning has infrequently kept pace with the changing programs; there is a wide lag in translating them into effective instruments because the courses of study and approaches, especially in required major subjects demanding substantial reading for background and comprehension, are meager and inadequate. Consequently there is minimum impact on the disadvantaged who must again face frustration.

The difficulty in developing viable curricula and approaches is not due to failure in properly identifying the students we are discussing; we now recognize that as a group—and compared to the college bound—they reveal a number of handicaps: reading retardation, poor work and study habits, poor command in oral and written communication, lack of confidence, a distaste for the formal part of schooling, and difficulties in personal and social adjustment. Rather, it is in not appreciating that their slowness and lack of achievement is merely descriptive of their present educational profile and belies their potential which is often much higher than their school records indicate; it is also in not underlining realism and directness, as well as direction, in courses of study with goals both discernible and achievable by the students.

To reach the disadvantaged, curriculum and instruction must assume broader meaning and flexibility. It should not be confined to a course of study with content arranged to favor only logical sequences for question-answer, stimulus (the question itself)-response; or, as in the case of history, a set of definitions, causes, effects, and dates; or the discipline of mastering mechanical operations in mathematics; the "what" in a fixed body of material. It should be concerned more with the "how" and "why," the understandings and applications that take into account psychological sequences and readiness situations for learning. Provision is then made for a variety of teaching and guidance techniques and materials for both the one-to-one and one-to-group relationships, individualized and class learnings.

A preponderance of courses in the lower tracks are outlines of content repeating, in list form, the conventional suggestions for activities or "learning opportunities": "Make a chart . . . develop a word list . . . draw a map . . . list the qualities of . . . ," and so on. This is helpful neither to teachers nor to students and carries little promise for educational growth. Instead, there should be practical examples and suggestions in depth, indicating with more specifics how the material may best be presented and carried through in culminating activities in a manner different from that employed for students who are not disadvantaged; the magic and know-how for vitalizing instruction. If reference is made to textbooks for readings and assignments, then, at the minimum, selectivity should be exercised and noted as to particular passages or sections that can be mastered by students seriously retarded in reading.

In history, for example, courses for students who are receiving their terminal education in high school frequently fall into the category of watered-down parcels of traditional content spanning a wide historical divide with little difference from what is offered to the college bound, except for some superficial rephrasing and change in format. In other cases, they are fragments of a less ambitious and abbreviated instructional program that is loosely connected—a product of skimming and scooping out sections of history. Teachers and students bear the strains and frustrations of racing through a mile course to "cover" the term's work; history is devitalized by dissections and cold outlines of topics neatly packaged into causes and effects, contributions, and political, economic, and social factors—but without much meaning or function to the disadvantaged.

MOTIVATION AS A PRIME FACTOR

A primary consideration is enlarging the role of motivation. Whereas motivation is important in the traditional lesson with regular-paced students, in the case of the disadvantaged it is paramount and all pervasive; it is not self-generating for them, they need extra and extended support from the teacher; it constitutes a major part of the lesson, in time and emphasis; it challenges and excites for learning when the disadvantaged perceive purpose as well as interest in the lesson. Otherwise the unit of instruction falls flat. For example, instead of motivating a lesson on the Articles of Confederation with a direct, analytical question—Why did the Articles fail?—a more adequate and effective building block is to have the class discuss the meaning of the word "league" (within the context of school leagues, baseball leagues), the need for rules, how they are enforced, and culminating in a question calling for simple research and purposeful reading—Why did this "league of friendship" fail?

GUIDELINES IN APPROACHES FOR THE DISADVANTAGED

Curriculum and instructional approaches for the disadvantaged should be the handmaiden to a number of factors or guidelines suggested by successful experiences.

1. *Personalize.* The line of communication for the learning process is the student rather than the subject, the warmth and tangibility of "you" or "we" rather than "they" or "the." A good example of writing in this vein is "You are about to undertake a journey that will last most of your adult life—your journey through the world of work. . . . This *Job Guide for Young Workers* has been prepared to help you get off to a good start on this lifelong journey by assisting in your choice of occupational goal. . . ." (Bureau of Employment Security, 1963).

2. *Orient to job experience or world of work.* Occupational mindedness is a dominant characteristic of these students. It is within the context of seeking a short-range, immediate goal—some vocational competence that bears hope and promise of erasing their disadvantaged state: it is their pragmatic test for judging the worth in subjects they are required to study. There is, therefore, more readiness to absorb instruction when identification or transfer is made to job preparation or improvement. This becomes especially meaningful and effective for students in supervised work-experience programs. Thus speech behavior in job interviews is woven into language arts; how we breathe and the production and transmission of sound are similarly part of this subject and are related to biology and science; protecting the worker is an assignment in social studies.

3. *Use the present and current events as a basis for understandings.* Although many students show achievement in subjects that include specific job training, they meet formidable hurdles in general education where concepts and trends are studied and developed. These have meaning to them only insofar as they help to explain their present world. Curriculum in history, for example, may well be built on flashback techniques motivated by present-day problems.

4. *Adapt or arrange text materials to fit reading levels, interests, and needs.* There is a dearth of good textbooks for the disadvantaged. The concern is not entirely one of vocabulary or sentence structure; it extends as well to the development and crowding of ideas and concepts in simple sentences and to demeaning simplification of material to elementary levels, not taking into account more mature interests. In truth, there cannot be ideal textbooks because of the wide range of abilities, attitudes, and previous scholastic achievement; the

task of custom-tailoring reading and text materials devolves, to a great extent, on the teacher who is in the advantageous position of knowing her students closely and at first hand.

5. *Correlate with more than one subject area.* Correlation will not only suggest additional instructional approaches, but also it will unify and strengthen achievement and upgrading in all subject areas. It encourages teachers to operate as teams, pooling information and testing suggestions and, of necessity, hitching guidance aspects (very often by individual case approach) to plans they adopt. For the students it means more teachers care about their total progress without fragmentation by subjects isolated from each other.

6. *Stress oral communication.* Unless oral communication is stressed, the disadvantaged state is frozen into permanency: not only is it a signal of surrender by the teacher, but it compounds the burden of frustration and negativeness students have accumulated. Nurtured cautiously and by degrees, students learn, by oral communication, to relate to others and share mutual acceptance. It is a humanizing process because they are now functioning as learners on a reactive basis.

7. *Work for standards.* The disadvantaged, including the slower learners, *are* learners who should be held accountable and encouraged to accept responsibilities. This firmness is not disciplinary but supportive; it is directed toward goal satisfaction and status building, their expressed needs. Implementation of this factor by the teaching staff is predicated on acceptance rather than rejection of the disadvantaged.

8. *Organize short, achievable units.* Realistic considerations dictate that the increased demands on attention and interest spans in extended, and often diffused, units of work—the area where the disadvantaged have been failing—be shelved for shorter units that facilitate mastery by gradation and provide for flexibility in size of units.

9. *Build in elements of success.* An overriding duty of the curriculum planner and teacher is to set the climate for raising the students' self-image, making it possible for them to achieve degrees of success. Within each lesson and unit, within each educational experience, these potentialities (the correct solution, the good judgment, the proper expression) should be sought for, demarked in advance, and incorporated as part of the instructional plan to act as propelling "ins" and sure steps for the students. This does not imply designing for easiness—a practice that is self-defeating; it does mean building confidence and extending encouragement in order to facilitate movement into more difficult assignments. The disadvantaged are provided the opportunities for discovering and whetting educational appetites —perhaps for the first time in their educational careers.

10. *Provide for exploration and discovery, including learning how to*

think. Learning should be an active process—not spoon-feeding information—leading to independence and maturity. By proper motivation an awareness of a question or problem is stimulated, a need and interest by students to seek out an answer or experience is uncovered. The problem is *theirs* without imposition and its solution is *their* formulation with guidance. The emotional approach and response, so largely responsible for many distortions held by the disadvantaged, is replaced by the more rational judgment and analyses.

All the foregoing factors are interdependent and mesh into one design to permit the disadvantaged to function and grow; to become advantaged and important to themselves and their community.

AN INTEGRATED NATIONAL EFFORT IS NECESSARY

Although there have been no radical curricular breakthroughs in reaching the disadvantaged, there is genuine need for gathering and integrating significant segments of work, experimental and tried, now in progress in educational systems alert to the scope and urgency of the problem; it will help to bring order out of the present haphazard and limited experimentation. The direction that this can take is exhibited by the impressive accomplishments of groups in biological sciences and mathematics, operating under national grants. The Biological Sciences Curriculum Study was organized in 1958 by the Education Committee of the American Institute of Biological Sciences to improve biology education in the high schools for the average student in the tenth grade. The curriculum work was done by teams of high-school teachers, research biologists, and other specialists who developed courses for the same grade level, but with different emphases; three versions with a core content that is 70 per cent common for all three levels. Summer writing conferences prepared experimental editions, and revisions followed after evaluation and testing (118 teachers and 14,000 students), taking into account wide geographic, socioeconomic, and ability ranges. The National Council of Teachers in Mathematics also prepared (in summer writing conferences) *Experiences in Mathematical Discovery* (EMD), textbooks, and teaching guides for students who have not achieved in mathematics.

But neither of these studies is geared to cover the major core of the disadvantaged students. The elements of direction in the studies, their careful operation and evaluation are, however, equally applicable to projects in other subject areas and for students in lower tracks.

A CAUTIOUS OUTLOOK IN MEASURING RESULTS

There is no magic formula or gimmick that will suddenly and permanently lift the disadvantaged into an advantaged state—the individual differences in abilities and attitudes are too wide to permit oversimplification, and the environmental influences are too critical. Curriculum work in this area is therefore appreciably more difficult and the dividends from investment of time and energy are not uniformly high. But, measured in personal terms, in a restoration of confidence and dignity in students who now share in a process of communication and learning instead of being consigned to custodial care or busy-work as "dead inventory," curriculum refinement and approaches (including guidance aspects) for these students is salvaging and rewarding. It is part of an abiding democratic faith built on a resolution that the disadvantaged, too, can and need be helped.

30 *The Culturally Deprived Child: A New View*

Frank Riessman

I have been interested in the problems of lower socioeconomic groups for about fifteen years, during most of which time there has been a lack of concern for the educational problems of children from low-income families. In the last three or four years, however, this attitude has changed markedly.

There is now an enormous interest on the part of practitioners and academic people in this problem. I think we are on the point of a major breakthrough in terms of dealing with this question.

After appraising a good deal of the recent work that has been done on the education of disadvantaged children, I feel that there is a considerable agreement regarding many of the recommendations for dealing with the problem, although there are some very different emphases. What is missing, however, is a theoretic rationale to give meaning and direction to the action suggestions. I should like to attempt to provide the beginnings of such a rationale.

I think that a basic theoretic approach here has to be based on the culture of lower socioeconomic groups and more particularly the elements of strength, the positives in this culture. The terms "deprived," "handicapped," "underprivileged," and "disadvantaged" unfortunately emphasize environmental limitations and ignore the positive efforts of low-income individuals to cope with their environment. Most approaches concerned with educating the disadvantaged child either overlook the positives entirely or merely mention in passing that there are positive features in the culture of low socioeconomic groups that middle-class groups might learn from, but they do not spell out what these strengths are, and they build educational programs almost exclusively around the weaknesses or deficits.

I want to call attention to the positive features in the culture and the psychology of low-income individuals. In particular, I should like to look at the cognitive style, the mental style or way of thinking characteristic of these people. One major dimension of this style is slowness.

SLOW VERSUS DULL

Most disadvantaged children are relatively slow in performing intellectual tasks. This slowness is an important feature of their mental style and it needs to be carefully evaluated. In considering the question of the slowness of the deprived child, we would do well to recognize that in our culture there has probably been far too much emphasis on speed. We reward speed. We think of the fast child as the smart child and the slow child as the dull child. I think this is a basically false idea. I think there are many weaknesses in speed and many strengths in slowness.

The teacher can be motivated to develop techniques for rewarding slow pupils if she has an appreciation of some of the positive attributes of a slow style of learning. The teacher should know that pupils may be slow for other reasons than because they are stupid.

A pupil may be slow because he is extremely careful, meticulous, or cautious. He may be slow because he refuses to generalize easily. He may be slow because he cannot understand a concept unless he does something physically, for example, with his hands, in connection with the idea he is trying to grasp.

The disadvantaged child is typically a physical learner and the physical learner is generally a slower learner. Incidentally, the physical style of learning is another important characteristic of the deprived individual and it, too, has many positive features hitherto overlooked.

A child may be slow because he learns in what I have called a one-track way. That is, he persists in one line of thought and is not flexible or broad. He does not easily adopt other frames of reference, such as the teacher's, and consequently he may appear slow and dull. Very often this single-minded individual has considerable creative potential, much of which goes unrealized because of lack of reinforcement in the educational system.

Analysis of the many reasons for slowness leads to the conclusion that slowness should not be equated with stupidity. In fact, there is no reason to assume that there are not a great many slow, gifted children.

The school in general does not pay too much attention to the slow gifted child but rather is alert to discover fast gifted children. Excellence comes in many packages and we must begin to search for it among the slow learners as well as among the faster individuals.

My own understanding of some of the merits of the slow style came through teaching at Bard College, where there is an enrollment of about 350 students. There I had the opportunity of getting to know quite well about 40 students over a period of four years. I could really see what happened to them during this time. Very often the students I thought were slow and dull in their freshman year achieved a great deal by the time they became seniors. These are not the overall bright people who are typically selected by colleges, but in some area, in a one-track way, these students did some marvelous creative work. It was too outstanding to be ignored. I discovered in talking with students that most of them had spent five or six years in order to complete college. They had failed courses and made them up in summer school. Some had dropped out of college for a period of time and taken courses in night school. These students are slow learners, often one-track learners, but very persistent about something when they develop an interest in it. They have a fear of being overpowered by teachers in situations where they do not accept the teacher's point of view, but they stick to their own particular way of seeing the problem. They do not have a fast pace, they do not catch on quickly, and they very often fail subjects.

At the present time, when there is a measure of public excitement for reducing the four-year college to three years, I would submit that many potentially excellent students need a five- or six-year span to complete a college education.

The assumption that the slow pupil is not bright functions, I think, as a self-fulfilling prophecy. If teachers act toward these pupils as if they were dull, the pupils will frequently come to function in this way. Of course, there are pupils who are very well developed at an early age and no teacher can stop them. But in the average development of the young person, even at the college level, there is need for reinforcement. The teacher must pick up what he says, appeal to him, and pitch examples to him. Typically this does not occur with the slow child. I find in examining my own classroom teaching that I easily fall into the habit of rewarding pupils whose faces light up when I talk, who are quick to respond to me, and I respond back to them. The things they say in class become absorbed in the repertoire of what I say. I remember what they say and I use it in providing examples. I do not pick up and select the slower pupil and I do not respond to him. He has to make it on his own.

In the teacher-training program future teachers should be taught to guard against the almost unconscious and automatic tendency of the teacher to respond to the pupil who responds to him.

HIDDEN VERBAL ABILITY

A great deal has been said about the language or verbal deficit supposedly characteristic of disadvantaged children. Everybody in the school system, at one time or another, has heard that these children are inarticulate and nonverbal. But isn't this too simple a generalization? Aren't these children quite verbal in out-of-school situations? For example, the educationally deprived child can be quite articulate in conversation with his peers. This is well illustrated by the whole language developed by urban Negro groups, some of which is absorbed into the main culture via the Beatnik and the musician, if you dig what I mean.

Many questions about the verbal potential of disadvantaged children must be answered by research. Under what conditions are they verbal? What kind of stimuli do they respond to verbally? With whom are they verbal? What do they talk about? What parts of speech do they use? Martin Deutsch (1960) of New York Medical College is doing some very significant research trying to specify these factors, and I surveyed some of his findings in my book *The Culturally Deprived Child* (1962). I think Deutsch is getting at some very interesting things. One technique he uses is a clown that lights up when the children say something. "Inarticulate" children can be very verbal and expressive in this situation.

Disadvantaged children are often surprisingly articulate in role-playing situations. One day when I was with a group of these youngsters, sometimes mistaken for a "gang," I asked them, "Why are you sore at the teachers?" Even though I was on good terms with them, I could not get much of a response. Most of them answered in highly abbreviated sentences. But after I held a role-playing session in which some of the youngsters acted out the parts of the teachers while others acted out the parts of the pupils, these "inarticulate" youngsters changed sharply. Within a half-hour they were bubbling over with very verbal and very sensitive answers to the questions I had asked earlier. They were telling me about the expressions on the teachers' faces that they did not like. They reported that they knew the minute they entered the room that the teacher did not like them and that she did not think they were going to do well in school. Their analyses were specific and remarkably verbal.

The quality of language employed has its limitations, however, and I think herein lies the deficit. As Basil Bernstein (1959) indicates, the difference is between formal language and public language, between a language in a written book and the informal, everyday language. There is no question in my mind that there is a deficit in formal language. Since this deficit is fairly clear, the question might be asked: Why make such an issue of the positive verbal ability of these children?

The reason is that it is easy to believe, that too many people have come to believe, that this formal deficit in language means that deprived people are characteristically nonverbal.

On the other hand, if the schools have the idea that these pupils are basically very good verbally, teachers might approach them in a different manner. Teachers might look for additional techniques to bring out the verbal facility. They might abandon the prediction that deprived children will not go very far in the education system and predict instead that they can go very far indeed because they have very good ability at the verbal level. In other words, an awareness of the positive verbal ability—not merely potential—will lead to demanding more of the disadvantaged child and expecting more of him.

EDUCATION VERSUS THE SCHOOL

There is a good deal of evidence that deprived children and their parents have a much more positive attitude toward education than is generally believed. One factor that obscures the recognition of this attitude is that although deprived individuals value education, they dislike the school. They are alienated from the school and they resent the teachers. For the sake of clarity, their attitude toward education and toward the school must be considered separately.

In a survey conducted a few years ago, people were asked, "What did you miss most in life that you would like your children to have?" Over 70 per cent of the lower socioeconomic groups answered, "Education." The answer was supplied by the respondents, not checked on a list. They could have answered "money," "happiness," "health," or a number of things. And I think this is quite significant. Middle-class people answer "education" less frequently because they have had an education and do not miss it as much.

A nationwide poll conducted by Roper after World War II asked, "If you had a son or daughter graduating from high school, would you prefer to have him or her go on to college, do something else, wouldn't care?" The affirmative response to the college choice was given by 68 per cent of the "poor," and 91 per cent for the more prosperous. The difference is significant, but 68 per cent of the poorer people is a large, absolute figure and indicates that a large number of these people are interested in a college education for their children.

Why then do these people who have a positive attitude toward education hold a negative attitude toward the school? These youngsters and their parents recognize that they are second-class citizens in the school and they are angry about it. From the classroom to the PTA they discover that the school does not like them, does not respond to them, does not appreciate their culture, and does not think they can learn.

Also, these children and their parents want education for reasons different from those presented by the school. They do not easily accept the ideas of expressing yourself, developing yourself, or knowledge for its own sake. They want education much more for vocational ends. But underneath there is a very positive attitude toward education and I think this is predominant in the lower socioeconomic Negro groups. In the Higher

Horizons program in New York City the parents have participated eagerly once they have seen that the school system is concerned about their children. One of the tremendously positive features about this program and the Great Cities programs is the concern for disadvantaged children and the interest in them. This the deprived have not experienced before and even if the programs did nothing else, I believe that the parents and the children would be responsive and would become involved in the school because of the demonstrated concern for them.

SOME WEAKNESSES

A basic weakness of deprived youngsters which the school can deal with is the problem of "know-how." Included here is the academic "know-how" of the school culture as well as the "know-how" of the middle class generally. Knowing how to get a job, how to appear for an interview, how to fill out a form, how to take tests, how to answer questions, and how to listen.

The last is of particular importance. The whole style of learning of the deprived is not set to respond to oral or written stimuli. These children respond much more readily to visual kinesthetic signals. We should remodel the schools to suit the styles and meet the needs of these children. But no matter how much we change the school to suit their needs, we nevertheless have to change these children in certain ways; namely, reading, formal language, test taking, and general "know-how."

These weaknesses represent deficiencies in skills and techniques. There is one basic limitation at the value level, however, namely the anti-intellectual attitudes of deprived groups. It is the only value of lower socio-economic groups that I would fight in the school. I want to make it very clear that I am very much opposed to the school spending a lot of time teaching values to these kids. I am much more concerned—and in this I am traditional—that the schools impart skills, techniques, and knowledge rather than training the disadvantaged to become good middle-class children.

I think there is one area indigenous to the school, however, which has to be fought out at some point with these youngsters; that is their attitude toward intellectuals, toward knowledge for its own sake, and similar issues.

These children and their parents are pretty much anti-intellectual at all levels. They don't like "eggheads." They think talk is a lot of "bull." I would consciously oppose this attitude in the school. I would make the issue explicit. There would be nothing subtle or covert about it. I would at some point state clearly that on this question the school does not agree with them and is prepared to argue about the views they hold.

SUMMARY AND IMPLICATIONS

I have attempted to reinterpret some of the supposedly negative aspects—for example, slowness—that characterize the cognitive style of disadvantaged individuals. I have given particular attention to the untapped verbal ability of these individuals. But there are a great many other positive dimensions of the culture and style of educationally deprived people which are discussed more fully in my book *The Culturally Deprived Child:* the cooperativeness and mutual aid that mark the extended family; the avoidance of the strain accompanying competitiveness and individualism; the equalitarianism, informality, and humor; the freedom from self-blame and parental overprotection; the children's enjoyment of each other's company and lessened sibling rivalry; the security found in the extended family and a traditional outlook; the enjoyment of music, games, sports, and cards; the ability to express anger; the freedom from being word bound; and finally the physical style involved in learning.

I have also indicated the basic weaknesses of the disadvantaged child which the school must work to overcome; lack of school know-how, anti-intellectualism, and limited experience with formal language. Others that should be noted are poor auditory attention, poor time perspective, inefficient test-taking skills, limited reading ability.

The school must recognize these deficiencies and work assiduously to combat them. They are by no means irreversible, but even more important, because neglected, the positive elements in the culture and style of lower socioeconomic groups should become the guidelines for new school programs and new educational techniques for teaching these children.

There are a number of reasons why it is important to emphasize the positive:

1. It will encourage the school to develop approaches and techniques, including possibly special teaching machines appropriate for the cognitive style of deprived children.
2. It will enable children of low-income backgrounds to be educated without middle-classizing them.
3. It will stimulate teachers to aim high, to expect more and work for more from these youngsters. Thus it will constrain against patronization and condescension, and determinate, double-track systems where the deprived child never arrives on the main track.
4. It will function against the current tendency of overemphasizing vocational, nonacademic education for children of low-income background.

5. It will provide an exciting challenge for teachers if they realize that they need not simply aim to "bring these children up to grade level," but rather can actually develop new kinds of creativity.

6. It will make the school far more pluralistic and democratic because different cultures and styles will exist and interact side by side. Thus each can learn from the other and the empty phrase that the teacher has much to learn from deprived children will take on real meaning. General cultural interaction between equal cultures can become the hallmark of the school.

7. It will enable the teacher to see that when techniques such as role playing and visual aids are used with deprived children, it is because these techniques are useful for eliciting the special cognitive style and creative potential of these children. All too often these techniques have been employed with the implicit assumption that they are useful with children who have inadequate learning ability.

8. It will lead to real appreciation of slowness, one-track learning, and physical learning as potential strengths that require careful nurturing. The teacher will have to receive special training in how to respond to these styles, how to listen carefully to the one-track person, how to reward the slow learner, and so on. Special classes for slow learners will not culminate in the removal of these youngsters from the mainstream of the educational process on a permanent second track, and longer periods of time in school and college can be planned for these students without invidious connotations.

31 *Some Psychosocial Aspects of Learning in the Disadvantaged*

Martin Deutsch

It has long been known that there is some general relationship between conditions of social, cultural, and economic deprivation and cognitive deficit. The environment that is associated with the highest rates of disease, crime, and social disorganization also has the highest rate of school retardation. Deficiencies are particularly striking in linguistic skills and reading. A significance of school dropout and failure, apart from what it represents in lost potential to the individual and his community, is that when the children who failed become adults, they will be confined to the least skilled and least desirable jobs and will have almost no opportunity for upward social mobility.

A large body of empirical literature lends support to the assumption that certain environmental conditions may retard psychological processes, including intellectual factors. This conclusion receives support on both the animal and human levels (e.g., Hebb, 1949; Hunt, 1961). One of the most comprehensive reviews of the effects of environmental impoverishment on intellectual development has been presented by Clarke and Clarke (1959), who present data collected on adolescents and young adults who have experienced severe deprivation as a result of cruelty, neglect, or parental separation. Bruner (1961a) writes that ". . . exposure to normally enriched environments makes the development of such (cognitive) strategies possible by providing intervening opportunities for trial and error. . . . [T]hat there is impairment under a deprived regimen seems . . . to be fairly evident" (pp. 203–204). Although Bruner does not specifically refer to the environment of the lower-class child, his remarks appear to be especially relevant there. The obvious implication is that disadvantaged children are often unprepared to cope with the formal intellectual and learning demands of school as a result of the meager environmental basis for the development of cognitive skills.

The conclusions from these data need not be wholly pessimistic, however: a fostering environment can facilitate intellectual development. Bruner, for example, suggests that certain types of environmental conditions increase the likelihood of learning cognitive strategies. And Clarke and Clarke (1959) report striking increases in I.Q. in the deprived group during a six-year program aimed at reversing the deprivation effects. Results also supportive of the conclusion that environmental conditions may have a positive impact on the intellectual development of children are found in the studies of the Iowa group (e.g., Skeels et al., 1938; Wellman, 1940; Skodak and Skeels, 1949). More informal observation shows that even in the most economically depressed areas, where school retardation rates are highest, there are children who have shown considerable school success and academic proficiency. If it is assumed that a causal relationship exists between environmental conditions and cognitive development, then variation in cognitive development can in part reflect variations within the environment. It can be assumed that a so-called "underprivileged" area does not possess homogeneous characteristics: there are indeed considerable variations in the home environments of children from such areas, variations ranging from large fatherless families supported by public assistance to small intact families having inadequate but regular incomes.

Just as environmental backgrounds are heterogeneous, so are learning contexts. Although the contexts are not really discontiguous, early socialization as mediated through home and neighborhood environments and mass media requires different kinds of responses than those demanded in the kind of formal learning that is the primary focus in this paper: school learning and subject mastery. Formal learning processes carry well-defined criteria of failure and success which are not mediated through behavioral indices such as group leadership, influence, and the like. This is not true of the informal learning environment where there are no explicitly stated criteria and marking systems. Instead, success might be more highly related to leadership, and failure to rejection or subordination by the group.

Just as the learning context changes when the child enters school, so does the psychological context for achievement. Here is where the amount of continuity between the home environment and that of school can be very influential in establishing the child's response to the learning context and the achievement context of the school situation. The discontinuity between the lower-class child's background and the school is detrimental to his successful response to the new situation.

The middle-class child is more likely to have been continuously prodded by his parents in the intellectual area, while being rewarded for correct answers. The lower-class child has, in the main, infrequently been subjected at home to the pressure arising from a formal adult-child learning situation. The middle-class child is likely to have experienced in the behavior of adults in his environment the essential ingredients implicit in the role of the teacher. For the lower-class child, relating to the teacher and school officials requires a new kind of behavior for which he has not necessarily been prepared.

The school curricula and the learning techniques tend to be based on an assumption that the child has had prior experiences in the complex learning dyad, where there are logical assumptions as to appropriate behavior and where success is rewarded and failure is disapproved. The teacher, trained in our not-so-modern teacher-education institutions, assumes, probably consciously as well as unconsciously, that the child is there as a quasipassive recipient of knowledge, and that he clearly sees the teacher in her educative and remedial functions. In this the teacher is as likely to be confused as to the child's expectations as the child is to be confused about the school's expectations.

There is an understandable tendency, in the absence of sufficient sociological sophistication, for the school authorities to expect of the children a level of comprehension and motivation that can only be built through positive experiences in the learning situation. What often happens is that children who are used to a great deal of motor activity and who have certain environmentally determined deficiencies in learning to learn, tend to respond with insufficient academic orientations. Teachers seem to meet this situation in a number of ways, most of which cause serious problems for the socially marginal child.

Some teachers establish low expectations, anticipate failure, and, true to the Mertonian self-fulfilling prophecy, find an increasing rate of failure.

Another reaction pattern seems to be, "they can't learn, they don't care, their parents are not concerned." This is a projective device that takes responsibility away from the professional, and at the same time contains a grain of apparent truth. Often older siblings and neighbors have experienced so much failure and so much class and cultural arrogance that a great apathy has been created in which no one expects positive consequences from the school experience. It is this apathy that is sometimes reflected in the attitudes of the educational apparatus toward the lower-class community.

There are still other teachers who say, "it is all the environment—impoverishment, economic insecurity, segregation, second-class citizenship, historical chains—and though none of these things is the child's fault, neither are they the school's fault." Here we have a more valid core, and one that invokes social circumstances that obviously are crucial to the developing organism. At the same time such a formulation often leads to a negating of the essential responsibility of the school and to a negation of the real strengths, both actual and potential, which the children have.

But most important, it induces an elaborate rationale for the further alienation of teachers from their primary function of teaching. The essential element, and a professionally and psychologically threatening one, is simply that if the child comes to school inadequately equipped to handle what the school has ready, then it is up to the school to develop strategies for compensating the child for environmentally imposed inadequacies and offering a program of stimulation appropriate to his performance level. In essence, the disadvantaged child is placed at a still greater disadvantage when the school, as the primary socializing and teaching agent, does not assume that it is more likely that *it* has failed when a child fails. To do this requires a constant self-criticalness and self-evaluation which has not been characteristic of educational systems, though there are some noteworthy exceptions.

My point here is that as teacher-training institutions and educational systems allow an atmosphere of critical evaluation of current procedures and establish high criteria for professional training and development, teachers will maintain a psychological connection with their children that today often gets lost, especially when the teacher must bridge social-class discontinuities with neither a theoretical nor a working model to accomplish this.

As regards much of the current scene, we would have to do a great deal of theoretical reconstruction if a higher proportion of children were succeeding and learning to read at grade level. The total atmosphere in the majority of our urban schools with large groups of disadvantaged youngsters becomes decreasingly conducive to the learning process and to the positive child-teacher relationship that gives rise to motivation and high standards of achievement.

The responsibility for this unfavorable learning situation cannot be placed only on the school. It is a combination of social circumstance, historical apathy, economic exploitation, and a society that does not put its money where its explicit values are. Despite the fact that the school is only one ingredient in the causal matrix responsible for the problem, the school most directly reflects society's failure, as it is the one institution that has the opportunity to directly affect the situation.

In this total atmosphere, what are some of the additional handicaps the disadvantaged child brings into school? If we expect the school to organize to meet the child on his own developmental level, then we must know a good deal about the specific intellectual sequelae more likely to be associated with economic impoverishment than with affluence. And we need simple and adequate ways of measuring each child's current status in the development of the abilities that underlie the skills that the school is going to teach him.

This type of information about the capabilities of each individual child will better enable the teacher to teach him and to present the most appropriate stimuli. But more than that, his probability of success will be increased when the material presented is most consistent with his developmental level. This is simply to say that if a sense of competence, in White's terms, is engendered, motivation will be sustained and learning thus will be further aided.

This discussion impinges on the issues involved in the self-image. The experiences in school can either reinforce invidious self-concepts acquired from the environment or can help to develop a negative self-concept not necessarily otherwise acquired. Conversely, they can create conditions in which positive self-feelings will be engendered by concrete achievements and some opportunities to function with competence, even if initially they must be in the most limited and restricted areas.

The evidence makes it inescapable to conclude that a number of children from disadvantaged circumstances have developed negative self-images by the time they enter school and that the school accomplishes little toward mitigating this.

There is another relevant element here, usually not considered, that probably plays a role in at least the perception of himself which the child develops in school, and that is the use of time. Generally, time is inefficiently used, there is a minimal amount of individualized attention, and it is possible for the child to spend a great deal of time in unproductive rote activities, as the teacher focuses her attention on remedial subgroups or the omnipresent paper work. The critical question is that there are few auto-instructional devices around, or preprogrammed curriculum elements that the child can go to, and at the same time there is a high pupil-teacher ratio.

This is part of a situation where responsibility cannot be placed on the teacher, and the frequent use of this downtrodden professional as the focus of the problem reflects in the main only her position as the psychologically operative instrument in the education of the child. In a sense, after passing through the whole of society's educational echelons, the buck stops with her (but not in her pocket). Nevertheless, this understanding does not neutralize the existing situation. Too often, there is very insufficient stimulation for the child, even in the classrooms of the best teachers, and there is little overall curriculum planning for the needs of disadvantaged children. Most important, society just has not furnished the funds, and educational leadership has failed to furnish the training, to introduce the new supplementary technologies that would enormously increase the effective utilization of time, and which in turn would help the child to develop a sense of purpose and belonging in the school context.

Another reason for serious consideration of auto-instructional and programmed devices and methods is that they might give the child a feeling of greater mastery over the unfamiliar environment. This they might do by reducing the passive element of the situation and by giving the child more control over the timing of stimuli, and thus minimizing cultural differences in time orientation. Further, in the self-corrective feed-back of programmed materials, the teacher's role of giving reward and disapproval would be shared, and for a child who is not accustomed to motivation for intellectual performance by means of such psychological influencing techniques, it might help to decrease the alienation between the child and the school. If these hypotheses are valid, then the new educational techniques could possibly be seen as socially facilitating the learning process.

The major emphasis of this discussion has been on the extent of alienation that the disadvantaged child experiences as a major factor in handicapping his performance and achievement. Much of this exists on the structural level, and much of the psychosocial problem is in the interaction between the child and the school. There are also socially influenced or determined cognitive variables, however, which contribute to the whole process of increasing alienation from each other on the part both of the school and the child. To consider just one of the major difficulties with which the lower-class child frequently operates, there is the often nonfunctional language system he brings into school. My colleagues and I have discussed this at length elsewhere (M. Deutsch et al., 1964a; M. Deutsch, 1964b, c; John, 1963).

What I would like to point out in the present context is the effect of social-class determination of linguistic styles and habits as an effective deterrent to communication and understanding between child and teacher. To illustrate, the child is not accustomed to attending to or to being the object of what for him are long, orderly, focused verbal sequences. Yet this is the primary scholastic teaching and discipline method. Further, the disadvantaged child is less familiar with the syntactical regularities and normative frequencies of the language, and thus has difficulty in ordering sequences and both deriving meaning from and putting it into context. This is a particular disadvantage for the lower-class child because of a short attention span for the verbal material to which he is exposed in school. As a result of this combination of factors, he is likely to miss a great deal, even when he is trying to listen. It therefore becomes extremely important for the child to feel some mastery in handling at least receptive language. This is made more difficult by what Bernstein (1960), the English sociologist, has described as the different dialects spoken by lower- and middle-class people.

This discussion keeps coming back to the need for helping the educator to develop a comprehensive consciousness of the psychological as well as learning difficulties the disadvantaged child has; the potential for change that exists; the specifics involved in training children, for example, to ask questions, or to become aware of syntactical regularities, or to use auto-instructional materials; and to maintain as high a level of stimulation and relevancy as possible in the classroom. This is where the research and the insights of the behavioral sciences should be able to make a significant contribution, if the educational albatross takes a few "risks" to accommodate social change.

32   *Teaching the Slow Learner*

Merle B. Karnes

Slow learners are children whose rate of intellectual development is about 75 to 90 per cent as rapid as that of average children. These children whose I.Q.'s range from 75 to 90 are often referred to as "dull normal" or "low average." Since their rate of mental growth is slower than average, their mental age always lags behind their chronological age. For example, a child with a chronological age of 6 and an I.Q. of 80 has a mental age of 4 years, 8 months. At age 12 his mental age will be 9 years, 6 months; and at age 16 his mental age will be 12 years, 8 months. The rate of achievement of the slow learner is about four-fifths to nine-tenths of a year as compared to the normal who ordinarily achieve at a rate of a year during each school year. The maximum mental-age scores of slow learners range from approximately 11 years to 13 years and 6 months and their maximum academic-achievement grade scores will be from grades 6 to 8.5.

Slow learners are not to be confused with educationally retarded children of average or above-average intelligence who may be emotionally disturbed or have sensory or perceptual handicaps that prevent their making educational progress commensurate with their abilities. If his intellectual functioning has been assessed validly, the slow learner, as defined herein, will never be able to catch up academically or mentally with his normal peers.

The best single method of accurately identifying the slow learner is by an individual intelligence test administered by a school psychologist. Since there are relatively few school psychologists, most schools attempting to identify slow learners will have to rely heavily on group intelligence and achievement tests along with observations by teachers and parents. If psychological services are limited then questionable cases should be referred to a psychologist for an individual assessment.

ARE SCHOOLS MEETING THE NEEDS OF SLOW LEARNERS?

Slow learners present one of education's most crucial unsolved problems. Every state in the union has legislation designed to encourage local school systems to establish programs for the mentally handicapped. As a consequence, programs for this segment of our school population are becoming more numerous. Many school systems have provisions for the mentally handicapped from the time they enter school through high school. At last and admittedly long overdue, the gifted are beginning to receive their just share of attention in many schools, which seemingly is resulting in marked improvement in educational provisions for children with superior intelligence—our potential leaders. Unfortunately, the slow learners have not received such attention. Nationwide the slow learner is the most neglected group of children in our school systems. Relatively few public schools are making special provisions and are developing curricula specifically designed for this 15 to 20 per cent of our school population designated as slow learners.

It is interesting to contrast educational provisions for the mentally handicapped (I.Q.'s 50–75), who constitute some 2 to 3 per cent of the general population, to the typical educational programs and practices for slow learners.

The educable mentally handicapped (I.Q.'s 50–75) in many schools are spared the frustration of grade failures and rigid demarcation of grade lines and grade standards. The educable mentally handicapped progresses through school in ungraded classes at his own rate and is provided with a special curriculum that is practical and functional. The adjusted educational program provides many opportunities for success which leads to the development of a feeling of personal worth. As a result of an educational program that is geared to his needs, he is able to develop the prevocational skills, attitudes, and habits he will need to make a good vocational adjustment.

The slow learner is usually initiated into reading before he is mentally ready and as a consequence fails miserably. After a preponderance of failures and retentions, his attitudes toward learning are so badly impaired that he develops modes of adjustment which are not acceptable to his peers, teachers, administrators, and the community in general. In most states, compulsory school-attendance laws force him to remain in school until he is 16. There is a limit as to how many times a slow learner can be retained at any one level of the school. Eventually he is given a social promotion whether he has mastered the academics or not. He is usually overaged and oversized for his grade placement. This tends to engender feelings of inadequacy and inferiority and generally undermines his self-confidence. As he is pushed along from grade to grade, the discrepancy between his level of achievement and that of his peers becomes greater and greater.

Usually at the secondary level, the slow learner is given the same program as provided for more capable pupils or at best a "watered-down" academic program. Even if there is a track type of organizational plan, this situation is likely to prevail. Such a program tends to be meaningless to him and does not motivate him to put forth his best efforts. His attempts to complete assignments and meet the standards imposed on him by the conventional curriculum usually lead to further failures. Sooner or later the slow learner ceases to try. Often he just sits through regular classes waiting for the day he becomes 16 and can drop out of school. Many times slow learners leave school psychologically long before they are permitted to leave school physically.

Teachers of the mentally handicapped are specially trained and provide a special curriculum that enables the mentally handicapped to graduate from high school. Teachers of the slow learners, however, usually are regular teachers who would rather teach the brighter. They seldom have any formal training that helps them understand this group of children. As a consequence, more often than not these teachers are not able to provide a meaningful program for the slow learners. Lack of success and a feeling of inadequacy literally "shoves" the slow learners out of school. Because they are problem children, school personnel often encourage them to leave school as soon as it is legally permissible. In fact, many educators wink at the laws and give up trying to keep the slow learner in school from six months to a year before he is 16. His name is just on the roll. In view of the foregoing, it is easy to understand why slow learners make up the large majority of the 30 to 40 per cent of youths who drop out of school between the seventh and twelfth grades.

To reiterate, lack of success experiences in school precipitates the slow learner's leaving school. He is not cognizant of the fact that the world of work does not have its arms extended to him. He is not prepared to take his place in the adult society which requires that he be able to hold a job. He has not acquired the knowledge, habits, and skills prerequisite for earning a living.

In the past, youths with low intellectual capacity and with limited education might have been able to obtain some kind of unskilled or semi-skilled employment. The dramatic changes induced by the scientific and technological revolution have and are continuing to reduce rapidly the employment opportunities open to such youth. This, along with the fact that youth are now with us in unprecedented numbers, will make it increasingly difficult for the slow learner with limited education to obtain and hold a job. The only hope for him is to educate him to the full limits of his capacity and prepare him to compete successfully in the labor market. The changes in the composition of the labor force have provided a mandate to the schools to improve their educational programs and to join forces with agencies in the community to provide the training and services necessary to enable the slow learner to acquire salable vocational skills and thus be able to successfully compete for a job.

It must be remembered that each slow learner is unique and therefore may not have all the characteristics that describe slow learners in general. When setting up an instructional program, one must hold in mind the general characteristics of the slow learner and within this framework design a curriculum that permits adjusting and modifying the program according to the needs of an individual slow learner. The educational goals for the slow learner are the same as for any other child in the school, but the manner in which the teacher helps each slow learner attain the goals must, of course, differ. The type of experiences, the materials of instruction, the teaching methods and techniques used in teaching the slow learner must be adapted to the special needs of the slow learner. The following presents briefly the characteristics of slow learners as they compare to the average and the implications of such characteristics for an instructional program.

Physically Inferior

As a group the slow learners tend to be somewhat inferior in size and in motor coordination. One may find a slow learner who is above average in size and well coordinated, but this is not generally the case.

Since more vision and hearing defects are found among this group, a school vision-and-hearing screening program is very essential so that those failing such tests will be referred to medical specialists. If a child has a marked auditory impairment, the teachers may need to use a visual approach in teaching the academic subjects, especially reading. If medical reports indicate the child has a visual impairment, an auditory approach to teaching would likely be emphasized.

Instruction should include more intensive teaching about matters of health than is necessary for brighter children since many of these children are from homes that are substandard so far as health procedures are concerned. This instruction is necessary because these children do not learn the good health habits that are a part of the health routine of most middle-class homes. Relatively few of these children receive the medical attention commonly afforded children from middle-class homes. Thus these children will need to be referred to clinics or agencies where they can receive medical care at minimum expense to them.

There is no law of compensation for the slow learner. In other words, because they are slow mentally does not mean that they will be strong physically or emotionally well adjusted. They are just as poor in manual skills as in reading or arithmetic. If they do better in the subject areas that require the use of their hands, it is because the activities are more purposeful and meaningful to them. Of course, academic classes then must be made more meaningful and purposeful. Shop work and homemaking activities should also be an important part of their learning experiences. An occupational therapist might contribute to the development of certain manual skills.

Even if their motor coordination happens to be normal, the limited intellectual ability of the children will hamper their competing athletically with brighter peers if the games are highly organized, complicated, and competitive. Nevertheless, they should be provided with opportunities to engage in physical activities that are geared to their level of intellectual functioning and at the same time ones in which they are physically able to participate.

Mentally Immature for Chronological Age

The slow learner learns at a slower rate than the average. For this reason he will start to have difficulty the day he enters school because he is mentally immature. At age 6 his mental age will be approximately 4 years, 8 months. Research indicates that a child needs to have a mental age of somewhere near 6 years, 5 months to ensure his success in learning to read. The slow learner, then, fails in reading in the first grade because he is too immature to learn this complicated task. Further, he observes his able peers learning to read and this causes him to feel inadequate. Repeating first grade is the usual method of trying to help the slow learner. Retention, however, is a questionable plan, especially when one considers the damage it can do to the child's self-concept and his peers' perception of him. A preponderance of failures interferes with good mental health. A prolonged readiness period followed by an adjusted program is suggested as the most appropriate means of coping with this problem. Ungraded classes seemingly have merits for these children.

Although the teacher should not expect these children to learn any of the academic skills at the same chronological age as their more able peers, slow learners will be able to learn many skills when they reach the necessary level of mental maturity.

Short Attention Span

Seemingly these children have a shorter attention span than the average. When the material presented is meaningful, interesting, and geared to their conceptual level, however, these children are able to attend to instruction for considerable periods of time. Serious attention should be given to providing materials at an appropriate level and lesser attention given to shortening the time requirements. Inattentiveness can be a symptom that the lessons are too difficult and, only to a much less degree, that they are too long.

Poor Memory

The slow learner finds delayed recall especially difficult. To ensure adequate retention he needs to repeat and drill more than most children. Repetition in meaningful context is essential to reinforce learnings. Moreover, the slow learner finds it easier to remember when the material to be learned has real meaning for him, when the learning task is purposeful.

Below-Average Incidental Learning

The slow learner does not have the intellectual curiosity or the ability to question why things happen or why things are the way they seem to be. Consequently, the slow learner does not pick up ideas and concepts that happen to be presented. For example, a bright student may make a tangential remark in the class that may lead to future learnings. Some of the average children in the class will remember this remark but not the slow learner.

Educationally, the slow learner needs to be taught skills sequentially and systematically. A developmental program is a must. Any gaps in his learning will not be filled incidentally.

Poor Abstract Reasoning

It is difficult for the slow learner to generalize. He is slow to see relationships, draw conclusions, and make inferences. He learns best when material is presented as concretely as possible. Whenever possible, the teacher should present material so that all of the senses are involved during the learning process.

Field trips provide especially valuable experiences for teaching these children. Firsthand experiences help them develop concepts more readily. Much use should also be made of audio-visual instructional materials. Alert and sensitive guidance must be given by the teacher to help these children profit from learning experiences. The teacher should structure concepts carefully and provide "thought bridges" from concept to concept. A thorough understanding of each experience seems to be more important than vague awareness of many bits of information.

Poor Response to Long-Range Goals and Delayed Evaluation of Their Work

Because of their limited intellectual ability, slow learners have difficulty anticipating future events or the consequences of their actions.

Short-range goals are easier for them to comprehend and to work to achieve. They become impatient when they have to wait until the end of a week or even the end of a day to obtain an evaluation of their work or rewards for their efforts because they have difficulty maintaining a relationship between an antecedent and its outcome. For these children the goals must be set in the immediate future to foster continued interest and maximum output of effort. In addition, lack of self-confidence increases their problems and makes it essential for the teacher to help them evaluate their work immediately so that they will get prompt feedback. They need far more encouragement, reassurance, and praise than pupils of average ability. The teacher should devise concrete ways of helping these children evaluate their own progress.

Poor Ability to Follow Instructions

Slow learners find it confusing and difficult to follow a number of oral directions. More time should be given in making sure directions are clearly understood. They are likely to flounder if they are given several directions all at one time. Again, directions should be given in as concrete terms as possible. Slow learners need closer supervision than the normal to safeguard against their making and reinforcing incorrect responses. It should be remembered that slow learners find it more difficult to extinguish incorrect responses than to learn them correctly.

Inadequate Self-Evaluation

Their intellectual limitations hinder their being able to critically evaluate their own work. The teacher must frequently help them evaluate their work rather than expect them to take a large portion of this responsibility. They tend to be unrealistic and then become discouraged and quit if the teacher does not give the needed help or a word of encouragement to continue with the task until it is finished.

Deficiency in Creativity

These children need considerable help and encouragement to develop their creative abilities. This is an area in which they seem particularly deficient. The teacher needs to become acquainted with various ways of stimulating children to become more creative. Once it was thought that the slow learner had no creative potentials to build on. This is currently not the thinking of the experts on creativity. It is thought that all persons have some creative potentials if they are but nurtured. These children should be encouraged to do divergent thinking to maximize any potential that they might have in this area.

Difficulty in Transferring Learnings

More help must be given the slow learner in transferring learnings from one situation to the other. Thus he needs help in developing word-attack skills even though he will have to expend more time and effort to learn such skills. He will need more help in applying or learning how to transfer these skills appropriately. The school curriculum should deal with real problems on the interest level of these children because it is easier for them to transfer learnings within this context.

Markedly Retarded in the Academic Areas

Slow learners tend to function academically two or more years below their chronological ages and many have been retained for two or more years. It is highly desirable to have a complete psychoeducational diagnosis of each child to determine his strengths and weaknesses so that an instructional program can be designed to help him in his specific areas of weakness. Most of these children are in need of a good developmental program that enables them to progress at a rate commensurate with their abilities. A remedial program is also a must for some of these children.

A percentage of slow learners may be mentally slow because of neurological damage. Such damage may hinder these children from learning through methods and techniques effective with the great majority of slow learners. In this event, a differential diagnosis is imperative to pinpoint specific areas of weakness. Clinical teaching methods and techniques must usually be used to enable such children to progress academically. Individual instruction for a portion of the day, especially in the initial stages, seems to be the best plan to ensure academic progress. Need for help in learning to read is the most common academic problem. Some, however, have learning problems in the area of arithmetic.

Slow learners tend to have poor work habits; this is largely due to the fact that they have either been given work that is too difficult for them or have been allowed to sit through classes with little or no expectations placed on them. The teachers in such cases will need to help the pupils establish good work habits. When they are provided with work at their level of achievement and ability, see meaning in what is required of them, are given reassurance that they are making progress, then their work habits improve accordingly.

In-school work and work-study programs at the late elementary, junior-high, and senior-high levels help slow learners develop an appreciation and understanding of work. These programs should reinforce learnings through both credit and remuneration. Participants in these programs learn such skills as taking directions from authority figures, getting to work on time, staying with a task until its completion. One problem of the slow learners, of course, is that they are prone to overestimate their abilities and set vocational aspirations higher than they can possibly achieve. Vocational counseling coupled with actual work experience helps them develop more realistic aspirations and attitudes that will help them compete in the world of work.

Poor Adjustment

They tend to have more social and emotional problems than other children. School failure has no doubt contributed to their poor adjustment. When so little satisfaction is obtained from school attendance, it is little wonder that they frequently present behavior problems. School experiences are generally frustrating to them. They are driven to using unacceptable ways of behaving to compensate for their poor progress and inability to successfully participate in the school activities. They are sometimes accused of being lazy and not trying. This impression of the teachers may be caused by a reaction to tasks that are too difficult or uninteresting rather than to lack of motivation to learn.

Their home environment predisposes them to be delinquent. As a rule they come from homes in the low socioeconomic range. The housing is poor. The home management is poor. There are inadequate play and recreational areas. There are more broken homes among slow learners than among the normal. Because both parents usually work, these children are left unsupervised. This is a particularly bad situation since slow learners are susceptible to suggestions from peers. They are so eager to be accepted and to feel that they belong that they will go along with and engage in antisocial activities if this promises closer peer relationships and acceptance.

Social casework with both individuals and groups of slow learners and with their parents is strongly recommended. The school and community must band together and provide constructive activities for these children after school hours. To leave slow learners unsupervised and on their own resources can be a breeding ground for the development of antisocial behavior.

Poor Attendance

Slow learners are likely to use every conceivable excuse to stay out of school. This situation is usually created by poor school progress and poor grades. The pupils are trying to avoid a situation that gives them little satisfaction. The school must devise ways of increasing its holding power. Curricular changes are imperative. The content must be interesting and meaningful to the slow learner. The learning task must make sense to him. Successes must far outnumber failures. Much criticism has been leveled at the content of basic readers for this type of child. Obviously the story content depicts middle-class experiences as well as middle-class standards. These concepts are foreign to the slow learners from low socioeconomic homes.

The services of social workers, psychologists, and guidance counselors must be made available to these children so that they can be helped to set realistic goals for themselves and be motivated to learn and stay in school until their education is completed. Also, prevocational counselors must be made available to these youths when they reach the junior-high level so that they can be provided with work experiences that will enable them to acquire desirable prevocational skills which will in turn aid them in ultimately obtaining and holding a job. Every effort should be made to develop joint efforts that utilize the services of those counseling agencies who have something to offer these children.

Administrative Plans for Slow Learners

Some plan that groups these children together for instructional purposes is indicated. Generally, special classes of slow learners provide greater opportunities for teachers to meet the needs of slow learners. Such classes should seemingly have a reduced teacher-pupil ratio, a class size being approximately 15 to 20. Another reason for homogeneous grouping is that regardless of how well a teacher is able to differentiate instruction, peer competition is usually keen in a heterogeneous class. Such competition reinforces the slow learners' feelings of inferiority and inadequacy.

Slow learners, however, should feel a part of the mainstream of the school and participate in learning and social activities of the school when success is possible.

TEACHERS OF SLOW LEARNERS

It is important for teachers to understand these children and know how to teach them; therefore any special training is advantageous. More important than training is the sincere desire on the part of the teacher to teach children who learn slowly. Too often new teachers or teachers who have not worked out so well with other groups of children are assigned to teach these children. This is most unfortunate because slow learners need good teachers even more than the average since they have so many problems associated with a slow rate of learning and often poor home environments. Teachers who teach slow learners should be held in as high esteem by administrators and other staff members as any other teacher.

GRADING SYSTEMS FOR SLOW LEARNERS

A grading system that takes into account the slow rate of learning of the slow learner and the extent to which each individual is working up to his expectancy is the only fair way of evaluating these children. If such children are graded according to a normal curve, they will likely always be at the bottom of the heap. A grading system that emphasizes individual growth rather than a comparison with others of varying ability is preferable. Ideally, an evaluation of progress which makes use of descriptive words rather than A's, B's, and C's or the like is more meaningful.

SUMMARY

When there is a discrepancy between what a person is able to achieve and the level at which he is achieving, the mental health of the individual is in jeopardy. Similarly, the mental health of an individual is in jeopardy when there is a discrepancy between what a person is expected to do and what he can do. Slow learners can learn at a level on a par with their capabilities if (1) they are expected to achieve at a realistic rate, (2) they are provided with an appropriate educational program, (3) services are provided to help them develop an adequate social and emotional adjustment, and (4) they are helped to bridge the gap between the school and employment.

Too long we have tolerated the waste of human resources among the slow learners. Technological changes make it imperative that we focus our attention on improved educational programs and services for slow learners so that they can become fully functioning, productive members of our society.

33 *Motivating Children with School Problems*

E. Paul Torrance

THE PROBLEM

Simply stated, the basic problem in increasing potential in educational achievement and reducing school dropout is one of motivating children and young people with school problems. Although the term "under-achiever" is woefully inappropriate in the light of new insights concerning the measurement of mental abilities and achievement, there is no question but that many children who are actually intellectually gifted are not motivated to learn and learn little, no matter how their achievement is assessed. Somehow there must be a will to learn. A recent national panel of educational leaders (Zacharias, 1964) identified this as one of the major problems for educational research. This panel pointed out that existing research makes it fairly evident that the following three major factors must be taken into consideration in stimulating the will to learn:

1. A recognition by the child that school learning leads to some worthwhile outcome.
2. Recognition that learning is, under certain circumstances, as pleasurable an activity as an arduous sport like baseball.
3. Recognition that such learning makes the child more like the adult he most admires.

The panel indicated, however, that much remains to be learned about these three factors.

It is not very helpful to explain the child who is unmotivated to learn by saying that he is "lazy," "indifferent," "uncooperative," "spoiled," or "bad." There are many reasons why teachers should be concerned about such children, even in the early grades. Research indicates (Frankel, 1961) that once a pattern of "underachievement" has been established, it

338

generally continues and becomes worse. The eventual outcome too frequently is delinquency, school dropout, and mental illness.

DEFINITION OF MOTIVATION

Research and theory concerning problems of motivation are so complex that it would be easy to become bogged down just trying to define motivation. Thus motivation will be defined very simply as involving all those variables that arouse, sustain, and direct behavior—in our case, the educational achievement of children. This means that a student lacking motivation is not sufficiently aroused and sustained to learn at anything like the level of which he is capable.

It is of course quite difficult to tell whether a particular child is learning at the level of which he is capable, because it is practically impossible to determine what is the potentiality of a child who is not motivated to perform well on the test or other indicator of potential. Yet it is important that teachers give attention to every indicator of potential available to them. Without a knowledge of potential, teachers may place too much pressure on a child who is already too strongly motivated and is unable to learn because he is overanxious, or be unconcerned about a potentially brilliant student whose achievement is only mediocre.

History is filled with accounts of eminent men and women, unquestionably gifted, who did not achieve very well during certain periods of their school careers. At least, they did not learn what their teachers tried to teach them. Albert Einstein, President Franklin Roosevelt, President John F. Kennedy, and Sir Winston Churchill are examples of men who at times appeared to be unmotivated to learn what their schools offered and made "C's." Wernher von Braun, our famous space scientist, failed his high-school courses in mathematics and physics. Of course, after he became enthusiastic about rocketry, he excelled in mathematics and physics. Thomas Edison's teacher thought that Tom was mentally "addled" and his mother withdrew him from school and taught him herself. Edison was motivated to continue to learn throughout his life and contributed numerous inventions even after he was 80 years old. Goertzel and Goertzel (1962) report that 60 per cent of the 400 eminent people in their study had serious school problems. They would have been classified as unmotivated. Their dissatisfactions in order of importance were with the curriculum; dull, irrational, or cruel teachers; other students who bullied, ignored, or bored them; and school failure.

Actually, it is sometimes difficult to distinguish the gifted child who is not motivated to perform well from average or slow-learning children. This difficulty is beautifully illustrated in some of the experiences of Ronald J. Goldman, educational psychologist at the University of Reading in England. He and his wife have been operating a youth club for adolescents of average and below-average ability. The school records of these youngsters indicated that their intelligence quotients are quite low —around 75 to 90—and that they were very low achievers. Besides this, most of them had been engaging in considerable vandalism and hoodlum-type behavior. After working with them in the club for some time and exposing them to a stimulating and responsive environment, Dr. Goldman asked them to take an intelligence test and to do as well as they could with it. Apparently, they were motivated then to perform in terms of their potential. The results showed that the average intelligence quotient of the group was about 25 I.Q. points higher than their school records showed.

Similar results were obtained in the Junior High School Project 43 in New York City (Clark, 1963). Of the 105 children who were tested at the beginning of the project and three years later, 78 of them showed an increase in I.Q. Forty of them gained more than 10 points and 13 gained more than 20 points. One child gained as much as 40 points in his tested I.Q. The dropout rate from high school for these children prior to the project was around 40 per cent; the dropout rate for the project children was less than 20 per cent.

Most teachers are familiar with the common symptoms of the unmotivated gifted child. Generally, he appears to be uninterested in school and in learning. He may not like his teacher or teachers, may have no friends, and may be unable to make any. He may feel insecure, be poorly adjusted socially, be intolerant of authority, and be fearful and anxious. These, however, might best be regarded as symptoms, so that attention can be given by the teacher to those things that he can contribute most effectively to the solution of the problem.

In a simple way, I will sketch what I regard as some of the most important basic reasons why children are not motivated to achieve.

NO CHANCE TO USE WHAT IS LEARNED

Perhaps the most fundamental cause of low motivation for learning is the school's failure to give students a chance to use what they learn as tools in their thinking. Thus students are unable to see that school learning leads to something worthwhile, and they are thereby robbed of the most important and powerful reward of learning there is. This leaves them unmotivated and unexcited about learning. What I have in mind is an inner stimulation, what is sometimes referred to as intrinsic motivation.

To many teachers, motivation means the application of external pressures (reward or punishment) to promote some type of desirable behavior. This may be due to the emphasis that has been placed in educational psychology on the stimulus-response approach to teaching. It has been my experience and observation that external pressure rarely promotes desirable behavior in unmotivated learners. In fact, we can seldom "make" a student learn, behave, study, or apply himself, if he chooses not to do so. With some children, the more we reward them the worse they behave and the less they learn, and likewise the more we punish them the worse things become.

Even if reward and punishment succeed temporarily, they do not supply the inner stimulation necessary for continued motivated learning. Such motivation is short-lived and requires continuous reapplication. If there is inner stimulation and more intrinsic kinds of rewards, such repetition of rewards and punishments is unnecessary. Although rewards are erratic as motivators, I am more concerned about the use of punishment to motivate gifted children than about rewards. Many observers of teacher behavior, even in special classes for gifted children, tell me that they are constantly amazed at the hostile and punitive behavior of teachers in the classroom.

Let us examine a couple of actual cases of unmotivated children who have apparently been victimized by punitive approaches to motivation.

You will recall the letter in Chapter 8 from the mother of a 13-year-old boy. You will remember that his teacher boasted about breaking the boy's spirit by shaming and ridiculing the boy. The counselor and teacher decided that failing grades would teach him a lesson and make him "buckle down and work or else." The principal reasoned that keeping the boy out of science clubs about which he was enthusiastic would force him to become "better rounded." As a consequence, we have a boy who is unresponsive in school, feels that he is in a "steel box," and that his only escape is to drop out of school.

The second case is that of a boy whose parents and teachers have been searching to find some punishment that will motivate learning and desirable behavior. Ten-year-old Graham's mother described their plight as follows:

Let me try to list some of the things that are driving his teacher, my husband and me mad. . . .

We have never found a punishment to fit Graham. If placed in a corner, he'd sing. If spanked, he'd howl like we were killing him, yet the minute we left the room the tears would snap off. If sent to his room, he'd simply lie down and go to sleep. Now that he is older, privileges are taken away. They too are taken with no hurt feeling on the surface.

Graham shows a great capacity for school work when he wants to. He refused to finish addition and subtraction drills at school. It was thought he didn't know the answers. When multiplication was introduced, he surprised everyone by knowing the answers. . . . His teacher reports that he is always raising his hand, walking up to her desk, and even trying to instruct the class (fourth grade).

. . . I want desperately to understand Graham. I'm sure his home life at the present time is not as happy as it could be. I'm anxious now because I know it will be more difficult as years progress. . . . Please let me know if and where I can get help. Believe me I'm shouting my plea.

Problems such as the two just presented would doubtless be much rarer than they are if teachers devoted more effort to motivating learning by providing more experiences in school for doing something with what has been learned—using them as raw materials in thinking. Some of the new curricular materials that have been developed in mathematics, physics, chemistry, and other fields should make it easier for teachers to provide such experiences. Zacharias (1964) suggests that the chief activating element in such instruction is what he calls the "teasing value of uncertainty"—the presentation of conjectural issues rather than laying out finished facts. Such experiences, he points out, capitalize on the disciplined use of curiosity, learning to draw suggestive inferences from minimum data, a habit of searching for relationships and analogies, and honest use of evidence.

Observations and recordings of what actually takes place in most classrooms indicate that such experiences are now rather rare. A recent study in Wisconsin (Fowlkes, 1962), for example, showed that over 90 per cent of the questions asked by junior-high-school social-studies teachers called only for the reproduction of what was contained in the textbooks rather than requiring students to think about such information. Those who have designed and experimented with systems for observing classroom behavior usually report that they do not find enough problem-solving behavior in the classroom to merit retaining such a category.

NO CHANCE TO COMMUNICATE WHAT IS LEARNED

There seems to be in every person a strong desire to communicate to others what he discovers and the conclusions he reaches. When children have no opportunity to communicate to their teachers, classmates, or parents what they discover and conclude, they are likely to feel frustrated and the resulting tension is likely to be manifested in lack of motivation. Two major problems seem to be involved here: (1) the rush and haste that prevails in most homes and classrooms and (2) the fact that some children are unable or unready to communicate according to the accepted classroom pattern.

In the rush of the classroom and home, the child who is not verbally facile and aggressive may have little chance to communicate his observations, discoveries, and conclusions. Learning how to slow down and shift gears with certain children is an important skill. Sometimes teachers are in such a hurry to "cover the lesson" and to tell their pupils something that they fail to listen to pupils. It is important to create an open conversational atmosphere at times, rather than a one-way communication system in which the teacher is always telling pupils something. Good questions with adequate pauses for thoughtful answers help but something more than question-and-answer periods are needed. There are times when it pays to encourage free conversation.

A number of kindergarten educators are beginning to learn that the learning potential of the preprimary child in mathematics and science has been largely overlooked and underestimated. This has been because children at this age cannot communicate adequately their thoughts and con-

Figure 1. *Performance on Picture Construction Task.*

clusions, either orally or in writing. These educators are now concluding that the child at this age is merely unready to communicate according to the accepted classroom pattern. As proof they are finding that preschool children can solve rather complex problems when permitted to indicate their conclusions in other than verbal symbols.

This problem, however, is not limited to the kindergarten level. In many fourth-, fifth-, and sixth-grade classrooms, there is in the back of the room a group of four to eight children labeled by the teacher as non-writers or nonreaders. When the author has administered these children batteries of creative-thinking tests, he has found that many of them are capable of some very high-level thinking and have at their command a rather unusual store of information. Some of these children perform at an even higher level when they do not have to report their solutions in verbal form. In some instances, it is clear that they are able to generalize a discovery but they are unable to verbalize it. Following such experi-

TASK 2: FIGURE COMPLETION

By adding lines to the figures on this and the next page, you can sketch some interesting objects or pictures. Again, try to think of some picture or object that no one else will think of. Try to make it tell as complete and as interesting a story as you can by adding to and building up your first idea. Make up a title for each of your drawings and write it at the bottom of each block next to the number of the figure.

Figure 2. *Productions on Figure Completion Task.*

Figure 3. *Productions on Figure Completion Task continued.*

ences, the teacher frequently becomes curious about these children, listens to them and observes them more closely, and is surprised that they know so much and are able to do such high-level thinking.

This matter of communication is especially important in working with children from depressed areas, foreign-language backgrounds, and the like. Figures 1–5 represent the performance of a 14-year-old Mexican migrant boy on the nonverbal or figural tasks of the Minnesota Tests of Creative Thinking. This boy has a measured I.Q. of 80 which would suggest little promise even in his ethnic group. Yet his performance on these tasks reflects a high order of fluency, flexibility, originality, and elaboration in his thinking, even if we disregard his artistic ability. We do not know how this boy would perform on either a written or oral test of verbal creative thinking. We do know that in some ethnic groups children perform disproportionately better on one type of creative-thinking task than on another. For example, children in New Delhi, India, perform disproportionately better on verbal than on nonverbal or figural tasks, while American Negroes in Georgia and children in Western Samoa perform disproportionately better on nonverbal, figural tasks than on verbal ones. We also find that many children who have learning difficulties in school, yet impress parents and teachers as being bright, perform better on the nonverbal, figural tasks than on the verbal ones.

INTEREST IN WHAT IS LEARNED RATHER THAN GRADES

Many children are keenly aware of the shallowness and inadequacies of the grading systems to which they are subjected. They would doubtless be more strongly motivated to learn if their teachers and parents were more interested in what they are actually learning and achieving rather than how well they do on some rather absurd test concerned with superficialities. This predicament can, of course, be remedied somewhat by the

TASK 3: LINES

In ten minutes see how many objects or pictures you can make from the pairs of straight lines below and on the next two pages. The pairs of straight lines should be the main part of whatever you make. With pencil or crayon add lines to the pairs of lines to complete your picture. You can place marks between the lines, on the lines, and outside the lines—wherever you want to in order to make your picture. Try to think of things that no one else will think of. Make as many different pictures or objects as you can and put as many ideas as you can in each one. Make them tell as complete and as interesting a story as you can. Add names or titles in the spaces provided.

Figure 4. *Productions on Lines Task.*

Figure 5. *Production on Lines Task continued.*

development of more adequate ways of assessing the outcomes of learning experience. The addition of tests that require creative problem solving, decision making, judgment, new organizations and syntheses of data, and the like would help.

Even discounting the inadequacies of present-day achievement tests, we find some interesting clues in the discrepancies between the teacher grades of some gifted children and their performance on difficult scholarship tests. Elizabeth Drews (1961) identified three types of gifted high-school students: social leaders, studious achievers, and creative intellectuals. Of these, the studious achievers attained the highest teacher grades and the creative intellectuals, the lowest. The creative intellectuals, however, excelled the other two groups on difficult standardized achievement tests, sampling a wide range of content and educational skills. During the usual preparation period just before examinations, the social leaders would be studying for the first time those things on which they would be graded, though they read very little in general. The studious achievers were also studying those things which would earn them good teacher grades. The creative intellectuals, however, might be reading a book on philosophy or a college textbook, none of which would earn them credit in the teacher's grade book.

Many conversations with parents and teachers of gifted children reveal a startling confusion about actual learning or achievement and the conformity behavior necessary for attaining a passing grade. For example, one third-grade teacher complained that a certain gifted girl was failing the third grade. She remarked that she could not understand why the child was failing because she was very bright, very active, and very alert. She further commented that in an arithmetic bee she outdid the best arithmetic students in the class. She was reading books well above her grade level. She could hold the class spellbound with her stories and could sit any of her classmates down in a spelling bee. This teacher with her emphasis on conformity to behavioral norms could not recognize that this child had perhaps learned more than any of her other pupils.

LEARNING TASKS TOO EASY OR TOO DIFFICULT

If learning tasks are consistently too difficult or too easy, students will be unmotivated and as a result will learn little. Let us examine first the case of a boy whose teachers consistently tried to keep his learning tasks too easy. It was not until Ted entered senior high school that it was discovered that somehow his intelligence quotient and his classroom number had been interchanged on his cumulative record during his elementary-school years. Ted's mother and older brother were aware that Ted was being treated as a mentally retarded child during his junior-high-school years. He was always being downgraded or ignored by teachers. He was discouraged from undertaking difficult projects. His junior-high-school science teacher told Ted's older brother that Ted had no ability for science and should be discouraged in his science interests. A nearby college physics teacher gave Ted some guidance, however, and this teacher remarked on several occasions that he wished that his science majors knew as much science as Ted knew at the time he was in the seventh and eighth grades. It was also at this time that Ted won first place in his region and in the state science fair for his linear accelerator with which he did biological research.

Ted's story reveals a couple of additional points on the motivation of students who are frequently classified incorrectly as slow learners. Ted received a rather low grade on his first physics examination. He could hardly believe his eyes, however, as he felt that he knew thoroughly the subject matter covered by the examination. Somehow he summoned enough boldness to talk with the teacher about his examination, explaining that his answers were compatible with certain recent experiments reported in college textbooks and physics journals. The physics teacher, fortunately an honest man, admitted that he did not know about these recent findings but that he would check up on them and give his answer the next day. This was a fortunate experience for Ted but the situation in chemistry was different. The chemistry teacher insisted that they stick to the "simple, fundamental things," and would not consider some of the more recent knowledge in chemistry, even though what was being taught was erroneous.

During his junior and senior years in high school Ted won eight major national and state awards for creative achievements in science and made high scores on the College Board Examinations, especially in science and mathematics, and was above average in English. Yet he was still regarded in school as a slow learner by everyone except his physics teacher. At the time one of the major awards was announced a newspaper reporter asked to interview Ted and his science teachers. The physics teacher was delighted and warmly congratulated Ted. The chemistry teacher's only remark was, "This is nice but think of how many good students knew nothing of the competition."

This is an example of the absurdities that occur when teachers do not challenge students occasionally to test the limits of their abilities and when they are blinded to what students can really do by the impact of a score on an intelligence test.

NO CHANCE TO USE BEST ABILITIES

Alert teachers have long been aware of the fact that when they change their methods of teaching certain children who had appeared to be slow learners became star learners and some of the former star learners become slow learners. They have also observed that when they change the nature of the test used in assessing achievement, such as from one requiring creative applications and decision making, the star learners and slow learners may change positions in class rankings. With some of the recent developments relative to mental abilities, some of these formerly puzzling phenomena are becoming clarified. There are now many convergent lines of research which make it clear that when we change methods of instruction or the nature of instructional materials children with different kinds of mental abilities become the star learners and nonlearners. Differences in methods of evaluation bring out still further differences in achievement.

A considerable amount of evidence regarding different mental abilities and different methods of teaching has been summarized in Chapter 24. These are very hopeful findings because, as Guilford (1962) points out, we can fortunately exert some control over the way in which information is learned and in this way we can influence unmotivated students to continue learning. In addition, Guilford suggests that if information is to be functioning later, it should be acquired with as many meaningful ramifications as possible, in an organized manner, so that cues may evoke the information at some later time.

NO CHANCE TO LEARN IN PREFERRED WAYS

Not only are there differences in "best abilities" but also there are differences in preferred ways of learning. Since I am frequently misunderstood on this point, I will make a further attempt to clarify the issue. In stressing the need for permitting children to learn in creative ways, I have not intended to imply that methods involving teaching by authority should be abolished. I maintain, however, that the weight of existing evidence indicates that man fundamentally prefers to learn in creative ways—by exploring, questioning, experimenting, manipulating, testing and modifying ideas, and otherwise searching for the truth. This does not mean that it is always good for pupils to learn creatively. Although the needs and abilities underlying learning creatively are universal enough to make this way of learning valuable for all children, creative learning should not be regarded as the exclusive method of education or even the exclusive method for any one child. Many things, though certainly not all, can probably be learned more effectively and economically in creative ways than by authority. Furthermore, many children have especially strong preferences for learning creatively, learn a great deal if permitted to use their creative-thinking abilities, and make little progress when they are taught exclusively by authority.

It is also man's nature to need anchors in reality, to want structure in his environment, and to want authorities upon whom he can depend. Just as individuals differ in the extent to which they prefer to learn creatively, they also differ in the extent to which they require authorities.

The matter of preferred ways of learning is especially crucial in the motivation of children who come from elementary schools where they are accustomed to creative ways of learning to high schools where instruction is almost exclusively by authority. Perhaps it will help if you can understand the panic and desolation of 13-year-old Alice when she transferred from elementary school where she had been permitted to learn both creatively and by authority to a junior high school where she had to learn primarily by authority. In elementary school she achieved a straight "A" record and was regarded as creative, imaginative, and intelligent by her teachers. Alice's mother describes the situation as follows:

She hated junior high almost from the first day. It frightened her. She complained that she felt lost in it, that it was cold, impersonal. . . . The teachers are no doubt well-intentioned but they are too overworked to do anything but get angry, pressure, threaten. These methods have never worked with her. As a result, she lost interest in her work, lost all her self-confidence. . . . She has given up her drawing and writing. She says she can't create or be artistic while she is unhappy about her marks. I am heartsick about this whole situation because I know she is very bright and that she has the scholastic potential to do well in college. It would be a terrible waste of talent and of a good mind for the teachers to give up on her at this point. I believe I have reason to have faith in her. She thinks for herself; that's important. On a recent Iowa achievement test, she averaged at the 95th percentile for the eighth grade (98th percentile in reading and 99th percentile for vocabulary).

Here we have a case which is the opposite of that of Bob cited by the author (Torrance, 1962a) to show how a boy who had been considered a hopeless case throughout elementary school and into the ninth grade can regain confidence in himself and begin learning. Bob's English teacher encouraged him to take his tests on the poems and stories read in class by illustrating them. His sensitive and brilliant insights about what they had read—insights which he could not express in writing or speech—amazed the other members of the class and brought praise. Soon he became interested in learning how to read and became a much happier and socially better-adjusted person. He was again able to excel in art and athletics.

NO REWARDS FOR CERTAIN KINDS OF EXCELLENCE

In the case of Bob, it might be hypothesized that he was not motivated to learn because he was never rewarded for those kinds of achievement in which he excelled and had little hope of achieving excellence in those things that were rewarded. Many kinds of abilities and achievements are needed in our society, and whenever we fail to recognize this we are likely to discourage youngsters who actually have the potential for truly outstanding achievements. Mark may be such a case. At any rate Mark has always been classified as a "slow learner," "low achiever," and as "not interested in school"—a "no good." His art instructor, however, believes that Mark is exceptionally gifted. Mark's mother wrote the author as follows:

The instructor tells us that Mark is an exceptionally talented craftsman, as well as an innovator of original ideas. He has recommended that Mark be sent to art school, and he predicts a promising future for this youngster as an artist or designer. On the other side of the fence, there is his counselor, a man thoroughly sold on verbal and word skills, who can see Mark *only* as a low-achiever. . . . His creative abilities and original ideas are recognized only by his arts and crafts instructor, so we are puzzled about what to do. The counselor tells us that the boy tests "above average" on a standardized I.Q. test; the art instructor believes, from observation, that Mark is far above average in intelligence.

We should be as concerned about motivating children in the areas of social adjustment and character education as we are in mathematics, science, and other curricular areas. The principle of rewarding different kinds of excellence is as appropriate here as elsewhere. There are dangers in rewarding social adjustment to the neglect of moral and intellectual courage. My contention is that we can have for all children both a higher level of adjustment and a higher level of moral strength.

LEARNING LACKING IN PURPOSEFULNESS

Motivation may be low in some children because they are asked to learn things that have little or no purpose for them. Perhaps this is one reason why so many theme-a-week experiments have turned out so poorly. Some students are not motivated to learn for high grades or to avoid failing grades. They need more of a purpose to motivate them to write than "writing to be corrected." There is much more purpose if they are writing to communicate something that they have discovered for themselves. This may be one of the reasons why students who spend most of their time reading and discussing perform as well in theme writings as students who have been subjected to a year of the theme-a-week treatment (Heys, 1962). When he discovers something new, a person seems to be motivated to tell somebody about it. This fact should be useful to teachers in motivating slow learners.

The motivating power of a purpose is illustrated in the case of Tim reported by Dinkmeyer and Dreikurs (1963):

Tim does well in creative work but is apt to be in such a hurry that his writing is messy. For an American history assignment, he wrote a poem about Captain John Smith which was so good that each of the other fifth grade classes wanted a copy. Thrilled by this recognition, Tim made three very neat copies for them.

As Dinkmeyer and Dreikurs comment, writing correctly and neatly took on new significance in that there was real purpose for the readibility of his poem. The teacher focused on his asset, his creative work, and seized the opportunity to let him recognize for himself the value of neat work.

McKeachie (1958) identifies two methods open to the teacher in developing motivation for learning, and both are related to purposefulness. One of these involves making learning instrumental for the motives a person already has. Using this approach we try to show students how our courses will contribute to their goals in life. The second approach involves the development of new motives for learning. The first step is to make learning satisfying, and this always involves beginning with the motives students already have. Thus we have to help unmotivated students see that their learning is really useful to them. By our own enthusiasm for our subject matter we can also make our students aware of the possibilities of joy in learning. McKeachie also suggests that a variety of teaching methods is another way of motivating learning. This is involved in the author's points concerning different kinds of abilities and different ways of learning.

CONCLUSION

Although the motivation of low-achieving pupils is inescapably a complex problem, there are some very obvious things that teachers can do to improve the motivation of these children. They can provide more opportunities for doing something with what is learned; be more concerned about what they are learning; adapt the difficulty of the task to the ability and experience level of the learner; teach in ways that give opportunities for using a variety of mental abilities in acquiring information; recognize and reward a variety of kinds of excellence, including social adjustment and character; and give greater purposefulness to what students are expected to learn.

Although these things can be done within the framework of a stimulus-response psychology, I believe that they will be more successful in motivating children—arousing, sustaining, and directing their behavior—if carried out within the framework of a responsive environment. What I have in mind calls for the most alert and sensitive kind of direction and stimulation (Ferebee, 1950). It means building an atmosphere of gracious and receptive listening; relieving the fears of the timid and the overtaught or overstimulated; fending off negative criticism and making the learner aware of what is good; stirring the sluggish and deepening the shallow; making sure that every sincere effort to learn brings enough satisfaction to keep the learner willing to try again; and keeping alive the zest and excitement of learning.

34 *Crises in Normal Personality Development*

Gordon W. Allport

There is one trick every teacher knows. When trapped in a state of ignorance, throw the question back to the class. Without suspecting the teacher's predicament, bright students will often rescue you.

This is the strategy I employed to learn something about "crises in normal personality development." I passed along the assignment to my class of 100 captive undergraduates, and they obligingly provided me, through their own autobiographical writing, with insights that I shall share with you. (Parenthetically, let me say that in my opinion no teacher or counselor has the right to require intimate autobiographical documents from students. Yet when given a completely free choice, the large majority will choose to write in the autobiographical vein. For the few who would find the experience too threatening, it should not be prescribed.)

I asked the hundred students, mostly sophomores and juniors, four questions, and found the results here indicated:

The Influence of Teachers

1. Approximately how many different teachers at school and
college have you had up to the present stage of your
education?

4632

*Percentage reported
as having various
degrees of influence*

2. How many had a very strong or powerful influence on your
development (intellectual or personal)?

8.50

3. How many others would you say had a reasonably strong,
well-remembered influence?

14.80

4. How many do you remember only vaguely, or who seem
to have had no substantial influence on your development?

76.70

100.00

We are immediately struck by the fact that more than three-quarters of the teachers are remembered only vaguely, and are credited with no appreciable influence, whether intellectual or personal. As teachers we all know the shock of discovering how little impact we have had. A former student of mine brightened my day by remarking, "Years ago I took a course with you, but all I can remember about it is that the textbook had a blue cover." He grinned pleasantly while I shuddered inwardly.

Only about 8 per cent of teachers are reported as having a very strong influence, and about 15 per cent are credited with a less strong but well-remembered influence.

Another way of stating this finding is to say that the average teacher (assuming all teachers are equally effective) "gets through" to less than a quarter of the class, and exerts a really strong influence on not more than one student in ten.

Asked to tell when and in what way they were influenced the students give us three facts of special interest.

1. About half of all their examples deal with experiences of intellectual awakening. For example,

She encouraged me to read poetry and drama beyond the class assignment.

In chemistry the instructor asked us why bubbles appeared overnight in a water glass. When we said we had never wondered about that, he told us that everyone must question even the most common and seemingly trivial things.

And about half of the examples deal with personal development:

She made me see that others did not judge me as harshly as I was judging myself.

He had so much warmth and humanity that I wanted to be like him.

She seemed tough and disagreeable, but was so kind and helpful to me that I realized I must think twice before passing judgment on anyone.

2. A second insight based on the large array of illustrative incidents reveals the remarkably casual nature of the influence. In hardly any case could the teacher or counselor have known that what he was saying at a given moment would make a lasting impression on the growing mind and character of the student. Elsewhere I have argued that in teaching values and attitudes it is not the deliberately adopted curriculum that is effective. It is rather the *obiter dicta*, the parenthetical remark, the "little true things," and above all the example of the teacher that count (Allport, 1961). And what holds for teachers no doubt holds for the counselor too.

3. Finally, and most relevant to our topic, is the finding that in elementary school there are few remembered influences of special strength.

Apparently development is gradual at this time, and the teacher does not often bring a sudden and traumatic experience of "dawn" to the pupil. Only 12 per cent report any strong or even appreciable teacher-influence in elementary school. Fully 88 per cent of the reports date the occurrences in high school (58 per cent) or in college (30 per cent, with the college years still incomplete).

And so it is in middle and late adolescence where the role of the teacher is most vivid to the student. It is in this period, according to Erikson (1950), that the identity crisis is in the ascendance. The young person seems to be moving from past childhood into present adulthood in a jerky manner. Development is not continuous like a hill; rather it is episodic like a flight of stairs. It is this episodic or crisis character of development that brings both challenge and opportunity to the guidance officer.

DEFINING "CRISIS"

What precisely is a "crisis"? It is a situation of emotional and mental stress requiring significant alterations of outlook within a short period of time. These alterations of outlook frequently involve changes in the structure of personality. The resulting changes may be progressive in the life or they may be regressive. By definition a person in crisis cannot stand still; that is, he cannot redact his present traumatic experience into familiar and routine categories, or employ simple habitual modes of adjustment. He must either separate himself further from childhood and move toward adulthood; or else move backward to earlier levels of adjustment which may mean becoming disorganized, dropping out of school, escaping from the field, developing hostilities and defenses, and in general becoming a thorn in the flesh of the teacher, the parent, the counselor, the dean, and occasionally the police.

Sometimes following a crisis the adolescent will become stabilized anew after four or five weeks of severe disorganization; but in many cases the trauma retards development for a year or more, and may even leave a lifelong scar.

THE PHENOMENOLOGY OF CRISIS

Turning now to my data, drawn from college undergraduates, we ask first about the phenomenology of crisis. What does it "feel" like to the student? Common is a sense of numbness and apathy. Upon entering college the youth finds fewer strict role prescriptions than at home. He is no longer tied to his domestic filial role, to the highly structured routine of high school, to his siblings, to his church connections, to his teenage subcultures. He has left his possessions behind: his stamp collection, his television, his girlfriends, his boy friends. All his familiar roles are in suspension. As one student writes,

The complete freedom of college is itself a crisis. For the first time I live in close contact with people who are not members of my family. They don't even resemble people I have known before. They have different opinions, different origins, and different emotions. I feel numbed by it all.

Interestingly enough, this sense of hollowness does not necessarily have its maximum effect during the freshman year. The excitement of new scenes, and especially frequent correspondence with, and visits back to, the hometown, keep the silver cord intact. The student feels that he should prove to his parents, teachers, and friends that he can master the college environment and thus please them and win their approval as he has done in the past. The impending crisis has not yet overwhelmed him (or her—for what I am saying is as true for college girls as for boys).

It is the sophomore year that seems (from my data) to be the year of crisis *par excellence*. Suddenly it becomes no longer tolerable to live one's life for the edification of people "back home." The time has come for the child of the past to be separated once and for all from the adult of the present. Here are typical phenomenological statements of this stage of the crisis:

I feel I have been dragged into something against my will.

I feel like a rat in a maze.

I want to be a law unto myself, but cannot.

It seems suddenly that the decisions I make must be valid for the rest of my life.

To shake off parental norms and values seems to me the most important thing I must do.

The life of the past and the life of the future seem suddenly to be at cross purposes. There is often an intolerable feeling of suspended animation. Recrystallization is not yet possible. The youth is waiting still to make a choice of careers, a suitable marriage, and to find an integrative philosophy of life which his diverse college courses are too discordant to supply.

It is small wonder that apathy and a paralysis of will often occur. But apathy is only a mask for anxiety. The whole framework of life is disturbed. Whereas the majority of students contrive gradually to build a new framework in spite of, or perhaps because of, the goads of anxiety, yet a large minority cannot cope with the situation unaided.

From my data I would estimate that three-quarters are able to take the progressive road in creating their new frame of existence. About one-quarter cannot immediately do so. Proof of this point is that the dropout rate during undergraduate years is surprisingly high—over 20 per cent at Harvard, about three-quarters of the cases representing voluntary withdrawals (Blaine and McArthur, 1962).

The dropouts present a special problem of guidance. Blaine and McArthur (1962) write:

The drop-outs as a group ultimately do quite well if properly handled. We attempt to establish a relationship, however brief or tenuous, with these students, not so much to prevent their leaving school, but rather in the hope of giving them some insight into the determinants of their difficulties so that their dropping out can be ultimately converted into a meaningful constructive experience instead of mere failure.

After a year or two of constructive work elsewhere the majority of voluntary dropouts return to college and graduate. But they could not have met their crisis by remaining in the environment that was the context of their conflict.

The regressive road is surprisingly common. Among eventual dropouts, but also among other students, we find such self-destroying behavior as quitting classes, a compulsion to do trivial things, playing bridge until 4 A.M., drinking bouts, feelings of unreality, fugues, and general debauchery. The candid documents received startle me a bit by the extent of plain juvenile delinquency among my innocent-appearing students.

One student, finding himself unable to handle his conflicts over choice of career and over friction with his roommate, indulged in plagiarism on a term paper in such a way that he would be caught and forcibly separated from college. In this case a wise instructor, catching him in the transgression, turned the occasion into constructive counseling, forgave the deed, and put the lad onto the progressive rather than regressive road.

Here I venture a theoretical digression. The problem, as I see it, is one of interiorizing motivation. To put it in a student's words,

I am fed up with having everybody else cheer me on. I want to work to please myself rather than others, but I don't know how to do it.

This plaintive statement points to a serious dilemma in our educational process. In school the child is rewarded and punished by good grades and bad grades. Even in college A's and B's are pats on the back, D's and E's are punishments. To gain love the student must read books and toe the academic line. Finally he obtains his degree (which is a symbol of academic love) and is freed from this external form of motivation. What then happens? Well, we know that a shockingly high percentage of college graduates rarely or never read another book after receiving their bachelor's degree. Why should they? Their love now comes from their employer, their wife, their children, not from the approval of parents and teachers. For them intellectual curiosity never became a motive in its own right. External rewards are appropriate props in early childhood. But we educators, being limited by current inadequate theories of learning, do not know how to help the student free himself from the props of reward and develop a functionally autonomous zeal for learning. With our slavish dependence on "reinforcement theory" I think it surprising that we arouse as much internal motivation as we do. In any event we cannot be proud of the many educational cripples who, lacking the routine incentive of college, sink into intellectual apathy.

CRISIS AREAS

The counselor, of course, cannot wait for better theories of learning. He is confronted here and now with crises in the concrete. Four areas of conflict, judging from my data, are especially common.

Intellectual Crises

First there are students whose problem is one of intellectual malplacement. Among my cases a large number report that in primary and secondary school they were too bright for their class. The penalty is one of boredom lasting into college work which they still do not find challenging enough for their abilities. At the same time, double promotions in elementary and high school are not a solution. To be placed with older children often creates social difficulties far more serious than boredom. In fact the evil consequences reported from double promotion are so numerous that we should challenge this particular solution of the bright child's dilemma.

The opposite type of intellectual crises is also common. It is the deep disturbance that often results in college from intensified competition. It is statistically impossible for most students to maintain the same relative superiority in college that they enjoyed in high school. Although this fact does not trouble the majority, it is a critical experience for those who depend on scholarship aid or who frame their self-image almost entirely in terms of scholarly preeminence. They are suffering a severe narcissistic wound.

Specific Inferiorities

A second area of crisis is the old familiar "inferiority complex." Besides the sense of intellectual inferiority just described, we encounter deep disturbance due to physical handicaps or to plain physical appearance, with resulting shyness, loneliness, and misery. To be poor at athletics creates a crisis for males, probably more acute in high school than in college. To be a member of a minority group likewise creates an inevitable crisis somewhere along the line. Here again I suspect the major adjustments and defenses are prepared before the college age. Occasionally the inferiority concerns guilt due to moral lapses. One student is still haunted by her dishonesty which enabled her to pass a certain course three years ago. She has felt miserable ever since about this critical experience, and badly needs a means of expiation.

In this connection we may speak of religious crises. Although they are uncommon in my sample, Havens (1963) estimates that at any given time 12 per cent of college students have a critical concern, and sometimes acute crises, due to their religious conflicts. I suspect the concern is even more widespread, but since it pertains to one's whole ground of being it is seldom configurated as a specific crisis at a given moment of time.

Another area, seldom mentioned but surely important, is the ideological crisis of modern society as a whole. Youth is inevitably worried, as are adults, by our uncertain future. Elsewhere I (Gillespie and Allport, 1955) have discussed the withdrawal of American youth from the social and political context of their lives. Both the earlier and present data show an almost exclusive concern among American youth with their own lives. Compared with autobiographies of youth in other cultures, the American documents are far more self-centered, more privatistic. They are too baffled to articulate their distress, and so take refuge in their private concerns.

Sex Conflicts

Needless to say our candid discussions of crises frequently, in fact usually, report acute sex conflicts. Extremely common are breakups in boy-girl relationships which are usually taken as a disaster only slightly less fatal than the end of the world. Such breakups are so recently experienced that college students do not realize that they will, in spite of their present feelings, eventually make a good recovery.

We should face the fact that at least in the early years of college life crises in the sexual sphere are for the most part frankly genital in their reference. The biological drive is so powerful that the youth is concerned with it almost by itself. Its integration into mature love, into marriage, into career plans, into an embracing philosophy of life, exceeds his present capacity. He is likely to think that genitality by itself is maturity. Sexual gratification is frankly the aim, often with devastating consequences. At this stage of development the students have much to say about sex, and little to say about mature love.

Family Conflicts

I have left until last the most pervasive area of conflict and crisis. I am referring of course to the situation that exists between every adolescent and his parents. It is not enough to say that adolescent rebellion against the parents is the rule. Of course it is, but my documents show that the whole history of the relationships from the time of earliest memories is important. Almost any irregularity in normal family life is felt bitterly, and may trouble a student even into adulthood. A mother who is neglectful or self-centered, or perhaps overpossessive and neurotic, leaves traumatic traces in the child's life. A father who is ineffectual and weak, or cruel, or absent (if only for wartime service), leaves the child with a lasting feeling of protest. Broken homes are, of course, a major dislocation for the child. The documents have convinced me that every child needs two parents. (A student points out to me that God had reached the same conclusion at an earlier date.)

One document of unusual maturity notes that many college students seem to need their parents as scapegoats. They find it comfortable to blame parents for their own shortcomings. Perceiving that their parents are not all-powerful, all-wise, and all-perfect, they can say, "Well, no wonder I am having a hard time growing up; they didn't raise me right." Thus the adolescent can soak himself in self-pity, not yet mature enough to relate his restricted image of his parents to the totality of human nature; not yet ready to appreciate the fact that his parents, considering human limitations, may have done a good job. Even if the job was not especially good, the adolescent seems not yet able to appreciate the parents' good intentions as an important value in its own right. From talking with many parents I hazard the hypothesis that normally it is not until the age of 23 that a child encounters his parents on a mature, adult-to-adult basis.

A THEORETICAL OBSERVATION

This brief account of crises emanating from the parent-child relationship leads me to a final point. My students were required to discuss their crises from the point of view of personality theory. They were free to employ any of the theories they were studying in my course. Most of them took Freud. (I may add that the reason was not because Freud was their instructor's favorite author.)

Now my observation is this: their Freudian interpretations seemed to fit well if and when the family situation in early life was disturbed. When the father was absent or ineffectual, when the mother was notably aggressive, when there was deliberate sex stimulation within the family—in such cases it seems that the Oedipal formula is a good fit, together with all its theoretical accouterments of identification, superego conflict, defense mechanisms, castration threats, and all the rest.

When, on the other hand, the family life is reasonably normal and secure, a Freudian conceptualization seems forced and artificial. If we say, by way of rough estimate, that 60 per cent of the students try a Freudian conceptualization of their own cases, about 10 per cent turn out to be wholly convincing and theoretically appropriate. The remaining 50 per cent appear to be somehow contrived and badly strained.

I am wondering whether the same ratio might be applicable to cases that come to counselors. If a counselor or a therapist approaches every client or patient with the preconceived belief that his life must fit a Freudian frame of conceptualization, he may win in a minority of the cases, but lose in the majority.

Even where a Freudian approach is clearly justified, exclusive adherence to it may distract the counselor from many significant developments within the life—for example, from the present functional significance of religious and esthetic values, from the competence and interests that extend beyond the neurotic core, from the client's conscious plans for the future, and from his "will to meaning," and existential concern with life as a whole.

Every person concerned with guidance, or for that matter with teaching, needs as background some general theory of the nature of human personality (Allport, 1962). Our tendency, I fear, is to draw our theories from the realm of illness and deviance. It is somehow tempting to apply psychiatric rubrics to all personalities, for psychiatric rubrics are vivid, incisive, dramatic, and easy. Our conceptual banners bear such sloganized concepts as Oedipal complex, character disorder, identity diffusion, schizoid, acting out, and maybe an array of dimensions drawn from the Minnesota Multiphasic Personality Inventory. All such concepts, of course, have their proper place. But personality theory for guidance and teaching needs also to be woven of less lurid fabrics.

Youth, whatever neurotic threads may lie in his nature, is busy with his realistic perceptions, with his gradual learning and quiet coping, with the slow extension of selfhood, with noncritical failures and successes, with developing a generic conscience and a personal style of life. Even in the throes of crisis he seeks in undramatic ways to consolidate his gains and continue on the path of becoming. A theory of personality adequate to undergird the art of guidance will keep such nondramatic facts in mind. Crises in normal personality development are important, but so too is the slow growth of each youth's unique style of life.

35 Comparison of Adolescent and Adult Behavioral Norm Properties

Robert D. Strom

In the past few years sociologists, psychologists, philosophers, and educators have expressed concern over the problem termed by Coleman (1961c) as, "the emergence of an adolescent subculture in an industrial society." Coleman refers to the changes in American culture which have served to bring about the separation of teenagers from the adult society, thereby encouraging youngsters to seek more and more peer approval for their behavior. Consequently, teenagers within their subculture have developed norms of behavior which are believed to be quite divergent from those held by adult society.

The purpose of this study was to investigate the norms of behavior for the adolescent subculture. The author sought to determine: (*a*) whether adolescents differ significantly on behavioral norm properties from adults, and (*b*) whether certain types of adolescents are more ready to accept adult norms than others.

METHOD

Subjects

As a consequence of the complex adult society, no individual or group can represent all of its facets, but it is generally accepted by adults that the teacher does at least a competent job of communicating the important values and standards of adults to adolescents. Therefore, assuming that the behavioral norms of teachers are somewhat representative of the standards of adult society, it appears logical to compare the norms of behavior for adolescents with those

The present research was conducted under the direction of A. Zander, Director of social research at the University of Michigan, and H. Bretsch, Assistant Dean of the graduate school at the University of Michigan.

The author gratefully acknowledges the help and encouragement of G. W. Allport of Harvard University.

Reprinted by permission of *Journal of Educational Psychology*, 54, No. 6, 1963, 322–330.

of their teachers in order to determine the extent this group of adults and adolescents agree. The adolescent sample of 303 seniors from Edsel Ford High School in Dearborn, Michigan, was to be compared in its norms of behavior with 30 teachers who represented adult society.

Subpopulations

Since some writers (Bestor, 1955; Rickover, 1960) insist that certain types of adolescents are more like adults than others in their norms of behavior, it was deemed desirable to consider these types within the sample for separate comparison to adults. Consideration was given to the assertion that students who are recognized by classmates as being leaders and those whose personalities are ascendant rather than permissive would correspond more closely to adults in their behavioral norms than nonleaders or submissive adolescents. Leadership and ascendance-submission became the variables in selecting the adolescent subpopulations. It was assumed that the ascendant person may be a leader or a nonleader; similarly, a submissive person may be a leader or a nonleader. Therefore, each individual was to be assigned to one of four subpopulations, namely: (a) leader ascendant, (b) nonleader ascendant, (c) leader submissive, or (d) nonleader submissive.

Desirability of Properties

The mere knowledge about agreement or disagreement is superficial if we cannot know in what ways and under what conditions adults and adolescents agree or disagree. In the absence of some scheme for representing the structure of a norm, much of its potential as a tool for analysis of groups fails to be realized. However, using a statistical tool called a "return potential curve" (Jackson, 1960), the essential properties incorporated in the idea of "norm" may be derived. The return curve enables the investigator not only to determine the extent to which teachers and adolescents differ in their norms of behavior, but also: (a) the limits of behavior that each group report they will approve or tolerate; (b) the intensity of approval or disapproval they state is evoked by certain types of behavior; (c) the proportion of the possible range of behavior that would be, in their own self-report, approved; (d) the point of ideal behavior as perceived by each group; and (e) the relative degree of crystallization for the norms of behavior of teachers and students. Hence the investigation concerned comparison of norm properties rather than merely norms themselves.

Behavioral Areas

Subjects in the study were questioned on six areas of behavior. Norms examined were of two basic types, namely, those which concern student behaviors that teachers might probably have direct influence on and those behaviors over which teacher influence is probably less direct. The more direct behaviors were (a) contradiction of teachers, (b) homework time, and (c) class-discussion participation. The less direct areas of influence considered were (a) dating, (b) clique deviance, and (c) physical-education participation.

A scale of approval-disapproval feelings, ranging from numeral notation of 4 for strongly approving to —4 for strongly disapproving through a midpoint of indifference at 0, was provided the respondents for their judgment on the eight frequencies of the behavioral dimension for each question. A sample question from the investigation follows.

Although there are no societal rules governing the frequency of dating, students have ideas concerning how often they should date while in school. For example, students who date only once a year may find their dating behavior disapproved by some classmates. On the other hand, students who date every evening may also be considered for disapproval by some classmates. If a student dates in the frequencies mentioned below, give your strength of approval or disapproval with the scale number of your choice in the column to the right.

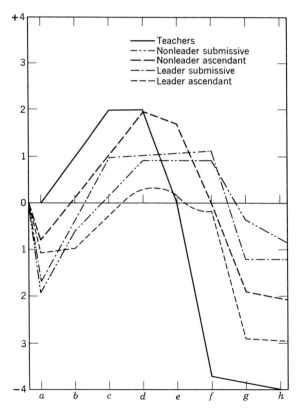

Figure 1. *Dating norm curve for all subpopulations and teachers.* (a, *3 times a year;* b, *once a month;* c, *twice a month;* d, *once a week;* e, *twice a week;* f, *3 times a week;* g, *5 times a week;* h, *daily.*)

(a) Three times a year   —
(b) Once a month   —
(c) Twice a month   —
(d) Once a week   —
(e) Twice a week   —
(f) Three times a week   —
(g) Five times a week   ---
(h) Daily   —

Major Instrument

The properties of a norm are derived from a return potential curve as shown in each of Figures 1–6. The horizontal axis is the dimension of behavior along which the frequency of action is cited while a dimension of evaluation is represented by the vertical axis. For any particular behavior di-

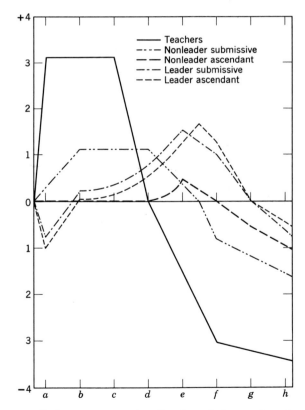

Figure 2. *Contradiction norm curve for all subpopulations and teachers.* (a, *Once a semester;* b, *once a month;* c, *twice a month;* d, *3 times a month;* e, *once a week;* f, *twice a week;* g, *3 times a week;* h, *4 times a week.*)

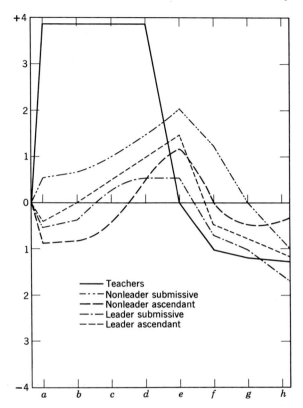

Figure 3. *Clique norm curve for all subpopulations and teachers.* (a, *Once a year;* b, *twice a year;* c, *3 times a year;* d, *4 times a year;* e, *once a month;* f, *twice a month;* g, *once a week;* h, *twice a week.*)

mension, the amount of approval or disapproval felt by members of a group toward a particular act may in principle fall anywhere along the evaluation dimension from strongly approving to strongly disapproving through some middle point of indifference. It is possible then in any concrete situation to plot a curve describing the feelings of the group members. Approved behavior would be revealed by positive potential return above the point of indifference whereas negative return characterizes behavioral frequencies which are disapproved.

Determination of Subpopulation

The seniors in their twelve separate homerooms were administered a leadership index. The names of all members of the particular homeroom were listed and after each name appeared a series of numerals from 1 to 5. Students were directed to circle the numeral after each student's name which would indicate to what extent the rater considered the ratee to be a leader. The numeral 5 indicated that the rater believed the ratee to be outstanding in leadership whereas a rating of 1 indicated that the ratee was not a leader. After the subjects had been rated by their peers, the subjects' leadership indices were computed by multiplying the circled leadership numerals by the

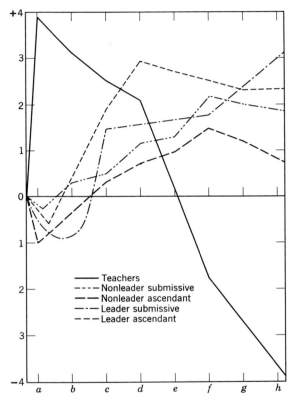

Figure 4. *Physical-education participation norm curve for all subpopulations ana teachers.* (a, *Once a semester;* b, *once a month;* c, *twice a month;* d, *3 times a month;* e, *once a week;* f, *twice a week;* g, *3 times a week;* h, *4 times a week.*)

frequencies in which each number occurred and dividing this product by the number of students who did the rating.

The Allports' (1928) *Ascendance Reaction Study* was used to assess the relative ascendance or submission in the personality of the adolescent respondents. A fairly large number of situations is verbally presented in the reaction study in which the respondent selects one of a group of standardized responses which most nearly characterizes his usual behavior in that situation. Each response choice is considered as having a diagnostic value for indicating ascendance (plus scores) or submission (minus scores). The final ascendance-submission score is the algebraic sum of scores for separate items.

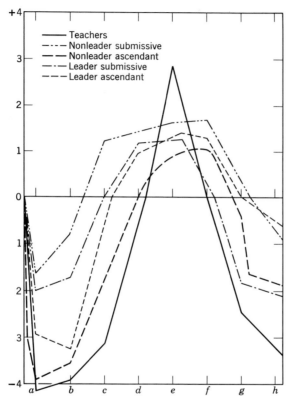

Figure 5. *Homework norm curve for all subpopulations and teachers.* (a, *1 hour a week;* b, *2 hours a week;* c, *3 hours a week;* d, *6 hours a week;* e, *12 hours a week;* f, *18 hours a week;* g, *24 hours a week;* h, *30 hours a week.*)

From a frequency distribution the median score in the leadership index was chosen as the separation for leaders and nonleaders and the ascendance-submission scores exceeding 0 in a plus direction categorized the ascendant persons. Individuals were then placed into one of the four subgroups depending on their scores, as shown in Table 1.

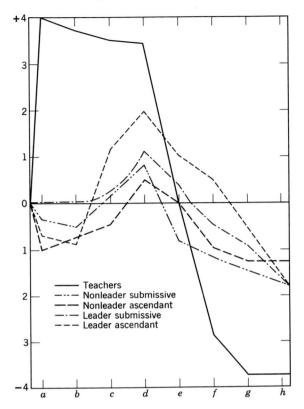

Figure 6. *Class-discussion norm curves for all subpopulations and teachers.* (a, *Once a week;* b, *twice a week;* c, *once an hour;* d, *twice an hour;* e, *3 times an hour;* f, *5 times an hour;* g, *7 times an hour;* h, *10 times an hour.*)

RESULTS

Before comparing the degree that various properties were assigned to the norms, it is useful to examine Figures 1–6, which contain the return

Table 1   *Number of Subjects in Each Subpopulation*

Group	Men	Women
Ascendant leaders	48	51
Ascendant nonleaders	28	22
Submissive leaders	39	14
Submissive nonleaders	56	45
Total	171	132

potential curves for all subpopulations on all questions. Note that the teachers render much stronger approval than students at the lower end of the frequency range and stronger disapproval at the greater frequency end of the behavior dimension in all norms except that in Figure 5 (homework). In Figure 1 (dating) and Figure 5 (homework), teachers and students seem to agree somewhat, but in Figure 4 (athletics), complete disagreement is evident. Throughout Figures 1–6, it is seen that teachers evidence much stronger feelings of approval-disapproval than do their students.

Subsequent to surveying differences in return potential curve structures between teachers and students, the comparative properties were computed for teacher and student subpopulations by summation of feeling on all questions, yielding a composite score which served as an index for the tests of significance. Index scores were used instead of one norm at a time as we assumed the aggregate score, representing a more general attitude about all norms among both students and teachers, was more relevant to our major interest than a detailed study of each separate norm.

"Range of tolerability," which is the part of a behavior dimension members of a group approve, was measured by taking the mean number of positive positions over the behavior dimension for all six norms as the tolerable score for each individual. Tolerable scores were then divided into categories for chi-square comparison. Table 2 shows that the range of tolerability for students does not differ significantly at the .05 level from that of the teachers. Also, there is no significant difference between the boys and girls in their ranges of tolerability.

The "intensity" of individual norms was measured by a summation of curve ordinates at each position on the behavioral dimension. Mean intensity of each question was computed for each group and then the mean of the six norms, as shown in Table 3, was used for comparison

Table 2 *Range of Tolerable Behavior for All Norms— Teachers versus Students*

Sample	Tolerable Score 1–3	Tolerable Score 4–5	Tolerable Score 6+	χ^{3*} Teachers versus Students
Teachers	5	22	3	—
All students	135	135	33	6.6663
Boys	73	75	23	6.6636
Girls	62	60	10	6.6691

* All comparisons are nonsignificant.

Table 3   *Mean Intensity for All Norms—Teachers versus Students*

Sample	M Intensity	t of Difference for Teachers versus Students
Teachers	18.1	—
All students	8.0	2.83*
Boys	8.0	3.02*
Girls	7.9	2.63*

* $p < .01$.

using the *t* test procedure. It is evident in Table 3 that there is a significant difference at the .01 level between the strength of feelings held by teachers and students on the intensity of the norms. The mean intensity of boys was slightly higher than that of girls but not significantly so.

Table 4 shows a comparison of "approval-disapproval ratios" between teachers and students. This property, which indicates the extent behavior is sanctioned by a group, is computed by dividing the mean intensity for positive return by the mean negative potential over the entire behavior dimension. Mean ratios for each question were computed for each group and then the mean of the six norms served as an index for comparison by *t* test. No difference at the .05 level was found. The boys seemed to sanction the behaviors less on the whole than did the girls but the difference was not statistically significant.

That behavior which represents the ideal in the eyes of group members is called the "point of maximum return." Computation of the mean maximal point for each student was determined after which individuals were placed in one of three groups for chi-square comparison. Table 5 indicates that both the total class and the boys were significantly different

Table 4   *Approval-Disapproval Ratio for All Norms— Teachers versus Students*

Sample	M Ratio	t of Difference for Teachers versus Students*
Teachers	.9	—
All students	1.3	1.61
Boys	1.2	1.46
Girls	1.5	1.76

* All comparisons are nonsignificant.

Table 5 *Maximum Return for All Norms—Teachers versus Students*

Sample	Maximum Points A–B	Maximum Points C–D	Maximum Points E+	χ^2 Teachers versus Students
Teachers	15	10	5	—
All students	53	151	99	8.3600*
Boys	29	86	56	9.2825*
Girls	24	65	43	7.4375

* $p < .05$.

in point of maximum return from the teachers. However, the girls were not significantly different from the teachers. Thus, in the property of maximum return, girls appear to conform more to the norms of teachers than do boys.

The crystallization or, conversely, ambiguity of a norm, drawn from the variance of the return potential curve, indicates to what extent members of a group have really established a norm or made up their minds. The mean variance of each group was computed for each question after which the mean of the means was determined for comparison by the F test method. In the cases of boys, girls, and the total class, Table 6 shows significance at the .01 level for the degree of crystallization between student norms and those of teachers.

At this juncture teachers were compared to the subpopulations, and to the subgroups (separate sexes of subpopulations). Moreover, the subgroups were compared with each other. The measures of comparison were the same as have been illustrated in Tables 2–6. Statistical differences for the properties of tolerable range and maximal point were found using the chi-square method; intensity and approval-disapproval ratio differences

Table 6 *Degree of Crystallization for All Norms—Teacher versus Students*

Sample	M Variance	F of Difference for Teachers versus Students
Teachers	5.0	—
All students	13.3	2.66*
Boys	14.1	2.82*
Girls	12.5	2.51*

* $p < .01$.

determined by the *t* test; and the degree of crystallization property compared by the *F* test.

The major findings of this study show that high-school seniors do differ significantly on certain properties in the norms of behavior from their teachers. The students as a group deviate from teacher behavioral norms on the properties of intensity, maximum return, and degree of crystallization. Statistical dissonance from teachers on the intensity property indicates that students do not feel as strongly about the behaviors studied as teachers do and therefore would not be as concerned about how their peers acted on these behaviors as would the teachers. The discrepancy in maximum return shows students and teachers differ in their perceptions of just what behavior is to be considered as ideal, indicating a behavioral goal conflict. Moreover, students do not have norms of behavior which are as crystallized or developed as norms of teachers. Thus on those behaviors studied the adolescents had not made up their minds to the extent that teachers had concerning what was to be approved or disapproved.

On the other hand, the adolescents in their norm properties of tolerable range and approval-disapproval ratio were not statistically different from their teachers. These results seem to indicate that the restrictions as to what behavior will be allowed or tolerated is nearly the same for adolescents as teachers. In addition, the proportion of possible range of behavior that would be approved or disapproved by the adolescents is in accord with the ratio accepted by the teachers.

The answer as to why certain discrepancies exist between the properties of teacher and student norms is not to be found by asserting that too few adolescents are ascendant in personality. Approximately half of the student sample was ascendant. Comparing these ascendant adolescents versus their submissive peers (ignoring sex and leadership) with teachers, it was found that ascendance does not seem to be an important determinant on most norm properties. Just as we cannot attribute the cause of statistical differences between adult-adolescent norms to the variable of ascendance, we cannot attach the cause to leadership. Leaders versus nonleaders (ignoring sex and ascendance scores) were compared with teachers and the findings indicate that leadership was not an important factor in determining the extent to which adolescents will differ from teachers. Similarly, girls versus boys (ignoring leadership and ascendance) were compared with the result that sex was declared unimportant as a determinant.

The possibility that certain of the subgroups would be more like teachers than other subgroups led the investigator to determine which of the eight subgroups (including boys and girls) would be most like and unlike teachers. The findings show that no one particular subgroup was in consistent agreement with teachers nor was any particular subgroup more unlike teachers than the others.

Finding the extent to which subgroups differed from one another was important in determining whether one or more of the subgroups deviated from their peers. With few exceptions, the uniformity of subgroup norms would lead one to accept as reasonable the assertion that students are mostly the same in their behavioral norm properties.

Of the three types of behavior in which teacher influence was more likely to occur, there appears to be no closer proximity to adult norms than those behaviors in which teacher influence is less likely. It would seem that direct teacher influence is of little importance in determining the behavioral norms for this group of senior students.

Some further interesting information emerging as concomitant outcomes of this study concerns the relative distribution of ascendance and submission within the adolescent subculture as well as the relationship between ascendance and leadership. This study shows that if a person is a leader the likelihood is twice as great that he will be ascendant than that he will not be. Conversely, if he is a nonleader, it seems twice as likely that he will be submissive as ascendant. The correlation between ascendance-submission scores and leadership was .28 ($p < .005$) for senior boys and .37 ($p < .005$) for senior girls.

DISCUSSION

This study demonstrates the success of a method by which the social climate of youth may be known. Adult concern with adolescent conformity may be shown to be valid or inappropriate depending on the direction of compliance and the types of behavior it may encompass. Nevertheless, to understand the ways in which peer pressures operate, to ascertain the areas of behavior in which these pressures are most influential, and to seek ways by which such forces might be redirected for personal growth will be helpful in effecting an improvement of the educative process.

In terms of educational setting, we have always known what teachers expect of students; however, our knowledge is both recent and sparse concerning the nature and influence of student expectations upon fellow pupils. Yet educators readily admit that both the amount and kind of learning are influenced by student climate. Indeed, to avoid rejection teenagers find it necessary to be cognizant of and in accord with peer norms regarding such academic behavior as class participation and allocation of homework time. No less expedient should it be for teachers to become acquainted with student norms lest they fail to offer an acceptable province for learning.

Evaluating the teaching of attitudes has been a task of anxious dimension for adults since time immemorial. It is now possible to measure whether desired outcomes of learning in human relations and conduct are being realized. This would encompass a host of concerns from patriotism to racial tolerance. Using dating as an area of personal relations, this effort illustrates how one can determine the kinds and limits of behavior youngsters will tolerate, the behavior perceived by a group as ideal, the intensity of approval-disapproval evoked by certain practices, and the degree to which ideas have been accepted.

Helping youngsters maintain satisfactory relations with their fellows is a difficult but necessary task of the educator. For the rejected child, something more than identification as an isolate is needed to produce adjustment. Comparing the deviant's norms of behavior with his peer group will reveal the conditions under which exclusion occurs and enable the counselor to provide direction for the student. To best foster adjustment and to increase our knowledge of personality development we need to examine behavioral norms for children of all ages. This would involve consideration of subgroups such as the creative and gifted. In the final analysis, a teacher's effectiveness is adversely affected if his understanding of student norms is not in juxtaposition to reality. It follows that to better know the student is to be a better teacher.

SUMMARY

Responses of 303 high-school seniors and their 30 teachers to a questionnaire concerning six behavioral areas served as data to determine whether adolescents and adults differ significantly in behavioral norms and whether certain types of adolescents are more ready to accept adult norms than others. Subsequent to selection of adolescent subpopulations (based on leadership and ascendance-submission), a return potential curve was employed to plot distribution of group feeling and serve as computational base for five behavioral properties. The chi square, t test, and F test revealed some significant differences between teacher and student norms but the discrepancies could not be attributed to the subpopulation variables.

36 *How Does It Feel to Fail?*

Lois French

Perhaps the topic appears facetious since each of us having failed at some time or another knows that it feels awful! The degree to which failure was disappointing depended on how much we cared, how many persons were present, who was disappointed, and the effect of our failure on others. Although unsuccessful students have been the focus of concern for numerous studies, we know little about the relationship between failure and mental health. Indeed, our research in overemphasizing promotion-retention problems has excluded consideration of those daily failing experiences to which children are subject. Little attention has been given to the significance of failure in terms of goals or standards set by parents for children or children for themselves. The youngster who aims for all A's and receives one B may have failed in his own eyes as completely as another who falters in every subject.

DIMENSIONS OF FAILURE

Since to fail implies personal insufficiency and since people do not like to accept limitations, it follows that any construct of failure lacks universality. Still, many persons envision failing experiences as having but one dimension, harm. Accordingly, they support any effort to lessen or eliminate the frequency of failing both in their life and in the lives of those for whom they have regard. Never so poignantly was this distorted view of failure shown me as in one of my college classes a few years ago. Curious as to what student teachers thought of failure in the classroom, I included the following item in a true-false examination: "No child should ever be allowed to fail."

All 150 students checked the statement "true." I was shocked not so much because of the interest in protecting elementary-school children from failing but by the strong assumption that a teacher should be able

377

to avoid failure for pupils. It was as though our potential instructors were unaware that:

1. Children make their own comparison of who is fast or slow, dumb or bright, in spite of interesting reading-group names.
2. Praise given a child who has done a poor job does not relieve the burden of failure.
3. Encouragement may be interpreted by the student as additional pressure to do something he knows he cannot do.
4. Comments about improvement can be poor substitutes for those satisfactions that come from actual achievement as seen by a youngster himself.

Viewing all failure as tragedy is common even among practitioners in our schools. The writer witnessed an interview of a young teacher who was applying for a post as physical-education coach at a large high school. In discussing competitive sports he remarked that his teams were not allowed to lose. The interviewing superintendent pointed out the inconsistency of such a view in lieu of the fact that in competitive games one team had to lose. Yet the young man remained firm in his assertion that failure was demoralizing and ought not to be allowed to occur. Certainly anyone who believes that a teacher or anyone else can prevent all failure in human experience is not thinking realistically.

Failure has another dimension, growth. From the time of our first tumble, failure is a part of living and the due of each who would approach new and difficult tasks. Through failing an individual learns what he can and cannot do. Therefore, adjustment after failure is a must for living, for mental health. Also, it is through failing that a person is toughened, develops courage and stamina. Success derives its joy from overcoming previous defeats. We should be aware that all progress of mankind has come about through the efforts of persons who failed, and failed again, but who would not give up. It is success after failure that provides the spur to keep us going, the experience that gives us hope and keeps us ready to endure more failure in the next difficult venture.

Two illustrations of failure's positive impact come to mind. Friends of mine have a young son who is affiliated with electronics research. After months of work on a complicated project, success was finally realized and its effect was shown verbally by long-distance phone: "I've got it! It works!" Similarly, my own boy evinced the usual symptoms of frustration, discouragement, and anger as he struggled all day with a difficult scientific formula. Having labored on into the night, he awakened me at dawn exclaiming: "It checks out!" If I did not know the meaning of algebraic symbols he waved at me, I did recognize failure vanquished and appropriately arose to drink a victory toast.

A FAILURE'S FEELING

Although periodic encounter with academic frustration may derive positive return for children, it is also true that no one can develop steadily in confidence while remaining in a situation where he fails constantly. As dissatisfaction with school increases, such a pupil evolves from dolt to truant to dropout. The understanding he needs is seldom forthcoming because teachers, as a rule, have not had personal failure with academic work.

How then can we better understand the feelings of those who daily experience learning impotence? During the past six years I became especially interested in fourteen failing children whose intelligence scores indicated normal ability. Seven of these students, ranging in age from 9 to 14, could not read even though referrals had been made to special tutoring and reading clinics. The remaining students were achieving far below grade level in other subjects. On the cumulative file of each was noted: "He could do better if he would try harder." Parents of these youngsters had received such advice as indicated by their prevalent recourse to disapproval and punishment for stimulation of school achievement.

All fourteen pupils showed discouragement in studies, dissatisfaction with teachers and peers, unwillingness to attend school, and reluctance to reveal in class that they did not understand what was going on. They were not, however, behavior problems of the type that disrupt a classroom. Some of them presented a cheerful demeanor in contacts with adults. Believing themselves incapable, all of them were sure they could never learn what was expected of them. Similarly, their teachers agreed the students could not learn but for other reasons than ability as evidenced by recorded comments: "Never pays attention, doesn't listen, doesn't try, doesn't finish homework."

My job was mostly trying to help these boys and girls arrive at a point where they were ready to try again. This task took time and love for they were not easily encouraged. I remember, after a period of getting acquainted, explaining to a 10-year-old a few reasons why children, especially boys, have trouble reading. After my covering things like mixed dominance and girls developing faster than boys in early grades, John looked at me with a new expression and asked: "You mean I'm not dumb?" I answered that was it exactly and that together we would locate his trouble. In another instance, it took six months before I could mention help with reading to a discouraged 12-year-old. One day, knowing I cared, he came to me with a book saying: "I guess you might as well know how bad it is." Renewed effort brought him the success of reading as was the case with four of his fellow nonreaders.

Working with poor students brought cognizance of the various ways by which such children protect themselves from their failure, symptoms which many of us fail to recognize for what they are. These include forgetting assignments, losing books or pencils, and not delivering to parents the suggestions sent home by teacher. Often comments bespeak the symptoms such as: "I lost it on the bus" or "I left it at school." Sometimes the signs are dawdling or persistence in not finishing work. Two children voiced the dilemma of their fellows as they asked: "Which is best—not to do it at all or do it and get it wrong?"

OVERPUNISHMENT AND LEARNING

One evening, in an attempt to temporarily put aside students' problems, I picked up a copy of the *Scientific American*. I was unable to understand most of the articles; yet, like my students, I periodically had hopes. The magazine contained an article entitled "Protopsychology"—the term applied to subtle types of behavior recently observed in a primitive worm. Heretofore such behavior had been associated only with animals standing much higher in the evolutionary scale. Here was something so absorbing that I forgot my troubles, for a time at least:

The fresh water planarian is a primitive animal that has bilateral symmetry, a rudimentary nervous system and distinct head that exerts control over the rest of the body. A member of the phylum of flat worms, it has a blind-ended gut and no circulatory system. Planarians are the contemporary representatives of what must have been a very ancient form of animal, from which many higher forms of invertebrates and also the vertebrates presumably evolved (Best, 1963).

Experiments of conditioned learning for the planarian were recorded. With a Y-shaped fork, one passage of which led to food and water, it was found that worms could learn to make choices culminating in reward. Cutting a planarian in two showed that head ends grow new tails and tail ends grow heads. Regenerated heads seemed to retain some learning when compared with untrained worms. Feeding bits of trained worms to untrained planarian seemed to enable the latter to better handle mazes than those untrained who had not eaten their relatives. Perhaps, as one researcher pointed out, human cannibals who lovingly ate ancestors in order to absorb their characteristics had a point.

Planarian research was interrupted when the worms became lethargic and refused to play their game when placed in the maze. Postulation that fatigue might be causing this behavior was discounted when, back in their home tank, normal activity resumed. Similar incidents had earlier been reported by those working with higher forms of animal life. For example, a cat sat down on an electric plate and absorbed the shock rather than try any longer to avoid it. Increased shock strength had no effect except to ruin the subject for further experiments. I wondered, were some of my students being ruined for further attempts to teach them? It was decided that the "lethargy phenomenon was caused by overpunishment and represented some kind of emotional response to the entire test situation." Pausing again I remembered the failer who said, "Everytime I get it wrong, my teacher tells Mom and I go to bed without dessert."

The planarian investigators stated that, aside from the trials themselves, nothing very punishing could be seen in the maze situation. Similarly, could it be that teachers see nothing very punishing about a classroom situation but that children familiar with failure find it very much so. Being sent to the board to work a problem one knows one cannot solve and having the whole class witness the misfortune, or being laughed at by one's peers following an outbreak of teacher impatience—these are little things, everyday occurrences, but each one emphasizing a child's inadequacy. Continuing the planarian article:

> At a loss for an explanation, I was glumly watching my cat trying to get into a closet past the closet door, which was slightly ajar. On the day before when I needed her out of the way briefly, I had put her into the closet with a plate of food. Instead of quietly eating, she had thrown a terrible feline tantrum, ignoring the food, yowling and scratching the door. Yet this same closet, a dungeon yesterday when escape was blocked, now, with the door ajar, became attractive. Why?
> I decided to present the planarian with a strategem analogous to the cat and the closet. A small piece of liver was placed on the flooded maze well as before. The entire maze block was put into the home bowl of the planarian and the water level adjusted until it was slightly higher than the top of the maze block. The planarian could now, remaining in water, pass between the well and its home bowl at its own discretion. The "open door" strategem worked. Under these conditions the planarian climbed into the well and ate (Best, 1963).

The fact that a generalized anxiety about environment could result in refusal of food seemed significant. I could see the similar dilemma of my students—overpunishment and no escape. Is there a more potent recipe for gradual and complete demoralization of a child's concept of self, his feeling of competence? Teachers' comments came to mind that learning would occur if "he would only try, only pay more attention." Just how long do any of us continue attentive if convinced that we cannot understand. We become psychologically deaf when, out of fear of failure, we close ourselves off.

Are we not all familiar with the inadequacies of listening to the spoken word, and some ensuing misinterpretations. Teacher experiences are replete with anecdotes about children who misunderstood because they did not hear clearly. "My country is a tree" represents a common first line of "America." The seventh grader on first reading of our Pledge of Allegiance was amazed that it wasn't "with liberal injustice for all." I re-call a little girl whose favorite hymn was "Gladly the Cross-Eyed Bear" ("Gladly the Cross I'd Bear"). Having concluded my remarks to a second grader concerning how I might help her prevent recurrence of certain unfortunate experiences of the first grade, she replied: "I love the way you speak Spanish." "I don't speak Spanish," I said. She ended our conversation, "It sounded like Spanish to me, it was nice!"

How often do we as teachers and parents speak Spanish to our chil-dren assuming that it is clear to them because it is clear to us. To quote again:

> There are great difficulties in working with a truly alien species. Nearly any experiment in learning is simultaneously an experiment in perception; conversely, almost all experiments on the perception of another animal are done by teaching it some kind of discrimination. When one does not know how an animal perceives the world, it is difficult to know whether an animal's failure to learn a task set by the experimenter arises from incapacity or com-municative failure.
>
> We are encouraged to believe as a result of our experiment with planarian that the strange, little-explored domain of protopsychology will shed new light on the ultimate nature of the human brain (Best, 1963).

An "alien species," a "human brain," a "little child's learning"—have we not been presumptuous in feigning erudite speech about the learning process when so often we fail to perceive its individual course in the lives of our students? We do know that youngsters go on learning in the face of many complications unless something happens to render expedient their closing off of self. Perhaps the major reasons for this isolation of self are overpunishment, little support, and no escape.

DIMINISHING UNDUE FAILURE

Interest in helping unsuccessful students reduce occurrence of their undue failures is commendable. Certain questions indicate directions in which understanding is needed. For example, what kinds of knowledge can we give parents so that home stimulation for achievement takes other than punitive forms? How can we lessen those instances where failure is imposed on pupils through assignments beyond their ability? In what ways can we diminish the social distance between teacher and pupil which so often leads the failer to self-isolation? Surely I do not have answers to these comprehensive queries, but the following suggestions may be help-ful in decreasing dissonance between our actual and ideal.

1. *We can recognize and explain more fully to parents variations in maturational rates of children.* Five-year-olds entering kindergarten are not equally ready. With some, total growth is accelerated whereas others ought to grow an additional year before enrolling. The term growth has come to mean more than just height, weight, and test scores in readiness or intelligence. Only recently have we found that "sidedness," an important factor in reading, does not occur until age 7. Then too, nearly a year's difference in age and maturity exists between youngest and eldest in early grades. These factors as well as individual growth patterns make comparison of children by teachers or parents undue pressures that contribute to failure.

2. *We can help parents understand that children ought not to be pushed in development.* Mother and father should not express severe disappointment about papers that first graders bring home. On the other hand, before school-staff members advise parents on ways of aiding youngsters who fail, we ought to find out what parents are already doing to help. Time-honored methods are disapproval, punishment, taking away privileges, promising rewards, and comparison with siblings or neighbor children. A child in trouble with learning needs support and reassurance along with whatever type of academic aid is given. Failure at school should not be compounded by failure at home.

3. *Do not compare boys with girls in academic work.* During the first few years of school, girls mature more rapidly than do boys. Generally, the girls are more ready to read, have better muscular coordination, and can do a more able job of writing. That these statements are true is evidenced by the preponderance of boys in classes for remedial reading. Unfavorable comparison of sexes at the elementary-school level results in angry boys and smug girls, hardly a beneficial base for wholesome relationships later.

4. *We can become more proficient in recognizing symptoms of learning difficulty.* Excessive parental dissatisfaction with work brought home may prompt a child to lose assignments as a way out, an escape. The youngster can always believe that he could have done the work if he had not lost it and still avoid any unpleasant experience of having another paper marked wrong. For some pupils, dawdling is a symptom of academic mishap. Time and again, I have found a child dawdling or daydreaming because he did not know how to begin his work and was ashamed to admit it. Copying is another symptom of learning difficulty though usually handled as a moral issue. Each symptom represents an escape from failure for those who are most subject to its occurrence.

5. *Teachers ought not feel threatened by student failure.* There is no reason to be antagonistic toward pupils who are unsuccessful in one's

classroom. Accepting them as they are one can extend sympathy such as "This is tough, isn't it?" or "You aren't the only one having trouble." Once while visiting a fifth grade, the teacher introduced a boy to me. "John has been having a lot of trouble with writing," she said, "I want to show you how much he has improved. Here is his paper for today, and here," she pulled out a drawer of her desk, "is one he turned in two months ago. I wanted you to see the difference." The child beamed.

6. *Listen to children.* This is difficult to do in a busy classroom but none-theless necessary. The suggestion is also important for parents as often adults and children talk but are not on the same wavelength. I have not forgotten a story told me of the father who took his 6-year-old daughter to the movies. The film was for children but the "short" re-vealed pictures of Christians being thrown to the lions. The little girl cried all the way home, refusing to be comforted. When she quieted, her father asked what it was that had caused her tears. "Well," replied the child, "there was one little baby lion that didn't get even one Christian." Incapacity or communication failure?

7. *We should lessen our attention to intelligence tests, especially those that are group administered.* In the main, group scores coincide with indi-vidual tests but from time to time this is not so. One of my students scored 68 on a group test and 110 when given an individual examina-tion. Why? No one knows really but my hunch is that with the group examination, he was sure he could not do it. In the individual test a skillful psychologist helped the student think he could do all right. We should stop saying to parents, "He can do it if he will try," when our judgment rests solely on I.Q. performance. There are all sorts of emo-tional and physical obstacles to learning, dozens of reasons why children are unable to use their abilities. We must continue to search for ways of overcoming these obstacles.

Help toward eliminating daily failure for students is steadily growing. There is good reason to believe that diagnostics in reading will become more able with current interest being expressed by neurologists and oph-thalmologists. Children suffering from aphasia are being recognized and studied as are brain-injured youngsters. Child-guidance clinics are amass-ing knowledge of the emotional factors involved in school failure. Teach-ers are being better trained to understand how children grow and learn. Finally, specialists in psychology, social work, and psychiatry are working in conjunction with instructional and administrative personnel to help school failures become successful.

37 *School Evaluation and Mental Health*

Robert D. Strom

Mental health is "that state of mind in which one is free to make use of his natural capacities in an effective and satisfying manner." If we accept this definition we will most likely view mental health as a determinant of academic achievement. Less often do we examine the converse of this reciprocal, that is, academic achievement's effect on mental well-being. The ways in which achievement has come to be misconstrued have resulted in an educational structure that necessarily acts as an impediment to positive mental outlook. The purpose of this chapter is to examine some of the misconceptions concerning school achievement and those concomitant outcomes that relate to the mental health of students.

THE MEASURE OF ACHIEVEMENT

The uses made of academic grades by both teachers and students require consideration. Throughout the educational scheme, from primary to graduate training, emphasis is placed on grades as a measure of academic success. Not only are promotions contingent on marks but the determination of honors, awards, and scholarships relates to grades. Matriculation in college is often based on past grades and continuation in higher education hinges on the maintenance of minimal marks. Under these circumstances it should not be surprising if some students make grades rather than growth their educational goal.

Teachers, in pointing out the true purpose of academic measurement as one of record keeping to interpret individual progress, lament the fact that grade seeking appears so prevalent among students. Yet the very method by which grades are determined and the significance attached to them belies whatever declared aim educators may assign to academic evaluation.

Reprinted by permission of *The High School Journal*, October 1964.

385

In elementary school the novitiate to formal learning finds emphasis placed on perfection as the standard by which his achievement is to be measured. Thus he is encouraged to make arithmetical computation without error, to spell perfectly, to exactly duplicate the letter specimens on the board, and to read with perfect diction. For high achievement the successful are given a "100," an "A," or an "excellent" label. Since every child is urged to achieve to the maximum (perfection) rather than his maximum (ability), a premium comes to be placed on the symbol of achievement rather than on achievement itself. The fact that young children can more readily grasp symbols than what symbols represent serves to further strengthen attitude direction toward the attainment of marks. So it is that, early in the educative process, grades emerge as the purpose of learning.

At the secondary and higher education levels of school there is acceptance of the fact that complexity of work renders any perfectable attainment extremely rare. Hence a new standard emerges as the criterion for measuring "achievement." Grades now serve to represent one's standing in relation to his peers. It is important to notice that in both elementary and higher levels of schooling the standard or criterion for "achievement" is outside and therefore unrelated to the growth of the individual graded. When pupils must view grades as an index of their work-product rank in relation to fellow students rather than as rough indices to denote whether they are progressing in their courses, it is natural that pursuit of grades will come to occupy a prime position while courses and learning itself becomes secondary. In this way scholarship is dealt a severe blow and overstrong attitudes of rivalry or competition are set up.

What mental-health consequences attend an educational-achievement program which is so structured that grades become goals, which is so measured that criteria are external to those being evaluated, which engenders a competitive atmosphere as most conducive to learning?

Grades—Symbols or Achievements?

To defend any competitive marking system on the basis of its motivational strength is untenable for it presumes that all persons are motivated in the same way by the same forces. Often competitive marking serves to dislocate student interest from the subject to the grade, from the real achievement to the achievement symbol. That this occurs is evident by the premium many parents place on high marks, often bribing, cajoling, or threatening a child to obtain them. Underlying this pressure imposed on children is the assumption that most if not all can have high marks if they just work hard enough. In many cases this results in a student's making lower marks than his intelligence and industry would normally permit him to make, simply because his concern impedes effective concentration. Some youngsters whose school work has become grade oriented are unduly disappointed as they perceive failure to obtain a grade as complete failure and hence lose even that which is within their reach. Although we cannot accurately assess the extent to which preoccupation with grades retards learning, few psychologists would deny the amount as influential.

All of us should be acquainted with the unnecessary anxiety, disappointment, and parental disfavor accompanying report time for some youngsters. By the nature of grading systems, the weaker student is forced to endure failure over and over again. Aside from the questionable desirability of such negative motivation, the blighting effects of constant frustration on personality development should be a matter of grave concern.

However, it is not just that pursuit of grades is predestined to fail for those who cannot "achieve" under prevailing conditions of measurement, but even for those who can succeed certain questionable results may occur. The real achievement of the more able is lessened when learning is in response to parental reward or teacher favor for a pattern develops in which these students seek cues as to how to conform. Bruner's (1961) studies of overachievers indicate they often become "seekers of the right way" and in their quest for authoritative learning fail to develop analytic abilities. Rote reports to the teacher of her own remarks (reproductive performance) hinder student capacity to transform learning into viable thought structure (productive thinking).

There is danger that those who choose grades as goals will cease to learn upon graduation when further incentives for effort are no longer forthcoming. If learning is to become a persistent part of personal existence the public schools must find ways in which to exchange the positions of reward and learning. How can this be done? Thorndike's law of effect states: "Behavior which is satisfying tends to be repeated." Although ostensibly satisfaction is a goal of education, the present structure relegates this aim to a position of secondary importance. Learning is not so satisfying as it should be in public schools. Part of the reason is that it is not personal. It is someone else's learning that children are taught. They do not experience the joy of using what they learn as tools for thinking. Elementary students must experience satisfaction from problem resolution and discovery if they are not to change purposes from progress to grade. This can only occur when thinking is considered a legitimate enterprise, and when production is not subject to the constant threat of evaluation.

We must ask ourselves whether or not grades should be used at all if they tend to distract students from desired educational objectives; if poor grades tend to discourage further attempts at learning, if good grades tend to cause future laziness on the part of the student? Should students perhaps grade themselves, so that they can learn to appraise their own achievements and be critical of personal growth? Should grades be based on effort, improvement, performance, or some ultimate standard? At this juncture the only thing clear is that there is no clarity in these matters.

Criteria, For or Against Achievement?

Tradition has dictated that pupils should be measured by comparison with others, although our knowledge of learners and the learning process has revealed that the valid measure is that which assesses the growth of an individual in relation to his previous position. Under present operations, "achievement" in the classroom is communal not personal.

Cursory observation of any school situation will indicate the negative motivation of marks on some pupils. When the same standard is set for every pupil regardless of his initial ability it follows that the motivating effect on some will be limited by the feeling that high marks are out of reach. If a mark compared the pupil with others of the same ability, each pupil might then have a chance for a high mark, but this would still not be an index of personal growth. One thing we have learned from research is that all men are created unequal; individual differences exist.

Our basis of assessing achievement by group standards may be likened to the efforts of an Arkansas farmer who sought to determine a fair price on the pig he was placing for sale. In order to ascertain price, the farmer found it necessary to devise a method to determine the weight of his pig. A long pole was placed in a horizontal position atop the back fence. To one end of this pole was tied the pig and on the opposite end was attached a large gunnysack. The gunnysack was filled with rocks until such time as the pole was balanced, the pig and rocks of equal weight. Then, to determine the weight of the pig, the farmer estimated the weight of the rocks.

To nullify individuality as a criterion for marking is to negate the validity of grades themselves if their purpose is, in fact, to record individual progress. To employ group curves as the standard for an individual's achievement is to guess the weight of the rocks in the farmer's case to determine the weight of the pig or in our instance the achievement of the individual. In both cases a pseudo-weight is assigned after first weighing something other than that with which we are concerned. It is fair to say that the concept of individual differences has been employed least in the area where it is most needed; namely, the assessment of achievement. Until individual achievement is based on personal progress, our schools will continue to perpetuate a fraud upon millions of boys and girls.

Even granting measurement's fundamental tenet that what exists in amount can be measured, by the same token it follows that what does not exist cannot be measured. And education is fundamentally interested in what does not yet exist, that is, in the student's future development and growth. The judging of achievement where growth is incomplete and still going on is bound to be different from measurement where growth is finished, where its evidences already exist (Dewey, 1928).

Competition and Learning

Competitive practices that survive from the period when little was known about the individuality of growth constitute a serious problem in academic evaluation. One of the hazards of normal growth and personality development is the discrepancy between what parents and teachers expect and what a child is able to produce at his level of maturity. There is a high emotional cost in those classrooms where pressures are brought to bear on all pupils to reach for average standards of achievement. Persons who exert such pressures imply that education can eliminate individual differences, that equality of education means identity of education for all.

Those who argue for inclusion of competitive grading at the elementary level insist that such preparation is necessary for the type of life one can expect to encounter in our society. This misguided premise fails to consider the fact that competition can occur only within a range of uncertainty, that is, the range in which both success and failure are possible. Competition cannot occur where each participant does not have a chance, where the outcome of victory or defeat is predetermined. It is to be noted that life's competitive situations are chosen where one perceives the possibility of success. "Competition" so-called in school is hardly chosen by children but is forced on them by compulsory school laws, anxious parents, and ill-trained teachers.

To compare the work product of one whose I.Q. is 85 with one whose intelligence quotient exceeds 130 ought to be a foregone conclusion. In a sense, school "competition" becomes a daily punishment for those of lesser ability. Under the circumstances where few participants have a chance to win, it is not strange that some students protect themselves by setting a low level of aspiration, that is, by not trying. In a spelldown some children are pleased only if they are not the first to make an error; winning is far from their minds.

Moreover, in competitive situations where immature minds are involved, defeating others becomes more important than doing the task well. In some pupils, competition arouses conflict; the threat of losing or the tension induced by working against others prevents whole-hearted participation. Repeated frustration in competitive situations produces a tensional state that makes large demands on a child's emotional balance and may alter his proper relationships with companions, teachers, and parents.

Competition is not the way to bring each person to his full potentiality. By emphasizing the false standard that he should take pride in what he excels in, we often discourage the pupil from developing his lesser talents. This is especially risky at the elementary level where strengths are only beginning to emerge. Youngsters ought not to be forced to capitalize on just those proficiencies that develop early lest other strengths which might develop later be excluded. Competition should never be made so important that failure to win is emotionally disruptive.

That "competition" can retain its antipathy, its sense of inequity is shown by the studies of Wilma Donahue (1962), Chairman of the Division of Gerontology at the University of Michigan, where it is stated that one of the prime difficulties in upgrading the skills of older workers is their persistent belief that age cannot compete with youth under academic conditions. Fear of competition in retraining programs renders some elderly folk reluctant to participate and not infrequently results in unemployment when their old skills become obsolete. Here is an example where "competition," the condition under which achievement was to flourish, has had an adverse effect on the stimulation of future learning and renders well-being and confidence uncertain. Donahue's postulate is the conviction that lifelong learning and activity are beneficial and will most probably take place if their occurrence is made satisfying.

DETERMINATION OF ACHIEVEMENT

In our fast-moving society it is natural that we should regard the rapid assimilation of knowledge and skills as desirable, even necessary; the sooner youngsters obtain them the better. Thus we concentrate on achievement, which is also desired, but in our eagerness to achieve we too often come to place emphasis on completion rather than on achievement itself. In other words, we are more interested in having lessons done with and over than we are in what we will know or be able to do. We want somehow to have our goal behind us and we make completion rather than achievement our goal.

Like the emphasis on grades as goals, so overemphasis on completion is not to be desired. At its worst, this emphasis results in an accumulation of courses taken as though each is another notch in one's gun, or another scalp at one's belt. Courses are taken for their own sake rather than for what one may know or learn. Too often students say "I had that course" as though it were another gold bar tucked away in their private Fort Knox.

It is certain that for some students the very termination of education—graduation—becomes a goal. This attitude has long-range implications for mental well-being. Luther H. Evans (Evans and Arnstein, 1962), Director of the NEA Project on Educational Implications of Automation, has pointed out that to lead a meaningful life in an age of automation will require a new kind of morale and educational outlook. An individual must realize when he leaves school that the traditional words of commencement speakers have become not just clichés; the education he has received really is just a beginning. No person can safely predict the kind of work he will be performing thirty years hence, but it can be predicted with certainty that he will have to update his skills and his general knowledge if he is to remain a productive member of society. The current rate of change makes it unlikely that any large number of people in our country can safely rely on the early acquisition of skills and knowledge to serve them for a lifetime. Failure to educate in terms of new developments can only mean unemployment and social disorientation. Educators must imbue youngsters with a positive attitude toward learning itself by effecting a transition from grade seeking or completion to growth as a personal goal. Although this is not a new idea, under the circumstances it becomes a new imperative.

Completion, A Misnomer for Learning

The concept of completion implies but does not ensure learning. Yet in some classrooms a major determinant of achievement is whether or not one completes assigned work. It is not that teachers are more interested in having things done than having them learned, but a persistent belief continues that practice will promote intellectual learning and the discipline of finishing tasks will develop personal responsibility as well as culminate the learning process.

This anachronistic concept of completion as achievement, so prominent in the days of mental discipline, is conceived again in modernity but this time as a miscarriage of gestalt closure. The gestalt principle of closure asserts that a student strives to reach a satisfying end-state of equilibrium through perceptive completion. This occurs as cognitive change allows new configurations of previously unrelated objects or ideas enabling the learner to resolve gaps in knowledge, find missing parts, or complete partial formations. In a sense we can say that closure-completion is synonymous with a certain kind of learning.

It is important to notice certain aspects peculiar to the closure principle as it relates to the classroom. First, intrinsic motivation is operative in order to reduce the need-tension created by the confrontation of a problem in which the student is ego-involved. Then too, the attention directed to the problem sustains until cognitive change (learning) occurs bringing new gestalt or configuration. Finally, closure results in satisfaction from resolution of the problem. It has been said that closure is to field theory what reward is to associationism.

Obviously, the mere completion of assigned tasks is different from gestalt closure. For one thing, the motivation is imposed, external to the learner so that the demand is made of him but not necessarily by him. Second, learning will take place only if a child experiences closure as his project proceeds toward completion. That completion is not necessarily learning has long since been demonstrated as has the fact that enforced practice is often required at the expense of antipathy. Finally, whereas closure culminates in satisfaction, completion more often than not terminates only in a feeling of relief. In fact, a displacement of satisfaction sometimes occurs when the teacher rather than the learner is pleased with completion of assigned work. The feeling that her authority has been accepted, her responsibility dispatched, need reduction occurs for the teacher; it is lamentable, however, when student work proceeds not for personal growth and satisfaction but to please or propitiate the instructor.

The most important problem with the completion hypothesis is that an overemphasis is placed on knowing rather than learning, on the end rather than the process. The prevalent notion among students is that the important thing is to write finis to the paper. Anxiety is set up as a stimulus. Physics may take several hours of work which if not spent will result in partial or complete failure so that if one does or does not do the work, either may be tension-provoking. Translating French, finding the unknown in math, or writing a composition is the same. Because the product is that which is evaluated, the student, in his eagerness to finish, employs short cuts rather than appropriate processes to determine answers. In modern education the answers should not be so important as the processes used in deriving solutions. The emphasis on completion often encourages careless haste and an attitude of finishing one thing and getting on with another until completion becomes a veritable compulsion and one comes to view achievement as that which one has completed or finished. This has ramifications for all areas of one's emotional traffic.

Teaching, Learning—Same?

In the minds of some the term "adjustment" has become freighted with anti-intellectual meaning and incites contempt. Yet Webster defines adjustment as "to put in proper position for use" and "to make necessary and desirable changes." That change is the lot of tomorrow's adult is certain; the result of change, however, is equally uncertain. Precisely because this is true, our schools must abandon the concept of retention as the epitome of educational purpose.

The most distinctive product of change or evolution is novelty. We cannot predict "answers" to questions that our children will need to resolve in their adult life. To attempt to predict the unpredictable is too prophetic for the teacher. Hence we must desist in emphasizing education for adulthood as this structure puts too much emphasis on past times, relies too heavily on the assumption that the future will merely be a repetition of the past. We can only prepare youngsters for the future by educating them for the present.

This venture can begin when the method of teaching and the method of learning become synonymous, that is, problem solving in approach. If classes operate in the hypothetical mode instead of the expository mode, students become learners rather than retainers for antiquity's store. A dynamic culture may require an exorbitant emotional expense of its constituents unless they are prepared to cope with change and encounter difficulty with a minimum of confusion. Armed with problem-solving techniques, there is reason to believe that those emotional barriers our children may encounter might be more easily overcome.

If educational achievement is to benefit personal development, certain of the present school practices need revision. Perhaps most important is that we properly locate the goal of the educative process inside the process itself, that is, growth becomes its own end. Since growth is personal, progress can no longer be determined apart from the individual. In this context, self-appraisal becomes a more legitimate and tenable base for the evaluation of achievement than does any judgment from external sources.

Up to now, educators have been more interested in what is taught students than in what students learn—the rationale follows that only the teacher could properly assess what advance students made. This idea is no longer tenable. The verb "educate" is not just transitive, it is also reflective; it is not something we do to the child; rather it is something that the child does to himself—a noetic process. Part of being educated is to determine or to evaluate one's own advance—to know what one knows and what one needs to learn to satisfy one's self for mental well-being. If knowledge is really subjective and therefore unique, it can best be evaluated by its possessor.

References

Allport, F. H., and G. W. Allport. 1928. *Ascendance Reaction Study*. Boston: Houghton Mifflin.

Allport, G. W. 1937. *Personality*. New York: Holt, Rinehart and Winston.

———. 1961*a*. "Values of Our Youth." *Teachers College Record,* **63,** 211–219.

———. 1961*b*. *Patterns and Growth in Personality*. New York: Holt, Rinehart and Winston.

———. 1962. "Psychological Models for Guidance." *Harvard Educational Review,* **32,** 373–381.

Altmeyer, J. R. 1951. "The School Social Worker and Problems of School Attendance." *Social Work,* **2**(4), 66–67.

Andrews, Elizabeth G. 1930. "The Development of Imagination in the Pre-School Child." *University of Iowa Studies of Character,* **3**(4).

Asch, S. E. 1960. "Effects of Group Pressure upon the Modification and Distortion of Judgment." In D. Cartwright and A. Zander (Eds.), *Group Dynamics: Research and Theory*. New York: Harper and Row. Pp. 189–200.

Babcock, Catherine Marly. 1962. "Did You Ever Read a Clock Upside Down?" Danbury, Conn.: Reeves Soundcraft Corp., 1962.

Baden Street Settlement House. 1964. "Stimulating Scholastic Achievement in a Socio-Economically Deprived Neighborhood." Rochester, N. Y.

Barron, F. 1958. "The Psychology of Imagination." *Scientific American,* **199,** 150–166.

Bedoian, Vagharsh. 1953. "Mental Health Analysis of Socially Overaccepted, Socially Underaccepted, Overage and Underage Pupils in the Sixth Grade." *Journal of Educational Psychology,* **44,** 366–371.

Bernard, H. W. 1952. *Mental Hygiene for Classroom Teachers*. New York: McGraw-Hill.

Bernstein, B. 1959. "A Public Language: Some Sociological Implications for a Linguistic Form," *British Journal of Sociology,* **10,** 311–327.

———. 1960. "Language and Social Class." *British Journal of Sociology,* **11,** 271–276.

———. 1961*a*. "Social Class and Linguistic Development: A Theory of Social Learning." In A. H. Halsey, Jean Floud, and C. A. Anderson (Eds.), *Education, Economy and Society*. New York: Free Press of Glencoe.

———. 1961*b*. "Social Structure, Language and Learning." *Educational Research,* **3,** 163–176.

———. 1962. "Linguistic Codes, Hesitation Phenomena and Intelligence." *Language and Speech,* **5**(1), 31–46.

395

Best, J. B. 1963. "Protopsychology." *Scientific American,* **208**(3), 55–62.

Bestor, A. 1955. *Restoration of Learning.* New York: Knopf.

Biber, Barbara. 1955. "School as an Influence in Developing Healthy Personality." In Ruth Kotinsky and Helen L. Witmer (Eds.), *Community Programs for Mental Health.* Cambridge, Mass.: Harvard University Press. Pp. 158–221.

———. 1958. "Teacher Education in Mental Health from the Point of View of the Educator." In M. Krugman (Ed.), *Orthopsychiatry and the School.* New York: American Orthopsychiatric Assn.

Binet, A. 1909. *Les Idées Modernes sur les Enfants.* Paris: Flamarion.

Birch, J. 1959. "The Slow Learner in the Secondary School and in the Junior High Schools." *NEA Journal,* **48**(2), 28–30.

Blaine, G. B., and C. C. McArthur. 1961. *Emotional Problems of the Student.* New York: Appleton-Century-Crofts.

Bloom, I., and W. I. Murray. 1957. "Some Basic Issues in Teaching Slow Learners." *Understanding the Child,* **26**(3).

Board of Education of the City of New York. 1957. *The Unit: In Curriculum Development and Instruction.* New York, N. Y.

———. 1962. *Curriculum Resource Materials for Meeting School Retention and Pre-Employment Needs.* New York, N. Y.

———. 1963. *Career Guidance Course of Study in Language Arts, Experimental Edition.* New York, N. Y.

Bonney, M. E. 1960. *Mental Health in Education.* Boston: Allyn and Bacon.

Boodish, H. M. 1962. "Educational Problems and Roadblocks." *The Social Studies,* **53**(6), 231.

Boroff, D. 1960. "American Colleges: What Their Catalogues Never Tell You." *Harper's Magazine,* **220**, 33–40.

Bower, E. M., and J. Holmes. 1959. "Emotional Factors and Academic Achievement." *Review of Educational Research,* **29**, 529–544.

Bowman, P. H., and C. V. Matthews. 1958. *The Motivations of Youth for Leaving School.* Report on Cooperative Research Project No. 200, United States Office of Education, Washington, D. C.

Braceland, F. 1963. *Emotional Problems of Contemporary Life.* Hartford, Conn.: Connecticut Mutual Life Insurance Co.

Brandel, A., and Barbara Hogan. 1964. "Adolescent Medicine: New Prescription for a Neglected Age." *Potomac, The Washington Post,* February 23, 1964, pp. 17–20.

Brim, O. A., Jr. 1959. *Education for Child Rearing.* New York: Russell Sage Foundation.

Bronfenbrenner, U. 1962. "Soviet Methods of Character Education: Some Implications for Research." *Religious Education,* **57**(4), 45–61.

Brookover, W. B., T. Shailer, and Ann Patterson. 1964. "Self-Concept of Ability and School Achievement." *Sociology of Education,* **37**, 271–278.

Brooks, D. 1962. "A Study to Determine the Literacy Level of Able-Bodied Persons Receiving Public Assistance." Chicago: Cook County Department of Public Aid.

Bruner, J. S. 1960. *The Process of Education.* Cambridge, Mass.: Harvard University Press.

———. 1961a. "The Cognitive Consequences of Early Sensory Deprivation." In *Sensory Deprivation: A Symposium Held at Harvard Medical School.* Cambridge, Mass.: Harvard University Press. Pp. 195–207.

———. 1961b. "The Act of Discovery." *Harvard Educational Review,* **31**, 21–32.

———. 1963. "New Curriculum." In Terry Ferrer (Ed.), *Classroom Revolution.* New York: Herald-Tribune, Inc.

————. 1964. "The Course of Cognitive Growth." *American Psychologist,* **19,** 1–15.

Burchill, G. W. 1962. *Work-Study Programs for Alienated Youth.* Chicago: Science Research Associates, Inc.

Bureau of Employment Security, 1963. *Job Guide for Young Workers.* Washington, D. C.: United States Department of Labor.

Burgess, E. W. 1957. "The Family in Changing Society." In P. K. Hatt and A. J. Reiss (Eds.), *Cities and Society.* New York: Free Press of Glencoe.

Byerly, C. L. 1963. "Pupils Who Do Not Respond." *Educational Leadership,* **20,** 309–314.

Byrd, R. E. 1938. *Alone.* New York: Putnam.

Carroll, H. A. 1956. *Mental Hygiene: The Dynamics of Adjustment.* Englewood Cliffs, N. J.: Prentice-Hall.

Cattell, R. B. 1955. *Handbook for the Objective-Analytic Personality Test Batteries.* Champaign, Ill.: Institute for Personality and Ability Testing.

Certner, S. 1949. "Teaching Over Their Heads." *High Points,* **31,** 9–21.

Chess, Stella, and A. Thomas. 1964. "Are Parents Responsible for Everything?" *Parents' Magazine,* **39**(11), 48–49, 118ff.

Chorpenning, C. B. 1946. *Alice in Wonderland.* (A dramatization of C. O. Dodgson's original work.) Chicago: Dramatic Publishing Co.

Chukovsky, K. 1963. *From Two to Five.* Berkeley, Calif.: University of California Press.

Clark, K. B. 1963. "Educational Stimulation of Racially Disadvantaged Children." In A. H. Passow (Ed.), *Education in Depressed Areas.* New York: Bureau of Publications, Teachers College, Columbia University. Pp. 142–162.

Clark, R. A. 1952. "Sociographic Analysis of Peer Group Status." Doctoral dissertation, University of Texas, Austin, Tex.

Clarke, A. D. B., and A. M. Clarke. 1959. "Recovery from the Effects of Deprivation." *Acta Psychologica,* **16,** 137–144.

Coleman, J. S. 1961*a.* "The Competition of Adolescent Energies." *Phi Delta Kappan,* **43,** 231–235.

————. 1961*b. The Adolescent Society.* New York: Free Press of Glencoe.

————. 1961*c. Social Climates in High School.* Washington, D. C.: United States Government Printing Office.

Colvin, S. S., and I. F. Meyer. 1906. "Imaginative Elements in the Written Work of School Children." *Pedagogical Seminary,* **13,** 84–93.

Community Progress, Inc. 1964. "The New Haven Employment Program." New Haven, Conn.

Conant, J. B. 1959. *The American High School Today.* New York: McGraw-Hill.

————. 1961. *Slums and Suburbs.* New York: McGraw-Hill.

Cooper, W. M., and associates. 1964. *Training the Hard-Core Unemployed.* Washington, D. C.: United States Government Printing Office.

Cowen, E. L., L. D. Izzo, H. Miles, E. F. Telschow, Mary Ann Trost, and M. Zax. 1963. "A Preventive Mental Health Program in the School Setting: Description and Evaluation." *Journal of Psychology,* **56,** 307–356.

D'Ambrosio, L. M. 1952. "Adjusting the Social Studies to the Non-Academically Inclined Child." *High Points,* **24,** 13–19.

Davis, A. 1948. *Social Class Influences Upon Learning.* Cambridge, Mass.: Harvard University Press.

Davis, K. 1962. "Urbanization—Changing Patterns of Living." In H. S. Simpson (Ed.), *The Changing American Population.* New York: Arden House Conference, Institute of Life Insurance.

DeHaan, R., and J. Kough. 1956a. *Identifying Students with Special Needs in Elementary and Secondary School*. Vol. 1. Chicago: Science Research Associates, Inc.

———. 1956b. *Helping Students with Special Needs in Elementary and Secondary School*. Vol. 2. Chicago: Science Research Associates, Inc.

Deutsch, M. 1960. *Minority Groups and Class Status as Related to Social and Personality Factors in Scholastic Achievement*. New York: Society for Applied Anthropology.

———. 1962. "Facilitating Development in the Pre-School Child: Social and Psychological Perspectives." Paper read at Arden House Conference on Pre-School Enrichment of Socially Disadvantaged Children, Harriman, N. Y.

———. 1963. "Reversing the Effects of Social Deprivation." Address delivered at the Washington Center for Metropolitan Studies, Washington, D. C.

———. 1964a. "The Role of Social Class in Language Development and Cognition." Paper read at American Orthopsychiatric Assn., Chicago, Ill.

———. 1964b. "Training Programs as Preparation for Social Change." Paper read at American Orthopsychiatric Assn., Chicago, Ill.

———, Alma Maliver, B. Brown, and Estelle Cherry. 1964. *Communication of Information in the Elementary School Classroom*. Cooperative Research Project No. 908, United States Office of Education, Washington, D. C.

Dewey, J. 1928. "Progressive Education and the Science of Education." *Progressive Education,* **5,** 200.

Dinkmeyer, D., and R. Dreikurs. 1963. *Encouraging Children to Learn*. Englewood Cliffs, N. J.: Prentice-Hall.

Dollard, J., and N. E. Miller. 1950. *Personality and Psychotherapy*. New York: McGraw-Hill.

Donahue, Wilma. 1962. "Adult Learning and Potentialities." In L. H. Evans and G. E. Arnstein (Eds.), *Automation and the Challenge to Education*. Washington, D. C.: National Education Assn.

Drews, Elizabeth M. 1961. "A Critical Evaluation of Approaches to the Identification of Gifted Students." In A. Traxler (Ed.), *Measurement and Evaluation in Today's Schools*. Washington, D. C.: American Council on Education. Pp. 47–51.

Dubos, R. J. 1959. "Medical Utopias." *Daedalus,* **58**(3), 410–424.

Educational Policies Commission. 1946. *Policies for Education in a Democracy*. Washington, D. C.: National Education Assn.

Erikson, E. H. 1950. *Childhood and Society*. New York: Norton.

———. 1959. "Youth and the Life Cycle." *Psychological Issues,* **1**(1).

———. 1960. "Youth and the Life Cycle." *Children,* **7**(2), 43–49.

Esfandiary, F. 1957. "Is It the Mysterious—or Neurotic—East?" *New York Times Magazine,* March 24, 1957, pp. 13ff.

Evans, L. H., and G. E. Arnstein. 1962. "Automation and Its Consequences." In L. H. Evans and G. E. Arnstein (Eds.), *Automation and the Challenge to Education*. Washington, D. C.: National Education Assn.

Farnsworth, D. L. 1959. "We're Wasting Brain Power." *NEA Journal,* **48,** 42–44.

Featherstone, W. B. 1951. *Teaching the Slow Learner*. New York: Bureau of Publications, Teachers College, Columbia University.

Ferebee, June D. 1950. "Learning Through Creative Expression." *Elementary English,* **27,** 73–78.

Ferrer, Terry (Ed.). 1963. *Classroom Revolution*. New York: Herald-Tribune, Inc.

Festinger, L. 1957. *A Theory of Cognitive Dissonance*. Stanford, Calif.: Stanford University Press.

Fowlkes, J. G. 1962. *The Wisconsin Improvement Program—Teacher Education and Local School Systems*. Madison, Wis.: University of Wisconsin.

Frank, L. K. 1959. *The School as an Agent of Cultural Renewal*. Cambridge, Mass.: Harvard University Press.

——, and Mary Frank. 1956. *Your Adolescent at Home and at School*. New York: Viking.

Frankel, E. 1961. "The Gifted Academic Underachiever." *Science Teacher,* **28,** 49–51.

Fraser, Dorothy M. 1962. *Current Curriculum Studies in Academic Subjects*. Washington, D. C.: National Education Assn.

Frazier, A. (Ed.) 1963. *New Insights and the Curriculum*. Washington, D. C.: National Education Assn.

Frederick, Marilyn, and Carol Ostrom. 1963. "The Slow Learner—A Challenge and Responsibility." *Illinois Teachers of Home Economics,* **7**(1).

French, J. R. P., Jr. 1963. "Social Environment and Mental Health." *Journal of Social Issues,* **19**(4), 39–56.

Friedenberg, E. Z. 1960. *The Vanishing Adolescent*. Boston: Beacon.

Fromm, E. 1947. *Man for Himself: An Inquiry into the Psychology of Ethics*. New York: Holt, Rinehart and Winston.

——. 1955. *Sane Society*. New York: Holt, Rinehart and Winston.

——. 1956. *The Art of Loving*. New York: Harper and Row.

Funkenstein, D. H. (Ed.). 1959. *The Student and Mental Health—An International View,* New York: World Federation for Mental Health.

Galbraith, J. K. 1958. *The Affluent Society*. Boston: Houghton Mifflin.

Gardner, J. 1958. *Annual Report*. New York: Carnegie Corp. of America.

Getzels, J. W., and P. W. Jackson. 1958. "The Highly Creative and the Highly Intelligent Adolescent: An Attempt at Differentiation." Paper read at the meetings of the American Psychological Assn., Washington, D. C.

——. 1962. *Creativity and Intelligence*. New York: Wiley.

Gillespie, J. M., and G. W. Allport. 1955. *Youth's Outlook on the Future*. Garden City, N. Y.: Doubleday.

Gleason, J. 1963. *Operation Liftup*. New York: Boys Club of America.

Glueck, S., and Eleanor Glueck. 1959. *Predicting Delinquency and Crime*. Cambridge, Mass.: Harvard University Press.

Goertzel, V., and Mildred George Goertzel. 1962. *Cradles of Eminence*. Boston: Little, Brown.

Goodlad, J. I. 1943. "Some Effects of Promotion and Non-Promotion upon the Social and Personal Adjustment of Children." *Journal of Experimental Education,* **22,** 301–328.

——, and R. H. Anderson. 1963. *The Nongraded Elementary School*. New York: Harcourt, Brace and World.

Goodman, P. 1960. *Growing Up Absurd*. New York: Random.

Goodykoontz, Bess (Ed.). 1963. *Basic Human Values for Childhood Education*. Washington, D. C.: Association for Childhood Education International.

Gordon, R. E., Katherine Gordon, and M. Gunther. 1961. *Split-Level Trap*. New York: Random.

Gordon, W. J. J. 1961. *Synectics: The Development of Creative Capacity*. New York: Harper and Row.

Gotkin, L. G., and N. Massa. 1963. *Programmed Instruction and the Academically Gifted: The Effects of Creativity and Teacher Behavior on Programmed Instruction with Young Learners*. New York: The Center for Programmed Instruction, Inc.

Griffiths, D. E. 1956. *Human Relations in School Administration*. New York: Appleton-Century-Crofts.

Griffiths, Ruth. 1945. *A Study of Imagination in Early Childhood*. London: Kegan Paul.

Grimes, P. 1960. "Indian Students, Too, Are Angry." *New York Times Magazine*, September 11, 1960, pp. 47ff.

Grobman, Hulda (Ed.). 1963. *Biological Science Curriculum Study, Newsletter No. 19*. Boulder, Colo.: University of Colorado.

Gross, N. 1958. *Who Runs Our Schools?* New York: Wiley.

Group for the Advancement of Psychiatry, Committee on the College Student. 1955. *Considerations on Personality Development in College Students*. New York, N. Y.

———. 1957. *The Role of Psychiatrists in Colleges and Universities*. New York, N. Y.

Gruenbaum, M. C. 1960. *Implications for Casework Treatment of Recent Studies of Learning Problems*. Boston: Judge Baker Guidance Center.

Guilford, J. P. 1956. *Fundamental Statistics in Psychology and Education*. New York: McGraw-Hill.

———. 1962. "What to Do About Creativity in Education." In *Educational Testing Service Invitational Conference*. Los Angeles: Western Division, Educational Testing Service.

———, N. W. Kettner, and P. R. Christensen. 1954. *A Factor-Analytic Study Across the Domains of Reasoning, Creativity, and Education. I. Hypotheses and Descriptions of Tests*. Los Angeles: University of Southern California.

Gurin, G., J. Veroff, and Sheila Claire. 1960. *Americans View Their Mental Health: A Nationwide Survey*. New York: Basic Books.

Haggard, E. A. 1957. "Socialization, Personality, and Academic Achievement in Gifted Children." *School Review*, **65**, 388–414.

Hanson, C. F. 1957. "How Can the School Best Provide for Slow Learners?" *Bulletin of the National Association of Secondary School Principals*, **41**, 79–81.

Hargrove, Katherine C. 1964. "Let the Angels Sing." *Living With Children*, **8**(4), 10–11.

Harrower-Erikson, M. R., and M. E. Steiner. 1945. *Large-Scale Rorschach Techniques*. Springfield, Ill.: Thomas.

Havens, J. 1963. "A Study of the Religious Conflict in College Students." *Journal for the Scientific Study of Religion*, **3**, 52–69.

Havighurst, R. J. 1958. "Dealing with Problems of Youth." *Nation's Schools*, May 1958, **61**, 43–45.

———. 1963. "Education and Social Problems of Big Cities." *New City*, February 1, 1963, **1**, 9–12.

———, and L. J. Stiles. 1961. "A Statement of National Policy for Alienated Youth." *Phi Delta Kappan*, **42**, 283–291.

Hayman, Charlotte. 1962. "Early Identification of the Potential School Dropout." Paper presented at the 61st Annual Board of Education Conference of the New Jersey Welfare Council, Asbury Park, N. J.

Hearn, A. C. 1956. "Increasing the Schools' Holding Power Through Improved Articulation." *Educational Administration and Supervision*, **42**, 214–218.

Hebb, D. O. 1949. *The Organization of Behavior*. New York: Wiley.

Hechinger, Grace, and F. M. Hechinger. 1963. *Teen-Age Tyranny*. New York: Morrow.

Henry, J. 1963. *Culture Against Man*. New York: Random.

Henry, N. B. (Ed.). 1955. *Mental Health in Modern Education*. 54th Yearbook of the National Society for the Study of Education. Chicago: University of Chicago Press.

Heys, F., Jr. 1962. "The Theme-a-Week Assumption: A Report of an Experiment." *English Journal*, **51**, 320–322.

Hiller, E. T. 1941. "The Community as a Social Group." *American Sociological Review*, **6**, 189–192.

Hillson, H. T., and F. C. Meyers. 1961. *Demonstration Guidance Project at George Washington High School*. New York: New York City Board of Education.

Hogan, Barbara. 1964. "The Silent Teens." *Potomac, The Washington Post*, February 16, 1964, pp. 4–9.

Holt, E. B. 1915. *The Freudian Wish and Its Place in Ethics*. New York: Holt, Rinehart and Winston.

Hudson Guild Settlement House. 1963. "Study Den Programs." New York, N. Y.

Hunt, J. McV. 1961. *Intelligence and Experience*. New York: Ronald.

———. 1962. "The Psychological Basis for Using Pre-School Enrichment as an Antidote for Cultural Deprivation." Paper read at Arden House Conference on Pre-School Enrichment of Socially Disadvantaged Children, Harriman, N. Y.

Hutchinson, W. L. 1963. "Creative and Productive Thinking in the Classroom." Doctoral dissertation, University of Utah, Salt Lake City, Utah.

Ingram, Christine. 1953. *Education of the Slow-Learning Child*. New York. Ronald.

Jackson, J. M. 1960. "Structural Characteristics of Norms." In N. B. Henry (Ed.), *The Dynamics of Instructional Groups*. Chicago: University of Chicago Press.

Jackson, P. W., and J. W. Getzels. 1958. "Psychological Health Criteria among Adolescents: A Study of Manifest and Latent Indicators." Paper read at American Psychological Assn., Washington, D. C.

Jansen, W., E. F. Huggard, and M. Krugman. 1956. *Experiment in Guidance in Potential Early School Leavers*. New York: New York City Board of Education.

Jenkins, D. H., and C. A. Blackman. 1956. *Antecedents and Effects of Administrator Behavior*. Columbus, O.: Ohio State University Press.

Jennings, F. G. 1964. "Adolescents, Aspirations, and the Older Generation." *Teachers College Record*, **65**, 335–341.

John, Vera P. 1963. "The Intellectual Development of Slum Children: Some Preliminary Findings." *American Journal of Orthopsychiatry*, **33**, 813–822.

Johnson, G. O. 1963. *Education for the Slow Learners*. Englewood Cliffs, N. J.: Prentice-Hall.

Johnson, R. T. 1963. "The Growth of the Creative Thinking Abilities in Western Samoa." Doctoral dissertation, University of Minnesota, Minneapolis, Minn.

Jones, R. J., E. Y. Williams, and W. E. Riddick. 1962. "Motivational Factors as Predictor Variables in Medical Success: A Pilot Study." Washington, D. C.: Department of Neurology and Psychiatry, Howard University Medical School.

Jourard, S. M. 1963. *Personal Adjustment: An Approach through the Study of Healthy Personality*. (Second edition.) New York: Macmillan.

Kaplan, L. 1959. *Mental Health and Human Relations in Education*. New York: Harper and Row.

Kaplan, L., and J. D. O'Dea. 1953. "Mental Health Hazards in School." *Educational Leadership*, **10**, 351–354.

Karnes, Merle B. 1959. "The Slow Learner—Administrative Plans That Help." *NEA Journal*, **48**(2), 22–23.

Kazarin, E. N. 1963. "Elementary Industrial Arts: Primer to Understanding." **52**(10), 14–15.

Kephart, N. C. 1960. *The Slow Learner in the Classroom*. Columbus, O.: Merrill.

Kirk, S. A. 1940. *Teaching Reading to Slow Learning Children*. Boston: Houghton Mifflin.

——, and G. O. Johnson. 1951. *Educating the Retarded Child*. Boston: Houghton Mifflin.

Kirkpatrick, E. A. 1900. "Individual Tests of School Children." *Psychological Review*, **5**(7), 274.

Klein, D. D. 1956. *Mental Hygiene: A Survey of Personality Disorders and Mental Health*. (Third edition.) New York: Holt, Rinehart and Winston.

Koestler, A. 1941. *Darkness at Noon*. New York: Macmillan.

Kuhlen, R. G. 1952. *The Psychology of Adolescent Development*. New York: Harper and Row.

Kunst M. S. 1959. "Learning Disabilities: Their Dynamics and Treatment." *Social Work*, **4**(1), 95.

Langworthy, S. B. (Ed.). 1961. *The Slow Learner in Secondary Schools*. Trenton, N. J.: New Jersey Secondary Teachers Assn.

Lazarus, R. S. 1961. *Adjustment and Personality*. New York: McGraw-Hill.

Leeper, R. W., and P. Madison. 1959. *Toward Understanding Human Personalities*. New York: Appleton-Century-Crofts.

Lichter, S. O., Elsie B. Rapien, Frances M. Siebert, and M. A. Sklansky. 1962. *The Drop-Outs*. New York: Free Press of Glencoe.

Lindzey, G., and E. F. Borgatta. 1954. "Sociometric Measurement." In G. Lindzey (Ed.), *Handbook of Social Psychology*. Cambridge, Mass.: Addison-Wesley. Pp. 405–448.

Luria, A. R. 1960. *The Role of Speech and the Regulation of Normal and Abnormal Behavior*. Washington, D. C.: Superintendent of Documents, United States Government Printing Office.

McClelland, D. C. 1955. *Studies in Motivation*. New York: Appleton-Century-Crofts.

——, A. L. Baldwin, U. Bronfenbrenner, and F. L. Strodtbeck. 1958. *Talent and Society*. Princeton, N. J.: Van Nostrand.

McConnell, T. R. 1934. "Discovery vs. Authoritative Identification in the Learning of Children." *University of Iowa Studies in Education*, **9**(5), 13–62.

MacDonald, J. B., and J. D. Raths. 1964. "Should We Group by Creative Abilities?" *Elementary School Journal*, **65**, 137–142.

McKeachie, W. J. 1958. "Motivating Students' Interest." In R. M. Cooper (Ed.), *The Two Ends of the Log*. Minneapolis: University of Minnesota Press. Pp. 36–39.

Maier, N. R. F., and J. J. Hayes. 1962. *Creative Management*. New York: Wiley.

Maryland Cooperative Study of Dropouts. 1963. *Our Dropouts*. Baltimore: Maryland State Department of Education.

Maw, W., and Ethel Maw. 1961. "Establishing Criterion Groups for Evaluating Measures of Curiosity." *Journal of Experimental Education*, **29**(3), 299–305.

Mead, Margaret (Ed.). 1955. *Cultural Patterns and Technical Change*. New York: Mentor Books.

——. 1959. "A Redefinition of Education." **48**(7), 16.

Mearns, H. 1941. *The Creative Adult*. Garden City, N. Y.: Doubleday.

——. 1958. *Creative Power*. (Reprinted.) New York: Dover.

Merton, R. K. 1957. *Social Theory and Social Structure*. New York: Free Press of Glencoe.

——, S. Bloom, and Natalie Rogoff. 1956. "Studies in the Sociology of Medical Education." *Journal of Medical Education*, **31**, 552–565.

Michael, W. B. (Ed.). 1962. "Mental and Physical Health." *Review of Educational Research,* **32**(5). (Entire issue.)

Millay, Edna St. Vincent. 1963. "Conversation at Midnight." In F. Braceland, *Emotional Problems of Contemporary Life.* Hartford, Conn.: Connecticut Mutual Life Insurance Company. P. 15.

Miller, Joyce. 1961. "How to Talk to Children." *Home Life,* **15**(11), 13.

Mitchell, J. V. 1963. "Self-Family Perceptions Related to Self-Acceptance, Manifest Anxiety and Neuroticism." *Journal of Educational Research,* **56,** 236–242.

Moskowitz, M. 1948. "Teaching the Slow Learner." *School Review,* **56,** 476–483.

National Council of Teachers of Mathematics. 1963. *Experiences in Mathematical Discovery.* Washington, D. C.

National Education Association. 1963*a. Deciding What to Teach.* Washington, D. C.

———. 1963*b. No Room at the Bottom: Automation and the Reluctant Learner.* Washington, D. C.

———. 1964. *Schools for the 60's.* New York: McGraw-Hill.

National Education Association Research Staff. 1943. "High School Methods with Slow Learners." *NEA Research Bulletin,* **21**(3).

Nesbit, E. 1951. "Finding the Causes of Non-Attendance." *Social Work,* **2**(4), 66–67.

Newcomb, T. M. 1962. "Student Peer-Group Influences and Intellectual Outcomes of College Experience." In R. L. Sutherland, W. H. Holtzman, E. A. Koile, and B. K. Smith (Eds.), *Personality Factors on the College Campus.* Austin, Tex.: Hogg Foundation. Pp. 69–92.

Nichols, W. I. 1962. "A Time for Heroes—Program for Youth." Speech presented to the Chamber of Commerce, Miami, Fla.

Niemeyer, J. H. 1963. "Home-School Interaction." Paper presented at National Education Assn. Dropout Symposium, Washington, D. C.

Ojemann, R. H. 1948. "Research in Planned Learning Programs and the Science of Behavior." *Journal of Educational Research,* **42,** 96–104.

———, and Karen Pritchett. 1963. "Piaget and the Role of Guided Experiences in Human Development." *Perceptual and Motor Skills,* **17,** 927–939.

Opler, M. K. (Ed.). 1959. *Culture and Mental Health.* New York: Macmillan.

Ornstein, J. 1961. "New Recruits for Science." *Parents' Magazine,* **36**(42), 101–103.

Orr, K. N. 1955. "Helping the Slow Learner." *Social Education,* **19,** 107–108.

Ort, Lorrene Love. 1963. *A Matter of Fences.* Washington, D. C.: National Education Assn.

Osborn, A. F. 1963. *Creative Imagination.* (Fourth edition.) New York: Scribner.

Otto, H. A. 1960. "Developing a Mental Health Program in a Teacher-Training Institution." *Mental Hygiene,* **44,** 188–196.

———. 1961. "The School Administrator's Mental Health." *Mental Hygiene,* **45,** 603–612.

Passow, A. H. (Ed.). 1963. *Education in Depressed Areas.* New York: Bureau of Publications, Teachers College, Columbia University.

Patterson, J. H. 1940. *Of Me I Sing or Me and Education.* Nappanee, Ind.: E. V. Publishing House.

Peck, R. F., and R. J. Havighurst. 1960. *The Psychology of Character Development.* New York: Wiley.

———, and J. V. Mitchell, Jr. 1962. "Mental Health." No. 24, *What Research Says to the Teacher.* Washington, D. C.: National Education Assn.

Philadelphia Public Schools. 1959. *The Key to Teaching Slow Learners in the High Schools.* Philadelphia: Philadelphia Board of Education.

————. 1960. *Guide to Teaching of English.* Philadelphia: Philadelphia Board of Education.

Pierce, J. V., and P. H. Bowman. 1960. *Motivation Patterns of Superior High School Students.* Report on Cooperative Research Project No. 208, United States Office of Education, Washington, D. C.

Pulsifer, Susan Nichols. 1963. *Children Are Poets.* Cambridge, Mass.: Dresser, Chapman and Grimes.

Raffle, F. A. B. 1963. "Automation and Repetitive Work: Their Effect on Health." *The Lancet,* **1**(7284), 733–737.

Ramseyer, J. A. 1955. *Factors Affecting Educational Administration.* Columbus, O.: Ohio State University Press.

Rapaport, D. 1945. *Diagnostic Psychological Testing.* Vol. 1. Chicago: Yearbook Publishers.

Redl, F. 1945. "The Psychology of Gang Formations and the Treatment of Juvenile Delinquents." *Psychoanalytic Study of the Child,* **1**, 367–377.

————, and W. W. Wattenberg. 1959. *Mental Hygiene in Teaching.* (Revised edition.) New York: Harcourt, Brace and World.

Revie, V. A. 1956. "The Effect of Psychological Casework on the Teacher's Concept of the Pupil." *Journal of Counseling Psychology,* **3**, 125–129.

Rickover, H. 1960. *Education for Freedom.* (Second edition.) New York: Harper and Row.

Riesman, D. 1953. *The Lonely Crowd.* Garden City, N. Y.: Doubleday.

Riessman, F. 1962. *The Culturally Deprived Child.* New York: Harper and Row.

————. 1963. "The Culturally Deprived Child: A New View." *Educational Leadership,* **20**, 337–347.

————, J. Cohen, and A. Pearl (Eds.). 1964. *Mental Health of the Poor.* New York: Free Press of Glencoe.

Rinaldi, J. N. 1962. *Early Identification and Prevention Program, 1961–62.* New York: New York City Board of Education.

Robinson, R., D. F. de Marche, and M. K. Wagle. 1960. *Community Resources in Mental Health.* New York: Basic Books.

Rockefeller, J. D., IV. 1960. "Students of Japan: An Intimate Glimpse." *New York Times Magazine,* June 5, 1960, pp. 21ff.

Roe, Anne. 1953. "A Psychological Study of Eminent Psychologists and Anthropologists and a Comparison with Biological and Physical Scientists." *Psychological Monographs,* **67**(2).

Rogers, C. R. 1954. "Toward a Theory of Creativity." *ETC: A Review of General Semantics,* **11**, 249–260.

Rosen, B. C., and R. B. Andrade. 1959. "The Psychological Origins of Achievement Motivation." *American Sociological Review,* **22**, 185–218.

Ruesch, J., and W. Kees. 1956. *Non-Verbal Communication: Notes on the Visual Perception of Human Relations.* Berkeley, Calif.: University of California Press.

Sand, O., and R. I. Miller. 1963. "Curricular Innovations." *The Bulletin of the National Association of Secondary School Principals,* **47**, 120–123.

Savitsky, C. 1961. *Curriculum Resource Material for Meeting School Retention and Pre-Employment Needs.* New York: Board of Education of the City of New York.

————. 1962. "Work Experience Programs for Potential Dropouts." *Bulletin of the National Association of Secondary School Principals,* **46**, 53–60.

Sawrey, J. M., and C. W. Telford. 1963. *Dynamics of Mental Health: The Psychology of Adjustment.* Boston: Allyn and Bacon.

Schuker, L. 1955. "The Slow Learner in the High Schools." *High Points*, **37**, 11–32.

Sears, Pauline S. 1941. "Levels of Aspiration in Relation to Some Variables of Personality: Clinical Studies." *Journal of Abnormal and Social Psychology*, **14**, 311–336.

Seidman, J. M. (Ed.). 1963. *Educating for Mental Health: A Book of Readings*. New York: Crowell.

Selye, H. 1956. *The Stress of Life*. New York: McGraw-Hill.

Shaffer, L. F., and E. J. Shoben, Jr. 1956. *The Psychology of Adjustment: A Dynamic Experimental Approach to Personality and Mental Health*. (Second edition.) Boston: Houghton Mifflin.

Simpson, R. M. 1922. "Creative Imagination." *American Journal of Psychology*, **33**, 234–243.

Singer, J. L. 1961. "Imagination and the Waiting Ability in Young Children." *Personality*, **29**, 396–413.

Skeels, H. M., Ruth Updegraff, Beth L. Wellman, and A. M. Williams. 1938. "A Study of Environmental Stimulation: An Orphanage Pre-School Project." *University of Iowa Studies in Child Welfare*, **15**(4).

Skinner, B. F. 1948. *Walden Two*. New York: Macmillan.

Skodak, Marie, and H. M. Skeels. 1949. "A Final Follow-Up Study of One Hundred Adopted Children." *Journal of Genetic Psychology*, **75**, 85–125.

Smith, H. C. 1961. *Personality Adjustment*. New York: McGraw-Hill.

Soddy, K. (Ed.). 1956. *Mental Health and Infant Development*. (Two volumes.) New York: Basic Books.

Solley, C. M., and K. Minden. 1962. "Behavior of the Mentally Healthy." *Bulletin of the Menninger Clinic*, **26**, 178–188.

Standing, E. M. 1962. *Maria Montessori: Her Life and Work*. New York: Mentor-Omega Books.

Stein, M. R. 1960. "The Slum, Street Corner Society, and Suburbia: Dream or Nightmare?" In *An Interpretation of American Studies*. Princeton, N. J.: Princeton University Press, 1960. Pp. 119–134.

Stolurow, L. M. 1962. "Social Impact of Programmed Instruction: Aptitudes and Abilities Revisited." A paper presented at the annual convention of the American Psychological Assn., St. Louis, Mo.

Strom, R. D. 1963. "Comparison of Adolescent and Adult Behavioral Norm Properties." *Journal of Educational Psychology*, **54**, 322–330.

———. 1964. *The Tragic Migration: School Dropouts*. Washington, D. C.: National Education Assn.

———. 1965. *Teaching in the Slum School*. Columbus, O.: Merrill.

Swarthout, G. 1960. *Where the Boys Are*. New York: Random.

Talbot, M., and I. Henson. 1954. "Pupils Psychologically Absent From School." *American Journal of Orthopsychiatry*, **24**, 381–390.

Terman, L. M., and Melita Oden. 1947. *The Gifted Child Grows Up*. Palo Alto, Calif.: Stanford University Press.

Thorpe, L. P. 1960. *The Psychology of Mental Health*. (Second edition.) New York: Ronald.

Torrance, E. P. 1962a. *Guiding Creative Talent*. Englewood Cliffs, N. J.: Prentice-Hall.

———. 1962b. "Fostering Creative Thinking During the High School Years." *High School Journal*, **45**, 281–288.

———. 1963. *Education and the Creative Potential*. Minneapolis: University of Minnesota Press.

———. 1964a. "Providing for the More Humane Education of Gifted Children." *Gifted Child Quarterly*, **7**, 135–145.

———. 1964b. "The Creative Child." In J. S. Roucek (Ed.), *The Difficult Child.* New York: Philosophical Library. Pp. 1–17.

———. 1965. *Rewarding Creative Behavior: Experiments in Classroom Creativity.* Englewood Cliffs, N. J.: Prentice-Hall.

———, and Ram Gupta. 1964. *Development and Evaluation of Recorded Programmed Experiences in Creative Thinking in the Fourth Grade.* Minneapolis: Bureau of Educational Research, University of Minnesota.

U.S. News and World Report. 1963. "Jobs in the Future—Where Biggest Gains Will Be." December 30, 1963, **55**(27), 67–70.

Van Egmund, E. 1961. "Socialization Process and Education." *Review of Educational Research,* **31**, 80–90.

Van Steenberger, S. 1940. "Techniques Useful in Teaching Slow Classes." *High Points,* **22**, 71–73.

Watson, G. 1961. *What Psychology Can We Trust?* New York: Bureau of Publications, Teachers College, Columbia University.

Wattenberg, W. W. 1955. *The Adolescent Years.* New York: Harcourt, Brace and World.

Wellman, Beth L. 1940. "Iowa Studies of the Effects of Schooling." *Yearbook of the National Society for the Study of Education,* **39**, 377–399.

Wheeler, Olive A., W. Phillips, and J. P. Spillane. 1961. *Mental Health and Education.* London: University of London Press.

Whipple, G. M. 1915. *Manual of Mental and Physical Tests. Part II. Complex Processes.* Baltimore, Md.: Warwick and York.

White, R. W. 1959. "Motivation Reconsidered: The Concept of Competence." *Psychological Review,* **66**, 297–333.

Whitehorn, J. C. 1961. "Studies of the Doctor as a Crucial Factor for the Prognosis of Schizophrenic Patients." Baltimore, Md.: Henry Phipps Clinic, John Hopkins University. (Mimeographed.) (Quoted in *Action for Mental Health,* Joint Commission on Mental Illness and Health, Basic Books.)

Whyte, W. H., Jr. 1956. *Organization Man.* Garden City, N. Y.: Doubleday.

Wilt, Miriam E. 1959. *Creativity in the Elementary School.* New York: Appleton-Century-Crofts.

Withey, S. B. 1962. "The Influence of the Peer Group on the Values of Youth." *Religious Education,* **57**(4), 34–44.

Wonnacott, W. A., J. Giovanni, and F. Hedrich. 1964. "Elementary School Industrial Arts." *NEA Journal,* **53**(1), 31.

Wrenn, B., and Kathleen Wrenn. 1949. *Fun for Everybody: Songs for Children.* Cincinnati: Willis Music Co.

Wrenn, C. G. 1962. *The Counselor in a Changing World.* Washington, D. C.: American Personnel and Guidance Assn.

Zacharias, J. R. 1964. *Innovation and Experiment in Education.* Washington, D. C.: United States Government Printing Office.

Name Index

Subject Index